Brother [illegible]
from
Jackie & Virgil
Parker
2003

Arm the Children

Photograph by Grace Stewart Clayton

Arthur Henry King, 1994

Arm the Children

Faith's Response to a Violent World

Arthur Henry King

With a Foreword by
C. Terry Warner

Edited by
Daryl Hague

BYU Studies
Brigham Young University
Provo, Utah

BYU Studies Monographs

B. H. Roberts, *The Truth, The Way, The Life: An Elementary Treatise on Theology*

The Journals of William E. McLellin, 1831–1836

Hearts Turned to the Fathers: A History of the Genealogical Society of Utah, 1894–1994

Second Crop

Behind the Iron Curtain: Recollections of Latter-day Saints in East Germany, 1945–1989

Educating Zion

Life in Utah: Centennial Selections from BYU Studies

Masada and the World of the New Testament

The First Mormon Temple: Design, Construction, and Historic Context of the Kirtland Temple

The Book of Mormon Paintings of Minerva Teichert

Letters of Minerva Teichert

Library of Congress Cataloging-in-Publication Data

King, Arthur Henry.
Arm the children: faith's response to a violent world / Arthur Henry King; with foreword by C. Terry Warner; edited by Daryl Hague.
p. cm. — (BYU Studies monographs)
Rev. ed. of: The abundance of the heart, c1986.
Includes bibliographical references and index.
ISBN 0-8425-2358-8
1. Spiritual warfare. 2. Christianity and culture. 3. Child rearing—Religious aspects—Mormon Church. 4. Church of Jesus Christ of Latter Day Saints—Doctrines. 5. Mormon Church—Doctrines. 6. King, Arthur Henry. I. Hague, Daryl, 1963– II. King, Arthur Henry. Abundance of the heart. III. Title. IV. Series.
BT975 .K55 1998
289.3'32—ddc21
98-25465
CIP

Printed in the United States of America
10 9 8 7 6 5 4 3 2 1

Acknowledgments

Dennis and Sandy
have taken my talks and made
them mean better than
I could. It's in others that
we become ourselves. I have.

I hope they have, too.
They applied themselves to me.
To apply me to
themselves may have proved not so
good an exchange. Time will show.

In the meantime, and
perhaps always, we're members
one of another.

AHK
September 1985

Colleague, friend, and Brother Hague,
barbering my loquacious, vague
parentheses to Figaro's pace,
colloquiality and grace,
what a difference you have made!

Studying my "style" to see
how far you could go with me,
you charmed my syntax to persuade,
lexis to purge—But schemes and tropes,
Rhetoric cried, "Keep within our ropes!"

AHK
March 1998

1986 My wife and I have been deeply glad to be under the wing of the Church at Brigham Young University, I think principally because when we came here we found affection, which is a quality of American people generally. Thanks to the University, expressing itself principally through Robert Thomas and Terry Warner, I have been permitted to do what I love to do for the last fifteen years.

This book has come about through the efforts of Sandra and Dennis Packard, my former students and present mentors. Thanks to Maxine Hanks and Lisa Brown Roper, who took unremitting labour to get the text right. Thanks are also due to my friends J. Reuben Clark III, Thomas Kent Hinckley, and R. Douglas Phillips; to my honorary daughters Jolynn Bennett and Camille Stilson Williams for running discussions on these topics over the years; and above all to my wife, my unfailing helpmeet and principal critic.

In addition to the acknowledgement of permission footnoted in specific chapters, I give acknowledgement to the Church and to Brigham Young University for lectures of mine that they have printed.

I am indebted to the Keter Foundation, a nonprofit corporation that supports the preparation and publication of selected Latter-day Saint books and that funded the preparation and editing of this manuscript.

1998 In the preparation of this new book, which is grounded in *The Abundance of the Heart* but which has moved well beyond it, Daryl Hague has carefully edited the transformation from spoken to written word. BYU Studies, the present publisher, under the leadership of John W. Welch, editor-in-chief, has undertaken to winnow the lectures of the past ten years and the chapters in the previous book to make something befitting our current world. He has done much to build a sense of teamwork amongst all who have worked on this book. Doris R. Dant, executive editor, has marshalled all of this into what, it is hoped, will be an inviting and informative book. Karl F. Batdorff, production editor, has captured all of this and laid it down on the pages. Thomas Kent Hinckley, an old boy and a lifetime member of the Institute of Printing, London, has made available his professional skills to reconcile important ideas in this book to give clarity and variety. In addition to being my liaison with BYU Studies, he has done a number of things to make the book attractive and readable.

Contents

Foreword

LAMAN, LEMUEL, SAM, and Nephi all heard the same teachings from their father. All of them received a bounty of information. Yet they did not have an equal understanding of the truth. Nephi and presumably Sam became truth's champions, while Laman and Lemuel knew nothing of it. It would seem that information, even accurate information, is not the same as the truth. 1986

Certainly, to the ancients, including the prophets of the scriptures, the various words that we today translate with the English word *truth* had a much richer meaning than mere "accurate information," which is approximately what that word means to most people in our culture. Our word *true* is derived from a word that, in earlier times, meant "faith" or "covenant." *Troth* is a related term. *Truth* signified "being true," the Oxford English Dictionary tells us, i.e., constant, steadfast, and faithful to a cause, person, or principle. The Hebrew word translated *truth* in the King James translation of the Old Testament had a similar connotation.

Put that information together with some of the scriptural passages about truth. In various ways, the Lord said that he himself is the truth. He said, "I am the way, the truth, and the life" (John 14:6). The truth is an individual, a living soul. "The Word was made flesh, and dwelt among us . . . full of grace and truth" (John 1:14). What is the connection between this principle and the ancient conception of truth? Of all the Father's children, Jehovah is the one who is completely true in this sense, and it is to the Father that he is true. In a manner or by a process I do not understand, he "ascended up on high" by virtue of his faithfulness, "as also he descended below all things, in that he comprehended all things, that he might be in all and through all things, the light of truth; Which truth shineth. This is the light of Christ" (D&C 88:6–7).

So the truth is more than, or different from, the words the Lord and his prophets have spoken. These words, it seems, are given to us to bear witness of the truth, but many hearing this witness do not accept it and remain as ignorant of the truth as before. "For this cause came I into the world, that I should bear witness unto the truth. Every one that is of the truth heareth my voice" (John 18:37). The truth to which the Lord and his prophets bear witness with their words is the Lord himself. And those who are of him are those who hear and receive this witness.

How do we come to receive this witness and thereby know the truth? The beginning of the quest, it seems to me, is to be receptive and responsive to the truth, which "shineth," rather than be resistant. These are our only options. "And the light which shineth, which giveth you light, is through him who enlighteneth your eyes, which is the same light that quickeneth your understandings" (D&C 88:11). We can resist this light or receive it gratefully. Though it is provided freely, we ourselves determine to what degree we will be enlivened and enlightened by it.

The image of a laser beam is a helpful analogy. Ordinary light consists of energy that is radiated in random frequencies and phases. The pulses of energy carried by this light bump into and interfere with one another, like roller derby skaters knocking each other out of the race. The radiation quickly dissipates; it takes a lot of energy at the source to illuminate even a small space because so much of it is canceled out by the way it interferes with itself in transmission. But it is possible to "amplify" light by radiating it in frequencies and phases that are highly coordinated. When this happens, the pulses of energy being transmitted do not bump into and negate each other. The result is a beam of such intensity that even a few watts can be used to light a spot many miles away, or slice metal cleanly, or perform precision surgery. Light radiated in this manner—light whose pulses are in harmony with each other rather than in discord—is called a laser.

Using the metaphor of the laser, we might say that when we receive the light of truth, when we are in tune with it, as it were, there is nothing in us that diffuses or obliterates it. Instead we resonate with it. To the degree that we do, our eye will be single to the glory of God. Our whole bodies will be filled with light. We will be yielding ourselves to his law, his power, and his love. Instead of merely receiving information (what a paltry conception this is!), we will, quite literally, be *informed:* we will in other words be taking on the *form* of the truth, coming under the formative influence of the Being who is its source, changing so that we are more like him, more "of the truth."

This means that learning the truth is a moral endeavor. It is a process of becoming truer, more faithful, and more responsive. Just as the light radiates from the Lord as it "proceedeth forth . . . to fill the immensity of space" (D&C 88:12), so, I think, do we irradiate our situations with this same light to the extent that we are resonating with it. I have sometimes pictured the cosmos as a vast field of light punctuated here and there by points of varying degrees of darkness, which are the resistant souls, and by points of concentrated brightness, which are the resonant ones. The latter are like television relay stations situated on mountain tops; they give to signals originating elsewhere a fresh "boost" that carries them effectively to further regions. Insofar as an individual is faithful, he is a substation of the Lord's radiance; the light of love shines on all around him.

Now when we resist the light rather than receive it, we continue to need it, but because of the state of our hearts, it works in and through us more like an ordinary incandescent bulb than a laser. We consume more power than we convey. We lose focus and concentration. The light of our understandings is conflicted, diffused, and finally dissipated. "If therefore the light that is in thee be darkness, how great is that darkness" (Matthew 6:23).

In this context, we can reflect again on our contemporary conception of the truth as mere information. This conception is not only false, it is dangerous. It leads us to suppose that we can pass bits of the truth conveniently to one another, as if they were coins. We are encouraged to regard the mind as a kind of purse in which we can collect and even hoard these coins. We believe we can buy, sell, and barter for them; we treat them as if they have exchange value. As far as we are concerned, evil people can get hold of them, as well as good people. Sinister men can control the world by acquiring these truths and withholding them from others. All of this is false. The idea that truth is information is, ultimately, a menacing economic metaphor.

Just how menacing this idea is can be seen in our approach to education. Because we have taken the economic metaphor seriously, we have come to think that learning is completely independent of morality. We have made it competitive rather than cooperative. We have turned our universities into vocational schools. Certain kinds of training have become not just occupationally, but socially, advantageous. We have made the most successful information mongers among us into snobs. Learning, so called, has become a divisive social instrument that reinforces class distinctions. It is not possible to calculate the devastating effects of these disasters.

Teaching is not a form of commerce. It is more like the radiance or influence of a resonant soul as it is felt by other souls. The teacher of the truth does not convey to the student valuable bits of anything, but by his presence and commitment, he points away from himself to something higher than himself, to which the student can have independent access. "And also trust no one to be your teacher . . . , except he be a man of God, walking in his ways and keeping his commandments" (Mosiah 23:14).

What sort of individual would such a teacher be? He would, I think, be a profoundly simple one. He would harbor within his heart no conflicting aims capable of canceling each other out. In public and private, he would cherish just one concern, which we might variously describe as a desire to do what is right, to keep his word, to complete his tasks. (The Danish thinker Søren Kierkegaard formulated a slogan with this principle in mind when he read from the book of James, "Cleanse your hands, ye sinners; and purify your hearts, ye double minded" [James 4:8]. The slogan was, "Purity of heart is to will one thing.") I doubt whether the prospect of compromising himself for personal advantage would ever occur to such a teacher; it would not appeal to him. The one use to which he would be willing to put his tongue would be to speak the truth plainly.

I have written this introduction to Arthur King's spoken words in an indirect fashion, by discussing obedience, radiance, and teaching. If I were to write of Arthur directly, he would disapprove. He knows that the Lord has instructed us to call no man good. When we praise a person, we seek to make a hero of him. Heroes populate a different sort of world from the one that Arthur has been searching for all his life. They are people to whom we have accorded an exalted status because in the half-light of our own inner conflicts and insecurities, they appear larger than they are. Even if Arthur has succeeded in living the kind of life he has desired to live and been the kind of teacher I have been describing, it would be wrong to admire or praise him for it—as wrong as it is to applaud in church. That kind of life, Arthur would be quick to say, is our simple duty, nothing more. If we serve the Lord all our days, we are still unprofitable servants.

Without violating his very proper concerns in these matters, I have tried to introduce the author of these talks. I have done so by writing, if not of him, of what he loves, and if not of his life, then of the life he has sought to lead. I have tried, in short, to follow him in diverting attention away from him and toward the Lord.

What I have said also sets the background for making the one point that is essential to this introduction, namely, that if these talks of Arthur's are taken to be informational, they will be completely misread. It would be wrong to suppose Arthur to be saying, when he comments about a subject, "This is the way things are." It does not matter whether we agree with what he says (certainly it would be of no concern to him); what matters is that in this text we observe this educated individual devoting his thinking to the Lord. What matters is that we see a man using his mind reverently and that as a consequence we will want to go and do likewise.

This has been the pattern with Arthur's students, of whom I have known many over the past fifteen years. He teaches them to write, but none of them writes like him or like each other. That is as it should be. A substation of Christ's radiance does not simply illuminate the darkness so that others can find their way. He inspires others to resonate with that radiance. Thus, if we read this book aright, we will honor the Lord in our response to it, as its author, and its editors, have honored him by preparing it.

❖ ❖ ❖ ❖ ❖

I have chosen the thoughts that follow to introduce you to **1998**
Arthur King's most unusual turn of mind, which you will find at once reverent and radical, gentle and challenging, sympathetic and alert. I cannot say I learned all of these thoughts from him or

that they exactly represent his views. But I can say I learned them with him, in long, animated discussions about many subjects over perhaps twenty years. He does not enter a conversation or a lecture prepared or even willing to say anything he has thought before. For him, to speak, to discover, and to create are synonymous. "How can I know what I think," he has asked on repeated occasions, "until I see what I say?" What I offer here has grown out of those discussions and my subsequent meditation upon them.

Whether Arthur offers his observations in conversation or in talks—and this book consists of talks given to students and to general Latter-day Saint audiences—they are not what you might think would issue from a man as profoundly educated as he. They do not flow like preformulated phrases from any accumulated reservoir within. Instead, they are responses—responses to you, if it is to you that he is speaking.

How this works in conversation amazes me. He exalts whatever you may have said by collaborating with it to arrive at a new understanding of the topic. He uses it to move both of you forward together. No one who knows him could call this merely a gracious manner. He perceives better than you the potential for insight or wisdom in what you have said and makes it the occasion for yet another fresh observation. And he then appreciates to the same degree whatever use you are able to make of what he says. Soon you get the hang of this collaborative work and start to take his remarks seriously in the way that he has taken yours—not by deferring to them, but by letting them rearrange your complacent opinions, causing you to consider matters from fresh angles and to discover as you speak what you never quite thought before.

You are not learning material here. You are learning to be; you are letting yourself be changed in "the inner man"; you are becoming yourself at your most engaged and responsive and disciplined. This happens because the teaching you are receiving—this is something that for me has been somewhat difficult to grasp—is an act of love. (Often hearing him take the conversation we are having to a new level of insight, I have been moved to say within myself, "This cuts against me, and I am glad to hear it.") In two decades, Arthur and I have never left a conversation without both having changed our minds—and yet the asymmetry of the collaboration has never escaped me: he ever my teacher, I ever his student.

Or his son. Of the highest relevance here is the fact that I and about fifty others like me have come in our adult lives to regard this simple, unpretentious man, who had no children of his own that survived infancy, as our father. His way with us has been a father's way, fostering our development in our own individual directions. For as long as I have known him, he has pondered the urgency and difficulty of the responsibilities of this parental calling, and that, I think, is why all he says in this book bears importantly upon every parent's task of preparing the next generation for a fullness of life. Who but a true father can instill in children, as Arthur has, the highest standards without resorting to any of the judgmental ploys or superiority of manner that often elicit resistance in the young and drive them obstinately to choose another way?

We cannot hide our inner condition. By our faces, our gestures, and our speech, we reveal ourselves. If our hearts are pure, we can speak with the tongue of angels. Otherwise, we conduct ourselves self-consciously, the way people do who have something to conceal. Said Joseph Smith, "It is in vain to try to hide a bad spirit from the eyes of them who are spiritual for it will shewe itself in speaking and in writing as well as all our other conduct."[1] As we respond to what life presents to us, so we are.

This principle, that everything is manifest, has not been widely believed. Many of us actually think we can cover ourselves with artful displays of graciousness, confidence, or piety. If more of us realized that this cannot be done, there would be less pretense and posturing.

But few of us do realize it. We are misled by the frequency with which others seem to be taken in by our efforts to manipulate or impress. We do not see that when they are taken in, it is because they allow themselves to be. They have a vested interest in accepting and believing in what is not quite right. All Korihor could see in Alma, for example, was a man with motives like his own—personal gain and self-aggrandizement. In Alma's face, he could see only a reflection of himself. On the other hand, when others have no such vested interest, we cannot dupe them for long. Instead of perceiving us as we project ourselves, they see us struggling insecurely to project ourselves that way. In Korihor's countenance, Alma could read Korihor's soul. That others may fail to see us for what we are has less to do with our skill as posturers or hypocrites than with their lack of discernment. They would see the manifestation we constantly make of ourselves if they had eyes to see—if they were righteous enough to be self-forgetful. Again from Joseph Smith: "It is also useless to mak[e] great pretentions when the heart is not right before God, for God looks at the heart, and where the heart is not right the Lord will expose it to the view of his faithful saints."[2]

One significant mode of self-revelation is language, spoken and written. The words we choose to express ourselves, together with the tone and rhythm and structure of our speech, convey to those with ears to hear the intent of our hearts. To the degree that we are self-forgetful and free of guile, our speech will be simple and straightforward and consequently beautiful and powerful—which is not to say showy or forceful or in any way cosmetic; we will not have contrived our speech to impress or to coerce or to hide. And to the degree that we seek to promote or conceal ourselves or to control others, we will craft our speech in convoluted ways. We will inhibit the manifestation to others of who we really are in favor of a contrived image we naively suppose will win more favor. We will corrupt the natural beauty of speech and weaken its effects.

We do not achieve any of this self-revelation by taking thought; we do not cast about in our minds for the words and the constructions that will best disclose us to others. Instead we simply speak, and the words and constructions that come to our minds reveal everything about our inward state—every anxiety, affectation, or manipulative intention, and all our humility, sorrow, or joy. In the details of our speech, we reveal that we have found suitable and appealing certain kinds of expression, either complicated or simple, tawdry or clean, agitated or calm. We are spontaneously drawn to language that best fits our interests at the moment. To the pure heart, our speech perfectly betrays our taste and our judgment. We can never hide ourselves under a cover of words.

Might it not be possible, by careful attention to the particulars of written or spoken language, to grow more and more discerning—to develop a discipline or art for understanding others through their speech? Yes. In simple terms, that is what Arthur Henry King has done. Some very important scholars have said that his treatise on Ben Jonson and the language of Elizabethan England, which appeared in 1941, created a new scholarly discipline.

At the very least, it consolidated this new discipline out of elements available in the tradition in which Arthur was rigorously trained, and thereby set a new kind of example in textual studies. Employing all the tools of philological and rhetorical analysis developed in the Western tradition, he collects with extraordinary precision every imaginable detail of the tone and structure of a text, until a rich understanding emerges of the speaker's (or author's) intentions and of the complexities of the speaker's relationships with everyone relevant to his act of speech. Arthur arrives at a critical understanding of the text through the intricate accumulation of facts that stand there, on the page, for all to see.

But that understanding, Arthur contends, cannot be completely stated in words. The meaning and truth of a text cannot be "boiled down" and restated any more than the fullness of another human being, which has been received in an intimate friendship over a long period of time, can be expressed in a carefully worded report. The understanding gained from Arthur's fruitful way of reading is what happens in and to the reader; it cannot be distilled in a paraphrase and passed on. Reading is more like conversion than it is like acquisition. It's the sort of thing we cannot be given but must undergo in consequence of diligent effort we ourselves have made (which incidentally is an important principle for those of us who aspire to teach the scriptures helpfully).

Here is another surprising wrinkle. When I called what Arthur has developed "a scholarly discipline," you might have thought I meant a technology of some kind, a skill that anyone with sufficient aptitude and training would be able to obtain and use. If you did, I misled you. The quality and degree of understanding that comes of this discipline depends on purity of intention, which is to say, on the openness and humility and self-forgetfulness of the soul who uses it. However technically equipped, a scholar will be able to discover in the rhetorical and philological and historical details he notices only what he is morally and spiritually prepared to accept; any personal agenda—any professional insecurity or arrogance, any shame or self-justification before others or God—will skew his interpretation. He will not see in the author or speaker what is there to be seen because there will not be enough love in him to accept that author or speaker without judgment and rejection.

This I think is why highly educated souls can be divided about the language of righteous people, especially the language of the prophets. Occasionally I hear an educated person say that this or that prophet does not speak or write particularly well and add, condescendingly and presumably by way of consolation, that prophets should be measured by what they say and not how they say it. Supposedly the prophets could express their message better if they were better educated. To those expressing this opinion, Arthur would say that the prophets' manner of speaking—the tone and rhythm and word choice and construction of their speech—is essential to their message. For in such aspects of their speech, we encounter these divinely anointed souls as they are being touched by the Holy Spirit, and we equally receive the Holy Spirit as mediated through them. We encounter in a prophet's words a living presence as surely as we would face-to-face. An individual soul is revealed to us; love is manifest. Whether we receive it is ours to determine. Everyone who has discovered the scriptures' living, nourishing substance understands what I am talking about.

So it is both true and not true that Arthur's unexcelled proficiency in textual analysis enabled him to recognize the authenticity of Joseph Smith when he first read Joseph's story. "[Joseph Smith] spoke to me, as soon as I read his testimony, as a great writer," Arthur has written, "transparently sincere and matter-of-fact. . . . Because Joseph Smith talked about his experiences in the way he did, I was able to believe him; and having that belief, I could then go on to say, 'This man tells the truth; therefore, I ought to believe other things he tells me, even though I haven't got the same evidence of those.'"[3] Any sensitive, righteous soul would have sensed the unusual straightforwardness and candor of the Prophet's words, but it took Arthur's technical skill to see why the Prophet could not have written as he did had he been perpetrating a deception. Conversely, if Arthur had lacked the humility and freedom from guile for which his honorary children respect him, the Prophet's own guilelessness would never have been so apparent to Arthur, in spite of his prodigious ability to read incisively. Reading of the profoundest kind is an act of true morality, which in turn grows out of faith.

Because profound reading requires faith and humility, the scholarly discipline Arthur created has little chance of broad acceptance in a secular and increasingly vulgar culture. On Arthur's own principles, his colleagues were not quite right who suggested that we would be able to go further in criticism of texts when we had others well enough educated to do the kind of fundamental and thorough-going work that Arthur has done. Education alone is not enough. Those so educated must also have attained to something of Arthur's desire for righteousness and generosity. In the study of matters human, scholarly work cannot be separated from the scholar's present spiritual condition. Concerning this inseparability, Arthur himself would be the first to add that the relationship between the scholar's work and spirit means that no individual can claim to have achieved a correct and complete analysis of any text; in other words, for the same reason that we cannot say that we are good, we cannot say that any of our interpretations is definitive. We are at best underlaborers to God, hoping that our efforts will yield something good.

This book strikes me as one small part of the good that Arthur has desired to come of his life's work. He means it as a call to arm the next generation—not with weapons like suspicion or wiliness or seductive appeal or any other so-called competitive advantage in this world, but with the armor of God spoken of in Ephesians. He thinks constantly of girding the children about with truth, fitting their feet with the shoes of gospel preparation for a long life's journey, and fashioning for them the breastplate of righteousness, the helmet of salvation, the sword of the Spirit, and the shield of faith. Since a righteous heart is able to discern both good and evil, it enjoys a natural protection from deception and seduction.

Arthur insists that the right place for arming the children is in the home. The work is to be done by parents and grandparents and siblings. As President Boyd K. Packer has taught, "Lest parents and children be 'tossed to and fro,' and misled by 'cunning craftiness' of men who 'lie in wait to deceive' (Eph. 4:14), our Father's plan requires that, like the generation of life itself, the shield of faith is to be made and fitted in the family. No two can be exactly alike. Each must be handcrafted to individual specifications. . . . The shield of faith is not manufactured on an assembly line, only handmade in a cottage industry."[4]

Children will want to love what their parents love. They can be introduced to intimate subjects in an atmosphere of trust and reverence, starkly different from the whispered or raucous settings that make these subjects seem forbidden and vulgar. They can learn about the horrors and temptations to be met with in the world while sitting in the safety of a parent's lap. They can be surrounded by objects and implements that are both true—in that they do not present themselves to be other than they are—and beautiful. (Arthur is very particular about this and gives a number of examples.) They can hear and learn to read the scriptures from their earliest years so that the language of these books becomes for them like a native tongue. Furthermore, they can orient themselves in life by the template of understanding given in the scriptures and not according to the confused principles of self-indulgence and self-promotion that structure life as seen in movies, on television, in posted advertisements that scream for our attention, and in the written materials available everywhere. Children can grow up in the presence of the best music and good art. Everything in a proper education has to do with the development of taste and good moral judgment. A home must be formative as well as nurturing. When the time comes, as it will, for the children to enter the world on their own, they must be equipped both to look at evil and feel revulsion and to look at good and feel delight.

"Touch not the evil gift, nor the unclean thing," Moroni writes, and "lay hold upon every good thing" (Moro. 10:30; 7:19.) Even early in his life, Arthur might have taken these to be his watchwords, had he known of them. He has gone about this world (throughout his academic and administrative career in various universities and the educational systems of the British Commonwealth, he has resided in England, Sweden, Germany, Persia, Pakistan, and the United States, and he has traveled extensively in most other places on earth) searching persistently for everything beautiful, good, and true—whatever has one of these qualities has them all—and decisively turning away from anything less. And while turning away, he has said to himself, "That is not what I am seeking for. That is not it at all." This is one of the many ways he has sought all his life to live what the Prophet Joseph called "the admonition of Paul"—to embrace everything "virtuous, lovely, or of good report or praiseworthy" (A of F 1:13) and eschew the rest.

The intensity and thoughtfulness of this search may partly explain why, as Arthur tells us in the story of his conversion, the definiteness and goodness of the doctrine of the Church struck him so forcefully. That intensity may also account for the entirely appropriate anxiety he feels and expresses in this book: the next generation must be armed against the treacheries that lie in wait for them. Our children can become so armed by having developed within them the same moral alertness that Arthur has striven to maintain in himself—the same antipathy to all that may be vulgar, sentimental, or inhumane and the same sense of homecoming in the presence of everything beautiful, good, and true.

—C. Terry Warner

NOTES

[1]Joseph Smith to William W. Phelps, January 11, 1833, quoted in Dean C. Jessee, comp. and ed., *The Personal Writings of Joseph Smith* (Salt Lake City: Deseret Book, 1984), 264.

[2]Smith to Phelps, January 11, 1833, quoted in Jessee, *The Personal Writings of Joseph Smith*, 264.

[3]Arthur Henry King, *The Abundance of the Heart* (Salt Lake City: Bookcraft, 1986), 25–26.

[4]Boyd K. Packer, "The Shield of Faith," *Ensign* 25 (May 1995): 8, 9.

Editor's Note

In 1986 a collection of Arthur Henry King's talks was published by Bookcraft as *The Abundance of the Heart.* All copies of that book were eventually sold, but Bookcraft did not issue a second edition. Over the last several years, therefore, people interested in Brother King's work have had to put their names on used-book stores' frustratingly long waiting lists in hopes of finding a copy.

With the publication of *Arm the Children*, the waiting is now over. In addition to providing five previously unpublished talks, *Arm the Children* contains all the talks that appeared in *The Abundance of the Heart.* We have also retained the topic divisions used in *The Abundance of the Heart.* In addition, *Arm the Children* contains a foreword by C. Terry Warner that includes his original introduction to *The Abundance of the Heart* plus new material written specifically for this volume.

A few technical points should be noted here. First, all references to Shakespeare (and they are abundant) are to *The Riverside Shakespeare* (Boston: Houghton Mifflin, 1974). Second, except for explanatory notes about Brother King's poetry, no endnotes appear in any chapter. Instead, source citations appear in parentheses within the text. Third, except for scriptural references, Shakespeare references, and a few long quotations, sources for most of the essays' short quotations or paraphrases are not provided. Fourth, with Brother King's approval, we have tried to edit the talks so that generic references are gender neutral. Readers will notice an exception to that policy with references to "the natural man" or "fallen man" (phrases that appear several times in the standard works). Nevertheless, we have tried to make the language inclusive where it was so intended.

Readers will find *Arm the Children* provocative, particularly because the talks often seek to distinguish the difference between popular culture and the gospel. "Arm the Children," the opening talk, provides a global perspective for the rest of the volume. That talk describes how we can help our children put on the whole armor of God, a theme central to the author's life as an English professor at Brigham Young University. As Brother King has no living offspring, he often notes that he considers many of his students and colleagues to be his "honorary" children. His talks are designed to arm those children—and the rest of us—for the battle between good and evil.

—Daryl R. Hague

Arm the Children!

For we wrestle not against flesh and blood, but against principalities, against powers, against the rulers of the darkness of this world, against spiritual wickedness in high places.

Wherefore take unto you the whole armour of God, that ye may be able to withstand in the evil day, and having done all, to stand.

Stand therefore, having your loins girt about with truth, and having on the breastplate of righteousness;

And your feet shod with the preparation of the gospel of peace;

Above all, taking the shield of faith, wherewith ye shall be able to quench all the fiery darts of the wicked.

And take the helmet of salvation, and sword of the Spirit, which is the word of God. (Eph. 6:13–17)

For we let our young men and women go out unarmed, in a day when armor was never so necessary. By teaching them all to read, we have left them at the mercy of the printed word. By the invention of the film and the radio, we have made certain that no aversion to reading shall secure them from the insentient battery of words, words, words. They do not know what the words mean; they do not know how to ward them off, or blunt their edge or fling them back; they are a prey to words in their emotions instead of being the masters of their intellects. We who were scandalized in 1940 when men were sent to fight armored tanks with rifles, are not scandalized when young men and women are sent into the world to fight mass propaganda with a smattering of "subjects"; or when whole classes of whole nations become hypnotized by the arts of the spellbinder, we have the impudence to be astonished. The suffering of any child shames a decent conscience. The simplest definition of evil begins with whatever makes a child suffer. The most terrible failure of adults has been their inability, or unwillingness, to shoulder responsibilities of adults and protect children not only from war but also from other, newer, non-martial forms of destruction.

(Dorothy L. Sayers, *The Lost Tools of Learning* [London: Methuen, 1948], 12–13)

The theme of parentlessness has become pervasive in the world. . . . Hell is answered prayers: greed has an omnivorous life of its own. During the 1960s, American fathers failed in their responsibilities to the young whom they involved in the Vietnam War. Now the moral abdications of adults in the economically successful world have brought down upon their own young inundations of drugs, guns, and a slithering, id-ridden chaos of cultural violence—all the highly profitable artifacts, legal and illegal, of a spiritual devolution as destructive as war.

("The Evil at the Dragon's Feet," *Time*, June 19, 1995, 66)

Christianity in one form or another is a world religion. The Founding Fathers, even Paine, one way or another believed in God. But the Fathers could hardly realize what would happen in the world and how fast it would happen. Two questions suggest themselves: (1) Has a country hitherto survived without a religion as grounding? and (2) Can Americans operate the Constitution of the United States if they are not Christian?

The United States is still the most Christian country in the world, but since the nineteenth century, the United States has not implied to its immigrants that they were welcome on the unspoken assumption that they intended to become Americans—that is, English-speaking Christians. Even so, racial prejudices in the United States have been too strong, brotherly love too cold. Indeed, the authorities are still allowing helplessly disoriented immigrant labor to be exploited (more often than not by already-established members of the immigrants' own race) to provide cheap clothing, fruit, and other products.

The United States has survived into a surround of minorities that separately may not amount to much but together form a politically decisive mass. Even so, for a long time Americans still had Christianity in common with the immigrants—or with most of them. That is no longer so. By now there are few indications about the education that can be undertaken in this country in this situation. Elder

James E. Faust called the religion of those who now determine the culture of this country a "civic religion." In so doing, he put his finger on it. The fact that this religion is civic does not mean, however, that it is all-embracing. As time goes on, the tensions between groups in this country—as in other countries—are tightening.

Violence and the Civic Religion

Violence is most noteworthy in the United States because it is a large place with high population in urban centers. Violence has increased also in European countries and all over the world. This violence is at its worst in Africa, where tribal rivalry simmers everywhere and has boiled over most recently in Rwanda and Burundi. These genocides are not characteristic of our own time—they have always happened. But in the past, they have happened on a smaller scale and less often because the population was smaller, whereas means of annihilation are now more powerful and the disposal of the bodies easier. This is the situation in which we find ourselves, and our children are going to face an even worse situation than we do at the moment.

Now this civic religion, which has its source in Satan, has its most obvious expression through bureaucrats (federal and local), teachers, and "priests" of the communicatorian and communicatrician churches. (The armed services are too close to fundamentals to be satisfied with a civic religion—they have chaplains.) Teachers—and especially physical science, life science, and social science instructors—are generally regarded as neutral in religion, but that is because civic religion refuses to regard itself as a religion; the anonymity resulting from that refusal is the movement's principal strength. Civic religion's High Church is the Establishment, in particular that of the Washington area. This religion's missionary propaganda is through the media. Its touch on the shoulder resembles the touch of death.

It is impossible for people to live without either religion or some kind of idolatry or private fetishism. Those in the last group construct for themselves some kind of fourth dimension. There have been other groups, in other times besides our own, who have made violence their god. Until the late nineteenth century in India, for example, a sect existed—in fact they lately show some signs of revival—called the *thuggees*. These thugs lived for theft and slaughter. So we have no new human situation on this planet, but the scale on which things happen has changed.

In addition to the scale on which things now happen, we must also face the matter of people's delight in violence. Sometimes that violence assumes the mantle of so-called righteous indignation. The problem is whether there can be such a thing as righteous indignation. True, the Lord has been wroth from time to time, but I don't think that is the kind of wrath we are liable to have as a reaction against cruelty we may perceive. We're liable to have pleasure in the violence and to have pleasure in our lustful indignation against it as well. A worse thing than the perpetrators of violence themselves is the far larger number of persons who enjoy, not committing violence, but watching it. They experience a vicarious joy, a pleasure at seeing people struck and shot. The media obviously would not produce such material were it not that millions of such people abound.

We are more prone to violence in the earlier part of our lives, in adolescence. I can remember violent feelings in myself, although I was restrained by my religion—I was a member of the Society of Friends (Quakers). I don't know what would have happened to me if I had not had that restraint—I was deeply affected by social conditions, as were some of my peers. I was always in a minority, resenting the majority. Some may say that the violence resulting from such youthful resentment reflects social rather than political realities. True, but on uninhibited talk shows, middle-aged and older persons have admitted suddenly that they found pleasure in a violent scene in a film or something like that, but they have been disgusted with themselves to find that violence was within them.

We find it too easy to hate cruel persons, and yet Christians are required not to hate. The civic religion, so-called, can do nothing for us because there is no religious force behind it. There is, however, a demeaning force behind it, and that is the force of natural scientists. Natural science is science about nature, and "the natural man is an enemy to God" (Mosiah 3:19). Natural scientists see human beings as part of nature—as natural man—not as supernatural; therefore, science sees human beings as enemies to God. Social scientists follow suit and have produced the "theology" of behaviorism for the use of civic religionists. Not that civic religionists necessarily realize it or that people who believe in science know it, but civic religionists' use of science is an inevitable consequence. Being restricted to the "natural" part of humanity, they can't believe in anything else but science. They have to have a religion, and human beings can make a religion of anything—a person, an idol, a stone, a blanket, a rag, even a philosophy.

For the last few generations, there has been much "well-meaninglessness" in society. In other words, society's true nature is hidden by favorable interpretations. Even we in our church are reluctant to think a thing is of evil unless we absolutely have to. One of the ways we can rectify this situation is to distinguish between the sin and the sinner. The sins of violence are serious sins and have serious effects on the sinner, but that must not affect our judgment of the sinner as a child of God. Such judgment may become extremely difficult, for we believe in the true faith, and we therefore often feel that we are in a better position to judge. The feeling that we are in a better position, however, seems ceasing to be so: we are prone to abandon conviction for mildness and thereby betray ourselves and others.

Social scientists have no problem here. They increasingly consider human beings as victims of their nature; therefore, human beings are not responsible for their conduct unless they make themselves responsible. In so doing, they think they know they evolved in a society of other natural men, those natural men also being enemies to God. So people become victims of their own beliefs.

Risks of Ignoring the Devil

This kind of thinking now gets support from the civic religion. Those working against us are subtly powerful and highly intelligent. If we compromise or collaborate with them, we permit the Devil entry. In a situation like this, to ignore the Devil as a driving principle and a person is to go with most of society. But if we do not believe in a devil in society, we do not believe sufficiently in the depth at which we really live. We inhabit ourselves in various "storeys." We may keep the basement and the attic locked because we don't keep them clean and tidy. There are cupboards into which we hastily throw things when a righteous soul comes to visit. But deep down somewhere the Devil works. And there is a devil or representative of the Devil in every department-block of ourselves. The reality of the Devil and sin is scriptural, but we do not sufficiently teach it to our children nowadays in the light of where they are and what they have to put up with and what they will have to endure.

We must understand that our children's problems are going to be more difficult than ours are now. We have to prepare them for that. A child who does not believe that the Devil exists can hardly imagine or worship anything profound. A world in which evil either does not exist or does not go down as far as good is a world which is unreal, superficial. The Devil is prepared to take any of us on at any point in ourselves if we give him the opportunity. And we constantly give him the opportunity by not making the best of ourselves and by not endeavoring to get our children fit for the struggle against an evil society, a society that will increasingly try to suppress our church because our church will not conform to the doctrine of a civil religion where the ultimate reality is generally taken to be the State and, hence, the body politic. That body politic believes in the tradition of Descartes, John Locke, Jeremy Bentham, John Stuart Mill, Herbert Spencer, Watson, and Skinner rather than that of Saint Thomas Aquinas, Bacon, Newton, Goethe, Coleridge, Carlyle, Emerson, William James, Whitehead, Santayana, and Gadamer.

Desirability of Faith

Education publicly undertaken without reference to religion is suspect. Education cannot exist that way; it becomes instruction, instruction about apparently objective "facts." But for human beings, there are no such things as objective facts. Rather, we have observations stimulated by experience. Our observations re-create the world inside us. What comes out and speaks to another person does not come out from facts but from creative interpretations of nerve phenomena; these phenomena bring to the center of our brain (however this thing works) impressions of things that are facts out there but not in our mind. These facts are at a point where we can't get hold of them; we can only get hold of our observations and our experience, not the facts themselves. That is the world without faith, without divine knowledge, without the light of Christ or the Holy Spirit. We should realize that in a world with that kind of uncertainty, our children need to have certain certainties, divine and eternal certainties, to enable them to live a moral and religious life. If children don't have certainties to live by, they become desperate and gang themselves together in their own kind of solution—and that is a solution of despair. The point is, therefore, that we have a duty to protect our children from the human environment into which they are born—not simply from the temptations of the world, but more importantly from the misinformation of the world, misinformation that leads to wrong life as well as to temptations.

The world presents its misinformation in seemingly objective ways. But objectivity is not possible. To illustrate, consider public broadcasting. I normally listen to public broadcasting in the early morning—I do that because it is more thorough than TV news. But because it is more thorough, one can more easily see the slant that any particular person takes. I noticed this morning, for example, that a man from outside the public broadcasting ring was asked to comment about the present situation in Washington. He was being interviewed by an interviewer who was sitting in for someone who would normally have been there. It became obvious to me within a moment or two that the interviewer was nonplussed, actively trying to keep his courage up in the face of a different kind of presentation from what he usually got. What one usually gets in this kind of broadcasting is opinions put by both sides as if they were objectively handled. On this occasion, however, the outsider was putting forth honest opinions, not pretending to be objective.

Human beings cannot write objective history; we can only hope to write honest history. Honest history means we recognize the contribution we make to our own writing. And that recognition is true not only of history and other humane academic subjects, but also of the history of our lives, our gossip, and so forth. What do our children need to be able to protect themselves from the seemingly objective misinformation of the world? Above all, they need a sense of values based upon the gospel—clear, simple, and not tangled in incompatibility. They should be taught in that clarity, clarity that has had to overcome generations of error and misunderstanding yet has sufficiently survived by tradition and revelation for our church to be able to work, as we now do work, to convert those outside, to educate those within, and to redeem the dead.

Advice for School Children

Within the Church, faith is growing in numbers and intensity, growing by the continued creation of large families and by better education in the gospel and regular attendance at meetings. Our young people need to be reminded constantly that they belong to a church that grows stronger every day. Our schoolgoers should go to school in the confidence of their beliefs, the ability to state and defend them in the playground or in the classroom. Our children must have the kind of warm interest in those around them that will form friendship groups. When they are in the majority, they should behave with modest ease to the Gentiles among them; when in the minority, they should seek opportunities of leadership. Whether in the majority or minority, they should be prepared for the official attitude of the nation as a whole as expressed through the media. That attitude encourages people to be at best cold and at worst dead against all forms of religion—in good times to be not intolerant, but in bad or critical times to turn against us, to single us out for condemnation, to envy us, and even to persecute us. Our children need to know the history of the Church; history helps to tell us what will happen.

TV announcers, programmers, journalists, academics, and people of affairs pretend to be unprejudiced; they think they are not prejudiced, but they also think religious people are prejudiced. These "writers" are more responsible than others for the permissiveness of modern society. When children are being misinformed by such people, especially in early adolescence (a crucial time for this upsetting of convictions), parents need to know enough about public affairs, science, and the arts to be able to deal with that misinformation. The crucial time for all this is between the ages of thirteen and sixteen. The young soul may choose to use school and state, national and media authority against parents and the parents' church. This use may just be teasing or it may be serious (for me it was a kind of political game played when I was fifteen to sixteen). If serious, the young soul may well use any weapon. Rock music is likely to come in. If we like jazz ourselves, we are in no position to argue—that would be like the man who uses alcohol yet tries to stop his son from using cocaine.

Lessons of Morality

The fact that society has lost its morality is clear and should be made clear to our children. One of the major causes of this lost morality is that people undertake business in the first place for gain, not for quality production. People interested in producing an article because they are expert in doing so are less likely to emphasize profit over quality. Those concerned solely with finance, however, are obviously more interested in profit than in quality. The tendency toward diminished morality that results from a focus on profit is exacerbated by the fact that at this time in our history—in the United States and Britain and Europe generally—we are moving towards providing services rather than maintaining industrial production.

Problems in a Megalopolis

Aside from aiding a loss in morality, our industrial and service-oriented society makes understanding the scriptures difficult for us. The metaphorical structure of the scriptures is based on pastoral and agricultural culture. That metaphorical base has not been adapted to post–industrial revolution or post–communication revolution conditions. The difficulty is not simply the language, but the societies about which the language is speaking. I have difficulty avoiding the idea that the agricultural and pastoral life is appropriate for humanity and that these other lives are not.

One example of these other lives is the oft-told story of the young soul going to New York or Washington or Hollywood to pursue a career; such stories provide the material for countless films. But going to a megalopolis is not a good idea. A better idea is to mature in our own hometown because the sooner we get away from our roots, the sooner our lives will become standardized and empty. For instance, I remember talking on my way back from England once with a group of young LDS lawyers who were working in New York City. They wanted to know how to reconcile their church life and their law life; in the light of their evidence, I had only one thing to tell them: leave New York. What can be done in a reasonably sized city with a reasonable amount of competition cannot be done in a megalopolis like New York where life is a rat race. And the existence of a rat race depends not just on the size, but the kind of place in which we live. There can be a real, royal rat race in Los Angeles or San Diego or San Francisco, but not perhaps in Salt Lake County. To seek a career is risky; to accept a career that appears to be coming to us may well be wiser.

Too Much TV

Taking off for a megalopolis might be a consequence of too much TV, although the problem is not so much the programs as the advertisements. Think about the advertisements created especially to attract teenagers. These ads are obviously not created for the sophisticated (who see through them) because the sophisticated prefer the kind of advertisement that addresses them. Think of young girls between, should we say, the ages of thirteen and seventeen, and consider the ads' emphasis on cosmetics; think of the lubricious sequence screens to advertise skin cream—the rolling body and glances building up the effect. Apart from these advertisements' pornographic nature, they also promote the false idea that one can become attractive by merely adding cream.

When I first joined the Church, I was shocked to find that sisters used make-up at all. My mother used to say that only duchesses and courtesans made up. The top and bottom of society are often similar in that each has its own morality; on the whole, they actually employ a lack of morality as opposed to the morality of the middle class. For example, a duchess or female factory head may swear, but the school mistress does not. Approaches to marriage similarly illustrate these class differences in morality. The lowest classes cannot afford to marry, while the upper classes marry for economic advantage and power rather than for love. (One may find, for example, the saying "You go your way and I'll go mine," concerning life after marriage among the upper classes.)

Need of Christianity in Capitalism

Communism is said to have proved itself infeasible, but that is not correct: communism may never have been tried. Any student of the Soviet Union could have told you, had you asked, that what we saw in Russia was state socialism. State socialism, too, has been weighed in the balance and found wanting, but it is still being tried in Western Europe. The inadequacies of state socialism mean that capitalism (muddling through with Keynes) is the only economic method available—it works more or less, but it needs to be tempered by regulation. Otherwise, it is stupid enough to force wages down to starvation level (as it did in the nineteenth century) and concentrate wealth into a small proportion of the population. That concentrated wealth is inherited by children who often are not given the opportunity to work hard and subsequently become weak members of the next generation. So they lose control to others, and their offspring find themselves back in poverty. The Old Testament shows this circulation repeatedly in the nation of Israel.

Hard work and intelligence may help people become wealthy; those intelligent enough to make money, however, may not be intelligent enough to be religious. Even if they are religious, they may still be fools enough to be hypocrites. Without Christian principles, capitalism will not work any more than the American Constitution. Christian entrepreneurs should pay fair wages, involve workers in governing the institution, and offer a reliable future. But few business owners nowadays take this point of view. There are many areas where the number of scoundrels in leading positions is increasing, and Christians may find themselves more and more compelled to a compromise as everybody steps down the slippery slope together.

As the economic system declines, rioting and counterrioting will spread more and more widely until martial law is declared, and it may be at that point (to judge from what happens and has happened in the Third World) that the armed services take over. The good LDS parent may well feel that the Church will take care of its own (and to some extent that may happen), but it seems to me, as to so many others at this time, that what I have suggested may well occur within thirty or forty years. By that time, the Church will not be numerous enough to cope with the entire situation. Of course, we in the Church have shown what we can do by providing relief after the disasters at the Teton Dam, other places in this country, and up and down the world, but at the moment such help is sporadic and is likely to remain so for some generations to come.

Parents to Confront Civic Religion

Should good Latter-day Saints wish to oppose these statements of mine as too gloomy, too hopeless, what alternative do they read out of prophecy? If we are wise enough to base our teaching on what prophecy tells us in the scriptures, why do we not apply the scriptures to ourselves, as we are bidden to do, and explain to the next generation what that prophecy is likely to mean? With the institution of the civic state becoming still more "civic" and with children being taught more and more by "civic" teachers (meaning agnostic or atheistic teachers), parents must realize that they need to try and keep ahead of their children in the kind of subjects that I have roused in this talk. By doing so, parents can help to keep the initiative over the civic state.

Young souls do not always come home from school with ideas implanted in them by their teachers. They may well have ideas of their own, and those ideas are the ones that parents need most carefully to investigate and to clarify. Parents should not lead their adolescent children in these matters so much as guide and criticize them. The situation in which the parent is critical of the child is much better than that where the child is critical of the parent. When the adolescent matures, nevertheless, the parent should be glad of criticism and take it seriously, as with an equal. The time will come when the parent will have to learn from the child.

Instruction in Faith and Reason

As parents confront the civic religion and their children's responses to it, they should always remember one fundamental principle: the theories of natural science are dependent upon observed "facts," and those observed "facts" may change as time goes on and theories change to fit them. Moral principles, on the other hand, stand firmly from the beginning and do not change, although in every society they have to be applied in such a way as to remain faithful to the principle itself. During a recent Education Week whose title was "Refinement by Reason and Revelation," for example, I should have preferred the title to be "Refinement by Revelation and Reason." For reason is the handmaid of faith, not its leader. Any intelligent scientist knows we shouldn't get out of bed in the morning but for faith. Get out of bed? We shouldn't even open one eye.

We cannot but feel confidence in certain basic things in order to depend on reason. We are confident, for example, that no large comet will induce the death of the Earth by collision during the next twenty-four hours, days, weeks, months, years, centuries, or millions of years (well, just possibly in that last time phase). Once we have started along this line of confidence in basic things, we cannot stop until we believe in a God who from our point of view (and this we have to teach our children) is omniscient and omnipotent; from his own point of view (which is not our business) he may, like ourselves, be following eternal progression an indeterminate interval ahead of us. But this way of thinking is absurd, for we don't know what an *eternal* progression is. An imaginative mathematician might be able to suggest an image. But let the eternal follow their eternal round, and let us be reminded that our children born under the covenant must be worthy and that they may well be at risk, and we as their parents—their teachers, bishops, stake presidents, and other leaders—must know more than the outside world.

Younger children are inclined to be rational; they can be taught at an early age about faith and reason. Reason frequently takes a form in young children of what is called in Shakespearean clowns "absoluteness," meaning taking absolutely literally what is said to you and replying accordingly, though the reply may be absurd. Children are apt to do that; they play a teasing game in which the parent replies in turn and is kind in making the situation even more absurd. From the age of eight or nine, children may enjoy the discussion in Lewis Carroll's "Alice" books. Parent and child may then collaborate in restoring common sense. When children reach that point, they may learn chess (some children will enjoy learning this from the age of six). They can try alternative moves and follow the consequences. While learning through such experimentation, they will also learn to have faith in the long-term wisdom of experience, when the steps of reasoning go beyond their power. Certain situations on the chess board, for example, look healthier than others: the consolidation of castling, realizing the rooks' potential, opening a bishop's file, and keeping the queen in reserve until the right bishop's moment.

Every one of the situations on the chess board is a metaphor of common life. Chess is a moral game—if things go wrong they're our own fault, not luck. In contrast, games of chance are immoral because success is not predicated upon ability but on the luck of the game. Gambling in all its forms must be prohibited—it becomes an unfit addiction. It plays upon weakness and superstition. Games of chance tempt the less able child to become less and less effective; that is dangerous because children have to learn to defend themselves from their own weaknesses.

Importance of Love in the Home

Chess and other games that require us to learn skills may combine with the life of imagination and the development of feeling, sensibility, and love by means of the arts. Love grows with shared experiences and shared joy. Nothing is so important to a young soul as the companionship of the parent, and a father in particular has no excuse in lack of time. The father nearly always has more time. People often say that "a woman's work is never done," but many men's work stops at a specific time. A man never knows how much he gains by missing the drudgery and frustration of daily living within the house. Unfortunately, the wage earner's leisure is at home, while the homemaker's leisure (far more rare) is away from home. The typical parent hopes to get this solved.

To face the world, children need the assured early background of a good home. The home is where children should learn love and collaboration, not quarreling and rivalry. One of our main points as Mormons, however, is that the home—together with the Church—is really responsible for much more than those things. Faced with the state-based "civic" religion, "education" will be better described as "public instruction." We therefore have to accept the real education that takes place away from school.

Economics and Childhood Education

So far, I have been speaking about our children's education more in terms of social and political background rather than economics. Simply said, both the well-off and the impoverished are more at risk than those who have neither too much nor too little. The difficulty of the impoverished home is obvious: there may not be enough to go round, that is, not enough to satisfy the children's and adults' needs. That the affluent home gets something is obvious. The affluent home can provide for the needs of the children and go beyond that: it can provide for the children's wants and demands and desires. In such homes, however, a greater probability exists that parents, burdened with added social responsibilities, will seek their own ways apart from the children. This situation may well lead to affluence itself being a substitute for love. The affluent sometimes delegate the care of their children, for example, to underlings.

Aside from economics, the number of children in a family contributes to the kind of education children receive. The home with but one child is obviously at risk; two means rivalry; three means switching loyalties; four is getting better; and five and upward may well prove safe. The more children there are, the less likely each is to sense not having enough attention to itself. That is because all lack attention instead of some having it and some not: they more easily perceive unsharing than sharing. Regardless of how many children there might be, however, the sense of inequality may remain. Early on, the tendency is for the older ones to do more ably than the younger; as times go by, the sense of rivalry and competition will be more marked because the early sense of hierarchy no longer exists. One or two of the older children may well not be so able as some of the younger ones. Such differences, in my experience, may last a lifetime.

Preparation for Realities of School

Childish logic insists on absolute equality, like counting how many chips we have on our plates. Parents do not do well to let children go into the world (that is, to school) unprepared. Instead, children must expect most of their peers to be normal. They must expect a certain amount of inequality and injustice. They must expect vulgarity. For example, my first day at council-school showed me a depth of depravity that remained with me as a private nightmare for years. I only hope most children won't have to face that. Unfortunately, the playground normally produces one or two bad-mouthed, loose-minded, thieving, bullying, envious, malicious, and cruel individuals.

Many parents will probably find—if the process has not begun before—that children develop some sense of privacy from the first time at school. Once their public schooling begins, children inhabit two worlds, and they will soon find it necessary to restrict conversation about either world in the other. Questions like "What did you learn in school today?" and "Did you make any new friends?" may be as embarrassing to the child as some of the questions we get asked sometimes in Sunday School. These questions may cause embarrassment because their answers are so obvious that anybody would be too embarrassed to answer. Rather than ask such questions, parents need to have a knowledge of details to be able to start from; once they have established their interest that way, they will find that it is possible to continue a conversation which may require brief information.

Children and Cynical Mentors

Parents particularly need to be able to establish whether there is a group or a single individual to whom their child "gravitates." Children are prone to be attracted to slightly older children who demonstrate an ability to deal socially. These older children may also be cynics and pose as such, and you may find your child imitating them. In some ways, this problem is worse than sex or drugs because it starts at the roots. The mentor children are anxious to break down anything positive, anything hopeful, anything naive, anything enthusiastic in your own child. Your children may well have a teacher that does this sort of thing; older siblings may do it as well. The child may be particular to keep the mentor relationship secret, especially if the influential child is a posing cynic. The cynical mentor is the most likely way of establishing in children a sense of superiority to or skepticism towards their own parents or, above all, their own religion. This process can start earlier than many people think.

Children may find their cynical mentor in a book, a film star, a criminal, or a rock hero. Beyond the hero looms the shadow of the gang; the secret group; determination against parents, society, and the Church; lies and hypocrisy. This situation may be regarded as the modern equivalent of the Robin Hood ideal: terrorism.

Public talk is increasingly liable to dwell on violence in humanity and nature, opening up vistas of horrifying decay and destruction. It is possible for people to behave anywhere as they have already behaved in Nazi Germany, Los Angeles, Africa, and the Far East. The constant grind of killings between the descendants of Abraham and Isaac and Jacob is sufficient example of how deep rooted these things are.

Need to Counter Advertising and Fads

To descend from the sublimely horrific to the apparently absurd—but nevertheless dangerous—small-scale detail of life, the cereal package on the breakfast table provides a good early lesson in defense against a voracious society. One side of the box describes the cereal's taste in affected and exaggerated terms; it is as if the manufacturer wanted to tell you what to taste and what the cereal will taste like so that you will know how to taste it. The example I have in my head at the moment is one which speaks of "scrumptious crunchy clusters." The repetition of sounds used to back up the description is the sort of thing Keats did. (The other part of this line of expression is a gourmet experience in misspelled words.) On the opposite side of the cereal box is a statistical analysis of the nutritional elements in the cereal. I don't suppose for a moment that a respectable firm like the one that makes "scrumptious crunchy clusters" would lie, but misrepresentation and misunderstanding lie in wait. Informed consumers will keep their own track of calories, fat content, and so forth.

Medicaments are a more serious matter than cold cereal. Misrepresentation in pharmaceutical advertisement might well be vital. Our offspring need to realize that there are souls in the world—even some in high places—who mean well to them. But there are people, many people, who simply don't want to do much about rectification. And then there are people who, if not possessed by the Devil, behave as if they were. I believe that I have had to deal with people who were possessed. Those who peddle addictive substances are wicked indeed. But cure-alls that postpone operations are just about as bad. Quacks are known by their quack-quack—their heartily universal salvation.

Advertisement's capacity for misrepresentation has not gone unnoticed. On the initiative of F. R. Leavis in the 1930's (see his *Mass Civilization and Minority Culture* and the periodical *Scrutiny*), for example, a movement was started in England to introduce the study of advertisement into the school curriculum. By 1970, the English colleges of education and the National Association of Teachers of English supported this movement; the study of advertisement—along with the study of affectation in literature—has since been incorporated into the education colleges' curriculum. This kind of teaching needs to be given throughout the teens. From the beginning, it is to parents' advantage that children should have a critical attitude toward advertisements and stilted language. Otherwise, children may see an advertisement for a product that makes them think they very much want it, and either that product is sure to disappoint or is expensive and unnecessary.

Advertisement plays a significant role in the desire to keep up with the Joneses. This desire arises in children (and parents) after they begin school; it remains constant with the false values of advertisement. Fashions, for example, are started at school; they become obsessive and compulsive (consider, for example, footwear and jewelry). This need to stay in fashion is exacerbated by the fact that children in the United States get too much pocket money too soon, and too soon do they earn money for themselves. In their teenage years, they may be particularly seduced by advertisement for clothing and cosmetics based on the desire to attract the opposite sex; such advertisements reinforce their message by visual pornography.

Why do young people who are apparently politically conservative—in the United States, of all countries—dress in proletarian working gear? This fashion trend has caught on in the world outside also. Are these young people deliberately undermining the capitalist system? By acting as they do, they are lining themselves up in dress, hair, and manners with the gangster and the terrorist. Such personal presentation seems to be an effort towards class suicide. Young people maintain, if you ask them, that they dress this way for comfort. Comfort, however, cannot be the purpose for having carefully crafted holes in the knees of the pants or for wearing Levi's in subzero temperatures. How can we help these young people to become one with the adult group in the Church? So-called primitive tribes have in the past practiced—and in some areas still do practice—difficult and painful rites of passage designed to create in their adolescents a sense of awe at becoming one with the adult group. Perhaps we should consider introducing into the rituals of priesthood advancement a scriptural competence that takes as much time, trouble, and interest as does qualifying to be an Eagle Scout.

Appropriate Education in Sex

Having mentioned the subject of rites of passage, now seems the appropriate point to discuss the question of how to help our children manage their sexual maturation. *Sex* used to be a neutral term, useful because most other words for it were filthy; but *sex* has been ruined by the term's casual use. I prefer the word *mate*, but people smile when I use it. *Mate* can be found early this century in popular novels; there, it is used mainly by men to describe their wives. Stevenson has "steel true and blade straight, the great Artificer made my mate." For a Christian with correct Christian doctrine, sex is a sacrament. It follows that we cannot teach sex by slides, films, and areligious teachers who usually cannot deal with sex's emotional aspect. In any event, most people still learn about sex inaccurately and degradingly. Education in sex (every time I repeat the term, it becomes less adequate) should be initiated and maintained for some fifteen years by parents and by Church authorities. If parents find themselves unwilling to undertake this task, they should find out why they feel that way and what is wrong with their own lives. Parents who are deeply religious and regard sex as a sacrament in their own lives should have no difficulty reaching the proper level in their children's minds.

Few people realize—and yet they should remember from their own lives—how early education in sex should begin. Quite young rural children may note the behavior of animals, while children anywhere can see the behavior of their own parents. This subject cannot be left until children inquire; if they do inquire, they may well do so because some other child has talked—and talked in such a way as to possibly ruin or seriously impair your children's highest feelings. We must not lie to or prevaricate with our children, for if we do they will probably find us out, and then they may well prefer to believe their coarse and vulgar peers. In matters of sex, parents should remember what they were like at the age of the child they are talking to. As a childless man (though I have many honorary children), it seems to me that one of the disadvantages of parenthood is that parents forget how ill-behaved (frivolous, flirtatious, wanton, affected, hypocritical, deceitful, faithless, self-seeking, careless, stupid, arrogant, self-pitying, sentimental, lustful, and cruel) they were in their early years.

The subject of sex will gradually extend to such matters as abortion, sterilization, AIDS, and sexual abuse; from these the discussion should continue to drugs, TV, pornography, the state of society and the world—all fulfilling prophesy, all pointing to the worldly end. These subjects should provide enough material for fifteen years of instruction. Can we really provide such instruction? We can if the tone is right. But we should never affect a tone for this purpose or for any purpose—that is manipulation. In no field has fallen man shown himself so fallen as in this one of sex. The largest Christian church, for example, has been warped through two thousand years by celibacy and has treated sex even worse than it has treated the Jews—and it has severely mistreated the Jews. Worst of all, false ideas about sex have made women objects of the worst abuse wreaked by men, abuse wreaked to punish the human female for supposedly tempting the human male. The story is monstrous in cultures all over the world. Above all else in our children's education in sex, the history of this abuse is what they need to learn.

A Broader Definition of Pornography

Religious parents need a far wider definition of pornography than that which satisfies the law. For me, *pornography* (which literally means writing appropriate for the brothel) includes all negative and debasing references to sex, all dirty jokes and stories—particularly those that put down women. I do not know how women talk when alone together, but I do know that when men are alone together in groups—especially in locker rooms, in camp, and in the military life generally—references to sex are debasing indeed. One might have hoped that equality of the sexes would be interpreted as bringing men up to the moral level of women, but equality seems to have taken the form (particularly with the invention of the "pill") of debasing women to men's level. Indeed, an increasing amount of pornography appears in advertisements and press periodicals, on TV, and on the stage. There seems to be a kind of unspoken—and inaccurate—belief that only certain things are pornographic and that most things are not; this belief is similar to the way that many people fail to regard alcohol as a drug when it is actually the most common and dangerous drug of all.

Link between Sentimentality and Lust

Sentimentality about sex belongs on the edge of this dubious world. It is so easy to pass from sentimentality and so-called love to lust. In fact, I am of the opinion that sentimentality and lust go well together and that most young lovers in particular have difficulty holding the balance between those two feelings. As an example of this link between sentimentality and lust, consider MGM's handling of the best actors and actresses in the world during the thirties and forties. What might MGM not have done with that crowd of male and female geniuses? Instead MGM sanctioned sentimentality and lust ("passion") in the language of mixed sentimental clichés and *double entendre*. All this pseudorespectable entertainment may be characterized as a "decent" extension of the meretricious. The acting of passion was allowed to proceed and then halt at the crux. Many in Hollywood objected that it was a very good tradition they had to follow. I fear, however, that the kind of art we were given was exactly the kind of art the MGM leadership wanted themselves to have and wanted us to have. They thought it was the best kind.

This standardized combination of sentimentality and lust, this "contraromance," has been largely replaced in accordance with the taste of the times by violence and cruelty. Matthew Arnold said, "We needs must love the highest when we see it," but what one has to say nowadays is, "We needs must lust after the lowest when we behold it." Our children need to realize—more than most things—the link between good manners, good taste, and the loving sensibility that can develop into the selfless tenderness of true married life. Children have the best means of learning about that link from the example of their parents. And if some parents realize already that they have failed, they can still help their grandchildren.

Sexual Abuse

The most recent panic of our human behavior is sexual abuse in the family. I believe that the proportion of incest to other sexual crimes has probably remained much the same throughout human history. The difference today lies in the willingness to reveal. When it comes to this subject, parents need to be as wise as serpents and harmless as doves. For the sake of our own and others' children, we must be prepared to imagine our children as other peoples' children. The retort "What? In my family?" reveals the need for humility.

It is a long way from the cereal box on the breakfast table to the sexual sins of a subcontinent, a long road between helping young children to pray and discussing the sins of society and the errors of government with adolescents. When the problem of preparing our children for the world is set out as I have done here, it seems simpler than it is. In actual fact, the matters I have discussed will not be addressed in any particular order; rather, they will be addressed as problems arise in the family. And problems can arise at any time because siblings—the children—are different ages, and they will communicate with one another accordingly. There will be a channel of information downward from the older to the younger that may anticipate your channel. I should not make recommendations about this aspect of the matter; you certainly know at least as well as I do how to teach your own children.

Preparing Our Children for the World

Throughout this talk, I have mentioned some important questions that arise in the relationship of the Church with society and of individuals in the Church with society. We obviously have to work outside as well as within and through the Church. We should think of a time when the home will have to take over more of the present services provided by the Church: the more teaching in the home, the better. It is natural that parents should as far as possible be the main teachers for their children. Parental teaching should be part of preparation for life, helping children to do much more than simply develop domestic and aesthetic skills. In how many households, however, do parents take the lead in reading the scriptures aloud, studying them, discussing them? With the scriptures' aid, adolescents may find their individual problems submerging into the problems of society. Parents should be able to comment critically on these matters.

Discussion and Family Activities

Social problems root deep. We can begin by involving children in terms of their full experience; above all, we should discuss society's ills with adolescents into their maturity. The problems of sin appear to be secondary when we are dealing with social, political, and economic matters because such matters may be remote from us. But the other problems, the deeper problems involving drugs and sex, are those in which all of us are potentially at risk. More drugs exist than the ones I have discussed: viewing, for instance, may be a passive substitute for action. Watching games on TV instead of playing them is an almost universal example of this kind of drug. Rather than simply viewing games, the well-balanced family should actually play games; furthermore, the family should have at least as much reading as games, and a good deal of that reading should be aloud.

The Role of the Arts

The united effort of the family should be to raise the level of its existence from entertainment to creativeness. This is where the arts come in; despite the differences of talent, there is no reason why all members of the family should not be able to read music and sing and explore music together. There is no reason why all family members should not have their own musical instrument. Outside and in we should praise the Lord with all the talents we have. But how can we find out what our talents are unless we try? The point is that entertainment sets out mostly to titillate, to excite, to arouse, to lull, to manipulate, to do a job on us. Admittedly it is possible to please and to edify at the same time. Purpose is the point. "Pure" entertainment is a kind of contradiction, because entertainment is purposeless. If morality is not present, some other element is present instead that makes for bad art.

The Battle against Civic Religion

This raising of the devil as entertainment is a matter for our wards as well as for our homes. We can do much to improve our standards in this area. Saints in the United States must not fail to see their responsibility for setting an example to souls in other countries. This example must be very different from that of the United States' cultural mass exports, for Christ cannot approve the export of violence, lust, and sentimentality. The responsibility for setting an example gives a serious national purpose to American citizens who are also LDS. To oppose and expose abortion is to show one of the offspring of murder, but the battle is not against the murders alone. Rather, the battle is against the cause and means of the murders, against the permissive civic religion of modern mass culture, against civic religion's craftsman, the Devil.

The Christian religion is being pushed out of its proper place in society; it will be replaced by several other things: ignorant, barbarous sects and cults. The gospel was taught in the Garden of Eden and was dispersed throughout the world in more and more adulterated forms. As a result of that dispersal, Christian elements appear in many non-Christian religions. All over the world now the dispersal seems to be repeating itself. Prophecy does not say that the world should evolve into a millennium; rather, it says that the world should decline into what the antiprophets might call animism—a chaos of superstitious tribes exploited and initiated to killings by gang chiefs under the influence of shamans and witch-doctors. The enormous task confronting us, therefore, is not so much to introduce the gospel to the world as to bring the world back to the gospel.

Falsehood of Being Masters of Our Fate

As a final example of what we are up against, consider the basic belief of the civic religion: "I believe in a cosmos that has constituted itself by natural processes." This being interpreted is as follows: "In the beginning were bootstraps, which produced boots, which produced human beings, who having donned boots by pulling on bootstraps proceed to hoist themselves up by pulling on their bootstraps so they might reach a level at which they themselves can make bootstraps." The inference we can draw from this belief is the following: "I believe that men and women are masters of their own destiny." A fundamental discrepancy exists, however, between the two tenets of a self-created universe and people as masters of their destiny. Specifically, how can we be masters of our own destiny when the universe is supposed to be developed by natural process? The ineluctable inference of civic religion's credo is that we are the slaves of our DNA.

Contrary to the civic religion's credo, we are not masters of our fate. We have free agency to choose, but having chosen, we are restricted or further liberated by the consequences of our choices. Our solution is that God's service is perfect freedom. God is, of course, the ultimate agent. Nature is not mistress of herself, nor are we the masters of nature. Just as in 1792 the French Revolutionists proclaimed reason as a goddess, so in our time have Darwin, life scientists, and others found it necessary to revert to nature. That is simply going back to the great goddess of interfering with times and places—a poor alternative to the Creator found in the New Testament. The Creator employs evolution as part of his means of creating. As to how the time goes, however, all the rest is to be seen. Some people talk about fourteen billion years; others produce a new species of fly in two weeks. DNA cannot be fully grasped. The scientists must spend a very long time trying to spell it out. And once they have done most of it, they will find increasingly a percentage of the remainder that they cannot account for and that causes all sorts of things to happen that they wouldn't expect.

Parental Responsibility

Our children need to understand the source of that remainder. They need to understand the tenets of the civic religion. They need, above all, to understand and to be protected from their own hypocrisy. As it is, they are liable to worship the goddess of nature at school and to give the Lord his due only at home. To ensure against that eventuality, parents must take responsibility for the level of education and religious practice in the home; they cannot devolve that responsibility upon anybody else. Parents need to provide education such that children make the best use of their time and realize that that is what they are supposed to do. In order to be able to realize this, children have to learn to enjoy the best. If they fail to do so, they will sink to the level of entertainment.

Entertainment is never sacramental, yet the Lord intended our lives to be sacramental. Our lives must become sacramental. If our lives and those of our children do not become sacramental, we shall not be worthy of the future that the Lord offers to those who believe in him and trust him.

CONVERSION

Late in August, early awake,
my windows wide on the mountain wall
and the full moon, I feel the winter cold
and, from the farm below,
I hear the cock crow.

The whisper of grass beneath a summer wind
rippling and veering like weed under running water,
and tree-spots of shade in the mist of shining grain
I must forgo
and wait for snow.
(It came one night on the heights and went next day,
and some night now it will return to stay.)

Nevertheless,
the harvest of the Lord is at all high times,
and most at the season of man's gathering-in—
not that I am part of a passive crop,
but though hired late, a labourer; so let me get to work.

AHK
August/September 1971

An Account of My Conversion

I AM NEW to the Church, and I wondered, therefore, what I could say from inside it that could interest you or, indeed, be knowledgeable. I have come in late, but I am addressing people here who have always been in the Church or perhaps came to it early. So it seems to me that what I could tell you of value is something of the quality of the wilderness outside. The wilderness is all about us, and the wilderness is inside all those who are about us. And we have to struggle sometimes to keep the wilderness out of our own hearts.

Some of you may sometimes feel an urge to go outside. Perhaps I, who have recently come in, can be of help to you. Some of you may even sometimes feel that you need to go outside to satisfy your intellectual honesty; I have heard of such people—perhaps I can say something of value to them; I hope so. It is only on that premise that I have agreed with myself to talk about myself, because oneself is the last subject in the world that one can properly talk about—others can talk about one much better than one can talk about oneself. But I thought it would not be too presumptuous to take you through the main stages of my intellectual life—not so much because they are mine, but because their disappointments and their contributions to my acceptance of the Church may be symbolic or typical, and, more particularly, because I can now describe them to you from inside the Church and so perhaps have a more objective view of them than I could when I was experiencing them. To begin with, I will merely say that my coming into the Church has, for me, brought all these stages together into focus and helped me to see what their disappointments were—for they were all disappointing—and what their contributions might have been to my own conversion and possibly might be to the conversions of others like me.

Early Family Life

I was reared as a Quaker in the Society of Friends. Some branches of my family had been in the Society from its very beginnings in the mid-seventeenth century. Some suffered years of imprisonment for their faith—I had to join the Mormon Church and do genealogy to find that out. My own father, during the First World War, being a Quaker, was a pacifist and, as a pacifist, a conscientious objector. Being poor, he couldn't go with the Friends' Ambulance Unit to the front because those men were volunteers and unpaid. So he took work as a farm laborer, and we went and lived in a slum in the country. Our neighbors' fathers, brothers, and sons were at the front, and here was my father, planting cabbages from four in the morning or feeding the beasts.

Life was hard for my sister and myself. I was seven at the beginning of this experience, and my sister was coming up to three. The village boys and girls would run after us, throw stones at us, call us names, and sometimes seize us and tumble us. I couldn't go to school because they would have teased the life out of me. So my father and mother taught me at home. I learned to endure unpopularity and even what a young boy felt to be persecuted.

We were brought up puritanically, against the following: movies, because of their debasing effect on society (that still seems to me to be the right view); dancing (I still do not understand how Christians can look with the least degree of allowance upon the use of dancing for erotic intoxication—a use that isn't characteristic of group dancing, though it is of rock dancing and dancing in which there is close and prolonged contact between men and women, as there is in the waltz); alcohol (I have never at any time felt comfortable in a public house); and betting or gambling (including, very properly, that on the Stock Exchange). I learned to mistrust all political parties and all government (and I still do). Comics never crossed the threshold, so between the ages of seven and nine, I read Dickens, Thackeray, Goldsmith, and others. And that kind of thing is what other children might do if they weren't open to the atrocious opportunities of today. In brief, I profoundly absorbed the view that our family was not of the world, that the world was sinful and vulgar, and that our enjoyments were superior to the world's enjoyments. This view led me, as it might well have led any child, dogmatically to look down on people—I must have been a prig.

The Quakers taught me something of the Holy Spirit. They believe that the Inner Light is with one and in one. From the age of thirteen onward in Quaker meetings, I had experience of the Inner Light: I would be forced from within on to my feet to speak. (All Quaker religious meetings are testimony meetings.) I would be red from the top of my head to the bottom of my feet, my pulse would be racing; I would resist, but I would be up and speaking because I had to be. Another thing for which I have to thank Quakers is that they have no paid priesthood. Every man and every woman stands before God in a personal relationship.

However, in my midteens I became dissatisfied with Quakerism. First, for social reasons: I felt that there were class distinctions among Friends, though this might not have been as clear in America as it was in England, where class distinctions are still more important than in the United States. Because my father was accidentally killed when I was nine, we were extremely poor. My family was therefore generously supported by the Quakers, but we were sometimes condescended to by members who were prosperous tradespeople and professionals. There were then few working-class members of the Society of Friends. It isn't comfortable to be dependent upon other people's charity unless those people are one's own relatives, and even then it is hard. One starts feeling condescended to even on occasions when one is not being condescended to.

Further, though I felt the promptings of the Spirit in meeting and would get up and speak, I felt that when I did, I irritated rather than edified others. I felt, also, that we shared a spirit that was too vague. It led to humane action on their part—the Friends' work is well known—but in my view, it was not vigorous enough. They were reluctant to take a political attitude. They did not have a God with a body, parts, and passions. They lacked dogma, something firm I could depend on to help answer my own and others' questions. Quakers hate to say they believe in something that might cause somebody to leave the Society because they think that people are more important than dogma. But they have gone so far that it is possible to be a Quaker and believe that Christ is merely human. Most Quakers don't seem to be concerned whether he is human or divine. What do they believe in? They believe basically in community, as so many religious people now do. They have gone mushy. There is no distinction between such religions. Dogma is important. I had the sense from an early age that dogma ought to be precise; I didn't like vagueness. I departed from the Quakers in spirit when I went to the University of Cambridge because I felt uneasy with vague dogma and I didn't like their middle-class attitude. It was important for me when I came into the Mormon Church to feel that it was not a class church. However, Quakers gave me much, and I shall be grateful forever to my ancestors who joined the Quaker movement and struggled forward, as Quakers had to do, for several centuries.

College Years

When I went to Cambridge in 1928, I found a generation trying to make the experience of literature and the other arts a substitute for religion. The text was Arnold's statement, "Religion has attached itself to the fact, and now the fact is failing it; but for poetry the idea is everything." He was writing at the time of the religion-science controversy, particularly the Darwinian controversy of the latter nineteenth century, and what he meant was that religion had attached itself to natural-scientific facts. Consequently, when other natural-scientific "facts" were found that seemed not to agree with religious "facts," the basis of Christianity had gone.

In saying that religion had attached itself to the wrong fact, Arnold was, of course, criticizing the churches that he knew. Joseph Smith also criticized those churches or ones similar to them. They were churches that were all wrong. We have the highest authority for knowing that they were all wrong. Matthew Arnold could see this, but he couldn't find the right church. He was not aware that there was a contemporary church in his time that was not a pastiche church, a church of the past, but a church of our time; he had not absorbed the message of Hebrews 11.

Arnold believed that art had to fill the gap left by the decline of religion and therefore had to take over the moral function that religion had previously had. The idea that instead of having a religious faith one could live from poetry, from fine art, from music was a common idea among undergraduates and academics when I was a young man; I think it may still be a common idea. Coleridge gave support to it by saying that when you are reading poetry, you have a willing suspension of disbelief, and you are able, therefore, to accept the poetry, to enjoy it, to have an emotional reaction to it although you know that from the natural-scientific point of view it is a tissue of untruths.

I was attracted to Arnold's idea for a number of years. The little book that most characteristically enshrines this view is I. A. Richards's *Science and Poetry.* The view is, however, an essentially individualistic one; it lacks the force to make a group cohere. There was a group—around F. R. Leavis's periodical *Scrutiny*—that had a good deal of influence in asserting the need for moral judgment in art, but we were at sea, and though we could learn about winds and tides, there was no anchor aboard and we had no destination. As Eliot put it in one of the *Four Quartets*, "Not farewell, but fare forward voyagers": not the comfort of going home, not the certainty of a destination.

I found Arnold's view insufficient in my personal life, so I went on looking. I found that you could take art until the cows come home, but it was not a substitute for religion. The arts are, after all, by origin and by practice, the servants of religion. It is only in modern times that the arts seem to have been freed from this, and, as a consequence, the arts have degenerated and now represent the world as a split and miserable place, as most people treat it. Most people are tolerably miserable most of the time.

Although we can get a good deal of satisfaction from artistic experiences, they cannot hold us up in the face of tragedy. I found that out because I had a pretty tragic life. And the idea that we can live *as if* certain values were true gives us no moral support. We cannot live a good life on the basis of a humanistic ideal because such an ideal will not give us the strength to do so. We cannot get the strength to live a good life except from the right religion; there is no other way. Morality is strong when it is derived from religion, just as all forms of art are strong when they are derived from religion, but if art and morality are cut off from their base, they cease to have their proper effect.

I also came to see that religion needn't have and shouldn't have "attached itself to the fact." The ideas we have about the physical universe change; it is the moral and religious truths that are permanent. The standards by which we live are from age to age and forever. Other ways of thinking pass and change. Much learned explanation is partial and uncertain. When I was a young man, the age of the universe was estimated at about one and a half billion years. Nowadays, the estimate has gone up to ten times as long. I am content to let the scientists continue (they have time). Facts we must accept, and we must know that our faith is never ultimately incompatible with them; interpretations remain a matter of continued discussion.

Writers of Importance

At this point, I should like briefly to comment on three important writers of my undergraduate time, their virtues and their failings, and the things I learned from them that helped bring me to the gospel. I think now they had those failings, and I thought so then, perhaps, too, but they are still important writers.

I speak first and most briefly of Yeats because he is the easiest to dispose of. He has his myths, his box of magical toys. We cannot take these toys seriously, but he did teach us a way—he gave us an example of a way—in which we might see the whole world and the whole of history in terms of images. That way of seeing history and that way of seeing the world is also the way of holy writ. And anyone who wants to write in that way can learn a great deal from how Yeats handled images.

The second writer I want to say rather more about, because he comes closer to our business and bosoms than Yeats does—Yeats is a little remote. But D. H. Lawrence is not remote; he is read, for mixed reasons, all over the world. He was an undisciplined and unhappy man. He never faced up to his tuberculosis, which he contracted at an early age. He always pretended it was something else. He ran away from life to enjoy life. He made something of it, but it was make-believe. He taught something of the sanctity and tenderness of the right relationship between man and woman in marriage; he was faithful to the woman he married. He idealized his sexual descriptions from his own not very satisfactory experience.

What was most important for me was that D. H. Lawrence had a profound instinct for the need of a patriarchal community—all the more intense because his own family was so matriarchal—and an instinctive feeling for the priesthood that perhaps came to him from his nonconformist upbringing. You see the dark shadowing of this in such books as *Aaron's Rod*, *Kangaroo*, and above all, that monstrous yet profoundly interesting work, *The Plumed Serpent.* He strengthened my sense and feeling that something like patriarchy and the priesthood was wanted, but as yet I couldn't define it. (My mother said to me from time to time that I was born to be a "priest" and I ought to be a "priest." I think she wanted me to exert spiritual authority. Well, I have become a priest but too late to help her on this side of the veil. However, her work has been done.)

The last person of whom I will speak—Eliot—I knew somewhat. I met him from time to time. I helped translate his verse into Swedish. He was aware of the difficulties of my life, and I was aware of the difficulties of his. He had a remarkable pair of large, pondering, reflective, piercing eyes—no wonder eyes play a key part in his poetry. He was a most sensitive and truthful seeker. He taught the value of a proposition that he expressed with challenging blasphemy, and yet it is a helpful proposition for our time: "The spirit killeth, but the letter giveth life." What he meant was that dogma is essential to religion, that dogma is better than free thought, and that what religion requires is exactitude; vagueness will not do. Only exactitude will lead to proper action. He certainly put that into my mind, and it stayed there. It was one of the things that brought me to the Church. He understood, too, better than any modern poet or writer, the steps leading to conversion and the final step that had to be taken. He phrased it thus, if I may run two of his quotations together: "The awful daring of a moment's surrender costing not less than everything."

And yet, with all that, Eliot turned from Presbyterianism, which is more exact, to the Anglo-Catholic wing of the Anglican Church, and few churches could be more apostate than the Anglican Church because it is preoccupied with manners. What did Eliot find? Not reality, but pastiche: an imitation of a life no longer lived. That is much of the picture of the Anglican Church today: an imitation of what was valuable, what came home to people three hundred and fifty years ago but does not come home to them now. This pastiche is reflected most clearly in that collection of essays called *For Launcelot Andrewes* and in Eliot's rather absurd definition of his position in favor of Royalism and of Anglo-Catholicism. He turned away from Presbyterianism and from the strength, integrity, and intelligence of so many nonconformist people. He made these values foreign to him. His social outlook was limited: he was, to my personal knowledge, a snob, and this comes out very clearly indeed in *Notes Towards a Definition of Culture.* So his conversion—which is an important symbolic step for our world today, a step that is worth pondering to those who are thinking about conversion either because they wish to be converted or because they wish to convert others—liberated him in some ways and desiccated him in others.

For some years, I attended an Anglican village church in the hope of finding some truth in it. While I appreciated the hymns and the ritual, I could not join because there was nothing to join—no community of the church, no true social group, no force. The upper people tended to go to morning service and the lower to evening service; it was so habitual for them that they didn't even know they were doing it until I pointed it out to them. Once I did point it out, they became very uncomfortable and, I think, promptly forgot it. That is one way of dealing with moral issues. Like Eliot, the upper-class people were pretending in good-taste, seventeenth-century pastiche; the lower ones in vulgar, evangelical, Victorian pastiche.

After College

After I left Cambridge, the wave of Marxist thought characteristic of the European thirties came to that university, as it did to others. I didn't become a Marxist. I didn't feel that I could commit myself in that kind of way. I believed in God—I always had believed in God—and Marxists deny God. Yet they have sometimes spoken for him without knowing it. Marx said in the *Communist Manifesto*, "As long as there is a lower class, I am of it." Devout Communists—among whom were some of my friends—taught me something of faith: faith must issue in energy, force, determination, organization. The Communists were rude, coarse, rough, wrong. But they had these other qualities that were not had by the Anglican Church, the Quakers, and those literary intellectuals who wanted to change the world but who hadn't the force or integrity to do so.

Faith is not content to leave things as they are but wishes to change them for the better, both inside and outside oneself. Many people don't wake up to what faith is. They may reject religion because they don't think that what they do and what they have is reflected in it, and sometimes they only realize very late, and sometimes not at all, that something they have been in the habit of doing or feeling all their lives has been faith. For example, I remember an atheist undergraduate friend of mine at Cambridge who was a physiologist and wore a golden beard in the days when beards were not the token of what they now are. He was ebullient and springy; he always got up in the mornings full of spirit, and he lived his life that way. He was never uncheerful. That man lived from some kind of fundamental faith that had to do not only with the health of his body, but also with the health of his mind. He lived in faith as he lived in air and drank water. In my opinion, only people who are full of faith could possibly have the courage to be atheistic. You can deny father if you know he is in the next room, but, if you have been taken away from him to live in a distant town, you may very well fervently believe in him. Many an atheist has not yet known what despair is.

The quality of my friend's faith may have been high, but its object was deception. The Stalin trials, the Russo-German Pact of 1939, and the suppression of Hungary in 1956 were fatal blows to that faith. My friends had been deceived; hundreds of thousands had been deceived. Nothing was left but disillusion—or else self-deception—for idealistic Marxists. They found themselves in a wasteland; they knew the kind of bitter disappointment that Wordsworth experienced in the French Revolution: "Bliss was it in that dawn to be alive"—but it was just being alive and young, the excitement of animal spirits, no more. Many of my friends fell back into an attitude of "Well, I suppose we'd better do the best we can with the kind of government we can get in a country like the United Kingdom." And that is the kind of compromising attitude that exists today in the United Kingdom and other European countries.

Overseas Travels

During a large part of my life, I have been overseas, moving about the world. I have seen something of religion in other parts of the world outside Christian countries. It is difficult to know what Christianity is like until you get outside, and once you get outside, it looks very different. For me, it still looked like something I wanted to get back into. During the fifties, I lived for about seven years in Islamic countries—two years in Persia and five years in Pakistan. Pakistan was then struggling to make itself an Islamic republic. I learned things about Islam that attracted me, but at the same time, I learned other things which made Islam unsatisfactory to me.

One significant thing about Islam is that it legislates for the whole of life. It is not just a Sunday religion like most Christian religions. It is not something that is put aside and brought out on certain days. It is something that pervades life. You cannot really be a Muslim unless the society around you practices the Islamic law because it is a complete law just as the Jewish law is an all-encompassing law (and, in fact, there is a relationship between them).

Three religious peoples—the Jews, the Christians, and the Muslims—are known as the "people of the book" because they all go back to the Old Testament and they all in one way or another accept certain things in the New Testament. Muslims, for example, accept Jesus as a prophet, and sayings of Jesus are quoted in the Koran with approval. There is one saying I like that is not cited elsewhere. I will repeat it in case you may not have heard it: Christ and the disciples were walking down a street in Jerusalem and there they saw in a gutter the body of a dead dog. The disciples were disgusted at the sight and stench, but Christ said, "Look at his beautiful white teeth."

Islam provides an organized way of living that is highly satisfactory to those who participate; it gives them a sense of security and confidence, a sense of social comfort. Islam is ritualistic, and ritual binds Muslims together as it binds the Jews together. The stress in the New Testament seems to be away from ritual. The emphasis in Paul is to discard the detail of the law. Christianity, especially in the nonconformist churches, moved away from ritual. But in their anxiety to discard the law, Christians sometimes throw the baby out with the bathwater because they also get rid of a great deal that controls, guides, and molds ordinary life.

My experience with Islamic peoples taught me that religion must be of the whole community in a way that no Christian sect that I knew of could be, since these sects didn't have an equivalent to the Jewish law. But Latter-day Saints have been given an equivalent, principally through the Doctrine and Covenants. Muslims have the Koran; Jews have the Torah and commentary on the Torah; Mormons have the Doctrine and Covenants. All of these books provide detailed guidance for daily living and for church administration.

The Doctrine and Covenants is an extraordinary document, and, of the documents the Mormon Church had to offer me, it was the one which, after the Joseph Smith story, impressed me most. The Doctrine and Covenants legislates for a new religious community, and the way in which its revelations apply to the details of people's lives seemed right to me. There has to be a connection between testimony, revelation, and ordinary practical life.

Islam also showed me the social value of plural marriage. Mohammed instituted polygamy so that single women and widows in the community might have a protected position and the opportunity of bearing and bringing up children, and so the faithful should engender more faithful as soon as possible in order to spread the movement more soundly and quickly. (My mother had another reason for plural marriage: she thought men were "naturally" polygamous and women "naturally" monogamous, and the world would be a much happier place if this were recognized and practiced.)

I also appreciated Islam for the democratic attitude it fosters in Muslim countries. Muslims are democratic in the sense that they believe that all souls are kin and that distinctions of color or race are irrelevant to that kinship. I am sure that the success of Islam today in Africa has to do with racial egalitarianism. I am sure, too, that the success of Islam in India was due to the fact that Islam is diametrically opposed to the Hindu caste system; people of no caste in India were attracted to Islam because they felt in Islam that they were the equals of everybody else. I am convinced that Muslims really are egalitarian. Arabs, for example, and other pale-skinned persons in Muslim countries have been perfectly prepared to marry blacks, and in India you find that Muslim people don't have any special feeling about people with dark skin, though Hindus very definitely do. I think that Muslims tend to think that other religions do not accept all souls are kin. Muslims haven't got this sense of class that we have in Christian countries.

But the unsatisfactoriness of Islam is plain. We are seeing something of it today in the struggles that go on in Muslim countries. This religion cannot reconcile itself to the modern world. Paradoxically, the only enthusiasts in Islam are those who are opposed to the modern world and therefore will not survive.

Muslims live ritualistically. They say their prayers regularly, they are good about going to the Friday mosque—much better than most Christian attenders—but it is still a ritualistic shell they have. Contact with God is rare because the God of Islam is not a personal God—he is a spirit. Mohammed they believe to be a great prophet, but he is a man, and God is inaccessible. God dwells remotely, and his purposes are not to be scanned by us. You may say that is in the Bible, too: "My thoughts are higher than your thoughts" (see Isa. 55:8–9). But that is not at all the same thing: his thoughts are higher than our thoughts, but they are not of a totally different kind. And the more highly we think, the more we discover that what we are thinking is like what God has revealed himself to us as thinking. I have always believed that God is reasonable. We may not always understand his reasons, but they are reasonable; they are not the expression of a whimsical tyrant, but of a supreme thinker who has made us in his image. And since he has made us in his image, we are able to think something of the kind of thoughts that he thinks, for to be made in God's image doesn't mean to be made a shell that resembles God, it means to be made outside and inside like God. And this means that we can begin to think like him and eventually become as he is. Most religions in the world, like Islam, haven't that feeling at all. They have the feeling that God is remote, and this is true of most Christian sects. The Roman Catholics, for example, have a strong sense of the removedness of God; you can't go straight to him.

Muslims see God as a providential spirit that does not deprive them of agency, but, on the other hand, they also see fate as an instrument of God, and that is a paradox I can't resolve. They have degenerated into a belief in God that is like a belief in fate—if God wills it, it will be so. If you are going to die tomorrow, you are going to die tomorrow, and you can do nothing about it. It is that kind of fatalistic belief they now have that has been popularized in vulgar literature. I think that some educated Muslims do not hold this belief, but most Muslims do, and it means that they have to submit to the will of a remote and arbitrary God. They cannot exactly do his will—willingly and obediently and freely—because they can't find it; they can't predict it.

Islam gave me a contrast between a God who remains above history as Allah does, influencing it in apparently arbitrary ways, and a God who not only presides over history, but enters it and becomes flesh in order to fully enter it. The Christian doctrine of the incarnation is monstrous to Islam, but most monstrous of all to the Muslim would be the doctrine that the Father and the Son both have bodies of flesh and bone.

A good historian is an important measure of the quality of the culture that produces that historian, and this is particularly significant for Islam, which is, like Christianity, a historically-based religion. There was a time, until the fifteenth century, when Islam had good historians. But in the end, the long-term effect of a wrong doctrine—the denial of incarnation and the incompatibility of that denial with Islam's historicity—was felt; Islam lost heart and the historians lost sense and ceased to be.

I have had some brief experience of other non-Christian religions: Hinduism, for example, with its combination of vague superstitions and caste prejudice. But it has a strong sense of the family. We should be ashamed if we realized what Hindus think of the way that the West nowadays treats the older members of its families—putting them away into institutions. This to a Hindu would be the abomination of abominations.

There is an easy-goingness about Hinduism. Hindus are eclectic. They can easily take another god into their religion. Queen Victoria, Empress of India, became a goddess in the Hindu pantheon. There are certain stable things about Hindu society, but that stability appears to be based paradoxically on the Hindus being so sophisticated that they can take in and absorb almost anything. The contradictions don't matter. You have only to read Forster's *A Passage to India* to see that.

The traditional scriptures of Hinduism contain a great deal we can appreciate. I will mention one work, which is anonymous, as all great work ultimately is: *The Bhagavad Gita*, or *The Song of God*, an ancient scripture that has been tolerably translated by the writer Christopher Isherwood (most great religious works in the Indian tradition are too vaguely translated). It is interesting to read from the point of view of how similar its teachings are in many respects to those of Christianity and how fundamentally different its teachings are in one respect that overshadows all the rest: depersonalization. There are gods, but above the gods is spirit, and spirit is not a person. The ultimate reality for Hindus is not a person, just as it is not a person for Muslims.

I have also had some experience with Buddhism, which is different from country to country: there is the whole gamut from the lowest of superstitions to the highest of philosophical conceptions. Buddhism is the way of purity; its final end is purification. To purify oneself means to strip oneself of all that is evil. Buddhists think that any wish to do anything is in the end evil because it leads to evil. Action leads to evil. But the moral teachings of Buddhism endorse the value of action (which at the religious level is denied) and are thus compatible with Christianity.

In its proper form, Buddhism is a matter of intense spiritual discipline and has no place for a personal God. Strict Buddhism really has no place for a god at all. Moreover, Buddhism isn't concerned with human personality, either: it posits the absorption of human personality into the infinite, which means the ultimate disappearance of personality rather than its intensification through eternity. The Buddhist says we shall get very tired of this existence and shall be very glad after a succession of lives to merge into the whole. But what—as I have always felt and as I feel more strongly now as a member of the Church—is most precious, if not the knowledge that we are individual persons of infinite worth, having free agency? That is what love starts from. To have love, there must be some sense of the individual; there must be individuals to love and to be loved. We can't really love ideas; we can't love abstract notions. We are made to love individuals. And individuals cannot continue to exist as such if they are transmigrated to camels or gnats or if they are merged.

Christianity is based on the concept of a loving individual, but it rejects the "self." And the Buddhist sense of the unimportance of self is compatible with Christianity in this respect. It reminds us of what our surrounding culture would have us forget: "Now, for this cause I know that man is nothing, which thing I never had supposed" (Moses 1:10).

Each world religion has fatal flaws, and each has in it something that points us toward, and prepares us for, acceptance of our church.

Conversion of the Soul

As a result of these various experiences, I was ready in 1966, when I met my second cousin—now my wife—and, through her, the Church. In March 1966, some years a widower, I had an impulse to pay an extra visit (I usually went to see him once a month) to my father's surviving brother. He told me he had just heard that he was to meet a female cousin from Canada, so I said I should be glad to see her, too. Five days later there was a hesitant tap on the door. There was my cousin Leonard (whom I had not seen for forty years), a woman who I felt must be his wife, and another woman whom I felt I had known all my life and to whom I immediately and unhesitatingly lost my heart. She was the Canadian second cousin. The three of them had not been able to find my name in the telephone book (they had looked it up just over the border in another county), and two of them had been very doubtful whether they should call on me unannounced. The third was not doubtful; they came.

During the next few days, she proved to have come seven thousand miles from British Columbia to take me just ten miles or so round some twenty farmhouses belonging to our ancestors in the seventeenth and eighteenth centuries. I had known nothing of them but had settled in their midst. We stood in an abandoned Quaker graveyard where the dust of hundreds of our ancestors and their collaterals lay under the primroses, bluebells, and beeches of an English spring. A hen pheasant was quietly brooding there, and the thrushes and skylarks were singing their heads off. My cousin bore me her testimony of the Church (to which she had belonged for fifteen years) and of genealogy (of which she had done much—she was at the time on a genealogical trip). But what I think I noticed most of all was that her faith had kept her whole through a life of considerable misery and strain. Five days later she left for Canada.

After our first meeting, I read the article on the Mormon Church in an old *Encyclopedia Britannica.* It was a good article. All I had known about before was Brigham Young and the great trek. I knew nothing whatever about Joseph Smith—I had never heard the name. What struck me then was that the Mormons had the kind of definite dogma for which I had been looking. I was attracted by the complete doctrine of incarnation, the doctrine that the Father is incarnate and has a body of flesh and bone, and the doctrine that he has a son Jesus Christ, who is his Son in the flesh.

The incarnation is the doctrine which rescues us from the nightmare of history as the natural man sees it—the nightmare from which James Joyce's Stephen Daedalus says he was trying to awake, the nightmare from which thousands of millions of people in the world at the moment are trying to awake. The nightmare is in history and in scriptural history from the beginning, from Cain onward. I would remind you in Isaiah of Rabshakeh before the walls of Jerusalem, cursing and despising the Jews (Isa. 36:11-21). I would remind you in the Book of Mormon of the Gadianton robbers. I would remind you of the jailers whom Joseph Smith rebuked. All this is part of history, but only a minor part—because God has entered history for us, and God guides history. The most fundamental sense of the incarnation is that Christ identified himself in and with human history to help lead it to completion. The song of redeeming love is the seed of history.

This is the point at which to say that a major reason for my attraction to the Church was that, of all the Christian churches, its doctrine was clear of gnosticism and, in particular, of the vicious belief (fostered by reaction against the fatigue of Levantine excesses) that spirit is good and flesh evil. Such a doctrine is contrary to our belief that the union of spirit and body is an opportunity for advancement and that we cannot perfect ourselves unless we undertake celestial marriage. Unfortunately, many Mormons whose ancestors came in from nonconformist sects tainted with gnosticism (Presbyterians, Baptists, Methodists, Congregationalists) even now have wrong ideas about the sanctity of sex in marriage. Marriage is the proper state for human beings; celibacy is an abomination.

I was also attracted by the logic that postexistence demands preexistence, the understanding that an immortal or eternal thing cannot just begin: things everlasting are from everlasting. In 1934, I spent a few days with Bertrand Russell when he came to my Swedish university of Lund to lecture against Hitler. He asked me then whether it was reasonable to suppose that something immortal could just suddenly begin in time. He set me thinking about premortal existence in a way different from the transmigration of souls. As far as I know, the Mormon Church is the only one to hold a reasonable doctrine about premortal existence that is not adulterated by the transmigration of the soul. Once the spirit is made flesh and thus becomes soul, it acquires its full potentiality, though it has not yet fulfilled this as actuality, and the soul remains unique.

A month after my cousin had left, I pursued her to British Columbia, and five months later she came back to Britain to marry me. We both felt that we had been guided to each other. After our marriage, I attended the LDS Crawley chapel in Sussex, England. We arranged for the missionaries to visit the house regularly. I am glad that the first thing they did was to give me the pamphlet on Joseph Smith's vision. The style of the Joseph Smith story immediately struck me. He spoke to me, as soon as I read his testimony, as a great writer, transparently sincere and matter-of-fact. That is what endeared him to me—so matter-of-fact. When Joseph Smith describes his visions, he describes them not as a man who feels that he has to make the effort to persuade. He simply states what happened to him, and he does it in a way that gives it credence. I am in this church because of the Joseph Smith story; my fundamental act of faith was to accept this as a remarkable document.

Because Joseph Smith talked about his experiences in the way he did, I was able to believe him, and having that belief, I could then go on to say, "This man tells the truth; therefore, I ought to believe other things he tells me, even though I haven't got the same evidence of those." The story of the finding and disappearance of the Book of Mormon plates seemed absurd to me. I comforted myself with that wonderful Latin principle: *Credo quia absurdum est*, "I believe it because it is absurd." When someone tells you an extraordinary story, the implication is that it is right to believe it. It is when they tell you ordinary stories that you have to be suspicious. A plausible liar is much more believed by the world than a genius who tells the truth. But the truth is rarely plausible.

It took me a long time to appreciate the Book of Mormon. When I started to read it, I thought it was an awful bore. Then I gradually found (it took me about two years) that I was wrong. I think my mind was closed to it in the beginning because it was so like the Bible and yet so unlike it. I couldn't solve that problem. I solved it later in my own terms. It has the same relationship to the Bible as American literature has to English literature. It is a different division. It broke off from the original stem and developed on its own.

I don't think I really was converted to the Book of Mormon until I began to teach it here at BYU. Having to teach it made me make the effort to see what it rhetorically was. I was trying to apply the principles of my judgment of English literature and poetry. I discovered my judgment was wrong. It didn't work on the Book of Mormon. The tradition of the language was different. What I was looking at as clichés weren't clichés at all. It is important to learn things like the fact that Archibald Macleish cannot be judged in the same way as Yeats. They come from different traditions. Their rhetorical patterns are totally different.

I am content to accept archaeological evidence for the Book of Mormon—the evidence that there were wheels in South America and other matters of that kind, but what I am principally interested in is that the rhetoric of the Book of Mormon is more developed than the rhetoric of the Hebrew scriptures. Look at Jacob 5, the parable of the olive tree, or 2 Nephi 9, the sermon about the Atonement. When we start working out the rhetorical patterns in those chapters, we have something more complex than anything in the Bible. That is another proof, incidentally, that not even Sidney Rigdon could have written the Book of Mormon.

I have heard some colleagues on the BYU campus sometimes describe the Book of Mormon in almost, shall we say, undue terms—that is to say, as if they were condescending or apologizing. A fine BYU scholar, when younger, is said to have written that the Authorized Version of the Bible is a magnificent cathedral, while the Book of Mormon is a plain, gray chapel. That is not so. The Book of Mormon is not in any way inferior to the Bible in its use of literary devices. The Book of Mormon, from the point of view of its style, is effective, full of great writing. There is no reason to condescend about the way it is written.

There were, at the time of my conversion, certain things in the Book of Mormon that I accepted instantly, particularly 2 Nephi 2, which is more compact theology than any chapter in the rest of the book. "Men are, that they might have joy" (2 Ne. 2:25) occurs in the same chapter as the doctrine of opposition. The two together gave sense to my life in a way far deeper than anything had before. I had undergone the death of my father when I was nine, the death of my only child when he was one week old, and the death of a wife from cancer protracted over four years. Now I came to understand that grief and joy are predicated upon one another, that we cannot know joy unless we know grief. That is why I am worried about those who are content with contentment. Content versus discontent is too slight an opposition and does not produce psychic tension. It is a facile soul that can be content in the world as it is, and even if we do not have griefs in our personal lives (and most of us have, if we face them, although we may pretend they are not there), we have plenty of grief around us in the appalling condition of the world.

The rhetorical differences between the Bible and the Book of Mormon, although they presented difficulties for me in the beginning, are actually evidence of the authenticity of the Book of Mormon. The Book of Mormon is obviously original, rather like the Bible, but nevertheless quite different in quality. It is clearly not written in normal Hebrew at all. It is written in something else. We are told that right at the beginning.

When I came to the Doctrine and Covenants and saw the extraordinary gamut of styles there, different styles for different occasions, that was further testimony to me that Joseph Smith was telling the truth when he said that he was inspired in these things. And how else but by inspiration could Joseph Smith have written those beautiful passages of the Doctrine and Covenants that lift and sing? And how I wish they were printed in a way that we could see how they lift and sing—I don't like division into verses. Joseph Smith was born at a time when the scientific revolution had not yet percolated down through society, and yet what he has to say under inspiration in the Doctrine and Covenants—that spirit is a finer kind of matter, not something totally different—is the only modern writing of its kind that is compatible with the true kernel of the scientific revolution as opposed to the philosophies of men. The facts of science as we know them are reconcilable with the Doctrine and Covenants. I don't think that they are reconcilable with the doctrines of the apostate churches.

At the least level, the Book of Mormon and Doctrine and Covenants are unique literary phenomena—by the test of stylistics, they are unique. They are quite different from Joseph Smith's own prose and significantly different from the Bible and from each other. They could not have been invented. They could not have been invented by Joseph Smith or (more importantly) by anybody else in the United States or in the world at that time, nor could anyone in our day have invented them, for that matter. Clearly the Lord made full use of Joseph Smith's remarkable mind, but equally clearly, only through inspiration could that remarkable mind have been made full use of, for Joseph Smith's education was small indeed—though better than most modern education, since it consisted mainly of the scriptures.

The missionaries gave me the lessons, but the lessons were not very successful. I didn't care for the flannelboard approach and didn't want to be corralled into a viewpoint. I preferred to read and ask questions. But as I look back at the process of my conversion, one thing that stands out is the look of authority that the three young missionaries who visited me had in their eyes. I felt able to accept their spiritual authority over me because of this look. They themselves were convinced; they themselves showed in their actions and their speech that they were sent of God. In addition, I had fruitful and helpful discussions with the president of the London Temple then, LeRoy Buckmiller, who was patient with me and who baptized me.

Now at this point, I should like to say something about my difficulties, because there were some difficulties, and the right time for difficulties is before, not after you have gotten in. A conversion cannot be such if you bring difficulties with you because conversion means a total turning, and I quote Eliot once again: "The awful daring of a moment's surrender costing not less than everything." Everything.

I had difficulty about the policy of denying priesthood to blacks. That policy made me think very hard about my experience of Africa. And I realized when I came to terms with myself that I had knowledge from my own experience that showed that the Church's teaching in this respect was not wrong: the blacks were not ready to come in and the Church membership was not ready to have them in. At the same time, I thought, and I realized that other people in the Church also thought, that this did not absolve us from a deep and profound social responsibility to that race. God had not cursed them, but humankind had cursed them; for a curse is not an arbitrary thing—it is a kind of acknowledgment of what is. And the nightmare of the blacks has been the most terrible of the human nightmares.

The second trouble—and it didn't last very long—was evolution. I may remind you that Darwin was trained to be a parson. When he began his investigation into evolution, he was trying to seek out the ways of God. I have a feeling that in his heart—and I think this is revealed by his remarkable prose style—Darwin remained a believer in God. However, the major point about this, which is clear to anyone who accepts God as a father and the Father of the universe, is that scientists may give us insight into the way that God works, but it is God who works. As perhaps some preliminary indication of the way in which God works, evolution may be a foreshadowing of greater knowledge on our part.

But we must not allow the acceptance of evolution as a natural-scientific hypothesis for research to cloud our knowledge of the divine origin of human beings or the actual (not symbolic) existence of Adam and Eve. Our first parents were individuals, not types. Sin, repentance, and exaltation are for individuals, not types. The individual is supreme.

About many matters that are not doctrinal, we need to remain open-minded, for science changes its statements as facts become available to it, and revelation continues. I do not see why anyone should want to exclude people from the Church for believing or not believing things that are not included under doctrine or deducible from doctrine. At the same time, I must regard with skepticism matters that seem to me irreconcilable with doctrine. Let us be very firm about Church doctrine and eclectic about anything else; such an attitude will leave us with a very great deal (and that is most important) to be firm about.

I discussed the theory of evolution and the problem of the blacks and the priesthood with President Buckmiller, as well as the Mormon doctrine of the relationship of spirit and body to soul and that relationship's consequences for sexual morality. He helped me to resolve these to my own satisfaction, and I am glad I did so before I joined the Church. Testimony does not consist in suppressing doubt. Testimony consists in getting rid of doubt, in eliminating it, in having it disappear. I saw that the Church of Jesus Christ is not puritanical (though some of its members seem to think it is), that eternal progression is a better evolution than Darwinism, and that a curse can be seen as a historical nightmare.

Any difficulties we might have are resolved by the determination to enter the Church and accept it as a whole—all of it; it belongs together; it has to be accepted as a whole. Conversion is not a matter of choosing what we like and ignoring the rest, but of whole-minded acceptance. We are not truly converted (and we need to be converted whether we are in the Church or outside it) unless we accept the Church as a whole. If we can make the step it takes to accept that, then everything else falls into place. When we have performed this act of faith, which is something that goes more deeply down into our minds, hearts, and spirits than anything else we can possibly imagine for the rest of our lives—once we have done this, all the difficulties are resolved by it. When we have laid down at Christ's feet all our scholarship, all our learning, all the tools of our trades, we discover that we may pick them all up again, clean them, adjust them, and use them for the Church in the name of Christ and in the light of his countenance. We do not need to discard them. All we need to do is to use them along with the faith that now possesses us. And we find that we can. Of course, if we want to preserve our own individual wills in order to assert our individual personalities, then we are free to do so. After all, our Father does not require obedience; he requires willing obedience. And our faith should give us willing obedience. If it does not, then there is something wrong that we must struggle to put right by prayer and thought.

To each person these kinds of difficulties will be personal ones and not general ones; there are no general difficulties, only personal ones. Suffice it to say that the Lord has yet much to reveal and I have much to learn, and so, for that matter, has the Church as a whole.

Before joining the Church, I still had to receive, in addition to all the promptings I had already received, the final sense of the rightness of it all. Such a sense that the gospel is true has to come from the soul and at a deeper level than reasoning.

Commitment to be Baptized

I had, at various points in my life, had a dream about a high mountain valley. It was pastoral and contained three classical temples. I remember once waking up at dawn in a bus in the middle of Iran on the way from Eṣfahān to Shīrāz and in my half-waking state thinking that the valley I saw in the mountains to my left was the one I had dreamed of. At another time, years later, I remembered my dreamed valley when I saw a green rift in the heart of the Andes while I was crossing that range in a low-flying Caravelle. Then, when I was on my way by light railway from Domodossola to Locarno, going up a transverse valley in the Swiss-Italian Alps, I thought I again recognized my dream. It was a beautiful evening, and the sun was shining from the west up the valley, and we were traveling eastward, so the light was perfect, and I felt a great lightness of heart. Then, at the beginning of October 1966, I had my dream of that valley again; when I woke up in the morning, I was resolved that I should join the Church. Not until 1968 did I see Utah for the first time. There are two places here that look like my dream—one at Manti and one at Heber City. For that reason, I have a special feeling for the Manti Temple and am particularly glad when one of my student friends gets married there.

Testimony

At this point, I feel that, having entered the Church, I should say something about my testimony of the Church. And so dear brothers and sisters, I will say to you in the simple terminology of the Church, which has become so dear to me—though the first time I heard it, I could hardly accept it—I know that God lives. I have always known it. But I now know that he has a body, parts, and passions. I know that he lives in and through history, that his Son was incarnate in the same flesh we have and has now the flesh and bone that we too shall inherit after the Resurrection. And we may become like him. I think this, to say the least of it, is profoundly satisfying dogma. It unites us with the universe in a way that nothing else can. And surely we are determined not to live in an empty universe. What is the use of doing it? What is the use indeed of doing anything if we live in an empty universe? It is a full universe that satisfies. Without faith, the universe is meaningless.

Secondly, I know the Church is true. Its social organization and indifference to class distinctions vouch for this at the superficial level. After I joined the Church, I became sensible of its extraordinary social organization and of how it gradually brings souls in to become part of the organization until that organization is the whole of their lives, but when I first joined, it was enough for me to attend minimal meetings. This is a better way than to come in with full enthusiasm and to wane later. I took cautiously the Church's taking hold of me, and that is the way the Church took me, too.

Now I am aware that there are some among us—and thank God, they are still among us and haven't left us—who believe only in the organization of the Church and that this will stand by itself. Brothers and sisters, it will not stand by itself. Swift (poor man, he went mad in the end) believed that the Anglican Church was just a very convenient institution for keeping the country in order. Now this is cynicism, as is believing any church to be a mere social organization.

So why am I impressed by the organization of the Church? Because I know that even a good organization, let alone a perfect one, must have behind it not merely concepts of morality, not merely the practice of good administration, but members who are informed by a common faith—a faith that they may reach deep down into every time they have to make decisions. Our church could not exist as an increasingly successful social organization unless it was inspired, for all other social organizations, after perhaps initial success, decline. The church's organization could not be maintained were it not for the urge behind, the religious drive. And so when we say that we know that the Church is true, we know not only that its organization is true, but much more as well, because unless we do know much more, we do not know even that.

Next, I know that Joseph Smith is a prophet of God and that the Doctrine and Covenants is revelation and that the Book of Mormon is an inspired translation, as Joseph Smith told us they were.

I know that there is a prophet upon the earth today, for there has to be succession and continuity. If you believe that Joseph Smith was a prophet, if you believe therefore that this church is true, then you must believe that God will so dispose it that the Church will continue to be true, to maintain the revelation. Otherwise, the thing is a mockery. As our prophet is sustained by our Father, so he is sustained by ourselves. Our Father blesses him and, through him, the whole of the Church; therefore we continue to accept and sustain him.

I believe in the work for the dead. The hearts of the fathers and the children may and must be turned to one another; otherwise, there will be a curse, and we see the beginnings of the workings of that curse more strongly than ever all over the world. How I managed to spend most of my life knowing very little about my ancestors, I don't know. But as a result of our collaboration, my wife and I have learned what our family was like in the seventeenth, eighteenth, and nineteenth centuries; that was a real revelation, because in our Quaker sect they kept detailed records, so we could learn a good deal about our ancestors. We learned about the way in which our ancestors sought truth. They were seekers (the technical term for those who didn't yet know what their religion was). We have an impression that for some three hundred years they were seeking, because even when they got into the Quaker sect, many of them were still trying to find something further (all Quakers do). To know that our ancestors were like that is a strengthening influence in our souls.

We learned that a fifth great-grandfather we have in common spent nearly twenty years in prison for his faith because he insisted on going to meeting, and most of the times he went to meeting, he was arrested and put into prison by the minions of Charles II. We also learned about a fourth great-grandmother who was the daughter of this man and whom we also share. Her name was Susannah Martin (born Garton). She was a mother of many children and, when older, a missionary who went up and down in England, Scotland, and Ireland. Susannah wrote her last letter in 1735, and it, rather than the usual recorded deathbed, was put into the Friends' Annual Register because she died suddenly of an apoplectic stroke, as they then called it, allowing no time for a recording. So this letter was in lieu, and there is only one phrase of it that is important, and it is so important to my wife and me:

> For I can say it is good to Serve the Lord, and to give up the strength of our Days to Honour him with it, who hath given it unto us; and having Tasted and felt how good the Lord is to them that are given up to follow him, I have wrote these few lines for the Encouragement of those who I may leave behind, to Serve the Lord in their Day.

You can imagine what feeling my wife and I had when we first read that extract in the minutes of the meeting, knowing that we had been raised up, as she said, to serve the Lord in our day. Sometimes I feel that our forebears for generations were seeking and that Patricia and I have found. We have done Susannah's work and the work of her father and her husband and all her relatives, and we now know that they wait for us on the other side. We feel convinced, having done their work in the temple, that most of our ancestors have accepted the gospel. My wife and I have a profound testimony of this work.

I have gathered with some shock that there are some among us who do not believe in temple work or are skeptical about it. But there are important reasons for engaging in temple work. When we go through the temple on behalf of our own families—or indeed, on behalf of others—we have the sense of the generations back and forward in time being drawn together. We have the sense that the family not only exists today, but it exists back in time to the Father of us all, and it exists forward into the future further than we can imagine. It is not simply our nearest and our dearest that are part of our families. It is our furthest and our dearest. They are all part of our families.

Another reason why I believe in the work for the dead is this: only through regular temple work can a marriage be regularly resanctified and become a true eternal partnership on this earth. To be married again as proxies for those who have given us life, perhaps centuries ago, is a profound experience of faith and wonder.

Someone once said to me, "You know, the Passion Play was so good at Oberammergau, and I think you should go in ten years' time." Well, I have never been, but I know how it is touristically exploited. I know about the intrigue that comes about when people are going to be given parts. I know about the pseudobeautification. This is another piece of pastiche. I am convinced that going through a live session in one of our temples is an experience of greater spiritual value than the pastiche experience brought to us by a combination of German scenery and Italian painting in a pseudofolk show.

Conclusion

I have come to the end. I would apologize for speaking so much of myself were it not that friends assured me, and I rather felt myself, that by so doing, I could perhaps say something of value to some of you—to those of you who may feel doubtful, also, possibly even more, to those of you who do not feel at all doubtful, but as missionaries want to go forth and want to know a little more about what sort of person I am because there are many like me who, perhaps for the same reasons I was, may be ready to listen to the voice of the Church and whom we need in the fold with us.

I have come, from the outside wilderness, home. I experience the love of that great home, the Church. I look forward to learning something yet of what the Lord has to reveal, and I am happy to know that those who come after me will learn a great deal more. I hope to help prepare them for that; that is what I am here for. I feel and know the office of the Holy Spirit in my affairs, both official and family. I have daily experience of this. I carry with me daily a sense of prayer. And it is because I carry it with me that I can write the kind of verse that I have been able to start writing in the Church. Although I wrote a great deal of verse before, I had no confidence in it. But now that I am in the Church, I have confidence in it.

The whole world is sanctified unto the Most High, and we may all say from the depths of our hearts, every minute of the day, "Holy, holy, holy, Lord God Almighty." For as Blake said in an inspired moment, "Everything that lives is holy." Home can, for us, be everywhere, because home is wherever the Saints meet. Home is in each of our hearts, wherever we may be. And I pray to God that it may remain so.

World Culture

THE DAYS OF nationalism are over. Europe is abandoning it at the very time when the new countries in Asia and Africa are trying to adopt it or rather to use it to the corrupt advantage of groups and individuals. (Remember Dr. Samuel Johnson's dictum, "Patriotism is the last refuge of a scoundrel.") All countries are now politically, economically, and culturally involved with each other. What is replacing nationalism and national cultures is a world culture. Africa, Latin America, and Asia are absorbing this culture, and it has already been established in the United States, China, Europe, and the Soviet Union, and, with some advantage due to Japanese loyalty, in Japan.

This world culture was made possible by the Industrial Revolution, which began in Britain and afterwards spread to this country and other European countries. The Industrial Revolution, with its mass production, has created a new type of existence and a similarity throughout the world that is more fundamental than the differences. We are all, ultimately, in this twentieth century, in the same economic and industrial boat. The Soviet Union has adopted mass production; China is beginning mass production on a large scale; mass production has absorbed Europe. Because mechanization creates similar conditions for people to work and live in, people become more similar. Differences of religion, differences of economic thinking, differences of politics are nothing compared to this uniformity of life, which is creeping over the globe as a result of the expansion of the Industrial Revolution.

This talk was given before the fall of the Soviet Union.

The similarity of one human being to another has always been greater than the differences between them, but the twentieth century is bringing people still closer together.

Even at the beginning, the Industrial Revolution left its mark on the quality of human life in no uncertain terms. I can see in the history of my own family, as I have followed it in genealogy, that the scourge of the Industrial Revolution and the scourge of tuberculosis hit England together in the late eighteenth century and took a terrible toll. This was also the time when five-year-old children were sent down into the mines. This was the time when industrial life in Northern England was such hell that it was possible for the Mormon missionaries to promise to thousands and then tens of thousands of converts from that part of the world, not only salvation in the next world, but also salvation in this world. Today, northern England is still a blighted place, just as parts of Pennsylvania and New Jersey are, and for the same reason.

You may say that the countries in which the Industrial Revolution took place went through a period of stress and strain and misery and tragedy in order to arrive at something better; the aim may have been profit, but that aim produced a higher standard of living for hundreds of millions of people. That is perfectly true. Mass production has raised the standard of living. But at the same time, it has done several other things. First, it has given mechanical work to hundreds of millions of people; that is to say, their work consists of sheer routine. We have a young friend who once worked in a bean-canning factory. She spent ten hours a day there. As the beans passed by her on the band, she took off the stalks. It was good pay, but I maintain that sons and daughters of God are not here to do that sort of thing. Sheer routine is not good for the soul. I do not believe it is right from the point of view of the gospel that men and women should have to repeat mechanically, thousands of times a day, insignificant actions that are incompatible with their dignity as sons and daughters of God.

The second result of mass production has been to fill our lives with mass art, inferior art, ugliness. Mass art pervades the mass media, advertisement, fashion. The United States is responsible for much of this art, particularly the pornography: American pornography circles the world. Moreover, American pornography and promiscuity have, I think, as a kind of reaction to American

Puritanism, gone further than they have even in Europe, though I must say that pornography and promiscuity have gone to most distressing lengths in the United Kingdom and in Scandinavia—further than in France, which went through this stage a bit earlier and got rather bored with it. People do get bored with it in the end, but getting bored with sex may be even worse than having promiscuous sex. Think about it. It is dehumanizing. Of course, the other countries contribute; they do the same sort of thing. But the United States does it on a much bigger scale. With its technical ability, money, and resources, the United States can express the Satanic better than any country in the world—including the Soviet Union and China. Those countries are inefficient, while the United States is still efficient. The Satanism in American culture uses American efficiency.

The mass media and advertisers propagate for the masses whatever is bizarre, tawdry, or unnatural in the world of fashion, exploiting the public's desire to be noticed. Women are induced to substitute for themselves some monstrous image that is antiart (fashion usually is antiart), and even men have padding in the shoulders of their suits to live up to some trapezoid ideal of maleness. Yeats has three famous, very serious lines:

> Maybe the bride-bed brings despair,
>   For each an imagined image brings
> And finds a real image there.

At this point, I want to share a story—one that hits rather close to home. Professor George Allen from the University of Sussex, who had been some years education advisor to the British Embassy in Washington, visited Salt Lake. I took him around Temple Square. He greatly admired the temple and tabernacle. He said they were unique. He took many photographs because, as he said, "These are superb buildings." Then I took him to the new visitors' center—not the newest one, but the then-new one. When he had gone around, he looked at me quizzically and then said, "Isn't it strange? The technique behind this is exactly the same as that behind socialist realism in Russia and the propaganda of the more modern wing of the Roman Catholic Church. I think it must be a matter of public relations." Mass art has become the servant of every master.

A third result of the Industrial Revolution's mass production, a result that is both a way in which people have become similar and a means to their becoming similar, is the mechanization of humanity. The Enlightenment aided people in producing more and more complex machines, and the more complex the machines became, the more keen people became on likening human beings to the machine. Human beings were reduced to automatons for the purpose of explaining, predicting, and controlling their behavior.

Capitalism and communism both premise deterministic, economic man, the maximizer of self-interest. The emphasis in capitalism is on the individual and/or corporation; in communism it is on classes. But capitalism and communism are more similar than different: They both pit people against each other in the struggle for power. They both allow groups to take power and exploit power for their own purposes, very often to the detriment of the rest of the community. The fact that capitalism and communism are on opposite sides in our modern world is a further indication that they are the same kind of thing because they couldn't struggle together unless they were using the same means. The obverse and the reverse are always aspects of the same coin, the same process; just as, for example, the trouble about the women's movement is that it is aggressively male; and, of course, the principal trouble with males is their egocentricity, fostered by their mothers. How could Winston Churchill win the war except by becoming more and more like Hitler as the war went on? How could Hamlet defeat and kill Claudius except by becoming more and more like Claudius? They belong to the same world. They belong, largely, to the same descent. They are uncle and nephew. But are they not, as souls, singularly different?

Evolutionary theory, survival of the fittest, is at the heart of both capitalism and communism—not historically, but in terms of moral justification. Both capitalists and communists justify their abuse of power and brutality by saying that in the long run, the struggle will allow the best (corporation or class) to survive. I think that we, one hundred years later, would find it incredible to think how grim and how naive nineteenth-century capitalists were in their application of Darwinism. They justified their practices in factories, for example, with reasoning such as the following: "If these people allow us to use them, we have a right to use them."

Darwinistic ideas were more emphatic in the development of American capitalistic society in the late nineteenth century than anywhere else in the world because American businessmen were more powerful than any businessmen in the rest of the world. The United States has led the world in the doctrine of economic success and in the doctrine of primacy of the self. And I say that these two doctrines are profoundly anti-Christian, antigospel. I don't think the founding fathers anticipated economic and political Darwinism.

Darwinism has become the center of the mechanistic view of the universe. Darwinism is, in fact, the prime explanation of a universe without God. From the point of view of evolutionary theory and its use, then, capitalism and communism are on the same side. The whole western world is on that side, and indeed, now, the whole world.

Many in the Church oppose evolutionary theory. We know it to be wrong. It is materialistic; it is mechanical; and above all, it is not respectful of humankind. Yet some of those who oppose it automatically introduce some of its consequences into their philosophy and practice. They look upon the business ethic of society, based on economic Darwinism, as something potentially good. But in the long run, that ethic always turns out bad because power corrupts. And we know what the Doctrine and Covenants says about that: give a man a little power, and he will "immediately begin to exercise unrighteous dominion" (D&C 121:39). And remember what the historian Lord Acton said, "Power corrupts; absolute power corrupts absolutely." This view complements that of the professor who was in charge of the history department at my old Swedish university of Lund, Professor Lauritz Weibull. He used to say inaugurally to his doctorate seminar, "Men, you have hitherto been treated as children. But from now on, remember that what I'm going to tell you is a sound principle of history: if anyone gets to a position of great power, he is a scoundrel, because the only way to get to a position of great power is by being a scoundrel." He would say, "It doesn't always work, but it works most of the time."

There is no ultimate religious difference between communist and democratic systems. They use the same methods—with different "goals" perhaps—and they use them in terms of self-interest.

Wherever you have a so-called communist government, it has established itself as a government of gangsters. Wherever you have a so-called fascist government, it, too, has established itself as a government of gangsters. And in so-called democratic states, look at the lobbying, the corruption, and gangsterdom, held barely in check, if at all, by governmental restraints on power. Although for simplistic purposes people talk about aristocracies, tyrannies, oligarchies, and democracies, the fact remains that in any state all those situations potentially exist and actually do exist side by side to some extent. I think that the word *democracy* is misused grossly, not only in the Soviet Union, but also in capitalist states, because democracy doesn't exist in any of them, and the reason is that where the money is, the power is. In capitalist states, lobbyists put pressures on elected officials, and those pressures are much more important than the views of the people throughout the country.

Modern world culture has socially denied the virtue of the individual; it is reducing human beings to a mechanism; it has allowed power to proliferate without control; and it has also allowed moral behavior to decline without control. We have results in law and in morality which are frightening. People today look at the promiscuity, the lack of values, as being new. But society departed from Christian standards much earlier than the twentieth century following the Second World War. The departure from Christian standards is coincidental with the development of the industrial and scientific revolutions, which threaten freedom of choice. The problem is not simply a matter of sexual morality. The decline of sexual morality is part and parcel of a general decline in the way of looking at human beings. And that general decline in the way of looking at human beings is a mechanistic way of looking at them that comes from looking at the universe without God. The fundamental thing is the belief in a universe without God or the practice of one's life as if it were without God. And, of course, for most people the universe is without God until some terrible crisis hits them, and then they may suddenly realize how wrong they have been or else commit suicide. A religious basis is essential. You cannot expect a country to maintain moral standards unless it has a religious basis. Without religion, politics degenerates. We are watching politics go to pieces now all over the world, including in this country, as a result of abandoning religious principles. Without religious life, there can be no decent political life.

Compensations

As faith withdraws from the world and the world becomes less and less Christian, the compensations the world seeks against misery and despair become more and more Satanic. As we go from generation to generation, the degeneration becomes worse. At the least damaging level, the world's compensations are amusements of various kinds that are not on a high level, but don't do much harm. But some compensations are so obsessive that they may be regarded as drugs. They are means of passing the time, of getting rid of the time, of forgetting. People get so bored with life they can't stand it without drugs. The more perfect life is from the point of view of modern technology, the more boring it is. There is no purpose, and drugs are taken to make up for that lack of purpose.

When discussing drugs, we must not make the foolish mistake of the surrounding culture. We mustn't think that coffee and tea and alcohol are relatively inoffensive compared with cocaine, for example, or marijuana; that is like thinking that fornication and adultery are not as bad as homosexuality or incest. We have to think of all these things as sins; we have to think of all the politicians and civil servants who make decisions for us when they are under the influence of alcohol or tobacco or caffeine and consider what effect these drugs will have on their decisions. In my former organization (the British Council), a man who worked as a controller of the Establishments Division—a position having a considerable effect on people's lives—often got drunk at lunch, so we had to be careful to see that he made decisions in the morning and not in the afternoon. Drinking alcohol and taking drugs are sins of a similar kind because alcohol is a drug, one of the worst drugs—perhaps it is the worst drug of all because it is the most prevalent of all. That is why it is completely illogical for a man who drinks alcohol to complain of his boy's smoking marijuana.

Drug abuse is widespread in our modern world. What saps the defense services of the Soviet Union? Drunkenness. What saps the armed services of the United States? Drug addiction. I am told there are even more drunken people in the armed services of the Soviet Union than there are drug addicts in the American armed services. So the United States still has a slight edge. Unfortunately, much of everything (including writing and scholarship) has been done under the influence of drugs, which certainly have had some detrimental effect.

Fundamentally, drugs are to be defined not as things which do us physical harm—because it may be possible to invent drugs that do not do us physical harm—but as things that do us mental and moral harm. All of us are taking drugs of this kind to some extent. They are drugs that we don't even recognize as such, and they come insidiously from all quarters. The mass media, the radio, and TV are drugs. Most video games are drugs. I remember going into a public house in England near Stratford a few years ago to get some bread and cheese and pickles. I saw a young man there with a glass of beer by his side—he was playing one of these games. My sister and I went in, had some lunch, and sat and talked, and about an hour and a half later we came out. The glass of beer was still there, and this boy—he was probably about nineteen or twenty—was still going on, on, on, and he would probably go on until the pub closed. These things don't harm the body (except that one exercises less when involved with them), but they may harm any soul. They are a great threat.

Gambling, both at the casino and on the Stock Exchange, is another drug which people don't recognize as such. Gambling frequently becomes an obsession. And it is a way of denying reality. People who gamble give themselves a wrong image of the universe, an image in which luck and fortune and chance see people through. Perhaps they are trying to escape from another wrong image of the universe, a deterministic one. But neither of these images actually reflects the universe. As Mormons, we know that we live in a universe of Providence and that there is no such thing as chance in this universe. We know that everything in the universe is purposive.

Anything in our surrounding lives that tempts us to think of luck or fortune instead of Providence is a sin. That is why it is immoral to play card games. Being able to win at cards depends partly upon intelligence, but it also depends very much upon luck, whether we get good or bad cards dealt to us. The best games are essentially like chess; that is to say, they contain no element of luck or chance. Chess is all calculation, so if we win a game of chess, we do so by our virtue, and if we lose a game of chess, the fault is ours. In chess we can never blame anyone or anything but ourselves, and that doctrine is fundamental to repentance. We make a move, we have to take responsibility for that move. Children need to learn this, and they badly need to learn it. I remember my nephew once throwing over a chess board when he saw he was losing because he didn't like to lose. A great many children will do that, perhaps most. But I do not believe when we are playing with children that we should play worse in order to let them win. Instead, we should teach them by saying why we made this move when we might have made that one, and so on. Then they will learn to do better. By the time he was eleven, my nephew could beat me, just as I in my turn had managed to beat my uncle, who was fifty-five, by the time I was the same age. And it is a wonderful achievement. It is an equality.

From the beginning, we need to teach our children that since they rely upon Providence, they should not rely upon luck. And we should be aware of chance in literature as well as games. Time and again, bad literature is based on chance. Now you may say there is chance in the greatest works of literature. But you and I know that what some people would interpret as chance is not chance, but the grace of God. Great literature does not base itself on chance.

Today, we are living in a world that, having gone down from religious principles, is looking for an escape. That is why we have drugs and gambling, and that is why these things will increase more and more. They are a substitute. They are a means of being able to endure a life that is unendurable outside the gospel. My own experience is that life is unendurable outside the gospel. That is the kind of thing that we have to get home to our young people.

The Gospel Response

World culture is, in my view, the great and abominable church. It is directly and fundamentally opposed to the principles of the gospel. The devil is there, manipulating behind world culture, and although appearances at times reassure us, the world is on its definite and prophesied way down. The cultural danger lies deep and goes through country after country.

As members of the restored Church, we should not be comforting ourselves with the superficial assumption that the surrounding culture is quite good, quite nice, getting better. Book of Mormon references to this kind of thinking will immediately spring to your mind. But most people do not think that the contemporary situation is similar to situations described in the Book of Mormon. Yet it is. And the kind of destruction that threatens us on an enormous scale is no different from the kind of destruction described twice in the Book of Mormon: large-scale annihilation the first time, total annihilation the second. The Gadarene swine are running down the slope; there comes a point at which the hill is so steep that all they can do is to fall into the lake.

I had two young German shepherds I got in Persia. When I took them back to England in 1952, they had to go into quarantine for six months. They were allowed their runs. It was a long, hot summer. At the beginning of their quarantine, they thought that all wasps were flies; at the end, they thought all flies were wasps. This is my answer to all people who are shallow enough to be optimistic: they will end up being pessimistic or hypocrites. I have in my own life found from the beginning that to anticipate the worst is helpful because when it doesn't happen you are grateful, whereas if you are an optimist you will be disappointed over and over again. But the thing to be is not an optimist or a pessimist, but a realist. The gospel is a gospel of realism. The gospel is, in fact, real. And nothing else is real in the same way.

We should be showing our own members what is wrong with the culture surrounding us instead of letting them slip into it. Such teaching is our duty, particularly with our young people. I know that many young people, and many adults, too, think at the bottom of their souls that the grass is greener on the other side of the fence, but I have spent a large part of my life trying to munch the grass on the other side of the fence, and I can tell you from personal experience that that grass is made of plastic, which is why it holds its color so well and doesn't need any watering. We must not let our members yearn for what they imagine to be the greater freedom outside. There is no greater freedom outside—there is only wilderness: wilderness and violence and despair.

As a people, we need to understand world culture, and then we need to work to save ourselves and others. An ideal Mormon is not one who spends hours in front of the television set, as the rest of modern civilization does, but one who is active, brisk, and busy. There are many good ways to be active: there is work, there is exercise, there is prayer. There is a time for all these things, and if we are doing none of them, then we had better sleep. How much better to sleep than to look at most television, because television detracts from our strength, but sleep at least builds it up. Mormons should not expect to be entertained. Life is too short for that. If they want relaxation, they should look for it not in passive entertainment, but in activities that are different from the ones they have been engaged in.

There is a great deal of sloth in our modern life. There is a great deal of passivity—and most passivity is sloth. Sloth is perhaps the most common sin. And "Satan finds some mischief still for idle hands to do" seems to point to the fact that sloth is a very grievous sin indeed. Sloth has to do with an attitude of "I don't care. I won't bother. I don't particularly feel like action." It consists, essentially, in letting ourselves go and deciding we don't want to do something good. Sloth exists all the time when, as Christians, we are not making the best possible use of our time. If we have chosen to look at a good program on television, good! But if we are just sitting idly in front of the television and watching whatever is happening there, that is sloth. If we need to catch fish, we should go out and catch fish. That is not sloth. But if we go out just to amuse ourselves by catching fish, that is sloth. To read the newspaper or a periodical for the benefit of finding out what is going on in the world is not sloth. But to sit in front of a newspaper or a magazine and go through it as a means of idling our time is sloth. We have to be careful of activities that require minimum intellectual effort and give us an excuse for really doing nothing. Every moment of our lives, we should be asking ourselves, "Am I doing at this moment the best I can?"

The Church's organization exists to help us rise to the greatest heights we can. And to what do we rise? I won't go into detail, only to say that we have to guard against listlessness in ourselves, just as we have to be aware of it in the world as a means and a background to the salvation we are to preach. A good thing in Puritanism was the belief that we should work. And the work morality is, it seems to me, the Mormon morality. So much so, that we are the only church that preaches a future state beyond the veil not of rest, but of work. We shall be in a state of spiritual peace, the peace that passeth all understanding. But peace is not the same as rest. That peace will be accompanied by intensive work for the Lord on a far larger scale than we have here.

Once when I was fourteen years old and a melancholy boy (I had just gone into long trousers, and we had not been allowed to go into long trousers before then), my teacher, who came from the Channel Islands and was partly French, came up to me and said, "I notice that you are not very happy. It seems to me that you think with Plato that happiness is a state of mind. Why not try, with Aristotle, to think of happiness as an activity?" My life changed from that moment on because I had learned something that I had not realized before, and I ceased to be a melancholy boy. I have since thought that this idea of Aristotle's, that happiness is an activity, is compatible with the Christian idea that we should be serving others.

The great work that we need to do is missionary work, and the foundation for doing that work must be a sound understanding of the difference between ourselves and the world. Our responsibility in the Church is not to sympathize with the world, but to empathize with it. Sympathy is fellow-feeling with another person. Empathy is the power to put ourselves into a situation that is foreign to us, being able to identify ourselves imaginatively with it, being able to understand. We need to identify with the unconverted, not sympathetically, but empathetically. If we are empathetic with them, we shall see the emptiness in their lives, not the "excitement."

We cannot smugly sit upon our hilltops. We cannot be fearful. It doesn't matter what the world thinks of us. We know by inspiration what the world needs: it needs the gospel. Not too long ago, I spent three weeks in England, going round and visiting my relations and friends. They're growing older; some of them are ill; some of them aren't getting on well with their children; some of them have grown-up children who ignore them. They have all these troubles and no reward, nowhere to go, no comfort—without the gospel, no comfort. And that is the state of most people in this country as well. Most people are tolerably miserable most of the time. But we in the Church have a purpose, which is the Lord's purpose. We have acknowledged that purpose. We depart from it sometimes; we sin, also. But we at least know what we are doing in life; we have an end. And our modern society does not, quite simply, any longer have an end. It may have ends, but they are temporary ends. The life of modern society is fading out.

Patriotism

AT THE TIME of my conversion to the Mormon Church, I was with the British Council working as an administrator in charge of British cultural and educational work overseas. I was traveling about from country to country, inspecting English teaching, advising governments. I was enjoying power. When I joined the Church, I felt that I had been sinning. I felt that what I must do was get back to teaching as soon as possible. So in 1968, two years after I joined the Church, when I came through Utah on a consultative Ford Foundation world tour, I took the opportunity of making contact at BYU. Later, President Wilkinson got hold of me, and in 1970, I came back for summer school. In 1971, I came back again and was taken by Robert K. Thomas, then academic vice-president, to meet Harold B. Lee, then President of the Quorum of the Twelve. He was to decide whether I should remain in Britain or teach at BYU. The decision was for BYU, for which I was grateful. That is what I wanted to do, what I had to do. That is what I felt the Lord wanted me to do.

President Lee, President Thomas, and I also talked, among other things, about my years of "going to and fro in the earth." And as President Thomas and I were leaving, President Lee said, with some good-humored irony, "So when you come here, you'll be a kind of missionary in reverse." In the context, he was speaking not of the gospel, but of culture. I would be a sort of bottled message from the peripherally insular survival of a *Pax* Britannica to the landlocked center of a subcontinent struggling to maintain a *Pax* Americana. I have taken President Lee's statement seriously. I have tried, in my talking at BYU and elsewhere, to talk, not so much to the Mormon in the American (that Mormon has no need of me), but to the American in the Mormon, who may find my intended wisdom foolish, but my unintentional foolishness of some profit (see 1 Cor. 4:10).

Although I have lived in the United States for fifteen years now, I am still a British subject. I think I am probably more useful to the Church as a British subject, and that view is shared by others, so that is what I remain. But I have not been a typical Briton. I was brought up in opposition to British imperialism by a father who was not a left-winger, but a Quaker. Not that as a boy of eight I understood my father's attitude properly. I had come to know a number of Bavarian prisoners working on the land under my father's supervision. I liked them. On November 11, 1918, I suggested to my father that we ought to fly the German flag. He tried to explain to me that it would be even less right for us to fly the German flag than to fly the Union Jack.

I learned early that patriotism does not connote slavishly following your country in all things. Patriotism does not mean, "My country right or wrong." That is moral nonsense. But it means, "My country insofar as it remains faithful to God's purpose." A true patriot doesn't pretend not to notice when his country goes wrong. He doesn't say, "All is well," when all is not well. And all is not well in the United States. (All is certainly not well in England, either. We have lost our empire, and now we are a small country. We are lost between the idea that we were once the most important country in the world and the reality that now we no longer are.) A true patriot says, "I love my country, and, therefore, I will do my best for my country. I will place my abilities at the disposal of my country; I will try to improve my country." A true patriot is prepared to help humbly bring his country back on to the right track again.

Some Americans like to say that this country, the United States, is the best country in the world. Now, do not misunderstand me, but I don't believe in "best countries in the world." It is obvious, from the point of view of the gospel and from the point of view of prophecy, that there are no good countries. But I would say that the United States is the least unsatisfactory country in the world, meaning that all other countries are less satisfactory than this country. This is the least unsatisfactory country because it has given more people than ever before in the world an opportunity to reach a decent standard of living under reasonably free circumstances and because that freedom came at least a half century before it did to many other parts of the world, including my own. Some of you are not brought up to realize that at the time you were fighting George III, most of the British people would have been glad to be rid of him, too. You did not complete your revolution. England, Wales, Scotland, and Ireland should have been freed together with your states, and then the British Isles would have achieved their liberty over 150 years before we did (not that we have yet quite achieved it: Britain is still highly class-conscious). You may not realize that your Revolutionary War and your Constitution were examples of freedom for a repressed intellectual class, a depressed peasantry, and a wretched working class in Europe for seventy years or more. Remember that Britain started the Industrial Revolution and that the Industrial Revolution produced in Britain circumstances of poverty, toil, and misery hardly exampled in world history until the "developing" countries of our own time.

We in the Church are told, and I as an Englishman also believe, that those who set up the United States Constitution were divinely inspired. But what do you think the founding fathers would have thought about the way in which this country has developed? Traditionally, the United States held the view of the rights of the individual, held the view of freedom of choice, and held the view that human beings are dignified creatures, responsible for themselves, with the right to decide for themselves and to make their own lives. This tradition has been departed from. And I believe the reason has to do with weaknesses inherent in a democratic system. Churchill said that democracy is the worst form of government, except all the others. And we, as members of the Church, can believe that because we know that there is no way people can adequately rule themselves independent of God. Lacking the kingdom of God on earth, all we can do is make do with what we have, be alert to its weaknesses, and prepare for something better.

American Democracy

Now, the United States, at its inception, was not exactly a democracy. It was something between a democracy and an oligarchy, most obviously because the franchise was limited. The Founding Fathers were representatives of the middle and upper classes. Washington was an upper-class person, Benjamin Franklin was a lower-middle-class person, and there was all the gamut in between. But the franchise was gradually extended, and from the presidency of Andrew Jackson, this country changed considerably. Up to that time, you had had presidents like Washington, Adams, Jefferson. Andrew Jackson was a very different kind of person from those people. Since that time, this country has had to struggle with the problem of demagogy and the fact that democracy can so readily decline into demagogy. Most elections in this country today (and in many European countries) are run on a demagogic basis. That is to say, candidates tell the public lies in order to get elected. Their statements are not based on true analyses of situations or on attempted true analyses of situations, but on considerations of popular appeal. In oligarchic states, candidates are less likely to lie than in democratic states because they are more likely to get caught. Informed persons vote for them, and voters are informed because it is in their vested interest to be informed: they have more to lose if the government acts irresponsibly.

The point is this: once you have a democracy, demagogy is usually not far away, and that means political and moral decline. It even means intellectual decline. Now one of the major characteristics of our upper-middle-class and our upper-class speech in Britain is stumbling and hesitating: anacoluthon has been fashionable for most of my lifetime. Politicians recommend themselves because they break the backs of sentences, because they are matey in speech. It is as if the upper classes in Britain were saying, "We will retain control over the lower classes by pretending to be more stupid than they are."

We are in a society now where people say, "sort of," "kind of," "in a way," "I mean," and all those other little ejaculations that we use increasingly. We use "I mean," "I mean to say," "you see," all those things—over and over and over again—like the gossips who say, "She said, she said, she said." They are a kind of stuttering, a kind of self-imposed idiocy, a kind of pretense very often found in people trying to show that they are just like everybody else—quite stupid really. Stupidity in a democratic society as a whole produces pseudo-stupidity in its leaders, with appalling results. Once there is television in the House of Commons—and I hope it will never happen—everybody there will be pretending to be as stupid as their electorates. This kind of manipulative pretense at being more stupid than the other person was first noticed by Wyndham Lewis in the twenties and documented in the speech of Bertie Wooster.

What underlies this stooping down of leaders is the desire in the common folk to see their rulers pulled down to their level. Look at what happened in your Watergate case or in similar cases in Britain: an enjoyment of scandal, a liking to see those in high places pulled down or denigrated or made to look absurd or comic. Most people, and I am afraid a large proportion of the people in our Church, too, like scandal. Scandal is the meat and drink of excitement to the dissatisfied, the bored. Yet the fact remains that it is incumbent upon us as Christians to hate the sin but love the sinner. We have no right to laugh at, or to be angry at, or to hate these people. We have the duty to pity them because people who are guilty in these matters are not hateful—they are pitiable. And it is a disgrace to drag other peoples' disgrace through the public street, for when you do it, instead of hating the sin, you hate the sinner. How many of us do not require a scapegoat? The need for a scapegoat is deep within us. If there is no one in a school who stands out for teasing, then the class will find some reason for using somebody. If he is not black, well, then red hair will do. I remember we used to torture the single red-haired boy in our class. Mind you, had all the boys but one been red haired, they would have tortured the one nonredheaded boy.

Socially, this leveling-down tendency is manifest in your peer groups. The desire to be like each other becomes a desire to be like the worst person in the peer group because the tendency is for the worst person to lower the group, not for the best person to raise it. And that is the problem of democracy generally.

Peer groups are most important among your teenagers, of course. And your teenage group as a whole is more anxious to establish likeness than any other teenage group I have known anywhere else. What has happened here is that advertisers have gotten ahold of teenagers and exploited them—advertisers have exploited teenagers' desire to belong in order to get money out of them. My theory is that the teenager was not an invention of the psychologist at all, but an invention of business and advertising: middle-class adolescents began to earn money, and therefore advertisers became interested in them as a target for advertising. I didn't know that I was a teenager when I became thirteen. I had no idea that there were special problems of adolescence; I just went through them. The root of the problem is that adolescents in this country are a money-earning group. In fact, the United States invented the middle-class, money-earning, adolescent male and female. They were and are a species almost unknown in Europe. European adolescents don't earn money for themselves. They are either working class and work in order to contribute to the family income, or they are middle or upper class, in which case they wouldn't dream of working while they were students. In this country, you think that working and earning money will encourage the adolescent's independence and ability to handle his life. What it actually does is to pour money into the pockets of those who exploit teenagers. What do teenagers spend their money on? Pop, cosmetics, games, records, cars, alcohol, drugs. And once adolescents have money, they gain a status which makes it more difficult for their parents to deal with them.

What a contradiction there is between the assertion of the individual and the assertion of the peer group! The great paradox of your American society today, as I see it from the outside, is your traditional political assertion of individualism and your contemporary social assertion of likeness. It is a tremendous paradox that faces you. You yourselves do not realize the tremendous pressure to conform that exists, not in your political system, but in your social system. If you come to think of it for a moment, you can see how that happens in an immigrant society such as the United States: the immigrants came into this country with a desire to be melted in the melting pot, as it used to be called, and their desire to be American, when they were not American, but had come in as immigrants, expressed itself as a desire to be like other people, to be 110 percent American.

Peer groups present a challenge to the political system. They are fundamentally protest groups. They challenge established institutions. And due to the tremendous assertion of peer groups in this country, the antiestablishment mentality often continues on into adulthood and right through into old age. One of its manifestations is voter apathy, which is considerably greater in this country than in European countries.

Let me now say something about democratic ideals in education. Look what has happened since 1870 in Britain, and since some other time in the United States, when education for all was decided upon. What has happened is that most students have been taught to read and few have been educated. Consequently, nearly everybody has chosen to read at the lowest possible level. Since that decision was made, we have had in Britain those vulgar weeklies, aimed at the servant and the apprentice, which have gradually proliferated until, today, this filthy flood covers the earth with inanity and lust and violence. Every airport bookstore, every book section in every supermarket, is a shame to humanity and a stink that reaches the bottom of the soul. So low has reading sunk that publishers make the pictures on the front even worse than the contents, to attract the reader. Only the illiterate countries of the world retain some human dignity. I do not advocate illiteracy, but teaching people to read without educating them means handing them over to exploiters of every kind, in patent medicines, in politics, in pornography, in moneymaking.

If a society decides to educate everybody, the standards go down, as they have in university general education, for example. Actually, general education wasn't even needed before education became what it is today. General education has had to develop at American universities as a result of the democratization of higher education, and even European universities have had to undertake it as oligarchic norms have declined. But general education today is becoming a less and less adequate substitute for "breeding"—the fundamental education that used to be received in the family and in society outside the school and university—because democratic educationists want to make things easier all of the time. Things that haven't any right to be there are now crawling into university education under all sorts of excuses.

I recognize the need for democratic education, but I recognize also the need to preserve the higher standards that the old oligarchic system had. The answer, in part, lies in achieving some kind of balance. America sends more than 60 percent of its young people into institutions of higher education. The percentage in Germany is 11 percent. The percentage in France is 13 percent. The percentage when I last saw it in Britain was 17 percent. You may say that European countries still have class societies and educate too few. And my reply is that you are right. But 60 percent is too many. It brings down academic values. They are difficult to maintain. We need to encourage nonuniversity alternatives, such as technical colleges, to satisfy the needs of those who do not really want a university education, but practical training. An undergraduate student who does not want education as much as training for a specific practical purpose does not belong at a university. At the undergraduate level, universities are for learning, not for the application of learning; they are for education, not for training. At the graduate level, education and training interact.

Mormons, of all people, believe that democracy ought to mean raising everybody to a higher level, not bringing everybody down to a lower level. If we aim at a lower level of spiritual and intellectual achievement for democratic man than for oligarchic man, we shall be going dead against the gospel. The democratic hope is that democratic education will bring everybody up. But that has not yet happened by any means, nor does it look as if it will soon. The right form of democratic education has yet to be worked out. And it may be that it won't be worked out until the Millennium.

Democratic thinking occurs in the Church, sometimes appropriately, sometimes inappropriately. And American Mormons particularly need to watch that their democratic cultural attitudes don't lead them, unaware, into religious error, as well as political, social, and educational error. There is a danger of bringing God down to the level of man or raising man to the level of God, which amounts to the same thing. Take that beautiful hymn "I Am a Child of God." It is an important hymn and an important concept. But we are not children of God in pride, we are children of God in humility. To be a child of God means to understand the greatness of God in a way that a person who doesn't think he is a child of God simply cannot do. I don't say that we should distance ourselves from God, but neither should we pretend familiarity with him. That is the worst way of distancing ourselves. To lose that sense of awe is to lose the concept of God, because God is tremendous in his power just as he is unending in his love. A child of God recognizes the fatherhood of God as the tremendous and "aweful" thing that it is.

American Culture

The problem for American Mormons is that, on the one hand, they have the teachings of the scriptures and the revelations that come from the Brethren, and on the other hand, they have the teachings of their culture. Two or three generations ago, these teachings were much more like one another than they are now. But whereas Mormon beliefs and Mormon morality are supposed to have remained the same, American beliefs and morality have changed. And when we are using the word "morality," we have to remember that we are not using a word of Hebrew or Christian origin at all. We are using a word of pagan origin, with certain limitations because it is a pagan word. The word "morality" is, by origin, Latin. The *mores* of society are its manners and customs, its habits. Something moral is something that conforms to the manners and customs of society. That is the original sense of it. The Romans, and also the Greeks, only understood that you either behaved as society expected you to or you didn't. And if you were out of line, it might be crime or it might be just bad manners. Now, that is not a religious viewpoint at all. It is a practical, social viewpoint practically hooked up with the social system. Romans and Greeks had no word for sin or righteousness.

The world's morality varies from age to age. But Christian morality is not dependent on the fluctuations of society. It is now moral (but not righteous), in your country and in mine, to murder—1.5 million abortions are performed each year in this country and a comparable number in European countries. Americans have murdered more babies in this country since abortion was legalized than the Germans killed Jews in concentration camps during the last war. The one is as monstrous as the other from the Christian point of view, but not from the point of view of society. The gap there is enormous. We think of as murder, more or less, what a large segment of society today does not class as murder at all.

There is a great difference between the customs of any society and the commandments of God. But in this country, particularly, there is a strange tendency to identify, without thinking about it, the morality of the surrounding society with the morality of the Church. When we start measuring our righteousness in terms of morality, however, we have made a step down. We have made a compromise, as very many of us have on the subject of abortion or women's rights or a number of other things about which it is crystal clear what we should think, but about which we prefer to think otherwise. There is an absolute difference between the morality of the only true church upon the face of this earth and the moral practices of any country you would like to mention, including your own. We have to understand that fundamental distinction. If we do not, we cannot understand the difference between being in the world and being of the world. And that is our responsibility—to be in but not of the world, to keep ourselves "unspotted from the world" (James 1:27).

As Mormons, we cannot fail to be in the world, because we live in it. Mormons nowadays have to live far more in the world than they used to. Their once fastness is overflown by the airplane, penetrated by the TV and public education, undermined by explosive ideas fashionably packaged and smuggled in, we live in Utah more or less as Mormons have to live elsewhere—cheek by jowl with non-Mormons. We need to watch ourselves that we do not become of the world by identifying ourselves with elements in the world that are not consonant with the gospel. And the greatest danger lies in accepting the world's values because we fail to notice that the world's values are creeping in and insidiously undermining our faith and our practice.

It is easier for Mormons outside the United States to see the difference between the world and the Church than it is for Mormons inside the United States. Most of us in other countries are under no illusion about the total difference between the Church and the surrounding cultures. Whether we come from Europe, Asia, or Latin America, it is the same. We know that Satan dominates in the surrounding cultures. And American Mormons are reluctant to admit this. But any country—even the United States—that is not endeavoring to follow the principles of the gospel is obviously not great. To assume too readily that America is great as it now stands is to jeopardize the future of true and traditional American values, which are in danger of being undermined by social decay in this country.

Most Mormons in the United States appear to be 100 percent patriotic; I doubt if Mormons in Japan or Britain or Germany are patriotic in the same sense at all. I can give you an example. We do not fly the Union Jack outside the English temple. I doubt if Mormons in other countries fly their flags outside their temples either. I once said to a president of the Provo temple, "Why don't you fly the flags of all the nations whose citizens have been through this temple?" (My question was ironical, for what national flag is not stained with national crime? The Union Jack has stains that can never be bleached out.) The temple president had no answer because he had never even thought of it. It does seem to me as an Englishman that American Mormons are often more comfortable about their own country than, as Mormons, they ought to be.

In the patriotic reflections of this third century of American independence, who in the Church is prepared sufficiently to remember the awful gap between the country this might have become and the country it has become? Who remembers the years between 1835 and 1890 in the Church and the attitudes that our predecessors must then have had toward Washington? Who sees the evil in contemporary American society? Mormons have not had the same attitude towards the American cultural setting after 1890 as they had before 1890, although the cultural setting today is more deserving of condemnation. We cannot say that 1.5 million abortions per year in a country is not evil. We cannot say that these pornographic and violent productions on film and on television are not evil. We cannot say that the rate of rape in this country is not evil, or the rate of murder. We cannot say that the rate of drug use is not appalling. We might say it is the same everywhere. But it is not the same everywhere. The number of murders in New York City in one month is greater than the number of murders in the whole of the British Isles in one year. There are countries that are worse—the Philippines, for example. In Manila, you find guards with tommy guns at store entrances. We have to face up to these things. The Church needs to bear them in mind all the time, and above all, we need to bear them in mind in the education and protection of our children. It is the imperfection we must see because that is what threatens us.

American Mormons, and Americans generally, are threatened at a more fundamental level by the material prosperity of this country. It is a curse in disguise. Prosperity per se is not an enemy to religion, but prosperity may often lead to idolatry. The danger of all progress is idolatry because the temptation all of the time is to set up something in the place of God. And the more tempting the progress is—and material prosperity is tempting—the more dangerous it is. Think of the idols of prosperity: the car, the camper, the boat (bane of bishops), the color TV, the football game, two weeks of hunting. These become idols when more enthusiasm and time are given to them than to the worship of God.

One of the fundamental tendencies of the modern world is to erect in the place of the priest, who no longer has credibility, the modern doctor, who has increasing credibility. The doctor and medicine have become a kind of idol. So on the one hand we have progress in medicine, and on the other hand we have progress in idolatry. Of course, progress in medicine is a good thing. But it is a very bad thing to give people the impression that because they are gaining more and more control over life and death, they are, therefore, becoming independent of Providence.

The idolatry of modern humanity was described to us in detail by President Kimball in the June 1976 *Ensign*. And he deliberately described it immediately before the Fourth of July, 1976, which was the two hundredth anniversary of the freedom of this country, to remind us of what we are doing in this country—worshipping false gods. That is perhaps the most trenchant thing that we ever had from that trenchant president, and it is worthy to be a section of the Doctrine and Covenants. In common terms, it is a piece of great literature. But I would not call it that. I would call it the Lord using a prophet to speak to us. I need only remind you of that article because most of you probably read it when it came out, and if you read it once, you have probably read it several times since. It needs to be read and re-read. I read it regularly to hearten myself and to make myself understand better. The point is, righteousness is important, not riches; the bread of life is more important than the cake. That is what the message of the prophets has always been about and is still about.

The materialism of American culture has corrupted many of this country's institutions. Even the great effort of religiousness, as far as I can see it nowadays in this country, is to sell salvation. It is a kind of commercialism, isn't it, persuading people that salvation is easy? Look at those ridiculous pontificators that take the pulpit on the television every Sunday morning, including that one I call Purple Wings. Think of the things they say. People think, "They're good men." But they are preaching heresy; they are preaching nonsense; they are preaching false comfort. Above all, they are preaching that religion is easy: all you have to do is acknowledge the Lord Jesus Christ and everything else will come. But we do not believe in our Church that salvation is easy. Conversion is an ongoing process, a day-to-day process lasting the whole of our lives. Repentance is an ongoing process. A moral life is a constant, hard struggle.

I remember my teacher Tillyard at Cambridge many years ago, lecturing on Milton, saying Milton was the kind of man who believed that you might commit a deadly sin as you stooped to do up your bootlace. And that, I think, puts it in a nutshell. That sense of sin is a good thing in Puritanism—that, and the realization that sin is not something easily categorized and got rid of, but something insidious, something threatening, all the time. Sin is like the tide. We know that the tide comes up the beach twice every twenty-four hours. It comes; we can't expect it not to. And some days it comes higher than others, and the wind is with it. And I think that image is relevant to the way that evil comes into our lives. It is there all the time; life is a constant struggle against it.

I want now to give you what you may perhaps call some rather superficial examples, but what I would call deeper examples—very often the "frivolous" things go deepest—of American practices that do not seem to me to be consonant with the gospel. Is it unimportant that males may keep a hand in their trousers pocket when they are praying or giving a talk at the pulpit? Ought members to chew gum in church? To me the former seems irreverent and the latter vulgar.

Or consider the example of wedding receptions. We get invited to a good many weddings, student weddings, and I discovered one summer that a number of my young friends that were getting married didn't want to have receptions. And so I started collecting the reasons why: expense, extravagance, conspicuous waste. To what extent are those receptions a Mormon phenomenon, and to what extent are they just a standard American phenomenon, a kind of social exhibition? Young people go to the temple, and one hopes they reach a certain standard of spiritual inspiration about their marriage. And then, isn't it coming down to go to these amiably easy wedding receptions the same day, perhaps a day or two later? What about the kind of music that is often played at those receptions? Reflect about the fact that people drop their wedding presents, walk along the line, sit down, sip a glass of punch, nibble a snack, and vanish. I went to one wedding reception this summer that heartened me. It was held at a home. The garden was not large; it was luckily a fine evening. The people who came stayed:

they did not come and go; they sat around. The members of the family did not form a line: they wandered about and sat down at this table and that, and so were able to meet old friends, relatives, etc. Obviously, there are some forms that can be devised for proper Mormon wedding receptions. But do we in the Church at this moment have the proper Mormon forms for wedding receptions? If we do, why do these young couples who get married (many of them spiritually serious) wish they did not have to have a reception and just have it because their family wants it?

Think also of the way dating is often practiced in this country. Surely one should not date in such a way that it is impossible to see who the other person really is. Yet that is what is done. Think of this business of dining by candlelight. Look at all those advertisements of that kind in the *New Yorker* and other objectionable periodicals. Think of burying oneself in the dark at the movies. How should one date? Surely one should date to find out about the other person the maximum that one can. I have a close friend whose family is an unalloyed success. When he was single and taking girls out at the university, where do you think he asked them to go on a first date? He asked them to join him for a spell on the welfare farm or in some similar Church task. He thought that was a good first test of a girl, and I don't see anything wrong with that. The right way to date, in my view, is in collaboration rather than in play: to share social obligations in the Church, to read the gospel together, to study together. These are the right forms of dating. And yet I find at BYU—and I am sure it is true elsewhere—that sometimes as many as four nights a week are spent in frivolity. Dating ought to take place, and dating is worthy of taking place, in the kind of context where it can really do what it ought to do.

Dating is practiced in Canada and in the United States, but it is by no means a universal practice. It has several advantages, which the Church endorses. One advantage is that young people are able to move from relationship to relationship until their minds are made up. The Church has refined the habit of dating into a proper (if properly followed) course of conduct between the young. But it may not be proper to introduce dating habits into other countries, and it certainly would not be at all proper to introduce the habits of necking and petting. In many social groups and in other countries, people believe (with some justification) that "dating" includes necking and petting. They may therefore reject "dating." British girls (and boys) look on the habit of having social engagements with more than one person of the opposite sex as a kind of promiscuity. It becomes that much more difficult, therefore, to teach Church practice on this matter in Britain. It has to be presented from another angle. We need to keep in mind that though it may not be difficult for good Mormons outside the United States to accept that the Constitution of the United States is an inspired document and to be concerned that its principles should be preserved, it may be more difficult for them to accept American (but not necessarily Mormon) social behavior.

The gospel is now spreading throughout the world; if the gospel is to gather the righteous in its net, American Mormons must exemplify and teach the gospel, not American cultural attitudes. They need to see that they are in the world, not to be of and for the world, but to try to bring everybody into their world. They and all Mormons have the difficult task of living in the world as the salt of the world, its true taste, its preservation and salvation.

When Elder Maxwell and I shared a fireside at Hyde Park in London seventeen years ago, he made a statement that I latched onto and have held to ever since: the younger generation can enable the Church for the first time to be a truly ecumenical church—that is to say, a truly worldwide church—because this generation is the first not to be caught up in racism and excessive nationalism. Our ecumenical movement is not like the wider movements sponsored by the Roman Catholic Church, the Anglican Church and so on, which are based on beliefs so weak that they can be shared by people who don't believe alike, but it is an ecumenical movement based on strong doctrine and developing its own culture. It is because we are the restored Church that we have this.

Other Cultures and the Gospel

It is not for American Mormons to accept American culture. But it is not for American Mormons to accept other people's cultures either: most so-called culture in the world is against the gospel, not for it. In Britain, for example, we are rotten with the class system; we prolong it in the mind. I felt it again when I last went back to England for a visit. My wife can tell you that I slipped back into this kind of class thinking before I had been there a day. From that moment on, there were hotels that were not good enough for me to go into, and there were other hotels that were too good for me to go into, and in every city, I had to find the hotel that was appropriate to our social class, rather than to our purse. This was not because I was consciously thinking about it, but because I had an instinct for the sort of place where I belonged. You probably don't know that feeling in America, but it goes deep in Britain. You in America, of course, have your equivalents to the class system that go even deeper and are even more difficult for you: your national minorities. And you know well that members of the Church sometimes have feelings about those minorities that are not desirable feelings, and members have those feelings because they are not up to their faith.

Another example: In Britain we are a litotic people. When we are about to give a public lecture, we get up and say, "Well, I don't know much about this subject, but . . ." When we are enthusiastic about something, we say, "Not bad." These habits are against the Holy Ghost. There is an arrogance of false modesty that is worse than the purest arrogance. It is like the arrogance of shyness, which is a terrible disease. If only the British could give up saying "not bad" for a time, and if only Americans could forget the adjective "wonderful" for a time, we might be able to meet, because the affectation of the English is to undersay everything. As for you, "wonderfuls" trip off your tongues. In England, you see people going around with melancholy faces all the time. You just sit in the tube (the subway) and watch them. Look around on a New York street and you will see a factitious cheerfulness over everybody because here that is the cultural mask. But cultural masks are not the religious truth.

There are examples from culturally more distant countries. I am thinking of the Shiite Moslems in Iran who are prepared to give up their lives in order to kill Americans. They think that they are in a state of the highest righteousness, and many others are inclined to think that at least they are heroic. Now, I have lived in Iran, and I know the Shiites well—I have had many friends among them. The fanatical element in their culture is caused, fundamentally, by the wretched poverty of the people who live there. And the difficulty is that Satan has expressed himself in this Shiite fanaticism in a way that is readily mistaken for heroism. But their "heroism" remains a sin. Satan has deceived them, not with obvious sin—not with wine, women, or drugs, nor even with hypocrisy—but with false righteousness. Being tempted of the devil at the highest level is being tempted in that kind of way.

It is very doubtful if we in the Church can make a culture by picking the best of other ones. In the Mormon Church, we are building our own culture, which flows from the gospel. It behooves us therefore not to be sentimental about either other people's cultures or our own country's culture, but to think of all in the light of the gospel. There are mistakes that we as British Mormons make because we are British, just as there are mistakes that you in the Church here make because you are American, and there are mistakes that Tongan Mormons make because they are Tongan. The mistakes occur where the culture contradicts the Church and the Church members don't realize it or ignore it. Each of us needs to watch and help the others, across cultures, from this point of view, and we now have a situation in the Mormon Church where we can do that.

I said that we make mistakes; I could as easily have said that we sin. We sometimes use patriotism to whitewash our sins. But that doesn't mean we should abandon patriotism. We should abandon our sins. Patriotism rightly conceived is a great and noble thing. It is part of religion, and therefore as patriots it is our deepest duty to help bring out what is best in our country—to fight corruption, tyranny, and moral decay, and to work to bring our people, wherever they are, back to God. We seek a country; we seek a city. They are the city and the country of God.

No Longer Strangers

I HAVE LIVED most of my life abroad. As a young man, I spent fourteen years in Sweden, where I took two higher degrees and taught American and British literature. I then joined the British Council and for twenty-eight years lived or visited abroad, covering a good deal of the world outside the Iron Curtain and South Africa. I was the British Council's representative in Iran for two years (1951–52), until British officials temporarily withdrew from that country. Iran's prime minister, Dr. Mussadeq, was a pleasant man who lived next door to me and for one whole summer took water from my streams because his own had dried up. I was happy about this until my ambassador asked me, "And what are you going to do if Dr. Mussadeq gets poisoned?" In addition to those two years in Persia, I spent five years in Pakistan, and I made various visits to Africa, Asia, Latin America, Australia, and the Pacific, attending the various conferences organized to bring Commonwealth countries together to discuss educational problems. Now, what I want to discuss, from the point of view of my experience in developing countries, is what I believe they need, how developed countries and others have been unable to help them, and how we in the Church have the opportunity to provide the help they really need.

On the surface, developing countries are very different from each other with respect to their dependence on developed countries. Persia and Pakistan represent the extremes. Persia is an age-old, independent country and very reluctant to let foreigners into positions of influence in its educational system or any other

---

This essay was written in the late 1980s.

part of it. Pakistan continues to lean. For example, to the Pakistani, the English university system is the system. There are not other university systems. But go to Indonesia and you will find that the Indonesians are convinced the Dutch university system they have inherited is the system. Not because it is Dutch, but simply because they don't know of any others and they assume that this is the one. Although former colonial countries repudiate ways in which they see that they are still colonial and don't want to be, it is extraordinary how they still remain colonial in ways they don't themselves recognize even though those ways are not good for them.

So there are age-old, independent countries like Persia and Ethiopia. And there are former colonial countries like Pakistan, Indonesia, and India. But although they differ on the surface, underneath the same thing is true of all these countries: they have failed to function as national units. There are apparently many reasons, but the underlying one is their failure to work, or perhaps to work as the northern-European Protestant tradition has inured us to work.

The age-old cultures of Persia and Pakistan are in a state of what I can hardly call other than existentialism. The existentialism of France is a generation old. But the existentialism of Persia is something like 2,500 years old, and by that time it really gets into the culture. Combined with other factors like diet and malaria (which affects the spleen, which affects the blood supply, which produces anemia), this existentialism controls the tone of work, the energy, the interest, the impulse. This is what lies behind the failure of Pakistan as an Islamic republic, and Pakistan has failed as an Islamic republic and knows that it has. It began with enthusiasm; the immigrants came in from the rest of India and set up this ideal of an Islamic republic. But the impulse went after a few years. It is kept artificially alive by things like excitement about Kashmir. But the impulse is gone; it was a quick brushwood fire. And now the state of Pakistan is very like the state of Persia.

Few countries have groups of people in which work and conscience are linked; few peoples feel responsible for how they do their work. And this link between work and conscience was, in my view, a necessary precondition for the development of the Industrial Revolution and the whole technological revolution. Northrop

Frye produced a nice little story in the 1952 volume of *The Yearbook of Technological Education.* He said, in effect, "Here is a ground crew on an airfield. It has an expatriate foreman. As long as the expatriate foreman is there, the ground crew will do what they are supposed to do. They will know what they have to do; they will know why they have to do it; they will do it. Remove the expatriate foreman, and the group will continue to know what they have to do, and they will continue to know why they have to do it, but they won't necessarily do it with the same thoroughness." Now that is a little parable. It may seem a harsh one. But I have in my forty years' experience of wandering seen so many problems like this in so many different fields. And the root of these problems is that, in so many countries, the conscience is only activated within the family unit, not outside it. Now if one of the members of the ground crew had had a nephew or a son on board, I guess the ground crew would have on that occasion performed with complete efficiency. Conscience may also be activated by other deep-rooted groups: tribal groups, linguistic groups, caste groups in India, and so on. But these are often the end of it.

People have thought it would be comparatively easy to export technology to developing countries because technology is international, being based on scientific procedures that are also international. I myself am very doubtful whether even scientific procedures are really international, and I am convinced that technological procedures are not because their exploitation, development, and use depend on the local cultural attitudes. International technological methodology cannot easily ride over these attitudes. They are at least bumps and ruts in the road, if not barricades across it.

Both in the professions and in education, we soon come up against the need for more than technological knowledge against this problem of conscience. In light of this, what can the developed countries export that the developing countries need and can use? Some think that what has to be exported is an attitude of mind, and they believe that humanism is the answer. But humanism is not the answer. It cannot raise education above rote because it does not motivate, and rote is the great enemy of education. Humanism cannot even foster the light "that lighteth every man that cometh into the world" (D&C 93:2), let alone the Holy Ghost.

Nor is the international fellowship of the professions the answer: the working together, the conferences, the interchange of information, the talk—talk does not raise standards. Oligarchic organization in politics, in education, and in the professions cannot survive into democratic organization without a dilution and an adulteration that brings standards steadily down unless there is religious motivation behind the movement towards democracy, as indeed there was in Britain and as there was in this country. What is the Hippocratic oath without a religious background that makes matters of life and death of real importance?

There is a general feeling that government aid has, on the whole, failed. Although host governments need aid, they resent it; they resent any kind of emotional attitudinizing or political capital made by resource countries out of giving aid. And so there has been an increasing tendency by your government and mine to devolve action upon nongovernmental organizations or upon international organizations. But when a government devolves finance and power upon independent or semi-independent bodies, it is still left with the problem of controlling the action of those bodies, and there is the unease, lest they go off and do something that is to their own interest rather than the national interest. I remember seeing with some apprehension, when I was last in Colombia, a project for nineteen schools financed by the World Bank. The schools were called "comprehensive" and were to give greater opportunity democratically. But what was actually being set up was simply a more diversified secondary system for the privileged. It requires experience of comparative education to spot this kind of thing. Such organizations as the Peace Corps in your country and the Voluntary Service Organization in my own, though commendable, are insufficient because their personnel are inexperienced.

There have been other failures in developing countries. Communism is and has been the twentieth century's false salvation to the developing countries of the world. (Mind you, there is no communism on the earth at all. What we have in both China and Russia is imperialist socialism or even state capitalism, not communism. These things ought to be called by their right names. "Communism" is just a bogie or a method of propaganda, but imperialist socialism is a wicked alternative system.) I don't believe in long-term communist persistence in any of these countries. What is now beginning to happen in China may prove to be one of the most significant turn-arounds in history. Insofar as communist governments are not able to deliver the goods, they will get into more and greater difficulties. They are already in serious difficulty. The problems in Poland are more obvious because they have been reported more. But they are present in the Soviet Union and the rest of the communist world as well. There has been no year in which the Soviet Union has not imported great quantities of grain. The Soviet government originally intended to be independent in supplying grain to its people by 1930. That is now nearly sixty years ago and they still aren't doing it.

Because the culture of countries is more fundamental than their politics, countries remain much the same, even when régimes change. This is true of communist countries. Before the Bolshevik Revolution, Russia was a semibarbarous country with an absolutist government relying on a secret police and an imperialist policy of expansion toward the Mediterranean Sea, toward the Indian Ocean, and along the Chinese frontier; the Soviet Union has inherited all that, and that inheritance is more important than communism. China was and remains a politically static country; its expansion is by export of its people, not by military conquest. It has the oldest civilization in the world. That may not have produced good government during the last hundred years or so, but it continues to produce patient, well-mannered, moral, hard-working people.

What has happened to religion in communist countries? In the Chinese world, religion tends to have become morality. In Russia, religion traditionally has been a great force, and that impulse must still be there—it was too fundamental to disappear. It is no accident that Tolstoy may be the most important and influential person so far to have recognized from outside our church the significance of our religion (to be followed, at some distance, by D. H. Lawrence). We should not underestimate what lies beneath the repression of an apparently stultifying philosophy and régime. I suspect the individual Russian is still sullen rather than stupid.

Roman Catholicism has not brought salvation to the developing countries of the world either. The Roman Catholic Church, although it still nominally has eight hundred million adherents, is a declining power. On the whole, that church has ceased to have the enthusiastic adherence of its disciples. It is being compelled to weaken certain beliefs or to recognize that a large proportion of Roman Catholics do not practice what the Roman Catholic Church would want them to. It is split between right- and left-wing thinking, as controversy about the issues of birth control, abortion, and women's rights shows, and it is tending towards greater devolvement of power from the Vatican to the periphery.

In Latin America, the Roman Catholic Church is split politically: there are priests in Latin America who speak for the régimes; there are other priests who speak for the "communists"; there are other priests who try to take their own independent position; and there are others who don't want to get involved in politics at all. Few in Latin America think of the Roman Catholic Church as political salvation. Comfort perhaps, salvation in the next world perhaps, but political salvation? By all means, christen your child in the church, marry in the church, go to the Easter service. But these are just ornamental excrescences.

When the Roman Catholic Church (or rather its priests) is radical, it will still inspire some enthusiasm in the common people—as it does today in Poland, against communism, and as it does in Central America, as the unwilling or unaware ally of communism. But insofar as the Roman Catholic Church supports reactionary regimes, the poor will look elsewhere, as they do in some Latin American countries. And insofar as it identifies itself with the social philosophy of the welfare state (that major step towards the commune), it will lose its own identity.

Other religions than Christianity have had little material effect. The one seeming exception is Japanese religions, but I wonder how long the Japanese system of loyalty will hold out against the vulgarization of the West.

We are the restored Church, and we may succeed where others have failed. When we say that only in our church is there salvation, we don't mean spiritual salvation alone; we mean salvation generally, and that includes political and economic salvation. If the religion is right, the politics will be right and the economics will be right, but not otherwise. Political salvation cannot be achieved by mass movement or by demonstration, but it can by conversion. Everybody who becomes converted to the Lord's work and serves the Lord is doing his best to achieve it. If tens of thousands do it, if hundreds of thousands do it, if millions do it, a change takes place. It is the only change that counts. The salvation of people in developing countries, like the salvation of those in developed countries, lies in the acceptance of the true Church, and through the true Church, the gospel. We must hope that those who join the Church in all these countries will be more in a position to influence affairs. That is happening as time goes on. It is beginning to happen in Mexico and Brazil. It will continue to happen as we respond to members of a particular class of people who now exist all over the world in developing countries. These people comprise not the upper, not the lower, but the middle classes. And it is about them that I want to speak.

Until very recently, many developing countries had practically no middle class at all. There was very little middle class in Iran when I was there over thirty years ago. But it is growing. This international middle class has risen because of the improved education for many that came with the development of mass processes. The middle classes throughout the world have improved their position, and not merely economically: they have a more developed intelligence; they read more; they think more; they are more tolerant; they understand better; and they have a certain sympathy with other people of this kind in other countries. I have come across plenty of these people in Latin America; there aren't very many yet in Africa, but they are in Pakistan and India and in large numbers in Japan and Korea. And they must be in China, too, because a country the size of China can't run itself. A billion and a half people can't run themselves; there has to be a middle class to keep things going. It is the professionals who keep things going in developing countries: the civil servants, the armed services, the doctors, the engineers, the teachers, the lawyers. Note, I say armed services; they have to be better skilled than they have been in the past to be able to manage more complex things. These professionals form a group with which I am familiar from my years of work in the British Council. I had ample opportunity to get to know these people well, and they are much the same in all countries. They are becoming international inhabitants of the world.

There are, of course, middle-class people in developed as well as developing countries. But in developing countries, there is a discrepancy between what middle-class people have been educated to do and what their environment allows them to do, and this discrepancy isn't present in developed countries. For example, I was once on board the same ship as a young Pakistani woman who was going back to her country after taking her Ph.D. in gynecology in London. She was a good-looking young woman, dressed in ordinary Western dress. But, by the day we got to Karachi, she had changed into Muslim costume with veil and hood, and that, she told me, was what she should continue to wear. She was going back to the north-west frontier; she was the daughter of a chief there. She had specialized in gynecology because Muslim men in that part of the world won't give male doctors access to their women, and women doctors are therefore needed. She did not intend to marry; she would be more useful to her people unmarried. She had a good degree and had studied at a good hospital, but she had to put on her costume and go back to the north-west frontier. It wasn't the same as if she were to be practicing gynecology in a rural district in the western world.

These middle-class people have more or less abandoned their faiths. They may give lip service to them; they go through the routines sometimes. But they are no longer religious. I am thinking particularly of India and Pakistan, which I know best. These people do, however, believe in certain things. They believe foremost in their children: they want their children to be healthy, and therefore want to have the means to keep them so; they want their children to be educated, and therefore want to have the means to educate them; they want their children to be happy. They don't want their children to starve. They don't want their children to be subjected to the horrors of nuclear war. There are many of these people in the world—not a thousand million, but probably a hundred million.

In the nineteenth century, it was the poor who needed salvation in this world as well as the next. They are still there; the poor we have always with us. But ever since I have joined the Church, my feeling has been that it is of the highest importance that these international, middle-class people receive the gospel. Conversions among them are a key to the spreading of the gospel throughout the world. The Lord has presented us with this group of people all over the world, and the Church is increasingly coming to them.

And I think we may find that they will increasingly come to us because they have, in spirit, left their own cultures and abandoned their own religions, and there is consequently an emptiness in their lives; they will come because they will find that the gospel enables them to lead richer lives, to have a purpose, and to achieve salvation for themselves and their children.

What about this class in communist countries? My work in the British Council gave me the chance to meet Chinese from communist China and Russians from communist Russia—scientists, engineers, teachers, who came to Britain to improve themselves, to attend conferences or take courses. I must have met three hundred people from the Soviet Union in this way and perhaps a couple of hundred people from China. These professionals from the Soviet Union and China were interested mainly in their professions, but they were fully aware of the oppression in their countries. And though they were under some sense of compulsion to be careful what they said about their governments—talking politics was dangerous for them, and they would often make mute appeals for us not to talk politics with them—they were nevertheless agreeable people to talk to, and they enjoyed themselves in the West. And when they went back to their countries, they went back with a knowledge of what the West is like that could not be taken away from them.

There are thousands of people in the Soviet Union who have gone through that kind of experience. I am astonished that the Soviet authorities allow people out at all when you consider what must be happening in this way. But then, think that most people these days go into politics because they are more stupidly cunning than the rest of us. That is something you in this country and we in mine have to put up with at every election, isn't it? The standards go steadily down. Think of people like Gladstone, Disraeli, and Lincoln, and even Woodrow Wilson. And then think about what we have had since: a solitary Churchill. The "nonviolent" Gandhi kindled more violence in India than before; Jinnah founded a failure; Sadaat's initiative came to nothing. I suppose the decline is even greater in China (no comparable successor to Mao Tse-tung) and the Soviet Union (since Lenin, only a paranoid bully, an exhibitionist, and a few mere bureaucrats). It is only the *really* stupid who endeavor to manipulate in the kind of way the leaders of modern countries (led by their experts in public relations) try to manipulate both their own populations and foreign opinion, for most people are not misled. And certainly these professionals, these inhabitants of the world I have spoken about, including the professionals in the armed services, are not taken in at all.

We can do more to reach these internationalized, middle-class people. We can bring them to us; we can also go to them. It seems to me that at BYU we ought to increase the percentage of foreign students to approximately 10 percent (it is 5 percent at the moment). By the year 2000, I believe it ought to be 15 percent. At English universities, by stature, the percentage of foreign students is (as I last heard it) 11 percent. There is room for BYU to give a higher education to more of these people from developing countries.

Historically, the Church first drew its converts to Utah. Then its missionaries went out, not to draw converts to Utah, but to convert and educate new members to stay in their own countries and develop the Church there. That was the second phase. Now, we are perhaps entering a third phase that will further widen and strengthen the Church in other countries. I am thinking of a long-term outward flow—of former missionaries, for example, who have married and established their families, or begun to do so, living and serving overseas in key positions. I am thinking of a minor family exodus. Families are popular in all these developing countries. Children, above all, are popular and loved there, and they can link up their parents with local people. Let me remind you how Christianity was spread throughout the Roman world: by the educated zealots in the great households and through the international movement of educated slaves and others.

I have come to the conclusion after my years of traveling the world that what the developing countries really need is devoted, warm, sympathetic, qualified people to help them without wishing to dominate them. What is needed is for Latter-day Saints to mingle and to live with those young professional men and women and their families all over the world in these various, almost despairing countries, with these people under the age of forty-five who have broken with their own traditional cultures, who therefore lack something, and who want in their children a hope for the future of the world. We have a unique opportunity to do this; overseas careers may readily follow missionary service because missionaries learn the language and gain the experience of their countries and the experience of living abroad. But we do not yet sufficiently encourage former missionaries to keep in touch, to increase their knowledge of their foreign languages, to go back to the countries they love, to live there.

Our church can surely develop a deliberate policy to encourage and train those who want to serve in careers overseas in the United States government's service, in international organizations like the World Bank, in the Food and Agricultural Organization and the twelve other organizations of the United Nations (even in UNESCO), in international firms, and perhaps most important of all, in the service of overseas governments and overseas educational institutions. I would remind you of such organizations as the Tropical Institute, founded in Basel by the Swiss pharmaceutical companies to train not simply pharmacists, but all sorts of professionals for work in the tropics. I became acquainted with this institute when I went to Switzerland to set up British Council work there after the war. It was good business for those pharmaceutical companies to have engineers and chemists and all sorts of other people in the tropics who had had this training. I would refer also to the educational work of the international oil companies. I remember my meetings with outstanding Mormons overseas: a brother who was in charge of the United States Binational Center in Bogotà, another who was working for USAID in Manila, and another who was a chemist researching with Del Monte among the pineapples in the southern Philippines. There can be more doctors, nurses, scientists, engineers, educationists, and administrators like these.

Our church can also provide service opportunities for its members overseas. Our schools in various countries and our health missionaries are growing points. With its students from developing areas, BYU campus at Laie offers a good training center in a state that acts as a bridge to living in developing countries. We may learn from the successes and failures of the medical and educational missions of other churches and from those of organizations like the Peace Corps and the Voluntary Service Organization.

I know that many young families (especially their wives and mothers) do not like to move away from places where the Church is dominant (sometimes even to other parts of the U.S.). There is the language difficulty, the need for educational and medical facilities, the absence of other members of the Church. But as one who has lived most of my years outside my own country, in Europe, Asia, and America, I can say with certainty that the problems are exaggerated. Cultural shock is more important than the ones I have mentioned, but many people do not suffer from this at all, and one stint in a developing country inoculates against cultural shock anywhere else. And I have always found that living abroad gave me a richer spiritual and intellectual life than staying at home among an insular people resigned to decline. The Mormons of America are neither insular nor resigned—though in the intermountain states they may be landlocked—but still their lives may be enriched by living in other countries. For many, the first missionary years should be only an introduction. Individual sacrifice is not enough; it needs to be family sacrifice. The reward, in the sense of feeling really helpful, of Christian living, of serving the Lord, is great.

What I have been trying to say is this: the main responsibility for the spread of the gospel to the world remains with the Mormons of this country. It will so remain for a long time to come, even though the number of missionaries in other countries will increase. You will have noticed, I am sure, as I have noticed, that by degrees the Church is calling upon us to contribute not less and less, but more and more, to give more, to do more. And that will continue. It must continue because of the increased responsibilities of the Church in all parts of the world, and we should not measure those responsibilities only in terms of our size. Size is not important. The original Christian Church was smaller after a hundred and fifty years than we now are. It is not size that counts; it is living the gospel, applying the principles of the gospel, and doing what the Lord wants. What can the pope do with his nominal eight hundred million? Very little. What can the prophet do with us six million? Much more—we are an integrated body; we believe in obedience. Roman Catholics are supposed to believe in obedience, but do they obey? The Roman Catholic Church has to reason with its supporters. The prophet of the Lord doesn't have to reason with us; he tells us what the Lord wants us to do, and we know by faith that it is right, and more than that we need not know.

We know that others will fail, and that is why we have the duty to succeed. We cannot say, "Oh well, someone else will do this." Someone else will not. The Lord has chosen us to do it, and we have not yet risen to that challenge. We have in the last several years been rising to that challenge more than ever before. But our prophet knows full well that we are going much too slowly. We have to go faster. What are we to go faster for? Because we have to help the Lord save the world. And the world has to be preserved in order that it may be saved. Both things have to be done. It can't be entirely destroyed, and prophecy does not say that it will be entirely destroyed. There will be survival. What we have to do is to work for that survival. That is our duty. I believe we shall succeed; I am certain we shall, for the alternative to success is the destruction of the world, and I don't believe the Lord intends to destroy the world because he said he came not to destroy, but to save. Ours is the great opportunity to prepare for the coming of Christ and the emergence of the Millennium from a world in hard labor, cynicism, despair, and mass destruction. It is we who have the inspiration and can therefore have the strength and intelligence to serve our divine Master in this, the greatest of all historical tasks that has ever been.

I remember one Sunday morning in February taking off at eight o'clock in the morning from Perth, Western Australia. I lunched with a colleague in Djakarta; I had dinner with another colleague in Bangkok; and I enjoyed a late supper with a third colleague in Delhi. This was one of the most exhilarating days of my life because right through it I felt the globe spinning beneath me, and I felt how the world now rolls beneath our feet. We are no longer to be strangers and pilgrims on this earth; this earth is to be our home, and we are to be brethren and servants of our Master here.

TRADITION

Age finds the way back
to childhood: past the yew-trees
into the cornfield.

AHK
September 1983

The Child Is Father of the Man

I HAVE TAKEN my title from a short poem that Wordsworth wrote on March 26, 1802, when we were about to leap again into the war with Napoleon:

My heart leaps up when I behold
A rainbow in the sky:
So was it when my life began;
So is it now I am a man;
So be it when I shall grow old,
Or let me die!
The Child is father of the Man;
And I could wish my days to be
Bound each to each by natural piety.

(*William Wordsworth: The Poems*, ed. John O. Hayden, 2 vols. [New Haven: Yale, 1981], 1:522)

He does not mean, by "natural piety," the piety of the natural man who is an enemy to God; man is "naturally" supernatural. Now, on that poem of Wordsworth's, a comment (by a late-nineteenth-century author) is worth quoting for the amusedly obtuse acuity of its wit:

"The child is father of the man."
How can he be? The words are wild.
The man is father of the child!

I would now ask you to search your souls about this: how far does your continued recollection and sense of continuity with yourself go back? I remember voices from before my continued recollection and before I learned to read. I can still hear the voice of my father reading the scriptures. His voice echoes from the deepest caverns of my memory, and it will echo right through my life, although he was killed when I was nine years old. I can remember his reading me to sleep at the age of five (very effectively) with *Hiawatha*, but I usually managed to hear quite a bit before I dozed off. That rhythm stuck in my mind until I broke out of it, on my own, at the age of twelve: I began writing hexameters, trying to imitate *Evangeline*'s beginning, which (oddly enough) was the first passage of nature poetry I had come across. I can hear the voices of my mother and my grandmother reading to me—not the voice of my grandfather; he preferred to be read to.

But my continued recollection goes back to the age of six. I very much doubt whether I have advanced from that age; I still feel fundamentally to be that boy of six. I have continuity with him, and I remember his life, and I remember his thoughts. And if I ask myself why, the answer is because it was by then that I had learned to read and was reading, and, of course, as soon as I had learned to read (in my generation the obvious way of amusing oneself was to read), I read and read. I have filled every vacant moment of my life ever since with reading. And that has been a continuity in my life; reading has helped to bind my life together with bonds of "natural piety."

Even after I had learned to read, my family continued to read to me for many years. My father, as I said, thought that *Hiawatha* was appropriate, followed by *Tales of a Wayside Inn.* Practically all the Quaker sect learned "Robert of Sicily, Brother of Pope Urbane and Valmond Emperor of Allemain" (probably no child learns that nowadays). And then we progressed. My father bought me *The Jungle Book* for my sixth-birthday present, and he bought me *Alice in Wonderland* for my seventh-birthday present, and he bought me *Alice through the Looking Glass* for my eighth-birthday present, and all of these were carefully read to me and my younger sister and became a permanent part of our literary lives.

I want you to go further on this biographical journey with me. I want to take you back to my childhood and show how certain major themes ran through my life as a result of the literature I read. That seems to me a better way of making clear to you the value of literature in one's life than pontificating in abstracts.

I lived as a child during the First World War, right in the heart of the country in Essex. Our Essex village cottage-slum was small—two tiny rooms down below, ten by ten, and an earth-floor kitchen at the back where the rats ran and the spiders lurked. I had a little cubbyhole by a window (a small window to the right-hand side of one of the rooms) that looked out on the farm and a field "of many one." This slum was afterwards known as Holly Cottage, but not at that time. It wasn't worthy of a name at that time, at least we never thought of naming it. And fifty years later my sister and her husband retired to a Norfolk cottage called *Holly House*, and about the field behind that house I have written the following poem, which I include to illustrate the bond of natural piety, field to field through a lifetime:

The Field behind Holly House[1]

Right at the end, I mean to see that field:
fifty-five hundred miles as crows make wing[2]
steady, deliberate, straight to their own end.
At any time of year now I am old,
that field I aim to scan: wheat-blades in spring
sprouting to blackbird whistles; grain-stalks bend
under the claw, as small birds thin the yield
in swarms and swoops of avid pilfering;
the stubble trampled into mud; the brand
of hoar frost on the furrow—a cultured wild,
not the Grand Canyon, or too tame to sing.
The kind of scene to give one peace of mind?

At the south end, one oak takes pride to be
isolate in the hedge, tawny in Fall
and April, ilex-green in August, bare
by my years' time, a sturdy, skeleton tree
that shows its stripped form best at the annual lull,
yet sleeps indifferent to my aging stare.
At the north end, the house end, in its lee,
grows from the ditch a crippled bush for all
titmice—blue, great, cole, marsh—and more that dare
a forage-base for suet or nut. I see
those many miles away the flick of a tail,
flirt of a wing, head's quirk, there—here—here—there.

The black cat through a tunnel of gold or green,
or slinking round the selion hugs his way,
following smaller bodies rarely seen
that save their lives or give them up as prey.
The stoat and weasel similarly pass

from east to west through oats, lucern, or grass,
from west to east. The cycle day by day
by month by season, the will be and has been—
present: right now I mean that field to stay
in all its times, as I in mine, one scene
in every scene, the field that is and was
my eyes and ears, my equal gain and loss.
This field's the one that Judas' crime lays waste;[3]
where Faust despairs,[4] and the Old Guard goes west;[5]
where Hector runs to kill or shed his blood;
where "country folk would lie,"[6] but the adder stings;
the field of folk where Lehi,[7] Langland,[8] brood;
the field by Mamre,[9] where all Israel clings.
The dark frown conjures, but the white brow sings: —
The soul has found a cross-tree in the wood.
The Lord of Easter, roused by morning's wings,
has risen, and here I stand as Maudlin[10] stood.
My days now one to me from first to last
I watch for sleep and wake my future's present past.

When I was a young boy, there was no school for me to go to. My parents taught me at home, and the only amusement I had apart from learning to milk a cow and picking up stones from flinty fields was my father's books. My father's library was not extensive—only about a hundred books—but they were there. There were all of Shakespeare and all of Dickens. Some of the books were trash. I read those, too, but I have forgotten all about them, except Marie Corelli's dreadful book (*The Mighty Atom*) about a boy of nine who hanged himself, but I did not take that example—the book was in too bad taste.

At the age of eight, I came to a turning point in my life. The winter that year was a bad winter; it was the winter of 1918–19, in which twenty-one million people died of the flu. I remember my father sitting downstairs with a temperature of 104°, while my mother was giving birth to my younger brother upstairs. There I sat that autumn and winter (sometimes with a candle and sometimes with a lamp) and read practically the whole of Dickens because at last I had got hold of myself and realized how much I was getting out of reading. It was a rather rainy year as I remember, but rainy years go with Dickens. I suppose that Dickens was my first introduction to real literature, and I think you know that Dickens can get across to quite young children. I recently reread Dickens *en bloque*, and going back to him after those many years, I realized that he is a great writer of the gospel, and we do ill in our church to ignore him. He has the quality that Tolstoy found in Victor Hugo's *Les Misérables:* the quality of human sympathy, which is of supreme importance in writing. Those who hate humanity may express themselves well on the surface, but they have nothing to do with the gospel.

I found themes in rereading Dickens that have run through my life as a result of my first reading of him when I was a child. And here I am going to cover four main themes: class, death, love, and creation.

Class

I think at the age that I read Dickens, although we were extremely poor and my father was then a farm laborer, I had no previous idea of class at all. I read *David Copperfield*, and there are several very distressing class events in that. There is the one in which Mr. Mell at Salem House School is dismissed because he has a mother in a poorhouse. And there is David's own shame—reflecting Dickens's shame—at going to the factory as an eight- to nine-year-old. When I reread David Copperfield, I realized that I distinctly remembered and have remembered all my life in detail, phrases, whole sentences, whole paragraphs, the names of unimportant characters like Steerforth's servant Littimer. That book has been with me all my life although I hadn't read it for fifty-seven years. I read *Great Expectations*, that superb study of class self-consciousness and class aspiration. Pip, the boy who is brought up by his blacksmith brother-in-law, a true Christian, inherits money from a convict (although Pip doesn't know his benefactor is a convict), and the boy's whole sense of values is turned upside down so that he falls in love with a girl whom he thinks belongs to a higher class (actually, she turns out to be the daughter of the convict), and he at last through illness and deprivation and despair comes to realize the value of that blacksmith brother-in-law of his and returns to sensible views on class. This lower-class position of David Copperfield and Pip appealed to me in my position, and I remember making up my mind that I never would do what Pip did—and indeed what David did—and I have not. I was born a lower-middle-class boy (perhaps, more correctly, an "outcaste"), and I have been a lower-middle-class boy and man all my life.

I have never sought affected or precious intellectual company. I have occasionally grazed it, but have managed by degrees to develop a healthy contempt for it.

I came into the Mormon Church, in part, because it is not a class church, though Mormons sometimes forget that. It took me a whole year to stop my brothers in the Crawley branch, to which I first belonged, from calling me "sir." Here I am sometimes introduced by a member of the Church to another member of the Church as "Mr." instead of "Brother," and it distresses me. I wonder what its significance is. This doesn't normally happen in Provo, but in Salt Lake it does happen occasionally. Sometimes Mormons become snobbish about their families. Sister Maryanne Sharp once made a very sharp speech at BYU on this subject of being too proud of one's family; she reminded us that, after all, it is oneself that is in question (Maryanne Clark Sharp, "Ninety-Ninth Annual Commencement Address," BYU, August 16, 1974).

We in Britain have been very clever in taking the more able people in the lower classes and bringing them up through into the higher classes so that they shan't be a nuisance. We have deprived our lower classes of their natural leaders. I believe you may be doing this, too. But it is essential that there should be highly intelligent people among the working classes to help lead them. One of the major reasons why we have such trouble with trade unions nowadays is that we have advanced the natural leaders of the working class into other positions in society, so they are no longer interested in and no longer feel with the working class.

Following on from my Dickens, when I was fifteen years old I came across Karl Marx's *Manifesto* (1848), and what struck me in there is something that again has never left me, because it seemed (and still seems) to me an absolute gospel principle embedded in the middle of that hateful tract, "As long as there is a lower class, I am of it." But in my life, I have interpreted that in a deeper way, I feel, than Marx himself did. "The lower class" is not simply the working class—it is all oppressed creatures: women, children, animals. I have felt of the lower class when I have seen the eye of the dying deer and the fish desperately flapping at the bottom of the boat.

Eliot said, following the mystic tradition, "The way down is the way up." That is diametrically opposed to the American doctrine that the way up is the way up. Americans believe in ambition, in achieving success. And this troubles and puzzles me. The ambitious person is not one who says, "I am trying to do what the Lord wants me to do." He says, "I'm trying to get where I want to get." Ambition is what made the devil fall. That is why he was cast down: he was a self-asserter, an ambitious fellow. Ambition without manipulation is rare indeed, and manipulation is a sin. But Americans seem to admire manipulators. Remember the abominable manipulator Tom Sawyer in the first chapter about painting the fence? It is a thoroughly immoral act, but Americans call it cute.

Apart from anything else, if we are ambitious, then we are so often disappointed. I was born extremely poor, but I had no ambitions; I was surprised every time something good happened to me. And I continue to be so. What one doesn't expect may prove to be a source of gratitude, and gratitude is a fundamental gospel attitude. It is what we have to feel; we have to give it back to the Lord in all things.

Here is a remark made by the headmaster of the Cathedral School in Lund, Sweden, to his most brilliant pupil, who was one of my best students and is now a member of the Swedish Academy (one of the eighteen), "Don't try to be remarkable in any way." The boy was precocious and affected because he was able. And how many boys are not precocious and affected when they are able? The ablest, of course, are not. But, then, the ablest don't know they are able. "Don't try to be remarkable in any way" is a hard saying, but it does seem to me that the gospel lies profoundly behind it.

Anyway, going down is the thing. And going down in this way, one finds oneself, like Milton in *Lycidas*, at "the bottom of the monstrous world," and it is at the bottom of the monstrous world that we meet death.

Death

Death seems, at least, to get rid of class distinctions. I met death in Dickens. It made more of an impression on me than anything else in Dickens. There was the death of Little Nell, the death of Paul Dombey, the death of Barkis in *David Copperfield*, the death (above all) of Dora. I remember reading about that in the autumn of 1918. It was October; it was a rainy day; and it was late afternoon when I read that chapter. I read it by the light of the fire. I can still remember all that. I can still remember my grief, and

I can still remember that it took me several months to overcome that grief about a fictive character in a book—not that I ever have really recovered. That experience at the age of eight prepared me to find value in the passing of loved ones. It helped me to endure and properly experience the real deaths that followed it. A year after I read *David Copperfield*, my father was killed under a bus. The last thing he said in his life was, "Get me out of here." The policeman came and knocked on the door, and I remember the heavy knock and wondering what it meant. And yet, even at the age of nine, as I did my boots up to go to school that morning—as I tried to go to school—I felt how much I loved my father and how much he loved me and how his death made that clear, much more clear than anything else could have made it. I lost my small brother in pneumonia a year and a half later, and I can still remember his little leaden face before they put him in the coffin. I had good reason to remember him fifteen years later when my own only son died at the age of one week, at 4:00 A.M. on Easter morning. I remembered then the feeling I had had about my father, and that was gratitude—I was grateful for that week. My late wife died after a four-year struggle with cancer. I can still remember how she felt when her lips were already cold and her forehead still warm. Then there was the death of my mother at the ripe age of eighty. She had been senile for the previous two weeks, and she died with a curious smile on her face, which, in my objective way, I knew was a result of the relaxation of muscles—no more, but these things always take on significance. At each of these deaths, I felt love and gratitude, and throughout my life, these experiences of death have built up into one of the most positive things in my life.

I have a testimony of death. That testimony is that without death we should not fully understand how much we love those who go, and this is equally true of our dying: when we are dying, we know how much we love those we are leaving behind. And I wonder how many of us sufficiently feel how profoundly grateful we should be to death for the way it intensifies our love as nothing else could do. And how many of us realize that it may intensify our love, not only at the moment it comes, but all our life, if we remember when we are with people that we may not, after all, be always with them? This thought comes to many people in old age, but it should be with us all our lives.

Now for Mormons, death is not much worse perhaps than a visit to an airport to say good-bye to someone for a long time—every absence is a little death, and death is just a long absence. But death is a hard separation and may take a great deal of recovery. It requires all the preparation we can get. We need to prepare our children for death, as Dickens's deaths prepared me to take as I should the deaths that came to me. It is wrong to bring up children ignorant of death. It is one of the things that they need and have a right to learn, and it is from literature that they can best learn it. It was there for me in *David Copperfield.* It might have been for someone else somewhere else, for example, in *The Story of a South African Farm,* by Olive Schreiner, which people read so widely at the beginning of the century.

Our grandparents and great-grandparents understood death better than we do. In the nineteenth century, one-third of all children died as children—died in their families, died at home, with others at their bedsides. In those days somebody died—your mother or father or one of the children. The experience of death came early. Today, we put our old people away into homes, and we put others with their incurable diseases into hospitals to die. They no longer die in their own families. And though I understand all the reasons for this, I think it is nevertheless terrible. The presence of death throughout the community is a religiously good thing. The absence of death is a dangerous thing.

As I reread Dickens, I found and remembered a death that greatly impressed me, and that was the death of Jo in *Bleak House.* Jo was a boy with no home, not even in the slums. No parents, no nobody. There were tens of thousands of his kind when Dickens was alive, in your country as well as mine. Jo, as he cannot fail to do, dies. A good young doctor is looking after him—Jo has made some friends. I am going to quote the very brief account of his death because it brings together what I have been saying about class and about death, which are deeply linked, because a class society is a society dead to the gospel.

> "—It's turned wery dark, sir. Is there any light a comin'?"
>
> "It is coming fast, Jo. . . . Jo, my poor fellow!"
>
> "I hear you, sir, in the dark, but I'm a gropin'—a gropin'—let me catch hold of your hand."

"Jo, can you say what I say?"

"I'll say anything as you say, sir, for I knows it's good."

"OUR FATHER."

"Our Father!—yes, that's wery good, sir."

"WHICH ART IN HEAVEN."

"Art in Heaven—is the light a comin', sir?"

"It is close at hand. HALLOWED BE THY NAME!"

"Hallowed be—thy—"

The light is come upon the dark benighted way. Dead!

If our lives are to be of quality, we need to comprehend that death is always around the corner. Those who are egocentric have no understanding of this. I am transported to the walls of Troy, and there is Helen on the walls, and she is looking at the Greeks assembling. As she looks around, she doesn't see her brothers, Castor and Pollux, and she says, "I wonder where they are. Why are they not here?" And then she has a purely egocentric and (for Helen) characteristic thought. She thinks, "I suppose they are not here because they are ashamed of me." And then Homer produces two wonderful lines, "But they were already lying under their own country's earth, in their dear Lacedaemon."

Love

I now come to the most important subject that I have to talk about. As I have tried to show you, the experience of death is perhaps the greatest experience of love that we can have in this world. And therefore, it is natural that out of the depths of death we should rise to this. There are so many kinds of love for us—there is parental love; there is spousal love; there is filial love; there is the love of brothers and sisters; there is love between friends; there is love of animals; there is love of God's entire creation—yet all of these loves contain that element of the love of God, which is essential to all love. The love of God is the love we have for God and the love that God has for us, and we are lucky in English to have that kind of genitive.

It is one of my strongest convictions that all love is ultimately one in the sense that all love partakes of divine love, no matter how twisted and perturbed a particular love may be. It is curious that Freud, too, should have thought that all love is ultimately one. Of course, he thought the one love was ultimately sexual. But we don't have to interpret that down. We can interpret it up. And that is what we in our church should do. There ought to be a physical element in everybody's affection. We ought to be able to put a hand on the shoulder or around the waist of a fellow female or a fellow male without people raising their eyebrows. I am not one who believes in the separateness of agape and eros. I believe that only in the Eastern Mediterranean (which was bored stiff with its physical experience) was such a division possible. But for us in the Mormon Church who believe in the oneness of spirit and body in soul, there is one love, and that love is divine love in all its forms.

Love begins in the family, and it begins much better in the family that spreads its arms. I had the good luck at the age of nine, when my father died, to have my grandparents move in, together with a maiden aunt, and we formed a multigenerational family. That was my salvation because my grandfather stood in for my father. And I hope in a world that travels so much, in a world in which people are a little casual about splitting their families and going to the ends of the earth, we remember that the multigenerational family has through the ages been the rule. On the farm, for example, it was the grandparents who were the keepers and educators of the children while the mothers and fathers went and did the dairying and the outside chores that had to be done. I believe in multigenerational families. Children love to meet their cousins. They feel their cousins are special to them. And let me ask, How can a father show his son how a son should behave to his father unless he behaves to his own father, that son's grandfather, how a son should behave? The multigenerational family is psychologically, economically, and theologically the right unit on this earth, and the unit in which our love can learn to spread.

Children learn various kinds of love earlier than most parents realize. I fell in love with a little girl—intensely, I remember—at the age of six. (It didn't surprise me, therefore, to find that Dante fell in love with Beatrice when he was nine and she was nine, too.) I fell in love with another little girl at that age. It lasted about a year. Parents need to remember what it was like when they were as young as their own children, because so many people underestimate all the time and have no idea of how mature their children are. They forget how mature they were themselves, and this causes difficulty and damage.

When I was twelve, I met a girl at the place where we yearly went down to spend our holidays. That year and succeeding years I saw her only a few times during the three weeks we were there, but I thought of no one else in the interim. At the age of fifteen, I saw her one evening, the first evening I had got down there. And that was, I suppose, one of the major points of my life. I shall never forget it. I moved away from that few moments of meeting so full of feeling that I did not know what to do with it. Luckily, I was alone, and I rushed off to the woods. I shouted and sang up and down those woods because what I had discovered for the first time was the priesthood and the power of the priesthood, though I didn't know that is what it was until I had got into this church. The power was just streaming through me; it was an exaltation of a kind which can rarely come later in life. It was an exaltation which began my true intellectual life because that summer I started to read intensively the higher things. (I was at the time luckily reading *As You Like It*, which has that wonderful interplay between Rosalind and Orlando.)

Well, that ecstasy remained with me for about three years, and when I came to it in books, I knew what it was all about. Act II, Scene 2, of *Romeo and Juliet* remains with me today as one of the greatest lyrical sweeps of the human spirit. That balcony scene between Romeo and Juliet—it never palls. It has an extraordinary strength and flow and sweetness. It is the greatest expression of young love that has ever been. Lust and sentimentality cannot be seen anywhere near it; it has nothing to do with them. There were many other experiences, too, like the wonderful experience of Florizel and Perdita in *Winter's Tale*. And so it went on through my life until I was reading Dante, Goethe, and others who have had that feeling.

My advice to people who come to me with questions about marriage is to wait for the thunderstroke. If you don't get it, you had better be careful. What is the use of getting married unless you have the thunderstroke? It hits you, and the decision is made. You cannot not get married. That is the position to be in. Whether you have known another person for five seconds, five minutes, five months, or five years is not something that you should consider by itself. You should depend on your personal experience and your knowledge of yourself. I offered my present wife marriage after knowing her for forty-eight hours.

It seems to me that the onset of sexual love, so-called (and I think we should call it so even in its highest reaches), is the onset of a deeper appreciation (if it happens rightly to one) of all love. But love is not just an ecstasy, not just an intense feeling. It is a driving force. It is something that carries us through our life of joyful duty. Here is another passage from Dickens, which I loved when I was a child and which helped me to understand divine love, because if ever there was a Christian marriage, it was that between Arthur Clennam and Little Dorrit; and, indeed, Dickens says that the light shone upon them through the image of the Savior in the stained glass window as they stood there at the altar. The passage is practical, but it is profound and has so much feeling behind it. They both sign the register and go out of the church. This is the end of the novel:

> They all gave place when the signing was done, and Little Dorrit and her husband walked out of the church alone. They paused for a moment on the steps of the portico, looking at the fresh perspective of the street in the autumn morning sun's bright rays, and then went down.
>
> Went down into the modest life of usefulness and happiness. Went down to give a mother's care, in the fulness of time, to Fanny's neglected children no less than to their own, and to leave that lady going into Society for ever and a day. Went down to give a tender nurse and friend to Tip for some few years, who was never vexed by the great exactions he made of her in return for the riches he might have given her if he had ever had them, and who lovingly closed his eyes upon the Marshalsea and all its blighted fruits. They went quietly down into the roaring streets, inseparable and blessed; and as they passed along in sunshine and shade, the noisy and the eager, and the arrogant and the froward and the vain, fretted, and chafed, and made their usual uproar. (Charles Dickens, *Little Dorrit* [London: Collins, 1910], 832)

I now want to read to you what I think to be the greatest passage in all literature outside the gospel. It is the reconciliation scene between Cordelia and Lear, and it is one of the demonstrations of how profoundly Christian Shakespeare is. You could almost place it somewhere near the parable of the prodigal son. This is an anagnorisis, a recognition scene, and time and again an anagnorisis is something most profound: it touches us deeply—more than anything else in the theater—because it is deeply associated with forgiveness and with repentance. I sometimes think that repentance might be better described as a recognition than as a turning back.

Cordelia and Lear are together. Lear, after a long sleep, has recovered from his madness and is waking up, and he recognizes that his loving daughter is with him.

Cordelia. How does my royal lord? How fares your Majesty?
Lear. You do me wrong to take me out o' th' grave:
Thou art a soul in bliss, but I am bound
Upon a wheel of fire, that mine own tears
Do scald like molten lead.

Cordelia. Sir, do you know me?

Lear. You are a spirit, I know. When did you die? . . .
Where have I been? Where am I? Fair daylight?
I am mightily abus'd; I should ev'n die with pity
To see another thus. I know not what to say.
I will not swear these are my hands. Let's see,
I feel this pin prick. Would I were assur'd
Of my condition!

Cordelia. O, look upon me, sir,
And hold your hand in benediction o'er me.
No, sir, you must not kneel.

Lear. Pray do not mock me.
I am a very foolish fond old man,
Fourscore and upward, not an hour more nor less;
And to deal plainly,
I fear I am not in my perfect mind.
Methinks I should know you, and know this man,
Yet I am doubtful: for I am mainly ignorant
What place this is, and all the skill I have
Remembers not these garments; nor I know not
Where I did lodge last night. Do not laugh at me,
For (as I am a man) I think this lady
To be my child Cordelia.

Cordelia. And so I am; I am.

Lear. Be your tears wet? Yes, faith. I pray weep not.
If you have poison for me, I will drink it.
I know you do not love me, for your sisters
Have (as I do remember) done me wrong:
You have some cause, they have not.

Cordelia. No cause, no cause.
(4.7.43–73)

This reconciliation is the climax of the play. Nothing matters in the play after this scene. Does it matter really that Cordelia is hanged and that Lear dies? With love reestablished, we can face the death of Cordelia and of Lear not with equanimity, but with joy, just as we in this church should face death. What I should like most of all to feel on my deathbed is that I love and am loved. I don't know anyone who couldn't pass with peace into the next world with that knowledge, and loving brings the return of love. Many of Shakespeare's anagnorises are celebrations of the resurrection of the dead. That is what lies behind Lear's speech, "You do me wrong to take me out o' th' grave." The last scene of *The Winter's Tale* shows how the statue of Hermione returns to life and how the whole family is reunited at the end of the play in harmony and in peace.

"And so I am; I am" and "No cause, no cause"—these are the simple words that Cordelia says. And when you go to the *Purgatory* of Dante, you find similar words. When Virgil has gone and left Dante alone, and Dante is in despair that Virgil has left him, there is Beatrice. And quoting Virgil himself, Dante says, "I recognize the traces of the ancient flame" (canto 30, line 48). And the first words that Beatrice says to him are these, "*Guarda mi ben. Ben son, ben son Beatrice*" (difficult to translate because of those three "ben"): "Look well at me, I am, I am Beatrice" (canto 30, line 73). "I am, I am": the simple repetition of love. When you read great literature and find echoes in it over the centuries, sometimes over the thousands of years, it is an extraordinary experience. It goes deep.

Creation

I come to my final section, and that is creation—God's creation, and our creativity as artists, as fathers and mothers. This is the most difficult section, but it is a section which subsumes all the rest. In Dickens, the sense of creation came to me that 1918–19 winter through the human richness and diversity expressed in such variety of language: I came to know Jingle and Sam Weller (*Pickwick Papers*), Mrs. Nickleby and Sairey Gamp (*Martin Chuzzlewit*), Micawber (*David Copperfield*), Flora (*Little Dorrit*), and Podsnap (*Our Mutual Friend*). Then, when I was ten, I got *Don Quixote* as a school prize, and another world opened to me. And so I was prepared for the worlds of Chaucer and Shakespeare when I came to them. Later, I found the human depth of Stendhal, Balzac,

Tolstoy, Dostoevsky, Proust, and Kafka, and the astonishing empathy of Joyce; later still, the power of Sophocles and Racine to merge the *persona* with action; last of all, the scope of Goethe.

This depiction of humanity in all its variety has been the main theme of the written and spoken word, from epic to gossip, as it has been of the visual arts, throughout the ages until the eighteenth century. Then came the surge and spread of music, the discovery of landscape, of the mountains, the opening up by Goethe of all nature artistically and scientifically (and who shall say the two conceptions are fundamentally different?) as the type and symbol of the divine process: the full entry of the German mind, with its intensification of both creation and chaos, into the European tradition.

My first real discovery of nature in life came one morning in April 1916. My father put me on the back of his bike where I had a little seat and said, "Off we go." And then he turned in the wrong direction, for I thought he was taking me down to Quakers' meeting—it was a Sunday. "No," he said, "we are going somewhere else today." And we rode for about eight miles, and we stopped at a wood. (It is now a housing estate. I took my wife there to see it, and there was nothing to show her.) We went into the wood, and there, suddenly, was a great pool of bluebells stretching for perhaps a hundred yards in the shade of the oak trees. And I could scarcely breathe because the impression was so great. The experience then was just the bluebells and the scent; now, when I recall it, it is also the love of my father who chose to do that that morning—to give me that experience. I am sure he had been there the day before, found it, and thought, "I'll take my son there." As we rode there and as we rode back, we heard the distant thud of the guns at the Battle of the Somme, where thousands were dying every day. That overwhelming experience of a natural phenomenon, a demonstration of beneficent creation, and at the same time hearing those guns on the Somme—that experience has remained with me almost more clearly than anything else in my life.

And again, when I met similar experiences in literature, I recognized them. I knew what Wordsworth was writing about in *The Prelude*, which is the greatest autobiographical poem there is. (Wordsworth is a good step to greater men. And I often think it is better to read Wordsworth in the original than Goethe in translation because so much of their message is so very similar, except, of course, that Wordsworth is so much narrower.) I cannot go through the landscapes of that poem now. I cannot even discuss in any kind of detail what landscape is about—obviously, it is not just about itself. Wordsworth called it "a type and symbol of Eternity." Those of you who don't know it might do well to look at a passage of *The Prelude* that was written separately and is often printed separately in anthologies. It is an account of Wordsworth and his companion (this was back in 1792) walking across the Alps. They were looking forward to the tremendous experience (they were Romantics, you know) of crossing the Alps. But alas, as they were walking along the road, they met a peasant who told them, to their disappointment, that they had already crossed the Alps without even knowing it. So in a state of great disappointment they continued. And Wordsworth describes it in his greatest passage:

> The brook and road
> Were fellow-travellers in this gloomy strait,
> And with them did we journey several hours
> At a slow pace. The immeasurable height
> Of woods decaying, never to be decayed,
> The stationary blasts of waterfalls,
> And in the narrow rent at every turn
> Winds thwarting winds, bewildered and forlorn,
> The torrents shooting from the clear blue sky,
> The rocks that muttered close upon our ears,
> Black drizzling crags that spake by the way-side
> As if a voice were in them, the sick sight
> And giddy prospect of the raving stream,
> The unfettered clouds and region of the Heavens,
> Tumult and peace, the darkness and the light—
> Were all like workings of one mind, the features
> Of the same face, blossoms upon one tree;
> Characters of the great Apocalypse,
> The types and symbols of Eternity,
> Of first, and last, and midst, and without end.
>
> (*William Wordsworth: The Prelude: 1799, 1805, and 1850*, ed. Jonathan Wordsworth, M. H. Abrams, and Steven Gill, 14 books, [London: Norton, 1979], book 6, lines 621–40)

Now there are two main aspects of creation. One is its intensity. When I rushed out into the wood that time after meeting that girl again at the age of fifteen, I had that evening as full an apprehension of the intensity of the creative force of the universe and of the feeling of gratitude as I could have, "This is in me! Astonishing! It is in me!" It is something to live up to. I wonder how I should have felt then had I known that I held the priesthood in the true church.

The intense activity down to the least particle of it is one aspect of creation. The other is its peace—the vast sabbath of the universe. In his greatest lyric poem, which may well be the greatest short lyric poem ever written (a few lines indeed), Goethe has seized that. I have tried to get these few lines right in English—I suppose I have got about a hundred versions. Of course, I haven't succeeded, but let me give you one of my translations anyway so that you may know more or less what the poem is about, and then I will give you the German.

Mountain and evening sky
Make peace.
Light airs in the high
Branches ease,
Breathe, and are through.
No birds now sing for the solemn wood.
Patience: soon you should
Be at peace, too.

Über allen Gipfeln
Ist Ruh.
In allen Wipfeln
Spuerest Du
Kaum einen Hauch.
Die Voegelein schweigen im Walde.
Warte nur: balde
Ruhest Du auch.

The peace of death, the peace of love, the peace of the most intense activity of creation are all aspects of the peace of God, which passeth understanding.

As I walk through my life, my years come along with me. They are all accessible from the age of six onward and occasionally present themselves from the age of three. In a moment of leisure or meditation, I may be anywhere in my life. We come here trailing clouds of glory, as Wordsworth said, and we do not lose them entirely: we glimpse them from time to time, as

Traherne and Vaughan did. And as we live, we find added to them variegated clouds that roll back to disclose a scene in detail, or even a dream we had half a century ago. The longer we live, the longer the prospect—if we believe in remembrance and strive toward righteousness.

NOTES

[1]Burston, Norfolk, England.
[2]*Macbeth*, 3.02.50–51.
[3]Matthew 27:3–10.
[4]*Faust*, between 4398 and 4399.
[5]Waterloo.
[6]*As You Like It*, 5.03.24.
[7]1 Nephi 8:9.
[8]*Piers Plowman*, Prologue, 17–109.
[9]Genesis 23:19; 49:29–31; 50:25.
[10]Mary Magdalene.

Finding Ourselves in Our Tradition

I HAVE A text, and I am going to quote it from the New English Bible version because it will be a little fresher to us in that version and because we know it well; there it is in Philippians, and there it is also in our Articles of Faith, and it runs as follows: "All that is true, all that is noble, all that is just and pure, all that is lovable and gracious, whatever is excellent and admirable—fill all your thoughts with these things" (Philip. 4:8).

I made a translation, or rather a paraphrase, of a quatrain of Goethe's the other day. The last line refers to Thomas Hobbes, who said about human life that it was nasty, poor, brutish, and short. I imagine that the "short" was said triumphantly on account of the other three. Here are my version and the original:

> Learn to know your way about in
> trimillenial tradition,
> or stay lost, a groping lout, in
> Hobbes's hand-to-mouth condition.
>
> Wer nicht von dreitausend Jahren
> Sich weiss Rechenschaft zu geben,
> Bleib im Dunkeln unerfahren,
> Mag von Tag zu Tage leben.

Goethe speaks in his quatrain of a trimillenial tradition because he is thinking of Troy. In the Church, we think further back than Troy; we speak of a four-thousand-year tradition that goes back to Abraham. Our tradition begins with the gospel in the Garden of Eden, narrows down to Abraham, and spreads again from him. Our tradition is, above all, the scriptures. Yet the true tradition is also to be found, as in a glass darkly, in the other cultures of the world throughout history and throughout the darkness of apostasy.

Since the gospel was taught from the beginning, we have a means of realizing in our church that moral standards were originally those of the gospel, although they became clouded as humanity spread. Therefore, we are not surprised to find in pagan literature reflections of the gospel. Homer, for example, teaches moral truths. Hugh Nibley talks about the fact that at the time of Isaiah there were Confucius and Zoroaster and Buddha—other great men teaching similar truths. There are, in history, people like Saint Francis as well as those like Pope Alexander VI.

If we are going to be able to live with sufficient vitality and richness in this world, we have to find our way about in those three or four thousand years dating from Abraham. That means knowing dates and places in order to have a frame of reference built in our brains for the history of civilization. A child should know where most countries and the most important cities in those countries are, and a child should know the most important dates. It is a grind to acquire those things, but one should acquire them. Yet the dates and the places do not count in themselves. They are merely a framework for us to use in order that we may build up our birthright for ourselves. (If we do not build up that birthright, we are behaving as Esau did. Jacob was a not very satisfactory young man in some ways, but he did take life seriously, and Esau didn't. Esau was a mere hunter. And I do say a mere hunter. I hope people remember that in October.) The point is, we have this remarkable birthright to which we have been born: the true documents and art of the past.

Tradition and Genealogy

The concept of tradition is one that in our church we should understand well because it is deeply linked with our genealogical work and our genealogical doctrine: the turning of the hearts of the fathers to the children and the children to the fathers. As we move forward in life, there is not only the whole tradition of our own lives behind us that we should not lose or forget, but also the whole tradition of our ancestors going back to Adam. And one of the major reasons that we need to find out as much as we can about our ancestors is so that we may interpret ourselves through them. Genealogy is important because our families are the extension of ourselves back infinitely and forward infinitely. It is by virtue of them that we are individuals. We do not act alone. The antecedents of our actions go back to our ancestors—what they have done, what they have passed on to us in the way of sin and in the way of virtue. And the consequences of our actions go forward to our descendants. Both the antecedents and the consequences are, in fact, eternal—there is no beginning and there is no end to our actions. That is why we have to thank our ancestors (that is one side of it) and to forgive them (that is the other side of it) and why our children will have to thank us and forgive us.

We need to take our genealogies seriously, and that means knowing our direct ancestors, knowing their collaterals, knowing what their lives were like. I am lucky because a quarter of my wife's lines and half of mine go back to Quaker ancestry, and Quakers kept detailed records. We have been able to find out from these records, for example, when our ancestors went to meeting and when they didn't, and we can wonder why particular ancestors suddenly missed meetings when they had been going regularly for several years. I remember one gap: my third great-grandfather in Somerset didn't go to meeting for three weeks. We discovered that he had gone off to the wedding of his son in Essex. We can build up much in this way.

We shall understand better the ways of our ancestors if we know about their times, even if we do not have records about them. We can learn from the literature of their times the kinds of problems they faced—how it was. My wife, for example, has a book of agricultural records. She can look up any year and discover what the weather and harvest were like that year, what kind of a summer a farmer ancestor had. We can learn about the cultures and histories of the countries in which our ancestors lived. We can learn the languages of those countries (and very often that means learning several languages). We can build all that up. We can expand from that into what impact there was from major events and from major figures. In my own family, we discovered by accident that one of our ancestors had some connection with Milton's secretary. There is a certain feeling one has on discovering that sort of thing. Somehow a great window opens. I believe that the more we know about our ancestors—the way they lived, the history of their times, their language and culture—the more chance we have that they will accept the gospel. I am sure that is so because if we turn our hearts towards them, they should turn their hearts toward us. That is one of the things that Malachi means.

We can change our ancestors, and by our learning about them, they can change us. In no other church can we find this doctrine, which is so profound and which is one of the main reasons why I am in this church. It is the image in our church of this general doctrine of tradition as a living thing. And tradition is a living organism like ourselves—it is in ourselves. A tradition is not a brick wall or a house; it is not something that is added to stone by stone. When a great work is written or a great painting is painted or a great piece of music is composed, it not only provides a new experience, but it alters the experience of everything else in that field forever. When we read a great modern work, we can no longer look at Homer or Shakespeare in the same way—they will never be the same again.

A particular tradition is not something that can easily be defined and circumscribed. It interacts across space and time with other traditions and, as a part, serves a purpose in the whole. So the more we understand of the wider tradition, the more we shall understand of our own. They are not separate. That wider tradition includes the tradition of our own countries, the tradition of the Western world, the tradition of the Hebrews and the Greeks that lies behind the Western world, and the contrasting traditions of those strange other cultures that are never more strange to us than when we go deeply into their religions and realize, not how alike religions are (as modern loose thinkers think), but how different they are from ours and how much they demonstrate to us by that means. The course of history is something that God presides over as a whole; he doesn't simply preside over the history of his chosen people. It is not merely that we are members one of another in our church; we are members one of another in a greater community than that: for better or for worse, we are members one of another in the whole human race as it was, as it is, and as it shall be. By entering that wider tradition, we enter more fully the tradition of ourselves, of our church, of our country.

Tradition and History

Tradition is what we have of the past. It is all we have of the past, except for the part of our lives we have lived in it. Tradition is what enables us to get back into the past, and it is only by that means that we can do it: we exercise our imagination in terms of our tradition to get back there. We can't go back, but we can imaginatively think ourselves there and have some idea of what it was like. I imagine that when we get beyond the veil, we shall have a different way of dealing with the past, but at the moment, the past is removed from us. A veil covers not only the future, but the past as well: we are between the two. The process resembles looking back on our own lives to see what we were like as children. Our thoughts are the thoughts of grown-ups thinking back to what we were like as children. We remember certain feelings we had; we think, perhaps, they were the feelings we now have, but of course they were not. They couldn't be because we have added to them the tradition of our lives.

A tradition encompasses much more than exact historical facts. And even about the "facts" there is considerable disagreement. For example, "Give me liberty or give me death" is thought by some to have been uttered by a famous person; experts say that it was invented by his biographer and put into a speech in the biography. We often have to choose between alternative "facts," and we may never be able to choose with certainty. Washington's cherry tree is part of tradition. Whether there ever was such a cherry tree is beyond our knowledge and, indeed, if there was this cherry tree, whether the episode ever took place. Some people think of Lincoln as a great religious character, but someone once told me that Lincoln wrote an unpublished book proving the non-existence of God. Tradition cannot always enable us to resolve these matters.

A more important point is that once you start putting facts together, they cease to be facts, putting them together is an act of the imagination. We may pretend it is an act of logic, but it is really an act of the imagination. Honest historians will not try to be objective because being objective in history is impossible; a historical situation is too complex. What honest historians will try to do is to express their total response in their histories. Historians are always biased. The question is whether they know it or not. Historians have a duty to express their bias. If they don't, they are leaving some of the truth out—the truth that is in them, the truth of them. Gibbon wrote *The Decline and Fall of the Roman Empire* with the whole of his mind, and that is the way

Thucydides and Herodotus wrote about the history of Greece. Their reactions, their feelings are there as part of the documents before us.

It is the honest reaction of historians to the situations they describe that is part and parcel of our tradition. That reaction enables us to know how people in the past really were, and it will enable people in the future to know how we are. The true documents of the past are not the histories of the past as written by modern people. They are what people have written about themselves and their contemporaries and their own pasts. Thucydides is valuable to us because he wrote about his time in writing about the Peloponnesian War. He revealed himself and the feelings of his contemporaries by revealing the war itself. That happens to all historians. Ultimately, their responsibility is to put their honest selves on the page. If they do not, they are hypocrites or self-mutilators.

In the Church, we are having a lot of debate now about history. Much of this debate has been naive because it has ignored the fundamental point that history is an art, not an objective process. Ultimately, history is a part of literature.

The tradition of any group of people is the product of the imagination of that group as a whole. That doesn't make their tradition invalid or untrue; it makes tradition more important. It is something that they have established about their history, something they take seriously and think of as an inspiration in their lives. So their tradition is a real thing because it exists in their minds, collectively, and because it influences their actions. And it ought to influence their actions. A French writer and patriot, Charles Maurras, who is decried because he was a Fascist, once opined that at an election French citizens ought to think of the tradition of their country and what their forebears would have wanted for it, and good French citizens must also think of what will happen in the future and what their descendants will want and will want their forebears to have done. The tradition of a country is the continuity of a nation, and if there are not citizens of a nation who believe in that tradition and who will vote in an election because of what their ancestors thought and what their children may need, then those people are in outer darkness, as most people are. Most voters in an election vote on the basis of their immediate needs and immediate desires.

That inverted saint Henry Ford said that history was bunk. I would agree with him that history is bunk in the sense that most histories are bunk because they contain a great deal that is false. But there is some truth in histories. And that truth we need to acquire.

History happens forward, but we are allowed to go back. We live forward, but we are allowed to return in our minds. And the further back we go, the further forward we can go. Going back in eternity is part of going forward. We walk into the future backwards. We can't face the future; we can't see it. We can see the present here and the past back there, and, in terms of the past and present, we can imagine what the future will be like. That is what prophecy is about. Prophecy can be expanded in our own lives by looking at the past. The past needs to become incarnate to us so that we can understand the present and feel for the future and, indeed, find the past in the envisaged future and the future in the envisaged past. To move to and fro in a great tradition is to give oneself something like the experience of eternity. It is an important experience.

The tree is for us an image of this process, and the tree is not the roots as the past and the trunk as the present and the branches as the future. The tree is the totality: the roots are still alive, the trunk is alive, the branches are alive; the roots are seeking the tree's sustenance and the leaves are seeking its sustenance; the whole thing happens together. The tree is an image of eternity: the tree of life, the tree of knowledge of good and evil, the tree of Jesse, the tree of the condescension of God.

Tradition and Literature

I should like now to move on to finding ourselves in the literature of the past. Much of what I have to say will apply also to the other arts, but I want to focus primarily on literature. One can't use the word "finding" without bearing in mind what the Lord said about finding and losing. It is by losing ourselves, not by trying to find ourselves, that we gain ourselves. If we try and go straight to our heart, we shan't find the way. We have to find the way through people and things outside ourselves—the Lord, our neighbor, and literature, which represents humanity in such a way that we may find in it an example for our own lives. Literature will help us find ourselves if we go actively to it and if we read it in the spirit of finding out what is there—not finding out what is here inside us, where, alas, there is very little wisdom. We need to look outward not only at today, but at the wisdom of all ages.

Literature deals with us therapeutically, on the whole without our notice, and it is better therapy than introspection. Let us be looking at what great men have said rather than poking around inside ourselves and listening to the burblings and meanderings of our own midnight thought. It is much better to be sitting there reading a great book than brooding things over without the aid of the Lord. Prayer is another matter, but all this so-called thinking things over, this self-indulgence in meanderings, is not profitable. One of the major reasons we should read is because we waste so much of our spare time just thinking. I remember the peasant from Skaane in Sweden who said, when asked what he did, "Well, sometimes I sits and thinks, and sometimes I just sits." The difference between sitting and thinking and just sitting is not very great. Sitting and thinking is like fishing or like watching cricket—perhaps not like watching baseball, though that is pretty slow, too, I must say.

Great literature helps us, as we are growing (particularly in adolescence), to widen our world from ourselves so that we can better choose what kind of person we are going to be. It helps us to choose ourselves out of the many selves that there have been. By losing ourselves in great art and literature, we can find what we ought to be, we can find our highest selves. Instead of recoiling upon ourselves, we can go out from ourselves stronger, better able to understand, more sensitive.

We may lead superficial lives with other people, or we may lead deeper lives with other people. And literature is a way in which we can learn to live deeper lives—husband with wife, parent with child, brother with sister, fellow member with fellow member. Most good authors are better than we are. They are much better company than our own friends. They are more intelligent; they are more sensitive; they are more experienced; they have wider backgrounds. Think of the amount of desultory conversation that takes place at any university at any time any day. Think of the time wasted—millions upon millions of academic hours wasted on desultory conversation when those same hours could be used for good reading, spent in the company of those who are much better than any of us.

What comes from good company? What comes from good company is better manners, greater sensitivity, greater sensibility, greater empathy, greater sympathy. Reading good literature makes us more capable of understanding other people, of loving other people, including those whom we don't particularly want to love, even our enemies. Literature is one of the ways in which we can learn to love our enemies as well as those closest to us. How can we expect to have full marriages when we are not going into those marriages with full minds and fine sensibilities? We are ignoring the tremendous possibilities of a delicate, well-poised, rich, sensitive life if we ignore the literature of the past. There is no substitute.

Literature is not a turning away from life. It is a way into life. We do not experience a book or a tale differently from the way we experience ordinary life. The difference between that which does not "really" happen in literature and that which "really" happens in life is irrelevant. That which does not "really" happen nevertheless does happen in its own way. I said to my father when I was seven years old that I had gone out that frozen morning and had seen a fairy dancing on the ice on a pond. I saw that fairy all right, but my father "sent me to Coventry" for a week because I would not say that I had not seen that fairy. Yet I had in my own way seen that fairy. It may have been a wisp of mist. Who knows? The lights of fantasy and nonfantasy are both part and parcel of reality.

Very often the experiences we get from books are even more intense, more living, than is our ordinary life, because they are monitored to us by authors who have seen more than we should have seen had we been with them, and we can learn to see through their eyes. The most important experiences of my life were not in my ordinary life at all. They were in the literature I read.

Matthew Arnold once said that poetry is a criticism of life. Let me explain a little what that word "criticism" means. It does not mean faultfinding. It means assessing, evaluating, judging. Literature is a judgment of life; literature is an assessment of life, by implication or directly. Now you may say, "Judge not, that ye be not judged." But if we look at that line in the Inspired Version we will find "judge righteous judgment" (JST Matt. 7:2). "Judge not, that ye be not judged" does not mean that we must not judge; it means that if we judge, we must be prepared to be judged. We must remember that we should judge in such a way that we shall not mind being judged in the same way. That is the point. To commit ourselves to a judgment is to be prepared to have someone else commit himself by judging us.

The dichotomy between critic and creator is a false one. The great writers are, of course, creators, but they are also critics, acutely aware of language, sensitively using it as a means of characterizing people in some detail. Eliot is the best modern example of the coexistence—rather the coalescence—of critic and poet. *The Four Quartets* is also a critical work; "Tradition and the Individual Talent" is also a creative work. The uncreative critic is a destroyer; the uncritical creator is a waffler (like Rabindranath Tagore). Creation and criticism go together: the Lord of Luke is also the Lord of Joshua. I see a great many students who come to me about their writing. Those that stay with me are the ones who take courses in criticism, and those that don't are the ones that would rather not; I am glad to say that most of them stay.

Literature is "a mirror held up to nature," to use Shakespeare's phrase—a mirror held up to humanity. It is given us to look into these mirrors and see ourselves as we are. "Thou art the man," said the prophet Nathan to David when he had caught David in the net of a parable (2 Sam. 12:7). We, too, are the men and women. Human virtues and vices have always been the same. What all worthwhile literature has to say about others is true of us, and we should liken it to ourselves to see what it has to say about our conduct at the deepest level, which is the level at which good and evil decide themselves.

For literature, as for music and painting, we need education. We need to be educated to look, not for the things that simply reflect us as we are or should like to be, that at worst flatter us, but for the things that will help us to become better. Most of us, after all, are not satisfied with ourselves as we are (though we may pretend to be). We need in our church to educate ourselves and our children to the point at which we can find in the best art sustenance for ourselves. The Holy Spirit does not do everything for us. It is there to guide us when we are unable to do what is needed for ourselves.

I have always strongly objected to the idea of reading for amusement. We can be amused, if we like, by Johnny Carson. A great deal of literature is not really better than that. In our church, we should not regard literature as an amusement; indeed, we should not regard anything worthwhile as an amusement. I had a Mormon once say to me, "Well, you know, it is a good idea to forget your religion sometimes and just relax." What kind of blasphemous nonsense is that? We must know in our church that to spend our time reading what is called "pure" entertainment when we have the opportunity of reading something of spiritual value is a sin, a plain sin. It is always sinful to do less well than we could. But we live our lives as if we were ignoring that fact.

Eliot once spoke of the life of the saint—and in our church we are all saints—as "a lifetime burning in every moment." That is what, after development, we may come to experience in the celestial kingdom. And we can be quite certain that in the celestial kingdom, about which we know little, the standards set will be the highest possible ones because no standard lower than the highest possible one can exist in the presence of God. Nothing impure can exist before God. Does anybody seriously believe that in the celestial kingdom there will be light reading in bed, or light music in cafés, or kitsch pictures like those on chocolate boxes? If we are struggling towards the celestial kingdom, must we not try to experience and find the best of all time all the time? Not just a good time. The world of light reading and café music, and the chocolate box is not the vision of Revelations.

We read books in order to learn more about life, but if we are going to learn, we have to work at it. We don't read a book as a substitute for another hour in bed. I gave a course at Brigham Young University called "Readings in the Classics." It was an intensive course, and students took no other classes during the term they took it. They had to concentrate all the time and promise to work from eight to ten hours a day, six days a week—reading, reading, reading. Adolescence traditionally has been the time during which the young of the middle class read hundreds of books. When I was young, I read somewhere between three and five books a week, I suppose, of about three hundred pages each. Many of my friends did also. It is surprising what you can get through when there is no television. Most students at BYU don't get through three or four books a year. And there are some who have never read a "whole" book in their lives.

We need to be unremitting in our study of the best because our lives are short. Only eternal progression is going to carry us all the way, and it is a long way that we have to go. It is, indeed, an eternal way. And learning to read is an eternal process. I doubt if it had its beginning in this life. There must have been something of the kind in the pre-mortal existence. We have forgotten it, and yet in some subtle way it must be working underneath.

Some people may ask, "Why bother about literature other than the scriptures?" They may say, "It is all in the scriptures." I remember a pastor of the Danish Church in Copenhagen; he was strongly Calvinistic. His study was full of books, and so I began to look at them. They were all trashy detective stories—shelf after shelf of violence. So I said to him, "You like reading detective stories?" "Yes," he said. "You see, as a Calvinist I believe that the scriptures are the only valuable literature, and since there isn't any other valuable literature, why shouldn't I read what I like rather than reading what people think one ought to read?" That man's attitude was the very reverse of Brigham Young's attitude or of Joseph Smith's; they wanted the Saints to take the riches of the world and interpret them according to the gospel so that those riches might refine the Saints and build them up. It isn't *all* in the scriptures except in the same way as the oak tree is in the acorn. The whole oak tree is there, but it has to grow out. And the scriptures have to grow out in our own minds.

We should not find great art to be contrary to the gospel. When art is great, in fact, we must expect very often that it will support the gospel. Even the greatest of art, of course, doesn't *always* tell the truth. Only scripture always tells the truth. Only scripture is inspired in that way. But unless we are familiar with great art, we are missing something that can help our own souls, because in great art, as in the scriptures, we may find power that enables us to live better. This is not a matter of highfalutin culture at all. It is a matter of the whole quality of the life we lead, minute by minute. Either we can look at the universe in the way of the greatest of art, or we look at it in a very dull light indeed. The difference is as great as that between a day with sunlight and a day without sunlight.

One of the great things about great literature is that the greater it is, the greater the scriptures are to us as a result of reading it. Why? Because the scriptures are even greater. We have a different sense of dimension when we know great literature. Where *King*

Lear (a play about pride) ends, Job begins; where *King Lear* (a play about envy and repentance) ends, the prodigal son begins, and so on. We shall appreciate the biography of David better, with all its fine observation and sensitivity, and we shall understand the subtlety and rightness of what the Lord said on any occasion (as when the Pharisees tried to trap him) if we are familiar with our Shakespeare and our Henry James. The sensitivity and truth that we can gain from great literature can help us to appreciate the greatest of literature—the scriptures. We shall know the scriptures better, too, if we are able to sing them with Bach and Mozart and to see them with Rembrandt and Michelangelo. These artists will strengthen our weakness, deepen our eyesight, make our ears come alive.

"I am the way, the truth, and the life," says the Lord. "No man cometh unto the Father, but by me" (John 14:6). That is true, but it is also true that great art—and it is only *great* art that can do it—can bring us nearer to him. Great art helps us to have a sense of mystery, a sense of sacredness, a sense of holiness. Great art helps us to praise the Lord.

What I am presenting to you is the alternative to the nightmare of history. It is the golden dream that enriches the waking respite. We can communicate with the past; we can live through the grace of the spirits of the past. We very often don't choose to do so: we are often preoccupied with practical things or inferior amusements. But the opportunity is there. The opportunity is there to read the scriptures, to see Shakespeare, to listen to the best music, to look at the best pictures. We need to experience the great works of the past through the whole of our life. Part of our life should be the experience of great works gone back to again and again, perhaps ten times, perhaps more. And every time we go back to them, they are different, and yet they are part of the tradition of our own lives.

Judgment

Oh yes, he had felt,
feeling through others' writing;
and yes, he had thought,
but thinking through others' thoughts.
Yet, being an inferior

person, in this way
he led, though at second hand,
a superior life:
Dante, Goethe, Shakespeare, and,
more than all else, the Bible.

A vicarious life?
This beggar lived like a king,
with seers, prophets, a
Saviour. Lived in tradition,
isn't all life vicarious,

empathetic, one's
neighbour as oneself? Yes, but
this man loved reading:
his neighbors were all ghosts, and
he spent his life seeing them.

AHK
March 1985

Judgment in Literature and Life

I DO NOT believe in literature as something special and set apart, what the French call *belles lettres* or the Germans *Schoenliteratur.* (You can hear the nineteenth-century cultural superiority in the German even better than in the French.) I am glad to say that we have not a proper English equivalent to it. The Oxford English Dictionary says, "This sense [of literature] is of very recent emergence"; indeed, it is only a hundred and seventy-two years old. It is itself an affectation and leads to affected behavior. It is very difficult for a person to write without being affected if he thinks he is doing something special, something that he has to be very conscious of doing differently. The gospel has nothing to do with that kind of behavior. The gospel has to do with simple, straightforward behavior. Literature does not exist apart from other written and spoken things. The language we speak, the language we hear on stage, the language we peruse in a doctoral treatise, the language we read in a novel, the language we mouth in a lyric are all different, but they are not fundamentally different. So the concept of "literature" as something special, something peculiarly beautiful, something set apart, is not a satisfactory one. The classical and Renaissance view is that literature is any good writing and, by implication, any good speaking. Literature is that which is well expressed.

It is possible to speak well or to speak badly, to write well or to write badly, and the way to define that word "well" is not in a highfalutin way. We must not be misled into complications and high theory not relevant to the point. The standards of judgment for literature are not tied to particular forms—novels or lyrics or whatever. The canons with which to judge literature are no different from the canons with which to judge our own friends' and relatives' talk. All forms of verbal expression come under the same canons and judgments, whether they are deliberately artistic, whether they are conceitedly artistic, or whether they don't seem to be artistic at all and yet are—and very often these last forms are the most artistic.

When we are listening to our friends, we do not think primarily of how "well" they are talking, do we? We think of whether they are telling the truth or not; we think of whether they are being loving or not; we think of moral qualities, and that is what we need to think of in literature. The object of art, after all, is not aesthetic contemplation; the object of art is the experience that incites us to better behavior, better doing. Art is there in order that we may live better, not in order that we may look at it and have a private aesthetic and mystical experience. We should be able to accept that in our church because we are that kind of church. We look askance at mystics.

The fundamental task of education is to teach us to discern the difference between the true and the false, the moral and the immoral. And that difference always shows itself in the language, spoken or written. Words are a part of conduct; they monitor conduct, reveal conduct. People reveal themselves completely by the way they speak and write. Whether or not they try to hide themselves, they still reveal themselves: indeed, the more they try to hide themselves, the more they reveal themselves. The greatest writers show us the connection between conduct and language. There are correlations between bad people and bad language in Dante and in Shakespeare. Dante, Shakespeare, and Goethe all make the most subtle, critical uses of language. They place people by language.

If people are good, they speak well; if they are bad, they speak ill. That is the classical and the scriptural view. That was the doctrine of the ancients, the doctrine of the Renaissance, the doctrine of all literary criticism until the late nineteenth century. It is an old, old idea that goes back thousands of years and has only been largely abandoned in the last one hundred. Let me quote a thing from Quintilian and others, which Ben Jonson quotes in his *Timber or Discoveries*, because it goes to the heart of the matter: "As a man speaks, so is he. Speak that I may see thee."

I am always prepared to demonstrate in any particular case that anybody wishes to bring forward, and I have done so in the past and will go on doing so, that, granted they have similar levels of technical achievement, a good soul will write better than a bad soul. Gifts are given to us all; we foster them or not; we behave with them well or not. It is true that very often bad souls have good moments. Very often bad souls have aspirations. Sometimes bad souls are struggling not to be bad, and in these cases they may well produce good work. We have to remember that. But we have to remember also that there are great writers who, because they were good, managed to maintain a high level through a great deal of their lives. It follows from what I have been saying that if our judgment of individuals and our judgment of their work do not coincide in our philosophy, there is something wrong with our philosophy. We cannot say that anyone is bad yet produces good work. We cannot say that a writer's style is wonderful yet the writer is depressed about life. We cannot make statements like those; we have to be careful about what we call "good" and "bad."

The more we know about authors, the more likely we are to find out that there is a connection between their conduct and their work. But it isn't necessarily our job to "find out about the author" because the authors give themselves in their style. Style has been defined in many different ways. I think it was probably defined best by the great naturalist Buffon, and I think he was all the better able to make this definition because he was a naturalist. He said, "The style is the very person." D. H. Lawrence once said something valuable here, and that is, "Don't trust the writer, trust the work"; that is to say, don't trust what writers say about themselves, don't trust what they say they are doing, but go to the work itself and see what they really are doing, which may be very different. The work will tell you. It is not what the author deliberately says that counts; it is the work that tells us about the author in the profoundest sense. It is that which comes which is true, not that which is willed or imposed.

I like students to come to me with their verse or short stories or whatever. I don't like them to come to me to talk about their problems—these are usually not my business. People may talk about their problems to somebody else because they simply want to have the narcissistic pleasure of exposing themselves in front of that person—all bishops and branch presidents know that happens. But if someone comes to me and says, "Here is a poem I have written," I can put that down on the desk and talk about it without probing or prying into that person's mind. What I have to say about the poem, of course, will tell something about the person. I may even say something directly about the person, as a result of the style, which the person may choose to take to heart. I remember a young woman who came to me with her poetry. She was so fluent in verse—it came out too superficially, conventionally, easily, but she acted so tense and nervous. I said, "If you want to improve your verse, you must improve your gestures. Study your gestures and find out why you make them in this kind of way, and then your verse will improve." She had this nervous, tense kind of way that was self-regarding, and it affected both her gestures and verse. What we can see in our friends—and we all see these sorts of things in our friends—is there in literature, too. And we should be monitoring the page as we do our friends or our enemies.

What I am suggesting is not something that is at all extraordinary. We spend our lives monitoring language in that way. We are not always aware we are doing it; most of the time, in fact, we are not the least aware. Nevertheless, in our daily social life, we are all the time monitoring what other people are saying. We assess what the tone is telling us about what that person is trying to do to us or not trying to do to us; we assess tone to determine goodness and truth. We work on hunch, on intuition, on study.

Sincerity

Of all the moral qualities we look for in language, spoken or written, and do find in the scriptures, the most important are sincerity and strength. When I speak of sincerity and strength together, I speak of something that is rarely achieved on the grand scale. It has been achieved by people like Shakespeare. In modern literature, the sincerity often precludes the strength: it is characteristic of modern literature not to believe in a combination of sincerity and strength, but to believe in a combination of sincerity and weakness, which leads to despair, self-pity, cynicism, solipsism, boredom. And, of course, when the combination is one of strength and insincerity, the strength itself is insincere. A great deal of popular writing is of this kind, from trashy novel series to pep talks. The Samsons of language flex their muscles in the popular TV pulpits, in political campaigns, in advertising, as mountebanks, but their linguistic muscles are those of liars and hypocrites, and their certainty of tone is a cloak or overcompensation for weakness.

There can be no real strength, no real edification, without sincerity. And so, I want to focus on sincerity. Sincerity is the preliminary criterion for goodness in literature as in our daily letter writing or speech: everything else is hypocrisy. That was the center of teaching at Cambridge when I was a young man; that has remained with me throughout my life; and that is one of the major things that brought me to this church.

Each of us has a sincere style of language that is natural to us. The style differs from person to person. But any sincere style has something in common with any other, and that is the effort toward honesty. Now, each person may vary from his natural style according to the company he is with. When I analyze a Shakespearean play, I note a difference when a role enters or exits because a person doesn't behave the same in one group as in another. All of us, some more than others, adapt to our company—in vocabulary, possibly even in accent, certainly in gesture and movement—because we are members one of another. And we are being sincere as long as we are adapting to our society naturally, out of human kindness. But if we adapt for a self-regarding purpose, our adaptation is hypocrisy.

In Britain, class aspiration has produced a great deal of hypocritical adaptation in speech over the generations: speech is the sign of one's social origin in Britain, and people notice very subtle differences. Edward Heath was born a small-scale builder's son in Kent, and at Oxford he changed his speech to upper-class English. Margaret Thatcher is the daughter of an East-Midland grocer. She may have changed her language before she went to Oxford—girls are more conscious of these things than boys. But to make an effort to speak better because you want to improve your social position is a kind of manipulation. You are doing something that is affected, adopting a different dialect from that which you would naturally speak, in order to impress other people; that is sinning because the effort to impress others is a sin—it is a moving away from yourself.

In this country, young people particularly are prone to pick up certain affectations in speech because they want to be like others in the peer group. When I first came to the Utah Valley, the expression "neat" was often used. Now it has pretty well gone out, but it was an affectation for a time. Think of other expressions like "sort of," "sort of this," "sort of that"; "kind of," "kind of this," "kind of that." "I feel sort of hot." Well, what does that mean? It is an unsatisfactory expression. You may think that the use of these expressions is not very important, but it is: it shows a desire to identify oneself with the group in a habit that is not a good habit because it is not a necessary one.

How difficult it is for the self-assertive to speak as members one of another. And yet, simple people don't find any difficulty because simple people are not preoccupied with themselves, and so, out of spontaneous fellow feeling, they adapt to people they find themselves around. As we talk to each other sincerely, we forget ourselves into the group and feel no barriers.

Sincerity is being oneself without thinking of oneself. When we come across authors who are just being themselves, what a relief! What a strain to read authors who are struggling to make themselves, to express themselves, to be more than themselves, or other than themselves, who are struggling to impress, who are struggling to shock (which is one of the things that modern authors love to do, one of the things that television now loves to do, to shock). If, in speaking, we express ourselves directly, there we are. But if, on the other hand, we wish to make an impression, there we no longer are, or we are merely the we that wish to make an impression; and the we that wish to make an impression are inferior to the we that do not think of making an impression.

Let me give you an outstanding example of sincerity between individual and group. I was present at the memorial service to T. S. Eliot in Westminster Abbey. The great actor Alec Guinness was there. He was a friend of T. S. Eliot's and was chosen to read from Eliot's verse during the service. I reflected as I sat there not far from him, now how is he going to do this? Is he going to do it as an actor? Is he going to do it as Eliot's personal friend? It was a complex situation. What did he do? He read it in such a way that I forgot my reflections and was afterwards ashamed of them. He just read it, and he was the voice of what he was reading. He did not act any part: he was himself. What does an actor do in order to be himself? Not think about himself. And in order not to think about himself, he has to be a righteous man. If John Gielgud or Lawrence Olivier had read that, he, too, would have produced a voice, but it would have been the voice of the actor reading Eliot's verse.

There would have been a flourish about it. Some people would have preferred it, because if there is one thing about good taste as compared with bad taste, it is that bad taste wants the exaggerated, the flowery, the gesture, the posture, the louder voice or the softer voice, anything to create a difference.

Self-forgetfulness is at the heart of sincerity. That means that if we try to force sincerity, we shall merely produce insincerity and hypocrisy. Once we start being self-conscious, we can't be true. Any self-conscious effort to express things is always against the grain. To attempt self-consciously to speak or write well means to fail; it is to forget that we are members one of another.

You may say, "Isn't education a means of becoming aware of yourself?" Let me give you an example as an answer. Learning a modern language, learning a musical instrument, learning to dance, learning any kind of skill—people can't help but be self-conscious to some extent when they begin because they are trying to make themselves do things. But if they work hard for years, in the end they can be spontaneous. They can be free. Being spontaneous may be the result of being inspired without effort, but it may also be, and more commonly is, the result of being inspired after great effort, after learning the thing so well technically that we don't have to think at all about what we are doing.

This has everything to do with being righteous. Living is also an art. We try all our lives to be righteous, and I do say *try to be righteous.* We have to work at it, just as the ballet dancer has to exercise on the bar and the musician has to practice a passage over and over again. Being sincere is not something that comes by nature—not, certainly, to the natural man. Naiveté is not sincerity. Innocence is not sincerity. We have to learn to be sincere. We have to try, just as we have to try to repent all our lives. It is an ongoing process. And eventually we can reach the point where we don't have to think about it. It comes spontaneously.

It is remarkably difficult to work out who is really sincere. Let me pose some questions about it. Are souls who decide to behave like Christians in order to try to become Christians actually Christians, hypocrites, or what? And if they are not hypocrites, at what point do they become hypocrites if they fail? May they spend a lifetime trying to do this? Is a soul who does good things without having any religious sense about them sincere? Is a soul who does good things out of duty but feels no pleasure in doing them sincere? Are souls who force themselves to do right and yet hate it being sincere? These are problems that go right down to the bottom of our souls, quite as much if we are religious as if we are irreligious, because they are points about which we have always some doubt. Those who feel absolute certainty may well feel that way because they cloud over, or are unaware of, their own uncertainties. Constantly, we are in trouble in the world because critics of profound discernment can see that we are being insincere, whereas critics of less profound discernment don't see that they are being insincere.

To know sincerity, we talk about it; still better we see it in others to know it. Literature is there to help us find our way. The scriptures are there to help us find our way, but they can be supported and helped by good literature to a surprising degree. Scripture and literature widen our field of vision because the hypocrites they portray are legion. Hypocrisy is what a large part of the New Testament is about; that is what the attack on the Pharisees is about. And I think that when one is a religious person, the greatest temptation one has is to be a Pharisee. The Pharisees were, after all, excellent people. They tried to behave well; they tried to live up to high standards; they worked at living respectably just like the elder son in the parable of the prodigal son. The elder son worked day after day for his father for many years, but look at the state of mind he was in. He wasn't a willing and obedient servant to his father, but one who harbored a grudge that gradually grew and broke open when his father did that favor for his brother that the elder son thought his brother didn't deserve. The elder son had no right to go against his father's judgment in that way, so he was fundamentally disobedient. The parable of the elder son may be a parable of our own lives.

In the end, sincerity is impossible to acquire except in a religious context because we can be sincere only if in some way we lose ourselves, and there is only one final way of losing ourselves. By placing our gifts in the service of the Master, we have, in this terrible age, the opportunity of reading, speaking, and writing as we should. "Whosoever shall seek to save his life shall lose it" (Luke 17:33) is true in the whole field of literature, as it is in our lives.

Religion, Art, and Morality

TRADITIONALLY, ART AND morality both spring from religion. Religion keeps both pure and makes it possible to create good art as well as good lives. But during the last hundred years, the world has been going increasingly astray in art and morality because it has not understood their relationship to religion.

Religion and Morality

Many people, especially nowadays, make the mistake of identifying religion—or what they see as worthwhile in religion—with morality. They believe it is possible to lead a moral life without religion. But we who are members of this church know perfectly well that without religion, morality is useless—it is theoretically comprehensible, but practically nonlivable. Religion provides the force, the living force, by which morality is endurable, enjoyable. It is not possible to live at the level that the Lord requires except through religion. Leave a society to act on the moral level, and it will decline, as society in the West during the last two hundred years has declined: in the eighteenth century, over all of Europe, religion became morality at the same time as scientific thinking came in, resulting in the permissiveness that we see in your country and mine and, alas, in other countries today.

Religion is more fundamental than morality. It is concerned with ritual, and ritual is extremely important. There are certain places in our church where ritual is very important to us, and there are other places, I suppose, where it is not so important to us. It causes us difficulty sometimes. Ritual goes beyond discursive language: it goes into gesture; into music; into poetic, rhythmical expression; into dance. The basic mental patterns are, after all, not discursive language patterns; the basic patterns lie behind discursive language. Morality is concerned with common-sense inferences from these basic suprarational principles of conduct.

Morality consists of formulations, and all formulations of what we ought to do fall short. The Mosaic law falls short; we know that later it was subsumed by the gospel, and the gospel is not a collection of formulae. The truths of the gospel cannot be set out like human laws. The gospel is always teaching something more than can be formulated in words.

The Bible is concerned with both religion and morality. Leviticus is concerned with morality mostly. Job is concerned with morality, except for chapters 38 to 42:6. The Psalms are concerned with religion. Isaiah is concerned with religion. Above all, the Gospels themselves are concerned with religion. In the letters by Peter, James, and John, as in those of Paul, we often get moral application.

Of supreme importance to the distinction between religion and morality is the chapter (Gen. 22) on the sacrifice of Isaac. Kierkegaard deals with this chapter in his book that is called in English *Fear and Trembling.* Kierkegaard reminds us more firmly than anyone else that the sacrifice of Isaac is the example that shows religion to be deeper and more important than any morality that may emerge from it. What he said was this: If, when Abraham raised the knife to slay Isaac, there had been the least trembling in his hand, then Isaac would have known that his father did not have faith and would have been in despair. But there was no trembling in the hand of Abraham as he raised that knife. The meaning of that chapter is that Abraham had absolute faith in God and therefore felt free to do what God told him to do, even though it seemed to be directly against what he thought God's teachings were. That is why Abraham is now a god.

Morality is concerned with deliberate reference to principles to find out what to do. Religion is concerned with spontaneous correct action. If we are righteous, we know what to do without having to deliberate and reason about it—it comes spontaneously to us. But at the moral level, we have to work it out. In the scriptures, we see Christ responding immediately, spontaneously, more often than not in awkward situations. "Render to Caesar the things that are Caesar's, and to God the things that are God's" (Mark 12:17). That can be said in different ways. I like to take an ironical tone: "This miserable little bit of metal belongs to Caesar, but give unto God the things that are God's." Christ was never caught. Christ was always ready from the whole of himself, from the whole of his training and the whole of his life, to do what was right at any moment among those people.

We cannot reduce to a moral principle what Christ did on any particular occasion. He told Martha that Mary had taken the better part. But ask yourself these two questions: Would he have said it at all if Martha hadn't fussed? And second, would he always be saying it? If there had been only one sister there, then surely that sister would have had to do the preparation for the meal and the listening to the Lord. And surely there must also have been times when Mary should have done the domestic work and Martha should have listened. And surely the person of all persons who knows that perfectly well is the Lord himself. Another example is the woman taken in adultery. The condemnation of such a woman in the law of Moses was death by stoning. But Christ's statement was, "Neither do I condemn thee" (John 8:11). Does that mean he would always have said that? Of course not. It would be utterly untrue to derive from the story of the woman taken in adultery (which no gospel could find place for and which later got attached to John because there was so much uneasiness felt about it)—it would be utterly wrong to derive from that story a principle that adulteresses, or for that matter adulterers, should be forgiven automatically. The story is not permission for adultery—it is a statement by Christ to that particular woman at that particular time in those particular circumstances. He sent her away without condemning her because he knew she was truly repentant—he saw that her mind had turned round. After all, she had been taken in the act and dragged through a hot, dusty street, anticipating death by stoning. But what Christ said to that woman is not something we should automatically say to all adulterers. That would be mechanizing what he did; it would be turning a living principle into an abstract one.

What is the difference between an abstract and a living principle? It is the difference between being reasonable and being wise. It is the difference between being sensible and being imaginative. It is the difference between having common sense and having uncommon sense. I am not talking about permissiveness; I am not even talking about flexibility in the superficial sense. I am saying that the principles of the gospel are twisted if they are applied in precisely the same way each time. But they remain true to themselves if they are applied in the way that is appropriate to the circumstances. And the way that is appropriate to the circumstances comes from following the impulses of the Holy Ghost, and the impulses of the Holy Ghost and the deepest workings of our minds are not things we can reduce to reason and clearly understand.

On BYU campus, they may talk about the difference between Liahona people and iron-rod people, but the opposition is superficial and foolish. I am perfectly certain that the river in Lehi's dream bent and wound, as all rivers do, and do you think that the iron rod went straight out into the river? Nonsense. It went round with the shore or cliff of the river because it was there to stop people from going astray. And they found their way to the tree of life, not by hanging on to a straight rod in mid-air over the stream, but by following the rod around, just as Lehi's family followed the Liahona's directions in the desert. This is the way that the Lord works.

We know that throughout history the Lord has been teaching people to live at a religious level. Even in the Mosaic law, the gospel was there. It was there in those two major principles that Christ enunciated from the Mosaic law when challenged by the lawyer: "Thou shalt love the Lord thy God . . . and . . . thy neighbor as thyself" (Matt. 22:37, 39). Those principles are enshrined in the Mosaic law (Lev. 19:18; Deut. 6:5), but the Jews did not live them. They were obsessed with tithes of mint and anise and cumin. And one of the invidious things people still do to the gospel is to erect it into rigid principles. Religion tends to attract fastidians who, in a kind of sadomasochistic frenzy, reduce it to very detailed laws about living, destroying the spirit of what was originally there. That is what the Pharisees did, and that is why they were whited sepulchers, and that is why they were abhorred by the Lord. That is why they, not the Romans, were his principal enemies; not even the constituted priestly authorities of the Jews were as dangerous as the Pharisees because the Pharisees had substituted an antilife of pseudomorality and hypocrisy for the life of the Spirit.

Plato found it impossible to define the good and therefore, in his *Republic*, symbolized the good as the progenitor of the sun. We symbolize it in a real individual—Jesus Christ, the Son of God. He is a man, not a principle—a man who includes all principles. And he underwent all the stresses souls should undergo; otherwise, it would have been just a trick. Christ had to undergo all stresses, as we have to undergo them, though he did so in a much higher and to a much worse degree. It is not possible to formulate the good. It is only possible to recognize the good in a good soul, and a good soul—a perfect soul—is what we are given to follow. And following a soul is very different from following a principle.

When we live the gospel, then we live a means of knowing, of learning to know and being able to do on all occasions what is right. And what is right is not something that we work out rationally in our heads. We do not have to work out philosophical complexities of ethics. It has nothing to do with that. We have to study the Gospels, see what Christ did, and try to identify ourselves with what he did. It is because we catch the spirit of the Master, the Master's love, and because we have soaked ourselves in the gospel, that we know what it is that we must do. The gospel, which we have stored within us, enables us at any moment to feel what we should do in a certain situation.

Years ago at Cambridge, I entertained a Buddhist priest. He was a pacifist—Buddhists tend to pacifism—and I remember someone in the university group whom I had invited over to meet him asked, "Now, what would you do if you saw a madman trying to kill a child?" His answer was this—and I have never forgotten it because it seemed and still seems to me a gospel answer: "I can't tell you what I should do, but I hope that my spiritual training has been such that if this event took place, I should then know what to do." Decisions taken beforehand about human conduct very often don't help.

If we do something spontaneously and it is a good thing, then it will be virtue unto us. But if we have to think whether to do it or not, if we have to reflect for even one moment, then the element of potential sin has entered because we are doubtful about what we ought not to be doubtful about. We ought to know what to do in situations. The right way to follow the Master is the way he teaches. And he teaches by saying unique things and doing unique things on every occasion that comes up. "Behold, I make all things new" (Rev. 21:5). That is one of the fundamental powers of the Lord. That means that when we are living a saint's life, we live life anew.

Religion and Art

A related mistake we have made in our age is to cut off art from religion. Art has been related throughout history by origin and practice to religion, and it cannot be great without religion: in all great art, if there is not an assurance of religion, there is a striving for religion.

Michelangelo is an example of an artist who did his art from a convinced religious background. And his art is profound and great because of that. I have no brief for Michelangelo's private life, but I say that when he was painting the Sistine ceiling, when he knew that Eve had a spirit body and painted it, he was under some kind of inspiration. He made the central panel the creation of Adam: there is God holding out his finger to Adam, and Adam is leaning forward, and Eve, in her spirit body, is encircled in the arm of her Creator, looking with intense interest at the Creation of Adam. We can be sure it is her spirit body because the next panel shows Eve in her physical body, which is not so young and immature as her spirit body—it is a beautiful body, but it is not quite the same. Where could Michelangelo have gotten that except by inspiration? There was no source he could have gotten it from.

D. H. Lawrence did not have the same kind of religious background, but he struggled towards religious concepts in a religious way. He failed to reach them except in bits and fragments, but he was trying, and because he was trying, he wrote some good things.

Art and Morality

When I went to Cambridge in the late 1920s and early 1930s, I. A. Richards and F. R. Leavis taught me that I was right in my instinct that there are no purely aesthetic standards and that a division between aesthetic and moral standards would not do. We cannot divide aesthetics from morality and say, "Aesthetically X, morally Y." It is no good having a compartmentalized mind that has some reactions in one direction and other reactions in another direction and no centralizing force. If we are to have an integrated life, we have to unite our aesthetic and moral standards. It is in terms of religion that we can unite them: religion is the source of the one ultimate set of standards to which all other standards must conform.

Most modern art critics don't want to make moral judgments. They are at a loss as to how to make them, anyway. Critics in the Church are capable of making moral judgments because they have the true standards, but they don't think that, as critics, they ought to be using those standards. That is nonsense. A split mind cannot produce something that is true and profound. If we have the true standards and refuse to take them into works of art and judge them by those standards, then we are not living according to the light within us; we are sinning.

To bring the moral and the aesthetic together is to get to the point in our lives where the good, the true, and the beautiful are the same. These three things are not different things; they are aspects of the same thing. If we think that something is good but neither beautiful nor true, our idea of goodness is wrong. And if we think that something is true but neither beautiful nor good, then our idea of truth is wrong. If we think something is beautiful but neither true nor good, our idea of beauty is wrong.

Art and morality are not linked directly, but indirectly through religion. Religion inspires them both, making it possible for art to revitalize morality and morality to keep art on the right track. Art does not draw directly from moral standards; it is too deep for that. It draws from the religious power behind those moral standards. If art and morality are connected directly, art etiolates. But if art gathers strength from religion and morality gathers strength from religion, there is that relationship between art and morality that we need in order that art shall be at all profitable.

A direct relationship between art and morality would be a tyranny. When a direct link is assumed, each tries to overrun the other. When an attempted direct connection is set up, one gets allegory instead of symbol, and allegory is always inferior to symbol because it is always more superficial. Allegory is a one-for-one correspondence, a simple, superficial thing. A symbol always has something more to give us. Take a work like Spenser's *The Faerie Queene*, which is a failure, and compare it to *Pilgrim's Progress*, which is a success. Spenser conceived of his epic poem as an allegory, and he wrote of types. On occasion, his inspiration ran away with him, and he produced a really living part. But for the most part, he was doing something that from the beginning was a dead duck. Bunyan succeeded with *Pilgrim's Progress*, not because the book is the allegory he superficially thought it to be, but because the spirit of the thing ran away with him, and he produced deep, feeling things. When the characters go down into the river of death at the end of *Pilgrim's Progress*, for example, that is no allegory. That is a profound symbol of what we, too, shall do.

We are greatly helped in judging art because we have the scriptures (and by the scriptures, I mean the ancient scriptures, the modern scriptures, and what the prophets tell us now—all these things that confirm one another), and we know that they are inspired writing. This means that they are the greatest writing, the greatest literature. They have the highest theological and moral teaching for us, and their method of expression is the highest. The scriptures are given to us in total speech, and the artistry of that speech reaches the height. It goes beyond ordinary discursion. The scriptures work more subtly than any other literature ever produced. The language of the scriptures reflects the rightness of the scriptures.

The scriptures tell us the truth about the people they describe. They do not idealize, but show us people as they are—not better, not worse. There are some people in the scriptures, like Joshua or Ruth, whose faults we know nothing of, and we do not need to know. Others, like Sarah or David, have faults that we are told of for our own good. We are meant to see their virtues and vices and to learn from both. There is only one perfect person in the scriptures: the Lord himself. From him we have the most to learn, for he was not magically perfect but had to make himself perfect, as we are to try to do (see Matt. 5:48 for "perfect," meaning "complete" or "whole").

The scriptures don't tell us half-truths. And we must not take half-truths from them: we must not pick out favorite texts that happen to suit us and reject others that we don't like. We need to be familiar with the scriptures not only in part, but in total. I was once asked to give a short talk on my favorite parable. My reply was that I didn't think I had one and I doubted if I ought to have one and even if I did have one, I shouldn't talk about it because the important thing is not to dwell on our favorite things in the scriptures—that is self-indulgence—but to try to get other things in the scriptures to be as favorite as the favorite things we already have. It is important that we concentrate on those parts of the scriptures that we don't much like—and I don't mean, for example, certain parts of Numbers. But I do mean that the scriptures are valid for us as a whole, and we must never run into the danger of interpreting to ourselves particular verses that happen to speak to us and ignoring other verses which don't seem to speak to us yet perhaps have a message that we ought to have. There are so many people who ignore the parts of the scriptures they don't "approve of." Be mistrustful of what you like most, and listen carefully to what you have an impulse to reject.

If it is in the scriptures, we had better accept it, because if we don't, we are going to lose something. "Don't read that chapter; it is not very nice." Who would dare speak of the word of God in that way? The word of God is the history of Tamar (2 Sam. 13) as well as the Creation (Gen. 1); Judges 19 as well as John 14. Let us never read the scriptures under the impression that we know better; we do not and shall not. We read the scriptures to find out what they, as writings above us, have to tell us. There is no question of naiveté, of primitivism, of coarseness, of insufficiency, of inappropriateness, about the scriptures. The inspired genius who wrote the history of the court of David was as "civilized" as Henry James and much more deeply certain about right and wrong.

The difference between the scriptures and other literature—and this is, of course, a profound difference—is that the scriptures always tell the truth (except insofar as men have tampered with them), whereas other great literature does not always tell the truth. The rest of great literature shares with the scriptures profound and broad comment on human life and tells a great deal of truth, but it does not tell the truth all the time. That difference is something we need to hold on to because that is what gives us the standard for judging all literature. By application of that standard, we can tell whether an author is speaking truthfully and sincerely or not. We need to apply that standard even to a writer as great as Shakespeare. Shakespeare's attitude towards obscenity, for example, is not altogether satisfactory. In his early work, he did not simply put it there because it was part of the life around him; he put it in because his audience enjoyed it. However, Shakespeare always saw marriage as an abiding relationship of supreme value. On the whole, his work supports the gospel.

The scriptures contain a variety of types of writing with which we may compare other writings. For example, once we have read the life of David in First and Second Samuel and the first two chapters of First Kings, we have got an example of the finest biography anywhere, and we may compare it with any other. It is an extraordinary biography. Under inspiration, the historian of David's court has interpreted a complete life to us in gospel terms. That interpretation is more insightful than any Greek tragedy. When he has trapped David in the net of a parable, Nathan says, "Thou art the man" (2 Sam. 12:7). There isn't any doubt about that line. The judgment is clear and profound, and we know that we have been told the truth about David. And once we have got that example, we can go to Carl Sandburg's *Lincoln* or Boswell's *Johnson* and immediately see the difference, and seeing that difference in that kind of way is important. We know that we have not been told the truth about Lincoln or Johnson in the same way as we have about David. It is not that Carl Sandburg's *Lincoln* is not useful in many ways, but it hasn't the quality that the life of David has. It hasn't the quality that a Shakespeare history play has. Neither has a Shakespeare history play the inspired quality the life of David has. Shakespeare himself has not that certainty of judgment that the scriptures must always have. With that certainty of judgment, we can go. If we want to judge love poetry, there is the Song of Solomon; if we look for drama profounder than that of Sophocles or Shakespeare, there is Job. If we seek a standard for what an epic or a novel on a family ought to be like, then we can read the book of Genesis, which is the finest book on a family ever written. It is perhaps the most interesting book in the whole Old Testament for that very reason. It comes home to us because it is the chronicle of a family, an astonishingly realistic chronicle.

When we have the scriptures in our heart and our mind and our soul, then we have a means of measuring all things; we have a means of judging everything else. My grandmother was not an "educated" woman. She left school at the age of twelve to become a kitchen maid. But she knew the scriptures, and because she knew the scriptures, she knew and could adequately teach me what was trash and what was not. She read me good things—Goldsmith and other classics; she liked these things. She was born in 1856, but she lived in her mind in the eighteenth century, and she found, quite rightly, most of the stuff written after 1780 pretty trashy. My grandfather was also "uneducated," having been apprenticed as a watchmaker at the age of fourteen. He, too, was soaked in the scriptures, and, like my grandmother, he also had taste in literature. He recited Shakespeare to me: he sprang to Shakespeare because he had learned the scriptures beforehand.

We should ask ourselves about literature other than the scriptures, "Is this literature before me worthy of being read in comparison with the gospel? Will this literature help me with the gospel?" If the answers are yes, read it; if they are no, leave it. If you felt when you were picking up a piece of trash (and most things that are printed are trash)—if you felt suddenly, "This doesn't compare with the scriptures"—wouldn't you throw it into the fire instead of continuing to read it? I had a young man come to me with a book and say, "Should I read this?" I pointed out to him that a way to find out whether you should read a book is to read the last paragraph or two of it—you will soon know. So we read the last page of the wretched book. He then threw it in the wastepaper basket. That was sensible.

What goes for literature goes for the other arts as well. If we are soaked in the scriptures, we shan't want to look at bad things on our walls or listen to bad music because those things won't fit. We shall intuitively reject them, just as we shall embrace what is good, because we shall have in our minds a firm and sound sense of what is in good taste. "Taste" is an unfortunate word for something so profound. But it is perhaps the best word because in tasting we discriminate, and the ability to discriminate—to discriminate between good and evil—is fundamental. Good and evil are there in every choice we make: what we eat, what we wear, what we read, what we look at on the television. Taste also implies preference—preference for what is good if we have good taste, for what is bad if we have bad taste. Taste means there is unity between what we judge to be good and what we like.

Great Art and Good Art

Good literature always supports the gospel, and there are two main ways it can do that. First, literature can directly reflect the gospel. The greatest of literature does that and gives us a sense of comfort just as the scriptures themselves do. When I say great literature, I mean Homer, I mean Virgil (their fundamental attitudes have more to do with the gospel than those of Thomas Aquinas or Calvin), I mean Dante, I mean Shakespeare, I mean Goethe. Goethe was a bit doubtful still when I was a boy. It takes a long time for these judgments to grow. Now I am convinced of Goethe. The whole of our literature in Europe and the United States and anywhere else in the West since Goethe is Goethe's aftermath, just as the whole of Greek literature was Homer's, the whole of the great period of English literature was Shakespeare's, and Italian literature is still Dante's. We can't expect great literature more than once every few hundred years.

What is the good of reading modern writers when we have left Goethe, Shakespeare, Dante, Virgil, and Homer unread? Even in translation they are greater than the other things. Of course, if we can, it is always better to read great literature in the language in which it was written; that is one reason why Shakespeare is important to us: he is the only one of the five great writers who wrote in English. It is true that English has changed since Shakespeare's time, but with patience and with the aid of the various handbooks that exist, using a good edition, we can still read the Shakespeare text. We may read the other writers—one is German, one is Italian, one is Roman, and one is Greek—in the original, too, if we are lucky enough to have their languages (and it has been known for people to learn these languages in order to read these authors).

Critics often don't see what there is to see in the greatest writers because they haven't the gospel to see with. For example, critics are sentimental about Faust. Yet Faust is an utterly selfish man who causes at least seven deaths, and Goethe does not endorse him or forgive him. People look at Shakespeare and they find in him what they themselves are. So, if an agnostic looks at Shakespeare, he finds him an agnostic, and if a Roman Catholic looks at Shakespeare, he finds him a Roman Catholic, and so on. Nowadays, when most critics are non-Christian, they like to pretend that Shakespeare was not a Christian. But Shakespeare's plays exhibit all signs of being written in a Christian framework, with undisputed acceptance of such doctrines as were common to the Anglican and Roman Catholic churches: baptism, sin, repentance, forgiveness, the Atonement, and life everlasting.

There is hardly a play of Shakespeare's that doesn't concern itself mainly with the punishment of sin, with the reward of virtue, with repentance and reconciliation. This is true of the history plays, which are under the dominance of the concept of God as Providence; it is true of the tragedies, where we get "great" people falling and being punished, not by whim, but by law; it is true of the comedies, where the foolish and the wicked are made absurd.

The family is dominant throughout Shakespeare. The history plays are chronicles of the decline and fall of families, of family deaths. The comedies are about the education of young men and women in order that they may marry more seriously. The tragedies, like the Greek tragedies, are, without exception, family tragedies, and the last plays are family resurrections. In these last plays, we see one generation being reconciled to the next generation, a theme that is important to us in the Church and one that we thoroughly understand because it is a genealogical theme. It is the theme of Malachi: the turning the hearts of the fathers to the children and of the children to the fathers. When we look, we shall find that everywhere in literature. Ultimately, reconciliation, repentance, and forgiveness are within the family—you may say, if you like, the human family. The human family is the macrocosm of our own family.

Shakespeare is concerned with good and evil. We can tell by the way he handles the characters what he means and thinks morally about them. In his language, he places evaluation of people all the time. This does not mean, of course, that his characters are either good or bad; for the most part, they are bad sometimes and good at other times. There are some consistently bad people. I can hardly think of a consistently good person, at least among the larger roles.

Now, if Shakespeare had been better as a young man (in which case he might not have written plays at all), he would not have followed the custom of bawdy wit. It was a theatrical habit, and he conformed to that theatrical habit and put it in. Gradually, though, he used the bawdy to illustrate character (Hamlet, Lucio, Iago) and to condemn the society that made so much use of it to defame women. He progressed from comparatively simple illustrations of sin (e.g., in *Richard III*) to very subtle and deep illustrations (*Measure for Measure*, *Othello*, *The Winter's Tale*). Shakespeare's moral discrimination is subtle and profound, more so than anything else we have outside the scriptures.

Shakespeare's plays are full of charity. He has pity or sympathy for practically everybody. It is a question of distinguishing all the time in Shakespeare between the evil of the sin and the pitiableness of the sinner, even in the cases of characters like Hamlet, Othello, and Macbeth. I do not believe that there is a single, solitary character in his plays with whom Shakespeare identifies, but I do think that he put something of himself into all of them because a writer cannot write of what is not inside himself. That is what has caused Shakespeare to be regarded as a universal genius. I think he is the most profound secular writer who has ever lived because other writers have not got his scope of human sympathy. When we read Dante, we see there are people whom Dante hates; he has put them into the cosmogony, but he hasn't been able to forgive them. But it seems to me that there is nobody incomprehensibly evil in Shakespeare, not even Iago, and I would hope not, because I fear that Iago is a portrait of a common man with the commonest of sins—envy.

Fundamental Christian themes in Shakespeare are very often given the "go-by" nowadays, but even the non-Christian critics more or less agree with the Christian ones on what the supreme passages in Shakespeare are: the reconciliation of Lear and Cordelia in *King Lear;* the final scene of *The Winter's Tale* (the reconciliation of the family); the death of Cleopatra; the finding by Pericles of his long-lost daughter. In some plays, for example in *Hamlet*, there are only a few lines of this sort. And in that play those lines aren't at the end at all—they are in the first scene: the description of what Christmas does to the world. And in *Measure for Measure*, there are a few lines in which Isabella refers to the Atonement:

> Why, all the souls that were were forfeit once,
> And He that might the vantage best have took
> Found out the remedy. How would you be
> If He, which is the top of judgment, should
> But judge you as you are? O, think on that,
> And mercy then will breathe within your lips,
> Like man new made. (2.2.73–79)

In these passages the true, the good, and the beautiful all come together. Great passages are more difficult to find in the history plays because the history plays are about distinguished persons, and most distinguished persons are scoundrels.

So Shakespeare's standards are ours; they are not those of the world at large. We Mormons have a community with Shakespeare that the non-Christian outside world has lost. We have a better opportunity of understanding him because we believe in Christian doctrine, and therefore we have that much in common with him and his audience. With all his imperfections, Shakespeare helps us to understand how close to gospel thinking somebody can come. It seems to me that the way in which Shakespeare portrays his characters in his plays is similar to, though at a distance lower than, the way Christ works in his parables.

Shakespeare has written the most subtle and profound things about humanity that we find outside the scriptures, and in his profound ambiguity, he leads us back to the certainties of the gospel. When you have studied Shakespeare for a lifetime, you realize (as I realized only a few years ago) with some surprise that most of Shakespeare's endings are as ambiguous as Ibsen's. There is a level at which human beings have to put up with ambiguity. Ambiguity is frequently the only way of telling the truth. To Christians, it should be fundamental to their art: that is what they must expect to find all the time. The only certainty is in the gospel. That is the only certainty we know. And we can move from that certainty into ambiguity, into dispute, into clouds, into confusion, and into chaos because we have that certainty. The rest of the world is compelled to flee the confusion by means of drugs of various kinds. But we are free to go down into the depths because of our certainties. As Shakespeare says in his farewell to the stage through Prospero in the epilogue of *The Tempest:* "And my ending is despair, / Unless I be reliev'd by prayer" (lines 15-16). Outside the gospel, there is nothing but despair.

There is an inferior but important kind of art that cannot give us the comfort of the gospel but can give us another kind of comfort, the comfort of destruction. Destruction is not a word that Mormons like to hear, but it is a most important word. You may say that destruction is evil, but I tell you that the destruction of evil is good. The power of art to destroy the evil in contemporary culture is good. We cannot speak in our day of great artists who are positive like Homer and Virgil and Dante and Shakespeare and Goethe. But we can speak of less great artists who portray the whole gamut of miserable life without the gospel. Most of the art of the twentieth century is, alas, not positive, but at its best powerfully negative. It is quite ruthless in its way of depicting what humankind is like without God.

The best literature of our times (outside the gospel) is miserable, uncertain, vicious, uncertain, cynical, uncertain, sardonic, uncertain. And it is no accident that this is the case. The reason is that faith has gone out to a lower ebb than it has ever been at before in Western civilization. Knowledge of the gospel, understanding of the gospel, and above all, following of the gospel are less common now outside the Church than they have ever been. Only the bad literature of our time is "happy," and it is bad because the happiness is synthetic. Bad literature tries to be happy with "romance" outside the gospel, and that is impossible. That is why it is so important not to look around outside the scriptures to try to find modern literature to comfort us. We can expect older literature to comfort us because it came from people who, though they lived under the cloud of apostasy, nevertheless had faith, as, for example, Shakespeare had. But in our time, we cannot hope to get gospel comfort outside the gospel.

The prophets are always emphasizing the wretchedness of humanity without salvation, and if we read them again we shall realize how important emphasizing that is. People, after all, have to be awakened to their wretchedness, just as they have to be awakened to their salvation. So many of them are so deep in boredom and sloth and routine that they don't realize how wretched they are. One of the great powers of modern art is to enable people to realize how wretched they are. Stravinsky, Picasso, and Joyce are the greatest artists of our century. They are far above anybody else. Why? Because they go deeper, because their despair is greater. Outside the gospel, we must expect despair, and therefore, those who give us the greatest despair are those who, if we do not already believe in the gospel, will drive us to it because there is nothing else. I assure you from my own fifty-six years before I joined the Church that there is nothing else.

Picasso underwent in stages, more profoundly than most artists, the experience of the twentieth century. The experience that he underwent was the experience of the natural man who is an enemy to God. And to undergo such an experience, with his ability, meant to portray the *impasse:* the impossibility of any decent life whatever in a nonreligious culture comes out to full expression. I needn't go through all his periods, but I should remind you of those tender, delicate, mildly ironical pictures of an acrobat's family that were produced just before the First World War. Contrast these with the paintings he painted during the German occupation of France in the Second World War, that terrible time for

France and all within her. In 1946 in London, in the Tate Gallery, there took place a great exhibition of these paintings. It was a terrible series of paintings. It was a depiction of hell. But then, France was hell when those pictures were painted. They were the revelation of a terrible period of human history that most people endured without God. The god of France was at that time a sect of torturers.

Tens of thousands, hundreds of thousands came to see Picasso's paintings in London. Some spat, some swore, some tried to get at the paintings to destroy them. People raved about them with anger, but that proved that Picasso had got home, that they understood him. They were angry apparently at not understanding him, but actually the kind of nonunderstanding they had of him was the understanding he wanted them to have. (Rage may be a very proper reaction to a work of art and may be learned from, and learning is better gained from experience with art than from experience with people.) Those who were most angry at those terrible pictures were those who knew most clearly what Picasso was doing and couldn't bear it. He was showing these people what they could not bear to see: what, in ultimate circumstances, the natural man is like. *Guernica*, for example (that memorial of a German bombing raid on a little Spanish town), is a superbly organized piece of human disorganization and agony, and that paradox holds us. It is one of the fundamental documents of our time, just as James Joyce's *Ulysses* is. We must recognize what Picasso was doing—he was making form out of the ugly, the noisome, the formless. There is a kind of form that can be made out of negative experience, and insofar as it is form, it is positive and teaches.

Picasso has been the greatest of all artists since I don't know who—possibly since Michelangelo, perhaps since Rembrandt, certainly since Goya. Whatever you say about him, you have to say that this man has presented to us the natural man who is an enemy to God in a way that no one else in our time has done. The appalling nature of human beings without God is shown better by Picasso than anyone else. In comparison, the rest of modern art is kitsch. Even Matisse seems to be kitsch compared with Picasso. We need to grasp the destructive power of people like Picasso and Joyce and realize how they had to move, by degrees, towards that destruction because they had no alternative in the Europe in which they lived.

People who live in Utah Valley and similar places need to know what life on the outside is now like. There are young people in our own church even—I have heard of them in California—who don't believe that the Holocaust, the wiping out of at least six million Jews, ever happened. Why not? They don't want to believe; they can't bear the thought. And yet thoughts of such things are proper thoughts of the religious person's life. We may say as Christians, "There is no tragedy because ultimately this is not a tragic universe. It is a universe that has a good, not a bad, end." But tragedy does mean something. It is not merely that millions are literally hungering to death; it is that they are in outer darkness spiritually, by the thousands of millions. And we are members one of another. Salvation does not consist simply in becoming converted oneself: it consists in going forth to others who are not converted. And in order to go forth to others who are not converted we must, by the aid of the Holy Spirit, understand the world as it really is, and that is where most of modern literature and art can help us. We may find it repulsive, we may find it unhappy, but it helps us to understand how people outside the Church live and think.

It is not for Christians to be optimists—that is not humble. The Lord has been the supreme optimist for us, and we cannot match his optimism. We can have an ultimate confidence, but we cannot have an ultimate confidence for most people. Read Matthew 24:22 once more: "And except those days should be shortened, there should no flesh be saved: but for the elect's sake those days shall be shortened."

Such great art as there has been in our time points to the terrible days to come. The great art of former times strengthens us to face these days and shows us the potential nobility of humanity. The scriptures, the greatest art of all, crown us with salvation, grace, and peace. Let us help our children to understand that art is a way to religion and that religion is the way to interpret art; then our children will have a better prospect to lead sensitive, loving, and moral lives.

Moral Significance in Anglo-Saxon Literature

FROM THE BEGINNING, in both oriental and western cultures, there has been a close link between art and religion and morality. All major cultures in the world have seen art as the assistant of religion. This is true wherever you go in the world and into whatever art you go. The Hebraic tradition, the Greek tradition, the Latin tradition, and the Oriental tradition are all concerned with the use of the spoken and written word as a means of improvement, as a means of education, as a means of teaching. Our own Anglo-Saxon literature is deeply religious and deeply Christian in the sense that it helps us understand what gospel principles mean. It has consistently dealt with moral issues from the beginning, and so is or can be useful to us in the Church. Anglo-Saxon literature has not been led away by the doctrine of art for art's sake to the same extent as European literature at the end of the nineteenth century was led away. Art for art's sake is a piece of self-indulgence; it is heretical; it is nonsense. Art reflects our total situation and above all our moral situation. The aesthetic category had little importance before Kant, but once an absolute aesthetic category was introduced, we got this split between art and morality, which has resulted in the development of so-called "good" art as an exclusive occupation—an occupation for those "in the know." The rest is thought to be bad. And, indeed, it almost always is bad; in these split conditions everything else turns out ultimately to be bad, too. The distinction we have made between highbrow and lowbrow in our modern culture is due to the severance between art and morality, which, in its turn, is due to the decline of faith and religious practice. Art for art's sake works as a divider between classes, between tastes.

Anglo-Saxon literature has its root in the classical period rather than in the early productions of northern Europe, so I will begin by saying a little about the Greeks and Romans.

The Classical Period

We might expect the Hebrews to have been morally preoccupied since they were the chosen people, and they were indeed morally preoccupied in a way that no other race ever has been. But the Greeks and the Romans were also morally preoccupied when it came to the arts. They didn't think that anything went. The moral function of art is fundamental to Greek critical thinking; it is there in Plato's *Republic* in his condemnation of certain immoral aspects of art and in Aristotle's *Poetics* in the seriousness with which he handles tragedy. It is fundamental to Roman thinking, as we can see in Cicero and in Quintilian.

The Greeks and Romans were aware that the arts had moral influence, and they were careful about that moral influence in education. "*Maxima reverentia pueris debetur*"—the greatest of reverence is due to youth, both male and female. Plato disapproved of art that weakened education. He thought, for example, that those disgraceful stories of the domestic habits of the Greek gods should not be revealed to young people who were being trained for leadership in the state. Music, too, he would not allow, except for the Dorian and Lydian modes, which were invigorating.

Horace, an urbane fellow who managed a fairly successful career but who always seemed to infuse a touch of melancholy into his cynicism (he felt he wasn't a particularly good man himself, but admired a good man), wrote of art that it should mix the instructive with the agreeable: *omne tulit punctum qui miscuit utile dulci*—"He gets everybody's vote who mixes the useful with the sweet." This line has been the source of discussion ever since. As we listen to the words and think of Horace, we cannot but feel that the remark is at much too low a temperature for us, and consequently the instructive and the agreeable do not fuse; they merely mix. Horace lived in a realm that had already abandoned its gods and was using them as political and social conveniences. He was in a position similar to that of post-Renaissance artists.

But lubricious as they occasionally may have been, and urbane, easy, and superficial though they often were, classical authors had views very different from those of our contemporaries about the task of literature: the object of pleasing readers was to attract them to be improved; pleasing readers wasn't an end in itself.

The Middle Ages

The relationship between faith and art in the Middle Ages has been traditionally regarded as intense and harmonious by aesthetes and religious pasticheurs. But there is dissonance. Some people have admired it for its artistic effect, but it is still dissonance. The greatest monuments of the Middle Ages are its cathedrals; but at the same time as we admire those soaring arches, we find at odd vantage points gargoyles and, carved under choir seats, grotesqueries. They express what the artists have not suppressed under the simplistic aspirations of their faith: evil pushing out through the creases, corners, and splits. I can therefore never feel that any Gothic cathedral, wonderful though it may be, is an example of perfect art because the evil is not under control or has not been sublimated; it breaks out. When we honestly face the artifact, the unity of faith and art is not there.

We Mormons can understand this. We believe there was an apostasy, and knowing that the Middle Ages was the high period of the apostate church, we can be more clear minded than those historians who have proclaimed the unity of faith and art in the Middle Ages. Even though the Medieval period was a period of so-called faith, there was a double morality: celibates writing one kind of verse for the religious public and another kind of verse for their own amusement. Their lives were not whole. How could they be? Celibacy is unnatural. Nevertheless, there were religious people and religious artists in the Middle Ages, including literary artists; the story of English literature in the Middle Ages is largely a story of religious literature. Moreover, the greatest literature of the Middle Ages is religious literature. Even the agnostics and the atheists can't avoid that fact.

The religious and moral preoccupation of these writers is obvious, for example, in the work of Langland, who wrote that long poem about the state of England, that tremendous social assessment, *Piers Plowman*. It is obvious in the devotion of that series of lyrical moments, *The Pearl*. It is obvious in the writing of that very humane and very worldly Chaucer with all his so-called liberality, not to give it a worse word. People seize on that because they are interested in that. But Chaucer is nevertheless a great religious poet. His *Troylus and Criseyde*, which is the greatest love story of the Middle Ages and a very tender, sad, and sometimes lubricious work, ends, as a medieval work must end, with a prayer. Chaucer produces this marvelous prayer, which wells up out of the totality of that work and which is an encouragement to fresh young people to seek God and not to seek the flesh, as did the lovers in the poem. It is the most moving passage in the work, and we understand by it that under this superficiality of sophisticated court behavior, Chaucer was a religious man. I will give you two stanzas and a rough translation:

O youngë, fresshë folkës, he or she,
In which that love up groweth with your agë,
Repeyreth hoom from worldly vaniteé,
And of your herte up-casteth the visagë
To thilkë god that after his imagë
Yow made, and thinketh al nis but a fayrë,
This world, that passeth sone as flourës fayrë.

And loveth him, the which that right for lovë
Upon a cros, our soulës for to beyë,
First starf, and roos, and sit in hevene a-bovë;
For he nill falsen no wight, dar I seyë,
That wol his herte al hoolly on him leyë.
And sin he best to love is, and most mekë,
What nedeth feynëd lovës for to sekë?

Oh young, fresh folks (he or she)
in whom love grows up (as you, yourselves grow up)
repair home from worldly vanity
and with all your heart turn your face up
to that God who has made you after his own image
and look on this world as but a fair,
this world that passes as soon as the beauty of the flowers.

And love the man who for absolute love of us
upon a cross in order to buy back our souls
first died, then rose and sits in heaven above.
For He will mislead no man, I can assure you,
no man who will rely upon him with all his heart.
And since this man is the best one to love and the most meek of all,
Why need one seek pretended loves elsewhere?

There is another poem about Troilus and Cressida—a favorite story of the Middle Ages—a terrible poem by Henryson, a Scot. (The Scots like to be terrible—more than the English.) After Cressida has been abandoned by one lover after another, she becomes a half-blind leprous beggar and begs of Troilus, who doesn't recognize her because her face has been destroyed by leprosy, and she doesn't recognize him because she can't see well enough. This scene is brought out very starkly and hard. People in the Middle Ages may have belonged to an apostate church, but they had a sense of sin as few others have had. And by the doctrine of opposites, in order to have a sense of righteousness, one needs to have a deep sense of sin, too. We have a lot to learn from Medieval literature about how deep-going a sense of sin can be.

Women in the Middle Ages composed mystical works (such as those by Dame Juliana of Norwich) and works about the rule of their order (for example, *The Rule of the Anchoresses*). These works are not as well known as they should be. There are also those magnificent play cycles which were produced on wagons by the guilds on St. John's Day (the longest day of the year), summarizing the history of the whole universe from beginning to end. Those people had that sense of the cosmos, which we can appreciate because we have it in our own religion. It rarely seems that these plays are obtrusively Catholic, and I recommend that members of the Church make use of them. I believe the Wakefield Series to be the best, but there are others as well.

The Middle Ages is a time of great religious art, not only in stone, but also in manuscripts:

> I sing of a maiden
> That is matchless.
> King of all Kings
> To her son she ches.[1]
>
> He came all so still
> Where his mother was
> As dew in April
> That falleth on the grass.
>
> He came all so still
> To his mother's bower
> As dew in April
> That falleth on the flower.
>
> He came all so still
> Where his mother lay,

As dew in April
That falleth on the spray.

Mother and maiden
Was never none but she;
Well may such a lady
God's mother be. (Anonymous)

The Renaissance

I come to the Renaissance. Renaissance artists had clear and explicit ideas about the relationship of art to morality, ideas which came from antiquity, from the Greeks and the Romans, as well as from the Christian tradition. Therefore, Renaissance writers were concerned with good and evil, sin and virtue; these are of supreme importance in their work. Shakespeare wrote in the Renaissance. As a youth, he went to school for seven or eight years, and during the whole of that time, he undoubtedly read practically nothing but Latin. He had to translate into Latin and translate out of Latin; he had to read the Latin authors. He had to read a little Greek as well—not as much. And with his brilliant mind, by the time he had had several years of Latin, he must have completely absorbed that pagan culture, which was reconcilable in terms of art and morality with the Christian culture.

Machiavelli also wrote Renaissance comedies, profound comedies. From the point of view of the nineteenth century, these comedies have a hard and cruel assessment of human beings. But we are not people of the nineteenth century, and our Mormon movement, our Mormon Church, has never been of the nineteenth century because it has never been sentimental. The nineteenth century clouded the distinction between good and evil by means of its romanticism and its sentimentality, and we have to get rid of the effect of nineteenth century sentimentalists like Bradley in order to be able to understand much more clearly what writers like Machiavelli and Shakespeare were doing with good and evil.

Imperfect though the Renaissance artist may have been, unable though he may have been—even in the case of Raphael, but certainly in the case of Michelangelo or Leonardo—to sum into himself the whole of his epoch and a complete faith, nevertheless he served a purpose. It did not occur to the artist in the Middle Ages or the early Renaissance that he was expressing himself: at the lowest level, he was placing his technique at the disposal of his patron, and at the highest level, he was placing his technique at the disposal of his church, of his religion. His art at the highest level was for his religion. This is true not only of much of the greatest painting of the time, but also of the greatest writing, and it is most profoundly true of the music. Our music, like our drama, sprang from the bowels of the church and has a mainly religious origin, and it is greatest, as is the painting, when it is faithful to that religious origin, however imperfect that origin may have been. The art of even an imperfect faith is better than the art of no faith at all.

But since the Renaissance, we have developed a heresy about the artist, which is one of the major heresies of the modern world because it has misled so many people—this heresy of the artist as hero, of man as the center, which is the characteristic humanist heresy. It begins with the Renaissance. It doesn't come into its own until the Romantic movement. As faith declined from the Renaissance onward, the division that was already there in the Middle Ages, and most definitely there in decadent Rome—the division between public and private morality—became greater and greater; the artist became the hero of people's private adulterous lives and of their public sentimentalities and violences.

The Seventeenth Century

In the seventeenth century, there is a wealth of religious poetry waiting for us in our church to discover. That poetry is from time to time inspired. The work of Vaughan, the work of Herbert, the works of Donne, Crashaw, and Marvell sometimes speak personally to us. The works of Vaughan and Herbert are particularly pure and particularly adaptive to our faith. I am thinking of Henry Vaughan's poem "Isaac's Marriage," in which he picks up on the wonderful verse in Genesis about Isaac going into the fields at evening when the camels were coming—when Rebecca was coming to be married to him. It is a magnificent poem, a patriarchal poem that immediately appeals to our patriarchal sense. It echoes the truth.

Milton, who also wrote in the seventeenth century, was a rebel. I think he might have been good material for conversion. He was Cromwell's foreign secretary during the great years when England was a republic (which republic set an example for your own), and he was radically against the restoration of a corrupt king. Certainly, he would have agreed with the fact that spirit is a higher kind of matter. There is also this sense of dedication and hard work in him and the sense of the sacramental in marriage. So in

Milton we have a thinker who is closely associated with the views of the Church. But I fear that even in our church he might have been rebellious about some things.

It is sometimes said that Milton identifies with the devil in *Paradise Lost.* I think this is a superficial judgment, although a man of no less profundity than William Blake made it. Blake was speaking as a romantic when he said that the devil is the hero of *Paradise Lost.* Milton knew exactly what he was doing with the devil's speeches. If we analyze *Paradise Lost* with care, we will find that the devil's speeches are all political speeches, carefully made, carefully crafted, but entirely devoid of feeling because they are intended to manipulate the other devils, humanity, and the devil himself. (One of the worst things that rhetoricians do is to manipulate themselves.) The devil's speeches are clever, but they are devilish, and as devilish, they are not magnificent.

I think that William Blake was somewhat confused about *Paradise Lost* and did not take *Paradise Regained* and *Samson Agonistes* into account. I myself think that *Paradise Regained* and *Samson Agonistes* are Milton's greatest works and that they are greater than *Paradise Lost. Paradise Lost* is too rich, too heroic, too "classical." There is also an imperfection in *Paradise Lost* that has something to do with what Blake observed. I would say that Milton's resentments arising from his private life, from his blindness, and from the wretched political situation he found himself in after the 1660 Restoration all combined for him to put into *Paradise Lost* some impure elements. This doesn't mean that he identifies with the devil but that the devil gets too much of the sort of obvious poetry that we admire. But by the time that Milton gets to *Paradise Regained* and *Samson Agonistes*, he has found another and deeper kind of poetry that is more difficult to learn to admire but is far more pure. At the same time, I still can't forgive the blind Milton for having taught his daughters Hebrew and Greek pronunciation so that they could read to him without teaching them to understand what they were reading.

The Eighteenth Century

When we come to the eighteenth century, we come to a period in which even apostate faith is declining. A second major heresy arises, which may be expressed as follows: "Well, I don't know about the Christian religion, but the morality is good, and it keeps people in order." This heresy contributed to a false and superficial morality in literature, which the Romantic movement was a partial protest against and which helped lead to the development of art for art's sake.

This heresy expresses the attitude of Dean Swift—that despairing man. Hardly anybody has been more deeply despairing than Swift. His typically Anglican view was that the Anglican Church was the right church to keep the people in order. There have been, no doubt, a great many thousands of Anglican divines and others who have thought this way and thanked God for the way the Anglican Church kept the English people in order. But no person of real intelligence could think that the morality of the Sermon on the Mount could possibly be lived, or even approached remotely, except by someone who believed in the Lord Jesus Christ and was trying to follow him.

Is it any wonder that in the nineteenth century Marx was saying that religion is the opium of the people when the apostate churches lay themselves open to that charge by actually being so and being cynically so? You need to have a revolution, such as you had in the United States, in order to destroy illusions such as Swift's. The English had their revolution too early. You probably had yours about the right time; in fact, I am sure you did. After all, the Lord intended that this country be a matrix for our church.

So the eighteenth century, alas, is the age of antienthusiasm, but it is also the age of enthusiastic protest, such as that of John and Charles Wesley. And what I want to draw your attention to is this: it is the nonconformists of the past with whom we may seek kinship, not with the conformists, because the conformists accepted the corruption around them and the nonconformists did not. We conform so well nowadays here in this country, just as we conform in Britain, that we must remember that, in the past, conformity was conformity with an apostate church. And so, we must look in the past to those who dissented as being those who, in some sense, were our forebears: Wycliffe, Luther, George Fox, John Bunyan, Charles and John Wesley, Blake—these are people who looked forward. They might not always have gotten the right doctrine. Bunyan was, after all, a predestinarian, but there is no more magnificent or convincing piece of Christian prose anywhere than at the end of part two of *The Pilgrim's Progress*. It is good that Christianity can sometimes overflow doctrine, but it is important that the doctrine be there because we don't want floods all the time.

When we come to the eighteenth-century poets, we find frequently that they have melancholia or nervous breakdowns or actually go mad or become drunkards because the attitude of pseudo-religion in that age was such, the atmosphere of propriety and decorum in that age was such, as to drive a poet to abnormality. If there is one thing a poet cannot abide, it is a restrictive code of manners interfering with genuine artistic expression. So we get that melancholy, which is evident in a great poem like Gray's *Elegy in a Country Churchyard.*

The eighteenth century is the age of emerging bourgeois morality, and it is the age of the emergence of that great bourgeois form, the novel. So many eighteenth-century novels were written purely at the moral level and not at the religious level, but there were some at the religious level. I speak of the works of our first and greatest novelist in English, Samuel Richardson. Samuel Richardson was a deeply religious man and a deeply moral novelist. He wrote what most modern people have found to be distressingly long novels, but his novels' genius lies in their length. Richardson was a printer, and he learned early to understand the hearts of women because from his youth onward, servant girls and others would have him write letters to their sweethearts for them because they couldn't write themselves. After many years of doing this, there was very little that Richardson didn't know about women. He knew the depths of the female heart, and he used that knowledge to the full in his novels. He had a high regard for women; they survived in his esteem. And he did produce one "ideal" man. As Latter-day Saints, we should become acquainted with the characters of Pamela, of Clarissa Harlowe, and of that ideal young man, Sir Charles Grandison, because these are almost unknown to us and yet they are profoundly Christian people endeavoring to lead Christian lives against difficulty. *Clarissa Harlowe* is a long book. It is a book about a young woman who gets into distress as a result of a mild fault on her part and finally dies magnificently. It takes many chapters for her to die. But the book is a wonderful experience, a wonderful spiritual experience, and it belongs to the gospel because it reflects truth. Richardson's novels are not well known in the Church, but they contain analyses of moral situations appropriate to our church, and we should become better acquainted with them. The tradition of Richardson runs on to the work of Jane Austen, who wouldn't have been what she was but for Richardson.

In your own literature, I draw your attention to two books, both of which are important books in English. One is the *Journal of John Woolman*. The other is the *Autobiography of Benjamin Franklin*. Here are two quotations about drink, one from each book:

> I perceived that many white people do often sell rum to the Indians, which, I believe, is a great evil. First they being thereby deprived of the use of their Reason and their spirits violently Agitated, quarrels often arise which end in mischief, and the bitterness and resentments Ocasioned hereby are frequently of long continuance: again their Skins and furs gotten through much fatigue & hard travels in hunting, with which they intended to buy cloathing, [these] when they begin to be Intoxicated they often Sell at a low rate for more rum, and afterward when they suffer for want of the necessaries of life, are angry with those who for the Sake of gain took the advantage of their weakness; of this their Chiefs have often complained at their Treaties with the English.
>
> Where cunning people pass Counterfeits and impose that on others which is only good for nothing, it is considered as a wickedness, but to sell that to people which we know does them harm, and which often works their Ruin, for the sake of gain manifests a hardened and Corrupt heart; and it is an evil which demands the care of all True lovers of Virtue [in endeavouring] to Suppress. (John Woolman)

> If it be the design of Providence to extirpate these savages in order to make room for cultivators of the earth, it seems not improbable that rum may be the appointed means. (Benjamin Franklin)

Most of you have probably read the *Autobiography of Benjamin Franklin*. Now do yourselves the credit of reading the *Journal of John Woolman*, which is immensely more to the sympathy of Mormons. Benjamin Franklin was deliberately self-assertive, ambitious, manipulative, and cute, and these traits have been expressed in American culture from Benjamin Franklin onwards. John Woolman sought the Spirit daily and hourly in order to make sure that he got the message of the Spirit and not another message. He was never clever. He was never anything but himself, and he was himself because he never thought about himself from the beginning of his life to the end. It was he who really started the American emancipation movement by gradually, throughout his life, persuading the Quakers first to stop selling slaves, then to stop buying them, and finally to release those they still had. He was a humble man to be classed with Thomas à Kempis and Dame Juliana of Norwich: they all three wrote with great limpidity.

The Romantic Period and the Nineteenth Century

And so I come to the Romantic period and back to that first great heresy, which is most dangerous to the arts—the heresy of the artist as hero. This heresy rose in the Renaissance but didn't come to full expression in Anglo-Saxon literature until the Romantic movement. Many of you are familiar with it. The artist found himself against society. He found it difficult to communicate. He was on his own and was proud of being lonely. He attitudinized; he strutted; he looked at himself in the mirror. He was concerned with himself because that is what happens to an artist of talent when he is either cut off from his religion or when he defies it. The artist becomes a replacement for God, and his art a replacement for religion. The heresy of the artist as hero is a dangerous one, and I sometimes see a pale reflection of this in the idea of the Mormon artist.

I invite you to consider the difference between Romantic poets like Wordsworth and Blake—who were partly successful in their lives and in their work because they were good men who were struggling toward morality, toward religion, who were honest and striving and also self-suppressive—compared with people like Coleridge, Byron, Shelley, and Keats, with their self-obsession, their self-pity, their self-aggrandizement, their mawkish sensuality (characteristic Romantic faults), and also with their drugs. Shelley was not technically a good poet, and Shelley was also an abomination as a thinker and a feeler. What did Matthew Arnold say about the company that Shelley and Byron kept? A very typical Victorian comment, but a very correct one: "What a set!" There is nothing like a sense of propriety to put the vulgar in its place. So much of the Romantic movement is profoundly vulgar. Compare the romantic faults of Coleridge, Byron, and Shelley with the irony, limpidity, and moral insight of Jane Austen, who was writing at the same time.

These romantic faults of which I speak are also the faults of Tennyson and Carlyle. They are not faults of Browning. Consider the married life of the Carlyles and the egocentricity, the indigestion, and the peevishness of Carlyle, and then look at his attitudinizing prose in *French Revolution.* His mannered style has something to do with his style of living; they belong together.

In the nineteenth century, there were so many authors imitating the romantics and strutting and caricaturing themselves, and one or two souls were doing their best in difficult circumstances, like Dickens, compelled after visiting a Mormon emigrant ship at the docks to go back and write a magnificent piece about that visit. I recommend that those of you who don't already know that particular article in the *Uncommercial Traveler* read it because it is a wonderfully heartening spiritual experience for us in our church to see what Dickens had to say—was compelled to say—about us. He went to scoff but came away and wrote the plain moving truth about that group of emigrants on that ship.

The novels of George Eliot are sound through and through—positive, loving. Look at all her moral insight in a book like *Middlemarch,* which is a gospel work in its delicate response to people in difficult moral situations and in its evaluation of them. Compare George Eliot with Thomas Hardy, who wrote a little later than Eliot and much admired her. Thomas Hardy failed, because of self-pity, to be a great writer. He handled himself very badly in his personal life and did not have a very strong physical constitution, so he responded with this miserable attitude to the universe which he shared with so many writers of the late nineteenth century. Yet people without vision see writers like Thomas Hardy and say they are great because of their self-pity and because of their complaints about the unfairness of the universe. Think about the last sentence of *Tess of the D'Urbervilles.* Tess has been hanged for the murder of her unwelcome lover. Her sister and her husband are watching the black flag go up. And the last sentence of the book is "The President of the Immortals had finished his sport with Tess." That, as the final sentence of the book, condemns the whole book.

Some Mormons that I know think of Oscar Wilde as great. People admire him for his worst works, like that terrible "Ballad of Reading Gaol" that he wrote when he had been incarcerated for two years for homosexuality. It is the worst example of self-pity and lack of repentance imaginable. It is miserable, it is unhappy, it is remorseful, but it is not repentant because it is full of posturing self-pity. And yet the same man wrote a play that most of you know, *The Importance of Being Earnest*, which is one of the finest castigations of Victorian hypocrisy. God gave Wilde a destructive gift, but he used it also to destroy himself.

In the American tradition, Hawthorne, Melville, Twain, and Henry James are all deeply and sensitively moral writers. Twain's *Huckleberry Finn* is one of the most moral books ever written. Its terrible irony is not lost even upon children. *Huckleberry Finn* has a religious depth, and one sees that Twain must have been struggling against that religious depth in himself all his life. That is why he produced superficiality from time to time. Twain is much greater than George Bernard Shaw, but he keeps reminding one of George Bernard Shaw when he tries to be amusingly rational. He had greater depths than Shaw, but he didn't fulfill them.

Herman Melville is sometimes sincere, sometimes so posturing, yet the same man. Think of Melville imitating Carlyle in *Moby Dick*—posturing. How much of that posturing is ironical? How much of it is narcissistic? How much of it is self-pitying? Both were attitudinizers, men with a sense of sin attitudinizing about that sense of sin, and at the same time so often able to produce points of remarkable religious insight.

Henry James is the greatest of all American novelists and one of the greatest novelists of all time. His sensitivity enabled him to follow sincerity and insincerity right into the crannies of the soul. He has a delicate moral discrimination that we in this church do well to put ourselves into because we shall find ourselves agreeing with it. It is fundamentally Christian because James was still coming out of a fundamentally Christian culture. Henry James is a more subtle writer than George Eliot: she adopted a male pseudonym; he might equally well have adopted a female one. If you don't know James, begin by reading *The Europeans*. He liked to live in Europe, but he knew that it had lost its moral force, whereas America had not yet done so.

The Modern Period

We do not commonly find moral discrimination to the same extent in modern literature. Art, in our time, increasingly represents what it has represented ever since the "Satanic mills" of the Industrial Revolution, of which Blake spoke, went up—the isolation of the individual. Now our church is one in which the individual need feel less isolated. But nevertheless, our insistence on individuality, even in the Church, is taking us towards that isolation. Our insistence needs to be on the family and, above all, on the multigenerational family, not the two-generational family, which came about as a result of the Industrial Revolution.

The isolation of the individual leads to a sense of insufficiency in the individual, and that leads, on the one hand, to individual self-assertion; art is the most profound way in which individuals have asserted themselves since, say, 1770. That self-assertion is deeply antigospel. On the other hand, that sense of insufficiency leads to various types of despair: self-pity, cynicism, solipsism, boredom.

We have not recovered from Romantic self-assertion, but we have broken down. At the beginning, it was self-assertive people like Byron; now it is self-pitiers like Faulkner. Self-pity is the dominant feeling of most modern literature in most countries. It is one of the greatest vices of our time. It is a very natural thing to have if one doesn't believe in God. What a pitiable universe it is if there is no God! No wonder that self-pity thrives. It is also a habitual disease of young people in societies that, unlike so-called primitive societies, tolerate a great gap between physical maturity and marriage. Self-pity is the insidious side of a demonic, satanic generation that has broken down and no longer even believes in its satanism. Baudelaire has given place to F. Scott Fitzgerald and Ernest Hemingway. Baudelaire seems almost magnificent by that comparison.

Self-pity is expressed directly enough in Hemingway and Fitzgerald, less directly in William Faulkner. I read Faulkner as he came out in the latter twenties and early thirties. He is a good second-rate writer. But nevertheless, self-pity is insidiously there in his books, not merely in the unfolding of his plots but in the details of his characterizations. I read my first Hemingway in 1929—*Fiesta* (sometimes known as *The Sun Also Rises*). This is the book of an adolescent influenced by Gertrude Stein. There is a dadaistic style throughout. He writes, not simplicity, but *simplesse.* And he expresses self-pity. The suicide of Hemingway was not an accident; he was an inferior writer for the same kind of reason as that which drove him to suicide. Competent to a certain level though they may be, Faulkner with his despair and Hemingway with his self-pity and his deliberate *simplesse* are not great writers. Yet we see, throughout the world, English departments asking their students to read miserable books because they think of those books as great. And it is the misery that makes them think of those books as great. I am horrified at the way in which people on the BYU campus also exalt writers like Faulkner and Fitzgerald and Hemingway to a high level when the fundamental thing these writers express, either directly or indirectly, is self-pity. Perhaps much of the praise given to this American literature comes from a perverted sense of patriotism.

Self-pity is never constructive. Destruction can be constructive because it gets rid of something bad on the site so that something better can be built there. There are good modern novelists (e.g., Joyce, Orwell, Kafka) who do not pity themselves or pity others as cloaks of themselves but describe the victims without sentimentality.

But self-pity is a morbid disease; it is a kind of self-indulgence instead of repentance. Self-pity is always a weakness, never a strength, and those who express it to any considerable extent in their work are suspect. We have to make up our minds that no amount of so-called technique will rescue such work from moral obloquy.

We are faced with two points about literary art in our time. One is its despair and the other is its difficulty. And for the most part, the difficulty isn't worth struggling over because when we find its solution, it is a despairing solution. Now difficulty in art is a matter of technique, but technique reflects the major ideas of the time, just as morality reflects the major ideas of a time. And permissiveness is a major idea of our time. Permissiveness has become characteristic of art, as it has of morality. Artists have permitted themselves to be difficult and have taken the lead in a desperate effort to attain through moral permissiveness a new salvation. But there is no good art that is immoral; there is not even the good deployment of technique where there is immorality since an immoral purpose vitiates also technical detail.

Today, in the case of art as in the case of morality, a center is lacking, a center which at the same time is outside and inside one. God is no longer the center, and therefore, in terms of Yeats's poem, "Things fall apart; the centre cannot hold." It is not holding in the world at large. The profound split between public and private morality that was manifest in the late seventeenth and eighteenth centuries and handled then in a sophisticated fashion by the aristocracy and covered up in the nineteenth century when it became a desperate middle-class underground war, causing a great deal of individual unhappiness and agony—this split between public and private morality has now broken out generally and is spreading everywhere under the head of permissiveness. It is as if the gargoyles and odd creatures under the choir seats had come down and out and were sitting in the pews.

When a society has ceased to have a religious center, when it has at most an official morality that is slightly permissive and a private morality that is definitely permissive, then the artist is at a loss. And what does the artist turn to? That great heresy, the artist as hero, the artist as center, the artist with the right to self-expression. And what does a right to self-expression mean? The artist may go so far as to consider the right to self-expression so great that he (it is usually a male) does not sufficiently consider the need to communicate, and lacking the common bond of religion between himself and his potential public, he really needs to consider communication more deliberately than the traditional artist needed to. Some artists may be so difficult that they fail to communicate even with themselves; they are not in touch with the part of them that is expressing itself. But expression and communication must go together in an artist. At least some degree of coherence is required of an artist if he is to function in society at all.

The greatest sin being committed by intellectuals in this church is that of accepting as they are the arts of the surrounding culture instead of attacking them by the strength that the gospel should provide. None of us should be ashamed of refusing to be fashionable by following artists into squalor when squalor is not significant, even though people develop a curious kind of taste for it, like children or foals who, not having been taught better, eat their excrement. Let us pray to be better educated in literature so that we embrace the scriptures and the other great writings in English: the works of Chaucer, Shakespeare, Milton, Bunyan, Samuel Richardson, Jane Austen, Charles Dickens, George Eliot, Henry James.

NOTE

[1]Archaic past tense of *choose.*

LANGUAGE

Tarry a little, there is something else.
Merchant of Venice 4.1.305

Address text without
concern for words, and you miss
green shades of meaning,
budding image-clusters, sharp
apropos, florescent schemes,
scent of 'something else,'
wind inspiring the whole bush
gently aflame; a voice.
'The thing wilts? Burns to ashes?'
It flowers beyond us; we fade.

AHK
August 1982

Total Language

WE BELIEVE IN incarnation. The Lord came into flesh as a means of advancement in the same way as we came into flesh as a means of advancement, in order that we might be able to do things we could never do before, as a step in eternal progression. The great incarnation of all time is the incarnation of the Lord, and though he is greater than we, though he is more than we, we are in his likeness—his total likeness—the likeness of his flesh and spirit.

Speech is an act of incarnation by an incarnate person. Every act of speech is an incarnation anew. Our voice is flesh and spirit together; our voice is soul. The word is made flesh for us daily. But people in the Church misunderstand about language in the same way and for the same kinds of reasons that they misunderstand the Church's teachings about sex and marriage. They have brought habits from their puritanical ancestry into the Church. They do not sufficiently realize that there is a difference between using language as an art to express a totality about human beings (just as music does) and using language rationally, nor that the latter is only a pale ghost of the former. This difference is quite fundamental, and even more fundamental when we realize that language has been used in a total way over most of human history and that not until the late seventeenth century did something fundamental start to change.

T. S. Eliot spoke of a dissociation of sensibility occurring at the end of the seventeenth century. He was speaking of the separation of sensibility from language, which made for an increasingly rational language. I doubt whether he fully realized the widespread European nature of what was going on. It began with Descartes in

France and spread later to Germany, but it had its most rapid, widespread, and devastating effect in pragmatic England and thence in America (contrast John Woolman's *Journal* with Benjamin Franklin's *Autobiography*). The Enlightenment, natural-scientific development, and technological development are all linked with Eliot's dissociation of sensibility. They were made possible by what Bishop Sprat advocated in *The History of the Royal Society* a few decades after the Royal Society had begun in 1660: a simpler language more suitable for expressing scientific thought. The founders of the Royal Society realized that in order to communicate scientific procedure, they had to write in a direct and limited way. It took time; they could not rid themselves of the Ciceronian style with which they had been brought up. Yet in the end, language was deliberately simplified in order to gain more control over it for certain purposes—in the first place for the promulgation of the scientific and industrial revolutions. That enormous leap forward of mathematics in the seventeenth century certainly had a great deal to do with the simplification of language. Mathematics took language with it. Language became more and more logical, more and more discursive. Mathematics helped to pull language into a rational, logical direction.

In the eighteenth and nineteenth centuries, rational language became a highly effective means of technical control, and its success led to its spread into other, more diverse educational fields. Being rational, being objective, being scientific became popular. Unfortunately, as scientific specialization increased and the quality of general education declined, scientists (and others) became less able to handle even rational discourse. What took its place was a "scientific" discourse characterized by jargon, periphrasis, passives, and complex syntax. The flow of metaphoric speech (still flowing freely in the Cambridge Platonists) was pruned first into simplification (as in Locke), then into a dangerous simplification through Berkeley and Hume, and has ended in cliché and jargon. As a result of this, academic language in the twentieth century is inaccessible to most people.

One of the characteristics of our culture is that the more learned we are, the fewer people we write for. A great deal of research now goes on with fewer and fewer people being able to understand what is going on in the language that is used. There are groups of scientists and scholars who have their own talk for themselves and who often do not realize or bother that the outside world does not understand this talk. I am thinking of the jargons of psychology, sociology, and the physical sciences, and perhaps worst of all (because it penetrates our newspapers and magazines more widely) the jargon of literary men, who have their own "scientific" language. These specialists use jargon in order, as it were, to protect, to build a wall around their specialties. The jargon keeps out other people who are not qualified. It says, in effect, "This is our closed group and we have this kind of way of talking, and other people don't understand this way of talking." Groups in the academic world often will not even consider the criticisms that outside people offer because these criticisms are not put in the "right language," which means that the language of these groups has become a wall instead of being a path. Yet learning should enable us to write for more and more people. And if the experts who use the language were educated, they could do what was done earlier on—put themselves not into jargon, but into cogent language. In the eighteenth century, educated people understood each other. I am thinking, for example, of Dr. Johnson's ability to handle a book on architecture or a book on mathematics. That time is gone.

As you in America developed mass production, so I think you were largely responsible for the jargon of the social sciences. There was a time during the war when we had an Allied Ministers of Education Conference in London. When the Americans entered the war, they sent sociologists and historians over to join this Allied Conference, which afterwards became UNESCO. The style changed, the minutes changed, the whole way of talking about everything changed. Jargon came into the documents, and plain prose fled out the window. And in spite of Ernest Barker's efforts to stop the rot, the rot was there to stay: the jargon was there to remain in international institutions. Today there are many institutions in the United Nations using their own kind of jargon, initiated by social scientists in the United States.

I do not suggest that the influx of jargon is a controlled process, but it is an extremely important historical process. We can follow it in some detail in Britain and France, but it has achieved its widest development in the United States, from which it has been imitated in the USSR and China. The effect is worsened because the most powerful minds internationally now go into science, engineering, and medicine and leave less able minds to look after the other subjects. There has, for example, been a decline in the quality of sermons in the Anglican Church during the last two hundred years and in the quality of journalistic prose during the last hundred. Weaker minds have been addressing themselves to what used to attract the best minds in the community—to literature—and by now perhaps only weaker minds are producing music and fine arts.

By now, so-called objective or scientific language and the jargons that, in our decline, we have developed from that language have spread everywhere. Total language is a dying memory. The desire for "objectivity" set language on an amoral course, which is, of course, an impossibility: if language is not moral, it is immoral. Whether or not this was due to the inevitable decline of faith that is linked up with the simplified natural-scientific approach, I cannot say for certain. We can say either that the decline of faith helped the decline of language or that the decline of language helped the decline of faith, or both. However it was, language became impoverished for moral purposes, for human communication, for our total selves.

Language of Religion

The language of religion has from the beginning been the language of the total soul, the most profound and widespread rhetorical language with the maximum amount of effect. The truths we find in the scriptures are not couched in the prose appropriate to a scientist announcing a discovery to the world for the first time and trying to persuade other people to believe it. The language of the scriptures is the language of and to the whole individual; by that, I mean language that appeals to the whole individual—language that is there not simply to give us plain sense (and there is plenty of plain sense in the scriptures), but to back up that plain sense with an appeal couched in emotive language that enables us to feel the truth and exhorts us to follow the truth. The scriptures ask us to be different, not to think different. That is what conversion is about. We can be intellectually converted without being converted at all.

The scriptures are written in the language of the whole individual in order that we might liken them unto ourselves, to feel, to see with the inner eye, to be made whole. The scriptures are history, but like all history, they must be a parable about ourselves, about us now. The language of the image, the metaphor, the example, the parable, the story, is the language of likening—we can liken it unto ourselves. The scriptures can teach us wisdom when, otherwise, if they were merely an abstract set of principles, they would teach us only inoperable rationality.

Only if we are naive and without learning nowadays are we able to approach the scriptures with that totality that is needed for them. If we are half-educated (and nearly all education nowadays is half education), we are at a loss with the scriptures. What do we do with them? We abstract principles from them. And when I use the word principle here, I don't use it in the way Joseph Smith used it in his writings. We abstract ideas. We abstract "concepts." That word "concept" has recently crept into our church, and we now come across it in the pedagogical material of our church. But I do not find the word in the Bible or the Book of Mormon. It is not "concepts" with which we are concerned in scriptural writings. When the Lord uttered his Beatitudes, he did not say, "Blessed is peace," but, "Blessed are the peacemakers" (Matt. 5:9). He did not speak of guilelessness, but said, "Blessed are the pure in heart" (Matt. 5:8). He did not say, "Blessed is persecution," but, "Blessed are ye when men shall revile you" (Matt. 5:10). Reality is not peace, but peacemakers, and peace exists only in peacemakers. Reality is not mercy, but people with mercy in their hearts. The ultimate reality is not love, but a loving person: God is a person, not an abstract. We must not lose the great traditions of our forefathers, who knew how to handle and respond to the language of scripture but would have raised their eyebrows at "concepts."

It is not helpful to think that all there is in the scriptures is a plain message that we can dig out and reformulate for ourselves. There are people who are willing (at the low emotive level at which they choose to live) to take the scriptures as a number of messages of plain sense that can be encapsulated, that can be learned, that can be called principles, and that one then lives by. But that is not living by every word that cometh out of the mouth of the living God.

We read in the First Epistle of John, the letters of Paul, and the Old Testament, about the bowels, "his bowels of compassion" (1 Jn. 3:17); "refresh my bowels in the Lord" (Philem. 20); "my bowels are troubled for him" (Jer. 31:20); "my bowels shall sound like an harp" (Isa. 16:11); "my bowels were moved for him" (Song 5:4); "his bowels did yearn upon his brother" (Gen. 43:30). What a wonderful image that is of the reaction of the whole soul. We don't feel that way nowadays. We have lost it. Something has happened in our thorax or abdomen to separate us into two pieces. Our bowels don't move with compassion—they don't move with any language of any kind. And yet they once did when human beings were total souls, before we introduced some kind of ideological-neurological plate into our middles.

The scriptures are the word of the whole God to the whole being. And so it is the whole soul of the scriptures that we are to find, and the soul is there as a powerful act of incarnation. What is the object of the parable of the prodigal son? It is to give us, by means of a piece of the highest art, Christ's own art, the Lord's own art, an experience—an experience of what it is like to repent, of what it is like to forgive, of what it is abominably like to envy—so that we may wish to repent and forgive and wish to shun envy.

Who was ever persuaded to repent by discussing an abstract concept of repentance? Who was ever persuaded to forgive by studying an abstract idea of forgiveness? What repentance is it that is not the repentance of the whole of us? What forgiveness is it that is not forgiveness by and of the whole individual? The parable is intended to be, not an illustration of a principle, but an example to be followed and a feeling to be conveyed. If we miss the experience, we have missed the point of the parable.

Christ taught in simplicity, and the parable of the prodigal son is an utterly simple story. Such simplicity is sometimes too much for some of us, and we proceed to try and explain the parable in language more complicated than the language Christ himself used. And indeed, in a culture that uses jargon a great deal, we cease to be capable of understanding simple things. Our ancestors were in this matter better off than we: they may not have had much formal education, but they did read the scriptures, and this helped to make their speech straightforward, simple, and expressive. The Church needs to try as far as possible to follow the pattern of the scriptures in simplicity, although this may require harder work than complexity does. The more simply we write, the more internationally understood we shall be.

Christ made that parable to touch our hearts, and it touches mine so much that I cannot possibly read it through aloud. I always break down at the same point, the point at which the father runs to meet the son. This is the greatest story in the world, and that particular verse is its climax. It enables us to have the overwhelming experience of what it means to be forgiven by the Lord of all mankind, this overwhelming feeling that no matter how far down we have fallen, we can nevertheless repent. The experience is there in that parable, and unless we have that experience, we have not got the ontology of our religion at all. We have something of ethics, we have something of philosophy, we have something of theology, but we haven't got the fundamental ontological fact, which is the love of God.

What is true of the scriptures is also true of the greatest literature: it is written in total language, and we must be whole men and women when we read it. If we read a great piece of literature in a total way, we go away with an experience that we haven't had before. But if we start trying to extract a message from it, we end up with a construct instead of an experience. People are always making these constructs, which are a kind of scaffolding. But the scaffolding is not the building. We put the scaffolding up in order to be able to reconstruct the building. The scaffolding gives the sense that the building is inside it, but if we take the scaffolding down, the building is not there—we do not know where it is.

Our experience of a work of art is fundamental, and we need to pay attention to it. When I went to Cambridge, Richards and Leavis taught me the necessity of discovering what one felt about a work of art in terms of minute observations of what was happening to one and not just a general kind of blur, appropriate perhaps (as some people thought, at least) to a lyric of Shelley's. (We didn't like Shelley at Cambridge in those days.) Some people say there is nothing to observe—they haven't got any responses. The answer is that not having any is itself a response and a starting point. What do you mean by saying you haven't got any responses? You must have some response. Is it disgruntlement? Is it fear? Is it disapproval? Is it boredom? Whatever it is, you start from there and say, "Why do I feel this way about this work?" And in answering that question, you have to look in your total mind for what is relevant and not merely in your rational mind. You have to draw on your own experience.

My Shakespeare classes sometimes get into trouble because they try to find out what reactions I want them to have. I don't want them to have any particular reactions. I want them to have their own, nobody else's. They expect to be taught how to respond. I can't teach anybody how to respond. I ought not to. A great deal of damage is done by people who say, "You ought to respond to a thing in this or that way." It is a satanic job to do that. What I can teach people, and what anybody else can teach them, is techniques by which they can discipline their own responses: ways for them to find out more about the work before them so that their experience of it may be a more profound one.

If we come away from an experience and ask ourselves what it means or what it is all about, we are asking ourselves the wrong kind of question because what we have just experienced is what it is all about. An important experience is an end in itself. It isn't something that is to prepare us for something else. It already contains the something else if it is worthwhile. Life is its own explanation. The meaning of life is in life. It is an aspect of the incarnation. God enters history and gives it meaning, so it is not for us to have ideas about history but to find God in history. The experience of a work of art is analogous to the experience of following the Master. It is as we incorporate the life of the Master that we can do what the Master wants us to do. The imitation that Christ makes of his Father is total and perfect. The imitation that we are asked to make of him is as deep, as profound, as total as we can make it. And it is through that imitation that we become children of Christ, having his image engraven upon us. In the same way, when we experience a work of art, we incorporate it into ourselves (and that is the word—incorporate), we change, become better, act differently.

Totalities and Particulars

When I went to study in Lund, Sweden, I learned by experience the way of philology, which is to study languages in order to study literature better. I learned Old English, primitive Germanic, Indo-European, Old Norse, and Medieval Latin in order to study English texts. Literally, philology means "love of the word," and we in our religion can regard that word "word" as meaning all that it can mean. And indeed, it can't mean anything with a small letter unless it means something with a capital letter—love of the Word. Philology is a way of saying, "I will deal with the words. I will take care of the pence, and the pounds will take care of themselves." It is saying, "Throw all the ideas out of the window unless they are based on actual words." Philology means that the first attention in studying texts is to the detail—all the time.

One of the tragedies of the twentieth century is the separation of philology into the study of literature and the study of language, and not only that, but the hearty dislike that literary people have for language and the hearty contempt that language people have for literature (or at least literary people). The two have separated widely, not simply in approach, but in the emotions they feel for one another; this is one of the worst examples of *invidia academica*, or academic hate. What happened was that literary people reacted against the tyranny and slavery of all the detailed philological work of going into the etymology, the pronunciation, etc., of all the words in a work, which they said destroyed one's reaction to the work as a whole. But the literary people reacted so strongly against philological study that they ignored the fact that the material collected by the philologist was extremely useful for literary purposes. I think that this split of philology into linguistics and literature is a very bad split indeed. It means that the linguists end up half-educated and that the literary people end up vague. The precision of linguistics is false and the vagueness of the literary critics leads nowhere.

Literary people had a point in their criticism of philology. The object of analyzing works of art is to enjoy them better as wholes. If, as a result of our analysis, we destroy what is in front of us, we have taken away the purpose of our enjoyment. It is wisdom to know which wholes can be explained by studying the parts and which can't—to know, for example, that we examine Milton with a telescope and John Donne with a microscope because these are the appropriate ways of approaching these people. If we did it the other way around, the effect would be monstrous. We can't just scrutinize Milton's style in the kind of way that we scrutinize Donne's. One of the great secrets of enjoying art is learning to know how a piece is constructed to a certain point. Beyond that point, analysis may not be profitable. That does not necessarily mean that the piece is vague. It may mean that the piece has a quality that is not definable and that, nevertheless, acts on our lives, but if we try to explain that quality, it is dissipated.

But the trouble with literary people is that they are not interested in literature anymore; they are interested in "ideas." They bring in "ideas" from psychology, anthropology, metaphysics, wherever, to replace the detailed study of literature. They do not understand what Blake wrote, "Virtue resides in minute particulars." Every particular of a work of art reflects the totality, and the totality is in all the particulars. The microcosms reflect the macrocosm, and the macrocosm encloses, in itself, the qualities of all the microcosms. We can find the totality of a work of art in its particulars, but we can't find it in "ideas."

All those disciplines that insist on a premature whole, instead of immersing in the parts, fail. Nearly all readers nowadays go for the premature whole and pass up studying the parts because they find studying the parts boring. I don't know why. Perhaps they haven't learned to study the parts. It is the most fascinating of studies. Boredom with words, boredom with the printed word is, of course, one of the principal diseases of our time, and it is so much the worse, unfortunately, because of the increasing predominance of the visual image.

In dramatic terms, the relationship between particulars and totality means that, if a director produces a Shakespearean play with the proper attention to all the details in the play, Shakespeare will look after himself, and his totality will appear on the stage. But if the director tries to impose a slant on Shakespeare or says, "I will use Shakespeare as an exposition of my own personality," which even some of the best of our directors seem to do, then of course the director won't get Shakespeare. I once heard a talk at an international Shakespeare conference in Washington by the then-director of the Royal Shakespeare Company, Terry Hands. I am grateful to him for it because I have spent my whole mature existence trying to fight for what he had to say. Hands said more or less that he had given up the notion that the director of a production should interpret the whole, put a stamp on the play by giving it a slant. He regarded the play as a poem, and he thought directors should pay the utmost attention to getting the details in each speech right for the actors; if they got all the details right, he believed that if the play was great the interpretation of the play would be there for the audience not by imposition, but by experience. Now that is essentially the point that I make about literary study. It should consist in learning the utmost about the language of the work in front of you, putting yourself into it, gaining your experience from that, and then being content because you have got what the author intended you to get. If the author had wanted you to get something else, something else would have been written; but it wasn't.

The thing to do with great works of art is to observe all the detail we can about them, not try to establish some kind of superficial philosophical grid to put them on because then they escape us. We gain by going into the utmost detail that we can, by not being vague or blubbery about what we have read, but by being keen about it, studying it again and again. This is hard work, but by degrees, by dealing with literature in this way, we become more sensitive to it and more sensitive to ourselves.

If we don't have the patience to go through a thing again and again, we shall never have the experience of discovering how unique it is. Remember Professor Agassiz's exercise on the fish. Students look at the fish for three hours and think they have observed enough. Then they look at it for three days and think that is enough. They stay nine days on that fish and they haven't exhausted it, and by that time they realize that that fish isn't exhaustible. There are poems I know that I can repeat from sixty years back and something will strike me that I have never noticed before. People get bored with the temple ceremony because they haven't the patience to get into it to the point at which they realize there is always more for them to understand and experience. The same can be said for the scriptures. But it all takes discipline. If we study something thoroughly and in detail, it leaves a model in our minds; we have broken through, we can raise our standards. All of us need to do something in detail because unless we have, we have not been educated.

Let me illustrate what I am saying about how to approach texts by saying something about how to approach both the Authorized Version of the Bible (KJV) and Shakespeare, which are similar tasks. The dialect of the Authorized Version is much the same as the dialect of Shakespeare. The Bible dates from the early seventeenth century but is based on other texts which were written between the fourteenth and the late sixteenth centuries. The language of the Authorized Version is not the language of 1611; it is a compromise between the language of 1611 and the language of the various other versions, from Wycliffe down through Coverdale and Tyndale, the Bishops' Bible, the Geneva Bible, and the Douay Bible. The translators had all these before them, together with Latin, Greek, and Hebrew texts, as they sat around that table at Hampton Court.

Because the dialects of Shakespeare and the Authorized Version are similar, the more Shakespeare we read, the easier we shall find it to read the Authorized Version of the Bible; and the more of the Authorized Version of the Bible we read, the easier we shall find it to read Shakespeare. There are various ways of coming to understand texts written in this dialect. I do not recommend books about the texts themselves but books that help us unlock the meaning of the texts—books that get us further into them.

Understanding both the Bible and Shakespeare entails learning the meanings of words as they were used in Shakespeare's and the Bible's day. We have the best dictionary in the world for that purpose, the Oxford English Dictionary. (The two-volume compact but complete set is much cheaper than the original thirteen-volume set.) This dictionary differs from others in that it gives not only definitions but contexts in which the words have occurred throughout history. Under each word, there is quotation after quotation so that we may pick up from the quotations, rather than the definitions, what the word meant. That book is a summary of the linguistic tradition of the English-speaking peoples. When you want to find out what a word in Shakespeare means, the Oxford English Dictionary will nearly always tell you—often it will even give the actual quotation. And when you want to find out what the scriptures mean when they say that David "prevented the dawning of the morning" (Psalms 119:147), you will discover by looking up the word "prevent" that David was not another Joshua.

The way to understand a word's meaning is through contexts, not definitions. A word inside a tradition is all the contexts in which it has ever been used in that tradition: it exists in the tradition as its history within the tradition. That is why one of the most important things in language study is etymology, and it seems to me so important that etymology ought to be taught in general education and not simply as a side subject incidental to other subjects. The Chinese, because of their ideograms, have something of the etymology of their words. But unless we learn Latin and French and the etymology of the Anglo-Saxon side, we do not know what our words mean as much as we could if we knew that.

A word is in a tradition only by being in our individual selves, and it is in our individual selves only as its history within us. A word inside us is all the contexts in which we have ever spoken, heard, or seen it. We walk through the world "trailing clouds" of glorious words, and these words have their value not because of precision and clarity, but because of suggestiveness and richness. We do not trail these words with us as groups of precisions.

There is no such thing as the meaning of a word nor is there such a thing as a category of meanings of the word. We can identify points, as it were, in a word's field, but they don't usually stand alone; other points come in. There are nuclei, if you like, and there are penumbras around the nuclei; the penumbras overlap, and sometimes the nuclei themselves overlap. The words we trail are groups of interacting nuclei. Therefore, when we look up a word in a dictionary, we want to remember that the word is not to be nailed down but to be pinpointed on the chart. The definition covers perhaps a number of senses that are aroused by its context. There may be a central sense, and there may be a penumbra of senses around it. I remember J. R. Firth once saying that language is an infinite number of infinitesimally small octopuses with an infinite number of tentacles each infinitely interacting. A word is, in fact, a thoroughly biological thing. It is very like a number of living cells. (J. R. Firth also said that there is no such thing as a language; a language is a proliferation of languages whose common denominator has sufficiently prompted us to regard them as one language, but the common denominator is a conglomeration of a number of languages.)

Besides dictionaries, other translations of the Bible can help us get at the meanings of words in the Bible. Maybe it is a simple question of whether Rebecca's ring (Gen. 24:22) was an earring or a nose ring. The Authorized Version translators were rather shocked to think that Rebecca should wear a nose ring, so they called it an earring, though it is not worse to wear a nose ring than to wear earrings. Those who are in the habit of wearing earrings might well remember that it is quite as sensible or silly to wear a nose ring as earrings. I like to use Bibles in all the languages that I read because I always get some slightly different impression from each translation. In our own language, we have modern translations—the worthy effort of the Protestants in the New English Bible and the perhaps somewhat more scholarly effort of the Catholics in the Jerusalem Bible. I use these two regularly, and there are other American versions with which you are familiar. And, of course, there is the Inspired Version. I also recommend a limited study of Latin and Greek. It is not difficult. With a grammar and dictionary, you can teach yourself what you need in only a short while. The Latin Vulgate is very easy to read. For the Greek New Testament, get an interlinear text with translation.

Here is a good exercise in using other versions of the Bible: Look at chapter 27 of Acts, which tells about Paul's journey from Palestine to Rome. Look at the prepositions in that chapter and make up your mind with the assistance of other versions of the Bible what those prepositions really mean. What does "under Crete" mean, for example? If you do that, you will find that that account, straightforward and simple as it seems, is detailed and factual, and you will have a much clearer idea of what happened to Paul during the voyage and when the ship ran aground at Malta.

Concordances are also invaluable reference books in studying Shakespeare and the Bible (and modern scripture also) because in any work, the words have to be understood in terms of the whole work: their meaning inside the work may be different from their meaning outside of it or in another work. For instance, the words "honor" and "honorable" are used differently in *Julius Caesar* from how they are in *Coriolanus.* We can't just work a cross between the two sets because "honor" and "honorable" are used in *Julius Caesar* in a satirical way and in *Coriolanus* in a positive way. We should ask and be able to answer questions like: How is the word "honorable" being used in this cliché speech of Mark Antony's? What is Falstaff doing with it on the field of battle? How is Harry Hotspur shooting his head off with it at the beginning of the play? These are fundamental questions about words that can lead us forward to a better understanding of Shakespeare. For Shakespeare, Marvin Spevack's *Harvard Concordance to Shakespeare* gives all the contexts of all but the very commonest words in Shakespeare.

Words may not mean outside scriptural contexts what they mean inside them. We should learn to understand contexts better by referring to other similar contexts and thus enrich the history of the key words in our minds. 1 Corinthians 13 is a great poem; as it proceeds with its statements about charity, we get a stronger and stronger sense of the word. By the time we have finished the chapter, the senses of "charity" have developed and become enriched in our minds, so "charity" means far more to us than it meant at the beginning of the chapter. And clearly, the word "faith" means something less in verse 2 than it does in verse 13.

I end by quoting from Alexander Pope's greatest poem, the greatest passage in that poem. The poem is *The Dunciad.* I might wish that I were capable of writing about modern criticism a poem like *The Dunciad,* which Pope wrote about his contemporaries' learning, but luckily I don't need to because Pope's *The Dunciad* has remained true about learning ever since it was written. His main target is critics who are interested in expressing themselves by importing their own ideas into a work of art. *The Dunciad* ends with that tremendous invocation of the goddess Dullness and a prophecy of our modern world:

In vain, in vain—the all-composing Hour
Resistless falls: the Muse obeys the Pow'r.
She comes! she comes! the sable Throne behold
Of *Night* primeval and of *Chaos* old!
Before her, *Fancy's* gilded clouds decay,
And all its varying Rain-bows die away.
Wit shoots in vain its momentary fires,

The meteor drops, and in a flash expires.
As one by one, at dread Medea's strain,
The sick'ning stars fade off th' ethereal plain;
As Argus' eyes by Hermes' wand opprest,
Closed one by one to everlasting rest;
Thus at her felt approach, and secret might,
Art after *Art* goes out, and all is Night.
See skulking *Truth* to her old cavern fled,
Mountains of Casuistry heap'd o'er her head!
Philosophy, that lean'd on Heaven before,
Shrinks to her second cause, and is no more.
Physic of *Metaphysic* begs defence,
And *Metaphysic* calls for aid on *Sense*!
See *Mystery* to *Mathematics* fly!
In vain! they gaze, turn giddy, rave, and die.
Religion blushing veils her sacred fires,
And unawares *Morality* expires.
For *public* Flame, nor *private*, dares to shine;
Nor *human* Spark is left, nor Glimpse *divine*!
Lo! thy dread Empire, CHAOS! is restored;
Light dies before thy uncreating word;
Thy hand, great Anarch! lets the curtain fall,
And universal Darkness buries All.[1]

That is one of the greatest passages in all literature. It is completely negative, completely destructive, but it is great. What it is destroying is the whole hypocritical world of nonsense. Prophetic Pope: he foresaw the appalling dullness of contemporary life. There is no alternative to universal darkness except light. That light we are given, within and without. And it is in that light that we should be able to reconcile—as they are reconciled in the light of Christ—the totalities and the details. Take care of the pence, and the pounds will take care of themselves. The words of scripture and the words of the greatest of literature are words that contain in their particulars the totalities that are relevant to us.

NOTE

[1]Alexander Pope, *The Dunciad*, in *The Best of Pope*, ed. George Sherburn (New York: Thomas Nelson, 1931), book 4, lines 627–56.

Rhetoric

WE LIVE ON the wrong side of a rhetorical watershed—we no longer understand the art of speaking and writing. The turning point came in the late nineteenth century. Many older people as I was growing up, even comparatively uneducated people, still understood and appreciated this art. I remember my grandfather eagerly looking into the paper the morning after a judge had made a great summing up, say, in a murder trial. My grandfather wasn't interested in the gory details, but he was interested in the way the judge did the summing up—in the way the judge spoke. I remember my grandfather talking about the speeches of Gladstone and the speeches of Disraeli. And there were hundreds of thousands of people like my grandfather in England and in this country, too. One of the interests in those days was public speaking; people took pleasure in going to a meeting and hearing someone speak well. It was an important part of life. Today this pleasure is almost entirely lost.

It is not so long ago since yours was a great rhetorical country, just as mine was. In your country, there were also great public figures who made great speeches. Americans, in fact, retained interest in traditional rhetoric rather longer than we did in Britain. I can think of twentieth-century Americans who were still writing and speaking in that way—for example, Clarence Darrow and William Jennings Bryan, two rhetoricians we followed during the "monkey trials" in Tennessee. There is only one example in Britain, and that was Winston Churchill. He made very good use of rhetoric during the war. Those speeches that he made in 1940 and 1941 were carefully worked on. He practiced them and learned them by heart; he worked on them as an actor. They had much more effect for that reason. When Churchill was composing his famous speech, "We shall fight on the beaches, we shall fight on the landing grounds, we shall fight in the fields and in the streets, we shall fight in the hills," he added, but did not say publicly, "We'll beat them over the head with bottles, if necessary, for that's about all we've got." That was his ironical comment on the speech he was building. At the same time, it was an accurate reflection of the situation. We had left all our equipment behind in Dunkirk. We had practically nothing. People were drilling with pieces of wood. I think you see the rhetorical point. Some of us would have preferred the beating over the head with bottles and would have responded better to that, though, for most people, it wouldn't have worked. But even Churchill didn't give that kind of speech much after he lost the election of 1945 because people no longer wanted to be addressed in great speeches—that is perhaps why he lost. A public-speaking manner didn't fit with the coming of radio and television. One had to have a private manner and a totally different style. Roosevelt seems to have been the first to try this.

When rhetoric declined in public life, political life, and social life, it also declined in the educational process because it seemed no longer needed in order to be successful in the community. Schools stopped teaching rhetoric shortly after World War I. (I am told textbooks can still be found in the BYU library.) Students today may even take English or humanities at a university without becoming familiar with rhetoric. The only place they are likely to meet it is in studying Latin or Greek. Those who learn Latin or Greek can't help but learn a good deal of rhetoric. Those who learn modern languages, if they learn something of the sixteenth and seventeenth centuries, will learn something about it. But for the most part, our schooling leaves this out.

What is taught nowadays is "modern rhetoric." And when we talk about "modern rhetoric," we are talking about rhetoric in the narrow sense. It is the false rhetoric of the sophists and orators that has become the false rhetoric of the advertisers, the journalists, and the politicians in our time. In contemporary society, rhetoric has come to mean decoration, a way of misleading, a way of telling untruths. But there is an important difference between rhetoric as manipulation and rhetoric as expression; expression need not be manipulation.

In the Middle Ages, they taught the disciplines of language in the following order: first grammar, then logic, and finally rhetoric. Rhetoric subsumed both grammar and logic. Logic dealt with means of persuasion; rhetoric dealt with modes of expression. Rhetoric prepared students to analyze writing and to write and deliver speeches. It attempted to describe the effect of language on attitude and feeling and what appeals to the "whole being."

We, for the most part, have lost the learning of language as a totality, and insofar as we have lost it, we have lost the power not simply to read the great classics, but also to read the scriptures. Learning to read the scriptures and learning to read the classics are much the same kind of activity because the scriptures and the classics come from the same rhetorical tradition. Although some rhetorical figures are more stressed in Greek literature and others more stressed in Hebrew literature, the fact remains that the use of rhetorical figures is very similar. Take the word *chiasmus*, which people are using in talking about the scriptures, especially the Book of Mormon, not realizing that there are other important rhetorical figures used in the scriptures. People are fascinated by that one, and it quite rightly is an important one, but there are more than twenty others that are at least as important. *Chiasmus* is a Greek word, but it is a favorite Hebrew device. *Parallelism*—saying the "same thing" twice or more in somewhat different words—is another Greek word that is also a Hebrew figure. It is, in fact, a staple factor of Hebrew verse. This rhetorical way of writing is characteristic of the scriptures, of Greek plays, of Shakespeare, and of much other great writing, so it is quite wrong to think that scripture is totally different in expression from this other literature.

When I talk about a rhetorical approach to the scriptures and great literature, I am always thinking about an approach that is helping us to understand the meaning, and I am using that word "meaning" in its fullest sense—the full amount of content that we can get from a passage, including that which is revealed by the voice. I want to be more specific now about ways to find that meaning.

Reading Aloud

It was the practice in the ancient world to read aloud to oneself as well as to other people, and it was a general practice in Britain and in other countries to do so until the nineteenth century. Many people in the early part of the twentieth century continued the art of reading aloud because, at that time, reading to each other was still one of the chief means of entertainment. And because it was, students learned in their schools how to read aloud. They practiced reading passages of great literature and reading, of course, the scriptures, which were still considered proper material for the schools. Now with television as our entertainment, the schools have completely abandoned the teaching of this art. They teach their students how to read to themselves, not how to read to each other. College graduates today know less about reading aloud than their great-grandparents knew in the fifth grade.

There are two habits that have developed in our time: silent reading and rapid reading. I have nothing against speed reading, provided that it is kept for the valueless material for which it is valuable. But those who read great writing and the greatest of all, the scriptures, silently to themselves are losing something inestimable. How many of us read the scriptures aloud daily? The scriptures will not give us what they have to give unless we read them aloud to ourselves and to others and hear them read aloud. If we hear them read aloud, we are much more likely to get a total response than if we merely read them silently. They are written in total language, and only the voice will help us to fulfill that and understand it.

Our voice knows things that we don't know it knows. It has been with us all our lives, and it has undertaken a lot of things. When we use our voices, we may be aware of some of the things we are doing, but most of what we are doing we are not in the least aware of. The voice carries us; the voice sums us up and coaches us in terms of our lives; the voice reflects our lives. It is the carrier to us of inflections, feelings (irony, bitterness, anything you like), and all sorts of things coming from inside us moment to moment, mostly things we have not planned for. We must therefore trust our voices to be able to tell us things that we wouldn't know if we didn't use them. If we are not in the habit of listening to our voices, we should tape ourselves and play ourselves back. We may find much. Perhaps most important is that we read to each other regularly, as couples, as families, listening to each other and telling each other what we are hearing.

I try to teach my students in religion classes to listen to what they are doing when they read. I show them that they may give a verse in the scriptures a number of different meanings or shades of meaning according to the stress that they give it. For example, the first two verses of the Gospel according to St. John may be read this way: "In the BEGINNING was the WORD, and the Word was with GOD, and the Word WAS God. The SAME was in the beginning with God." That is one way of doing it—a way in which to get the plain sense, the plain antithetical sense out of that verse. There is another way of doing it, which might almost be called worship, that goes like this: "In the BEGINNING was the WORD, and the WORD was with GOD, and the WORD was GOD. The SAME was in the BEGINNING with GOD." Now that is what I call rhetorical stress intended to convey the supreme importance of Deity. It is a very different way of reading from the first way. The possibility of reading it either way is there in the Greek, too, or in any language. The point is not that one or the other is the correct reading, but that they are doing slightly different jobs, so that we have one experience when the passage is read one way and another experience when it is read another way. And both of those experiences are valid. But if we just read it to ourselves, without reading it aloud or hearing it read aloud, those differences will not be clear to us. Listening to ourselves read the scriptures aloud, then, is one of the best ways to see what we have got is a shimmering jewel that will show different lights according to the way in which the light plays upon it, and not just a plain piece of dull stuff.

In a lay church like ours where everybody has the opportunity of participating, we all need to learn to read aloud, beginning as young as possible. We need to learn to speak, and I imagine that in our church there is more attention paid to this than in most places. As a result of our tradition for public speaking, we can expect people in our church to be better at reading aloud than people generally are elsewhere, just as they are better than others at forming committees and other things that have to do with the relationship of soul and soul. We can expect them to do better, but you and I know what they do is inadequate. Women's reading is perhaps, on the whole, better than men's when there is no particular instruction on the matter because women are more willing to let their feelings come through than men are. I should like to see everybody who goes to the pulpit read sufficiently well, not merely to be understood, but to convey something of what is there to be conveyed, which is after all not simply plain sense but high emotion, too.

Conveying emotions is important. But how ought one to do that? When I was at Cambridge fifty-five years ago, there were two opposing schools. One school said, “Read to make yourself clear, but don’t read in such a way as to impose your emotions on other people. Let them have their own reactions to the piece.” The other school said, “Read with your whole soul; put into it whatever feelings you can find to put into it.” But alas, those who do that may readily degenerate into second- or third-rate actors. It is one thing to read with feeling that you genuinely have, but it is another thing to read in order to make other people feel. It seems to me that that is manipulation and a sin. To make other people feel without feeling yourself is profoundly wrong unless you are an actor. When I was an undergraduate at Cambridge, I held to the other school, which said, “Read as well as you can, read warmly if you will, but allow other people to have their emotions for the piece, and don’t impose what you affect to be your own.” There is a great deal to be said for that. So rather than try to *put* feeling into our reading, let us just read and then afterwards listen to what feelings came out.

Rhetorical Figures

I want to go on now to other ways of getting at the full meaning of a passage. To get that, we should learn the common rhetorical figures, including their names. Some of these you know already. The important thing is to be able to feel the impact of these figures, but we feel their impact more when we can identify them. I never realized until I went to stay with an uncle who was a botanist how much more I could enjoy flowers when I knew their names. “A rose by any other name would smell as sweet,” but Juliet had her Romeo to make the rose do that. I am concerned here to tell you that a rose without a name would not smell as sweet. When we know the names of the flowers, we know the flowers better, we can identify them better, we know more about them.

I want to discuss two categories of rhetorical figures—repetition and implication. Repetition includes repetition of words, phrases, syntax, and sounds. Let me give you a few examples.

For repetition of words, phrases, and syntax, let us look at 2 Nephi 9:50: “Come, my brethren, every one that thirsteth, come ye to the waters; and he that hath no money, come buy and eat;

yea, come buy wine and milk without money and without price." There are a number of rhetorical figures in that one verse. First, anaphora—repeated initial words: "*Come*, my brethren, every one that thirsteth, *come* ye to the waters; and he that hath no money, *come* buy and eat; yea, *come* buy wine and milk." Next, phrasal anaphora—repeated initial phrases: "*come buy* and eat, *come buy* wine and milk." Epanalepsis—irregularly repeated words: "no *money*, without *money*." Finally, parison—repeated structures: "*without money, without price*." Of course, the whole verse is a metaphor, and that is another rhetorical figure, but I am not going into that now. The whole chapter of 2 Nephi 9 contains wonderful, interlaced patterns of repetition; so does Jacob 5. Repetition of words and structures highlights organization and creates emphasis and rhythm.

Sound repetition is more difficult to learn to pick out. Let us look at Psalm 121:

> I will lift up mine eyes unto the hills, from whence cometh my help.
> My help cometh from the Lord, which made heaven and earth.
> He will not suffer thy foot to be moved: he that keepeth thee will not slumber.
> Behold, he that keepeth Israel shall neither slumber nor sleep.
> The Lord is thy keeper: the Lord is thy shade upon thy right hand.
> The sun shall not smite thee by day, nor the moon by night.
> The Lord shall preserve thee from all evil: he shall preserve thy soul.
> The Lord shall preserve thy going out and thy coming in from this time forth, and even for evermore.

There are many sound patterns. "I will lift up mine eyes unto the hills, from whence cometh my help": *I*, m*i*ne *eye*s, m*y*; w*ill*, *l*i*ft*, h*ill*s; *u*p, *u*nto, c*o*meth; wh*e*nce, h*e*lp. "My help cometh from the Lord, which made heaven and earth": *he*lp, *hea*ven (and in Shakespeare's dialect *ai*rth); *M*y, co*m*eth, fro*m*, *m*ade. "He will not suffer thy foot to be moved: he that keepeth thee will not slumber. Behold, he that keepeth Israel shall neither slumber nor sleep. The Lord is thy keeper. . . .": H*e*, b*e*, h*e*, k*ee*peth th*ee*, h*e*, k*ee*peth, sl*ee*p, k*ee*per; s*u*ffer (u=oo), f*oo*t, m*o*ved, sl*u*mber (oo—the sixteenth-century pronunciation); su*ff*er, *f*oot; *B*ehold, slum*b*er; kee*p*eth, sl*eep*; wi*ll*, s*l*umber, Beho*l*d, Israe*l*, s*l*umber, s*l*eep. “The Lord is thy shade upon thy right hand”: Lor*d*, sha*d*e, han*d*. “The sun shall not smite thee by day, nor the moon by night”: r*ight*, sm*ite*, n*ight*, internal rhyme; *day* and *night*, *sun* and *moon*, antitheses (antithesis, the use of direct contrast, is, of course, not a type of sound pattern, but another rhetorical device). “The Lord shall preserve thee from all evil: he shall preserve thy soul”: sha*ll*, a*ll*, evi*l*, sou*l*—the *l* runs right through and gives it weight. “The Lord shall preserve thy going out and thy coming in from this time forth, and even for evermore”: L*or*d, f*or*th, m*or*e; preser*v*e, e*v*en, e*v*ermore; co*m*ing, fro*m*, ti*m*e, ever*m*ore; go*ing* out, com*ing* in. There are other things going on; I have selected some. But the point is that if we study this passage in this way, it takes on a musical reality.

In giving you these examples of sound patterns, I am not suggesting to you that they were deliberately devised. They were not put in according to a set of clever tricks. Rhetorical language springs from the feelings spontaneously and is then afterwards analyzed and discovered to be what it is. Those sound patterns are an integral part of the language of learned men under inspiration. They are there because the King James translators who sat around that table in 1611 were brought up in a rhetorical tradition that gave them a speech richer than that of our public men nowadays. The voice comes out with different sound patterns according to the tradition that lies behind it; all of those figures had from seven to ten years of Latin in school, and they instinctively applied those lessons to their own language. Their voices came out that way, so the translation came out that way. But we live in another time and speak another dialect, and if we don’t know the sound patterns are there, we won’t realize that one of the ways in which this psalm reinforces our courage is through these sound repetitions.

Were these sounds in the original Hebrew? Of course not, but equivalent sound patterns were. The translators of 1611 are closer to Isaiah than they are to us—they shared much the same tradition. Now that tradition has gone. If you compare the New English Bible—well meant as it may be, fairly accurate as it is—with the Authorized Version, you will see that the main difference between them is the lack of this rhetorical tradition, and you will also see how weak and colorless the language of our time is when compared with the rounded, rich, sonorous, and determined English of the Authorized Version. The Roman Catholics, too, have lost something by moving away from Latin into modern English. Most modern English is abominable—the words get stuck together. Our church still stands by the Authorized Version. It will be a sad day if we give it up for something of inferior artistic value because we shall have lost a help to live a holy life.

Implication is perhaps the most important rhetorical figure of all in studying great writing. Think of implication as a way of reading between the lines. Under implication we have the following: juxtaposition, which means that certain things are placed side by side for a certain reason; inclusion, which means that a thing is deliberately put in; exclusion, which means that a thing is deliberately left out; and omission, which means that a thing is left out, but not deliberately—the author didn't seem to realize that it could have been put in. We need to train ourselves to ask questions like these: Why are A and B placed side by side? Why are A and B placed one after the other? Why is A in but B not? And why has C been added? And why doesn't D come in, which we would expect? We don't reflect on questions like these by thinking that something ought or ought not to have been put in or ought to have been put somewhere else. But we ask ourselves, why was it put in when it seems that most people would have left it out; or why was it left out when most would have put it in; or why is it here when a more logical, or apparently logical, place would be there?

Let me give you some examples—first, of inclusion and exclusion. Turn to chapter 22 of Genesis, which tells the story of Abraham and Isaac—that stark chapter. It is a bare, almost bleak story, or it would be, were it not for its joyful conclusion (vv. 15–19). The Lord spoke to Abraham, told him to go and sacrifice Isaac, perhaps only an hour or two before Abraham rose and made ready. And Abraham went to sacrifice Isaac and then was stopped at the last second. Why, in that story, are we told so much about Abraham's preparations for the journey—the fuel, the knife, the donkey, the two young men that assisted—and nothing whatever about his state of mind? Could it be that he was not introspecting and worrying? We have one question from Isaac in that story, and only one, but it is a very pregnant question—it is a weighted question: We have the knife, the fire, we have the wood, but where is the victim? Think how effective that question is when there is nothing whatever said about what Abraham or Isaac were thinking. Then, after the story is told, we get that bit of genealogy at the end of the chapter (vv. 20–24). Why? And why are we not told what Sarah felt? Perhaps she did not feel anything, for she may have been left in complete ignorance. Did it not occur to the writer to mention Sarah at all in that chapter? Or did he deliberately exclude Sarah from that chapter? Sarah made some important decisions in the life of Abraham, like the decision to send away Hagar. Abraham didn't want to send Hagar away. Sarah insisted, and the Lord spoke to Abraham in the night and told him that Sarah was right and that he must send Hagar away. So why isn't Sarah in the chapter about Isaac? I don't suppose a modern teller of that story would have dared to leave Sarah out, but she is left out and those genealogical details are in. If we try to figure out why these things are included or excluded, we give ourselves a better chance of understanding what the story is all about.

For an example of juxtaposition, look in 2 Samuel 23:8–39 at the list of David's mighty men. These are the men who were with David in the cave of Adullam, who journeyed with David in the wilderness, who supported David in those lean years before Saul was killed. There are thirty-seven of them; the list goes on and on and on. And at the end, in the final verse of the chapter, the thirty-seventh name is "Uriah the Hittite"—the man that David had killed in a way that amounted to murder. This is the only other mention of Uriah in the Bible outside the story of David and Bathsheba in 2 Samuel 11 and 12. Don't you think the person who wrote that list under inspiration put Uriah the Hittite right there at the end on purpose—the Hittite—to hit you in the eye? There is no reference back to chapters 11 and 12, nor is there any reference forward from chapters 11 and 12 to chapter 23, but there it is for us to find and realize. And when we are left to find and realize it for ourselves, it hits us that much harder, doesn't it? After writing "Uriah the Hittite," the scribe finishes, "thirty and seven in all." It would have been plain enough if he had finished the verse with "Uriah the Hittite," but he slipped in that "thirty and seven in all," too. And what a curiously perfunctory feeling we have about those words. It is as if all that heroism had been reduced to just a number by the introduction of the name of Uriah, as if David had canceled out the heroic part of his life and the heroism of his companions by his sin.

Now turn to Luke 15, the parable of the prodigal son. Notice that just as that chapter begins with the Pharisees accusing Jesus—"This man receiveth sinners, and eateth with them" (Luke 15:2)—so it closes with the elder brother accusing his father in similar language (Luke 15:29–30). That chapter begins with the Pharisees, and it ends with a Pharisee. What is to be inferred? I shall not infer it for you. These are examples of juxtaposition, the placing of things—at the beginning, at the end, side by side—rather than a comment on them: the placing is the comment.

In Shakespeare, we need to ask ourselves why one scene succeeds another. Why, for instance, do we get clowning and fooling after there has just been a tragic scene? What is the point? In *Antony and Cleopatra*, the armies are tramping on and off the stage the whole time, and the whole of the Roman Empire is being deployed in front of us. And in the middle of it all, we get a drunken scene where the rulers of the world make fools of themselves. (It might have been Tehran, where your Roosevelt and my Churchill were both drunk together with Stalin, who probably didn't get quite so drunk.) And what comes after the drunken scene? The Roman army on the outskirts of the frontier is solemnly coming in with the dead body of the son of the Parthian King. Here in the middle of the empire are these disgustingly great men getting disgustingly drunk, and there on the borders of Asia Minor are the tired Roman troops who had done their duty and had won their victory. It is a contrast. Nothing is said about it. The one thing is presented to us, and the other thing is presented to us, and it is our job to see what juxtaposition has to tell us.

Literary artists don't say all they mean; they have silences and gaps, and these have their effect on us as well as that which is explicit. These silences and gaps are a part of the writer's artistry that is frequently forgotten but which is nevertheless there, and supremely there in the scriptures. Writers who don't tell us their point but leave it for us to find have much more opportunity of gaining our consent because in the finding we identify ourselves with those writers by going through their own thought processes. In the rhetorical tradition, people would have been alert to look at these juxtapositions, inclusions, and exclusions and to give them sense. We also need to learn to see what is not said because it is being said more effectively by not being said.

Tone Rhetorical figures often give us insight into a writer's tone or attitude, and this is crucial for understanding his work. It is important for us to ask ourselves, "Is this writer being straightforward or ironic?" People seem to think that irony is not everywhere, whereas it is practically everywhere most of the time. Irony occurs in situations in which there is a conflict of values, which means that one set of values invalidates another or that the existence of those values side by side produces something absurd or grotesque. Whenever we profess to do one thing and do another, there is irony. Shakespeare, Goethe, Dante, Virgil, and Homer are always acutely aware of the difference between what human beings profess to do and what they actually do. The inspired writers of the scriptures are supremely aware of it.

Whenever we have two sets of values in our mind, one that we act upon and one that we ought to act upon, there is irony. The contrast between what we actually do and what we ought to do is very ironical indeed and is constantly present to the Godhead. That is why they must feel about us a high degree of loving irony. If there is no irony in the Deity, then there is no comparison between lower life and higher life.

The major theme of the whole of Israel's history is that ironical contrast, that circle: hard work, success, riches, depravity, collapse, hard work, success, riches, depravity, and so it goes around and around and around, over and over again throughout the Old Testament. That is an ironical situation. To do the wrong thing once is bad enough, but to go on doing the wrong thing is ironic, even funny. For example, in the old days, if a man slipped on a banana skin, it was funny. But if he went down the street another two or three hundred yards and slipped on a banana skin again, it was howlingly funny. But if he went on and slipped on a third banana skin, well, then of course anybody who had observed all three would have collapsed with laughter. That would have been a characteristic response throughout the ages, from Aristophanes to the nineteenth century. (We have become a little more civilized nowadays.)

A great deal of artistic work is ironic, except there is not so much of it in the romantic period. I think it was Eliot who once pointed out that the difference between classicists and romantics is that romantics forget everything except the mood they happen to be in at the moment, but classicists never forget the alternative. It is always present in their minds. If they are making love, for example, they are always remembering death.

Look for irony in the scriptures. It is there. It is there in the Old Testament, in the New Testament, and constantly in Christ's dealings with the Pharisees. Irony is superbly there in the account of David and Bathsheba in 2 Samuel 11 and 12; look at 11:1 and then look at 12:27–29. The first verse of chapter 11 reads:

> And it came to pass, after the year was expired, at the time when kings go forth to battle, that David sent Joab, and his servants with him, and all Israel; and they destroyed the children of Ammon, and besieged Rabbah. But David tarried still at Jerusalem.

"When kings go forth to battle," a generalization, and then at the end of the verse, "David tarried still at Jerusalem." The point of the verse is clear enough, especially if we notice in the second verse that David seems to be bored and not doing very much while his men are at Rabbah. Now look at verses 27–29 of chapter 12:

> And Joab sent messengers to David, and said, I have fought against Rabbah, and have taken the city of waters. [This means he has taken the cistern; the inhabitants now have no access to water, so the city will fall in three or four days.] Now therefore gather the rest of the people together, and encamp against the city, and take it: lest I take the city, and it be called after my name. And David gathered all the people together, and went to Rabbah, and fought against it, and took it.

Take that ending to the story together with the beginning verse in chapter 11, and you will see the ironical intention of the writer, especially in the light of all that has happened in between—the interchange between Joab and David, and what Joab knows, and what David knows Joab knows. David must now put up with this impertinence from his mere nephew, "lest I take the city, and it be called after my name."

Read chapters 10–12 of Second Corinthians. What is Paul doing? We can make out what Paul is doing if we are prepared to see irony in the scriptures. But we can't make it out if we are not prepared to see irony in the scriptures. We should not exclude anything from the scriptures that is intended for our edification.

Moral Judgments When we have gotten a hold of a writer's attitude or the attitude of one of his characters, we can make moral judgments about that writer or character. That, ultimately, is what the rhetorical approach is about, and that is the difference between the rhetorical approach and the modern linguistic approach. The rhetorical approach is always aiming at an evaluation, a judgment; it is always asking, "Is this bad or good?" Modern linguists are concerned, they say, with describing. And yet the poor modern linguists can never describe language irrespective of bad or good because the sense of its being bad or good always creeps in. Evaluation is not easy, but it is what we have to do in our daily lives, and we have to do it when we are reading, too, and it means study and careful reading and slowness.

Let us take a look at Polonius's advice to his son Laertes in *Hamlet* and ask ourselves what Shakespeare is telling us about Polonius:

> Give thy thoughts no tongue,
> Nor any unproportion'd thought his act.
> Be thou familiar, but by no means vulgar:
> The friends thou hast, and their adoption tried,
> Grapple them unto thy soul with hoops of steel,
> But do not dull thy palm with entertainment
> Of each new-hatch'd, unfledg'd comrade. Beware
> Of entrance to a quarrel, but being in,
> Bear't that th' opposed may beware of thee.
> Give every man thy ear, but few thy voice,
> Take each man's censure, but reserve thy judgment.
> Costly thy habit as thy purse can buy,
> But not express'd in fancy, rich, not gaudy,
> For the apparel oft proclaims the man,
> And they in France of the best rank and station
> Are of a most select and generous chief in that.
> Neither a borrower nor a lender be,
> For loan oft loses both itself and friend,
> And borrowing dulleth th' edge of husbandry.
> This above all: to thine own self be true,
> And it must follow, as the night the day,
> Thou canst not then be false to any man.
>
> (*Hamlet*, 1.3.59–80)

This speech is given on a comic occasion when Laertes is trying to get away to the ship. He has already had a farewell speech from his father, and now all this is being added unto him. It is perfunctory advice from a worldly father to a worldly son who has no intention whatever of carrying any of it out, and the father knows that, but he is doing the correct thing on the occasion. The sentiments of that speech, perfunctory as they are, are directly opposed to the sense that Shakespeare has of the generous soul, the magnanimous soul. This is a miserable and meanly prudential speech, and I hope never again shall we have Polonius quoted at General Conference or anywhere else. Polonius was a wicked old man and is so presented to us. He was a coarse and vulgar old man. He was capable of saying to the king, "I'll loose my daughter to him," using the image of a sow being loosed to a boar or a mare to a stallion. That is the coarse image he used: he would loose his daughter to Hamlet to get some knowledge of what was in Hamlet's mind. The only good thing about Polonius is his poor daughter's grief at his death.

Now look at some of the things in that speech. "Grapple them unto thy soul with hoops of steel." What an extraordinary image of friendship—grappling your friends to your soul with hoops of steel. What an uncomfortable and possessive process in the extreme. Five lines further down, "Give every man thy ear, but few thy voice." Prudentiality. And then so characteristic:

> Costly thy habit as thy purse can buy,
> But not express'd in fancy, rich, not gaudy,
> For the apparel oft proclaims the man,
> And they in France of the best rank and station
> Are of a most select and generous chief in that.

What gets more attention than anything else in this speech? Costume. What very English advice this is. Spend all the money you possibly can on your clothes, but make sure they are neat and not gaudy because your affectation must not seem to be affectation.

The last lines of Polonius's speech give us no different opinion of him: if the false man is true to himself, what is he? Think about that. And think about that metaphor, "as the night the day." That is very different from "as the day the night." The night is a symbol of evil, and the day of good, and that makes the sentiment ludicrous. Think about Polonius stabbed behind the arras with Hamlet's comment afterwards, "I'll lug the guts into the neighbor room" (*Hamlet*, 3.4.212).

Here is a very different simple line from Horatio that places Hamlet in a way we don't like to think of, but it is true. Hamlet has just told Horatio how he has sent Rosencrantz and Guildenstern to their deaths.

> *Horatio.* So Guildenstern and Rosencrantz go to't.
>
> *Hamlet.* Why, man, they did make love to this employment,
> They are not near my conscience. Their defeat
> Does by their own insinuation grow.
> 'Tis dangerous when the baser nature comes
> Between the pass and fell incensed points
> Of mighty opposites. (*Hamlet*, 5.2.56–62)

That simple line of Horatio's is in my view the key line of *Hamlet* because the whole moral issue, the greater likeness of Hamlet to Claudius as the play goes on, is there admitted ("mighty opposites"). Horatio has made the point, and after Hamlet is dead, we have to remember the point because the English ambassador is brought onto the stage deliberately to tell us that Rosencrantz and Guildenstern are dead and that Hamlet is an accomplished murderer. That has to be taken into account. We must remember that in Shakespeare's time everybody sitting in that theatre knew well that vengeance was a sin.

Othello in all his flourishing rhetoric is "placed" in the same way. Desdemona's maid Emilia comes to the bed and says:

> *Emilia.* O, who hath done this deed?

This is what Desdemona replies as she dies the second time:

> *Desdemona.* Nobody; I myself. Farewell!
> Commend me to my kind lord. O, farewell!
> (*Othello*, 5.2.123–25)

Her kind lord is the man who has broken her neck.

Conclusion I hope these examples have shown that we need to get back in touch with the rhetorical tradition that the scriptures and the great classics were written in. It is essential that we know the gospel, but we cannot know it if we cannot read it. We need to relearn, maintain, and develop this tradition. We don't need to adopt something new; we need to return to the age-old practices—as we can see from their writings—of the inspired authors of the Old

Testament from Moses to Malachi, of the New Testament from Matthew to John the Revelator, of the Book of Mormon from Nephi to Moroni, and of the Restoration, as well as of the great secular writers. I do not think our predecessors fully understood the tradition they were part of. They didn't need to understand explicitly. They were reading the great writing as it was meant to be read. For us, the language of great writing is fast becoming a foreign language. It is imperative that we try to understand, more than ever before, how to approach it.

Style in Shakespeare

"LET YOUR COMMUNICATION be Yea, yea; Nay, nay: for whatsoever is more than these cometh of evil" (Matt. 5:37). The evils in speech stretch out along a long line, from profanity and obscenity to the highfalutin affectations of social, scientific, political, and religious hypocrisy. And Shakespeare, more than most of us today, was aware of these evils.

I want to begin by saying something about the state of language at the time Shakespeare wrote. I need to go back to 1066, the time of the Norman conquest. The Normans established themselves as rulers in England and made serfs of the tribes they conquered. The Normans spoke French; the conquered tribes spoke Old English. And French is a different kind of language from Old English. French developed from Latin and is an analytical language, which means, in the first place, that French constantly, instead of using unique verbs for unique actions, uses common verbs like "make" or "have" and puts them together with nouns. All these constructions that we now use—"make an effort" (instead of "try"), "make love," "do this," "do that," "have a shave," "get married," and so on, came in during the twelfth and thirteenth centuries by the hundreds because of the influence of French. French also uses noun phrases instead of simple nouns—for example, "man at arms" instead of "warrior." Old English, on the other hand, was not an analytical language.

After 1066, the ruled classes in England went on speaking a development of Old English, but at court, in the law courts, and in administration, from 1066 until the middle of the fourteenth century, French was spoken. That was three hundred years of it. So there existed a situation like that in some foreign countries today—Pakistan, for example. English there is still a language of rule, but the Pakistani have their own languages as well, and they move between languages. They don't stay in one or the other. You may be speaking in English to a Pakistani, and he may be speaking in Urdu to you, and then he may go over into a phrase or sentence of English and then back into his Urdu again, to-ing and fro-ing in that kind of way.

Over that three-hundred-year period in which the English were moving between English and French, upper-class English developed into a language more like French than lower-class English. Upper-class English became more readily precise and, therefore, fit for use in administration, law, and other specialist areas, and eventually for use in science. Lower-class English, though it gradually absorbed some of the French element also, continued to reflect the rural farming habits of the common people. So in the Renaissance there was, on the one hand, this upper-class English that was used by the rulers in administration, in the court, in manners, in the upper class itself as a means of communication; on the other hand, there was the simpler language of the people. This created a tension that has existed ever since between the sort of language we use for public life, in all its variety, and the sort of language that we use for what we might call the natural purposes of life, like communication within the family, and so on. There became a tension between the artificial, manipulative, in-group language used to run the country and the genuine language that poets and others wanted to use. And from this point on, we can distinguish in English what we call levels of language, registers of varying formality.

Language differences between the upper and lower classes preserved class distinctions, just as language differences between classes still do today. Basil Bernstein at the Institute of Education at the University of London in our day has carefully observed the differences between working-class communication and middle-class communication. The differences he found in Britain probably exist also in this country to some extent, though not so markedly. He found that members of the working class communicated with fewer words, more gestures, and more extra-linguistic noises, but managed, nevertheless, within the family or within the peer group, to communicate very well. Middle-class language was like the language I am using now, connected, ratiocinative, and discursive. But this kind of language doesn't easily touch matters of the heart, and, if you get a linguistic distinction between heart and head in a community, it is very difficult to deal with.

The gospel does not advocate upper-class language, nor does it advocate lower-class language, but the tension between the two has existed in the Christian community from the beginning. It is recorded in the scriptures: Paul grumbling about Peter's behavior, and Peter grumbling about the fact that Paul was often incomprehensible. Since then, that grumble has been frequently heard in society. The peasants in England, when they rose, said, "Let's kill all the lawyers" because they didn't understand the lawyers' language. And, of course, if you don't understand the lawyer's language, you are at his mercy, just as, for example, if you don't understand the language of the income-tax form, you are at the government's mercy. Specialized languages are or may become means of ruling others by keeping them ignorant. The anthropologist has something to say about these languages because all communities have them, and they are used by some within the community in order to dominate or manipulate others in the community. Such manipulation exists everywhere, although in some countries it is more highly developed than in others.

There is a term for the language that the rulers imposed upon the people in Shakespeare's own time, and that is "complement." It comes from the Latin *complementum*, which means "a fullness." It was a periphrastic style of language—hence the sense of fullness—that was often used in an affected, posturing way. And posturing or affectation came up in the Renaissance very strongly, partly because of class circulation. By the time of the Renaissance, there were not only the upper classes speaking in their kind of way and the lower classes speaking their dialects, but there were also the middle classes trying to imitate the upper classes in order to rise in society. That rising in society was very important in the sixteenth century. It was important in most European countries, but much more so in England than anywhere else because the bourgeois pressure was strongest in England.

As long as classes are sure of themselves, they don't assert themselves. Once class movement begins, then a class asserts itself either to defend itself or to attack. People want to move into the upper class, the upper class rejects them, and affectation and posturing begin on both sides. It started at the court; it started with the king and queen. The Renaissance kings and queens were actors on a stage, supported by their courts. This acting and affectation then passed down through a striving community, many members of which were trying to move up.

Class assertion meant that the sixteenth century was a great century for education; people were anxious to acquire education as a means of acquiring power. They wished to gain the kind of language that would enable them to rise in the community. Many books were written in the sixteenth century about how to speak and how to write, and that is why we know so much about what writers were trying to do in Shakespeare's time.

Shakespeare lived and worked in this kind of atmosphere, and the social background of posturing and affectation was one of the major reasons why the drama was so successful in his time. There are writers before Shakespeare in whom this is almost the only thing. The supreme example is that satanic writer Marlowe, by whom Shakespeare is said to have been influenced. (I think myself that they developed side by side.) Shakespeare shows us in his work this posturing, this affectation, to the full. Everybody can see affectation in some of the fools and clowns and characters like Don Armado. But it is also there in the figures of true evil, who express themselves in Shakespeare in the Senecan style—a style of melodramatic posturing common in the tradition of tragedy. Let me give you some examples, starting with this speech by Lady Macbeth in which she asks to be "unsexed" (and may therefore almost be regarded as a contemporary character) in order that she may be strong enough to commit the murder that she fears her husband will not be strong enough to commit:

> Come, you spirits
> That tend on mortal thoughts, unsex me here,
> And fill me from the crown to the toe topful
> Of direst cruelty! Make thick my blood,
> Stop up th' access and passage to remorse,
> That no compunctious visitings of nature
> Shake my fell purpose, nor keep peace between
> Th' effect and it! Come to my woman's breasts,

And take my milk for gall, you murth'ring ministers,
Wherever in your sightless substances
You wait on nature's mischief! Come, thick night,
And pall thee in the dunnest smoke of hell,
That my keen knife see not the wound it makes,
Nor heaven peep through the blanket of the dark
To cry, "Hold, hold!" (*Macbeth*, 1.5.40–54)

That is a piece of satanism. Lady Macbeth is one of the four witches in the play. Her speech, as Johnson noticed, is mean and low. They are dismissed, she and her husband, by Malcolm at the end (5.7.97) as "this dead butcher and his fiend-like queen." (Macbeth is introduced to us in act 1, scene 2, butchering on the battlefield, "till he unseam'd him from the nave to th' chaps"—a line which indicates that the wretched man, his enemy, was already lying on the ground supine in front of him).

In the light of that, we can turn to the "Tomorrow and tomorrow and tomorrow" speech, which Lord Clark thought was an expression of Shakespeare, but which actually is the chaotic, nihilistic expression of a satanic villain on the verge of his unheroic death:

To-morrow, and to-morrow, and to-morrow,
Creeps in this petty pace from day to day,
To the last syllable of recorded time;
And all our yesterdays have lighted fools
The way to dusty death. Out, out, brief candle!
Life's but a walking shadow, a poor player,
That struts and frets his hour upon the stage,
And then is heard no more. It is a tale
Told by an idiot, full of sound and fury,
Signifying nothing. (*Macbeth*, 5.5.19–28)

This is a posture, and it is not a great posture. It is a self-pitying posture with no real content. There are no magnificent figures of evil in Shakespeare, though the self-assertive philosophy that began its rise in the Renaissance and reached its height in the romantic period has led people to think they see magnificent figures of evil in the "great" sinners of Shakespeare.

Another tradition in Shakespeare's time was the tradition of the *sermo humilis*, the plain style, the simple style. *Humilis* means more than just "plain"; it means "humble," "straightforward." Plato argued for this in his *Republic*. Saint Augustine, in the sixth century, said that this style should be used to express the gospel and to teach the gospel. Thomas Aquinas and Erasmus reassert this. The gospel is simple. It must be simply expressed and taught so that it is accessible to everyone; it is for everyone.

The *sermo humilis*, to reach its heights, needs to have the musical endorsement of a lift in language that lifts up our hearts. Notice the way the language lifts as Marcellus describes Christmas in *Hamlet* 1.1.158–64:

> Some say that ever 'gainst that season comes
> Wherein our Saviour's birth is celebrated,
> This bird of dawning singeth all night long,
> And then they say no spirit dare stir abroad,
> The nights are wholesome, then no planets strike,
> No fairy takes, nor witch hath power to charm,
> So hallowed, and so gracious, is that time.

This is the only place in the play where the language does so lift, and the last time I saw the play the director had chosen to cut this passage, presumably because he thought that it was redundant and that its Christian sentiment would no longer appeal to the audience; more deeply, perhaps, he hated it for its beauty.

The Bible (the Authorized Version) is not all written at the same level; but its expressions of the highest feeling have this simple music of endorsement:

> For whither thou goest, I will go; and where thou lodgest, I will lodge: thy people shall be my people, and thy God my God: Where thou diest, will I die, and there will I be buried. (Ruth 1:16-17)
>
> In my Father's house are many mansions: if it were not so, I would have told you. (John 14:2)
>
> Peace I leave with you, my peace I give unto you: not as the world giveth, give I unto you. (John 14:27)

Saint Jerome used the plain style when he revised the old Vulgate into what is now the Vulgate. He wrote in the most beautifully simple and lucid Latin. In the middle ages, the greatest poet of perhaps all poets, Dante, wrote in this style—he wrote his *Divine Comedy* in this style. Many sermons of the early sixteenth century are written in this style. I am thinking particularly of the sermons of Latimer and Ridley, which are extant. I always think of those two because they were burned at the stake at Oxford for their Protestant beliefs, and when they were being burned, Latimer made a joke to Ridley, which has been recorded, "Be of good cheer, Master Ridley, for by God's grace we shall this day light such a candle as shall never go out!" But the candle was themselves burning at the stake. (Humor is deeply enshrined in religion; it is one of those things that distinguish the believer from the hypocrite.) But in Shakespeare's time, the change came, and in the late sixteenth and early seventeenth centuries, we find people of posture and affectation like Launcelot Andrewes and John Donne, who did not write for ordinary people at all but who were much admired by literary persons. They were exhibitionists, narcissists who liked to see their clever selves reflected in their prose.

Shakespeare (and his audience) was familiar with the plain style as well as the other styles I have been speaking of. And now and then, about one percent of the time in Shakespeare, we get the plain style. It comes at the points where something very deep and very moving and profound is happening on the stage. It is the language that most affects us and makes for the supreme passages of Shakespeare. But it would not be what it is unless there was all that posturing language around it to show it up. I want to conclude by giving you a few more examples of Shakespeare's plain style.

Coriolanus, reacting against his city, having it in his power, giving up his advantages as the result of his mother's intercession, and knowing that this means his death, breaks down in utterly simple language:

> O my mother, mother! O!
> You have won a happy victory to Rome;
> But, for your son, believe it—O, believe it—
> Most dangerously you have with him prevail'd,
> If not most mortal to him. But let it come.
>
> (*Coriolanus*, 5.3.185–89)

Shakespeare's *The Tempest*, which is his last play, summarizes, to me as an old man, what he has done throughout his whole life and what he is there saying farewell to, for his magic in putting things on stage was like Prospero's, and Shakespeare was not certain of the validity from a religious point of view of everything he had done. He, too, like Prospero, had sins of which to repent. Prospero studied too much magic; Shakespeare perhaps exercised too much magic. But it was not his wand that he was waving when he was writing the passages that I am going to quote; he was writing those under the inspiration of the gospel.

Prospero repents. He repents at the prompting of Ariel, who is not even a human being.

> *Ariel.* Your charm so strongly works 'em
> That if you now beheld them, your affections
> Would become tender.
>
> *Prospero.* Dost thou think so, spirit?
>
> *Ariel.* Mine would, sir, were I human.
>
> *Prospero.* And mine shall.
> Hast thou, which art but air, a touch, a feeling
> Of their afflictions, and shall not myself,
> One of their kind, that relish all as sharply
> Passion as they, be kindlier mov'd than thou art?
> Though with their high wrongs I am strook to th' quick,
> Yet, with my nobler reason, 'gainst my fury
> Do I take part. The rarer action is
> In virtue than in vengeance. They being penitent,
> The sole drift of my purpose doth extend
> Not a frown further. Go, release them, Ariel.
> My charms I'll break, their senses I'll restore,
> And they shall be themselves.
>
> (*The Tempest*, 5.1.17–32)

But the moral channel in *The Tempest* is not Prospero; Prospero is a sinner who has to repent. So is everybody else in *The Tempest.* So are we all. But old Gonzalo is the man who rescued Prospero and Miranda from death and who sums up the play in terms of Providence, saying as it were, "Yes, Prospero. You were a magician to a point. You couldn't bring the ship near the island, but you could cause a storm. You could cause Ferdinand and Miranda to meet, but you could not make sure that they would develop between them the affection that was needed. This was Providence." Shakespeare uses the word only four times, twice in *The Tempest.* Not a safe word to use on the stage in those days, with ears listening to make trouble at court or in the city. Here, then, is old Gonzalo:

> Was Milan thrust from Milan, that his issue
> Should become kings of Naples? O, rejoice

> Beyond a common joy, and set it down
> With gold on lasting pillars: in one voyage
> Did Claribel her husband find at Tunis,
> And Ferdinand, her brother, found a wife
> Where he himself was lost; Prospero, his dukedom
> In a poor isle; and all of us, ourselves,
> When no man was his own.
>
> (*The Tempest*, 5.1.205–12)

"And all of us, ourselves, / When no man was his own." Those words summarize to me the essential point about the gospel, about the Atonement, about the kind of language we ought to use, about the kind of attitude we ought to take to ourselves, because we find ourselves when we are not our own. There is more than one sense of that in the play. The obvious sense is that they were restored to their senses after having been put out of them for a while by Prospero's charm. But the deeper sense is that they had lost themselves to find themselves, and that is what the whole of this play is about: we lose ourselves to find ourselves. These simple passages of Shakespeare point to just that.

Education

Stripped of their fruit and
leaves, the boughs reveal the trees'
effort out and up.

If competitive
outward, then upward too; not
seeking for the Lord.

AHK
November 1973

Education in the Home

Everything human begins with the child in the home. The young child needs to be given opportunities to develop fine sensory discrimination: to touch, see, and hear a variety of things.

Touch: Before they even hear or see properly, children touch fabrics, toys, room surfaces, human hands and cheeks, themselves. All this touching may form either a rich experience or the experience of mere uniformity. Synthetic fibers produce a great variety of textiles, but they are more uniform in texture. Wool, cotton, linen, silk, and velvet need to be felt in their variety. Plastic toys are safe and cheap, but they are smooth; they don't feel like wood or metal or textile.

Sight: The eye sees form and color—lines, angles, and curves; shades, tints, hues. Plastic objects are made in molds, and these molds produce approximate lines and depths; they smooth everything out. The colors of plastic are often a searing contrast with the delicate colors of the natural environment. A child reared on the strong colors of substitute materials will not respond to finer shades.

The eye likes to see and the finger likes to feel precision and refinement in the object, but they need to have the experience that will enable them to do so. Tumblers of molded glass are clumsy compared with cut-glass ones. Cut glass is more finely shaped and/or decorated, precisely angled and edged, and polished by wheels. The light refracts more definitely. Everybody knows the difference between a molded and a cut-glass chandelier—the light shows it at once.

It would be good to have one or two objects of sterling silver that are the child's own possessions: the difference of weight and appearance from stainless steel is part of our children's and our own education. We were very poor when I was a child, but I had an engraved, eighteenth-century, silver christening mug that I have treasured all my life.

Think how superior those small metal automobile models are compared to the plastic ones. It isn't merely a matter of their appearance, but of their weight, their dignity, their importance. My father made me big, heavy, wooden models of a locomotive, tender, and cars. True, locomotives are not made of wood, but at that age sharp metal might have injured me, and I trundled those heavy toys about the floor with a sense of pleasure mingled with respect.

Hearing: Young children flinch at loud noises, but in modern society they soon learn to endure and then to enjoy excessive decibels. Loud noise, however, prevents the development of discriminative refinement. Our civilization shouts so loud that the value of a whisper is forgotten.

Continuous background noise—from the radio or television, for example—discourages the development of perception and discrimination. Something that is there the whole time no longer draws proper attention: it dulls; it becomes a kind of drug; it floats us sluggishly along. It is like a stream of dirty, lukewarm water—a kind of inferior bath taken disgustingly in common. Whatever encourages our inattention diminishes our ability to make wise choices because, of all the things that are required to make wise choices, a delicate and sensitive attention is the most important.

The Truth and Beauty of Objects

But we need more than the experience of sensory discrimination; our intelligence also discriminates other qualities—like the truth and beauty of objects. "Beauty is truth, truth beauty," said Keats. This means that all beautiful things are true and all true things are beautiful. The equation of truth and beauty in the home translates into the principle of functionalism: objects are most beautiful that are adapted to their purpose; these have their own consequential beauty, the beauty of their practical truth. The most practical shape is the one we should recognize as also being the most beautiful. If we think a thing is more beautiful because it has been fashioned to be less useful than it might be if it were another shape, then there is something wrong with our judgment. The world knows of the fine taste that Swedish people have in the everyday things they surround themselves with in the kitchen and elsewhere in their homes. But that is not just a modern development; that is the flowering of peasant culture over many centuries. Useful objects have developed to be as useful as possible and to show their use in their form.

The principle of functionalism applies all over the house. It applies perhaps best of all in the kitchen. We are under various pressures to buy things, and as a result of this we may get out of balance in our kitchens. There are certain cooking jobs for which aluminum is best, or cast iron, or copper. We should not then go all out for one or another. I believe we use wooden utensils, like the wooden spoon, less than we should. After all, a wooden spoon is much better than a metal spoon for stirring porridge, soup, or sauce in a metal pot.

Plastic can provide satisfactory heavy objects of good quality, but it cannot satisfactorily replace other objects that have qualities plastic cannot have. Plastic plates may be good for a picnic (and paper plates even better, because they are disposable); plastic plates are light, they can be produced in pleasant colors, and they are easy to handle. But the very lightness of plastic products is sometimes an inconvenience in eating—for example, the lightness of plastic cutlery. And you cannot clean plastic plates as well as you can glass or china.

In light of the principle of functionalism, there is a point to be made about ornamentation: we should not use as ornaments objects with a use that they are never put to. There is no point to a silver mug on the mantelpiece or to those copper objects that are left about the house to inculcate a certain "folk" atmosphere but which never come into use in the kitchen. A copper kettle that is never boiled in, a silver mug that is never drunk from, a vase that is left to stand empty because of its shape—these are a kind of hypocrisy. So are cushions that are placed on a couch just to provide a contrasting blob of color.

Art in the home should spring from the purposes of the home. This principle has relevance to the decoration and color and general layout of every room in the house. The sitting room needs to be peaceful without being somnolescent. Children's rooms need to be more animated than adults' rooms because adults prize rest but children do not. And there needs to be the common meeting ground between adults and children that is not disturbing but harmonious. There are proper colors for everything. We do not want to increase the possibility of quarrels by using too much red or orange; green and blue are reconciling colors. We need to use less beige and cream, which are too predominant. We could go on in more detail concerning the textures of curtains, carpets, bedspreads. Every single object in a room is of relevance to our education and to the education of our children.

We need to remember that rooms have no right to an existence of their own; they exist only to serve human functions. There can be no truth of a room in itself, only a truth of its relation to the human beings who use it. The home is there to serve us who live in it. It is not to be a demonstration to our neighbors of our better taste, conspicuous waste, or exhibitionistic ornamentation. If there is anything in our home that is there to impress our neighbors rather than to be used by ourselves, then there is something wrong with it, so closely are art and morality allied.

Another principle to be derived from the equation of truth and beauty is the principle that real things are better than imitation ones. From very early on, the child may be given the unreal instead of the real—for example, the dummy (pacifier) and the bottle. How can they compare in quality with a mother's breast? None of my grandfather's grandchildren ever had either dummy or bottle. His great-grandchildren, alas, have had.

There is a story of the father who drove his family in an air-conditioned car to the edge of the Grand Canyon and then, inside the car, in comfort, showed them slides of the Grand Canyon. I also remember the sad story of a friend of mine who was in charge of the household of the Governor-General of Sudan in the Imperial days. He was seen one evening before an official dinner putting artificial lilies-of-the-valley in vases on the table and spraying them with lily-of-the-valley scent from a bottle. Better cactus and dried grass than that. We should not use artificial flowers in our homes. It may be argued that artificial flowers can be made to look like real ones so that it is difficult to tell the difference. But it is not simply a matter of sight, but of touch and of scent. No artificial petal can provide the soft brush and cool feeling against the cheek that a real petal can. Artificial flowers are sometimes said to look "better" than real ones. At the point that we think so, that we prefer plastic flowers to the ones that God has made, we are in serious moral danger. Even some highly bred real flowers are offensive to good taste: I don't like a chrysanthemum head to look like a mop.

We do not want things pretending to be what they are not. The trouble with plastic is that it often pretends. Plastic footwear may be efficient, but it usually *sets out* to look like leather and, therefore, to be a substitute for leather instead of a substance in its own right. Neither do we want things hiding other things that one wants to hide. I need not speak of the Boston ladies who kept whiskey in a teapot in a corner cupboard. That was an obvious piece of sinful hypocrisy. But there are also the wide-crinolined dolls that are put over telephones, and the knights in armor holding pens for spears, and the hundreds of things that we may not be prepared to have in our own houses but may be prepared to buy to give other people. Tastelessness is rarely exemplified so completely as in the whole field of gifts.

We do not want objects to be made unlike themselves, and we do not want objects that are deliberately made to look like other objects. Both of these are evasions of the truth. And truth is beauty. All these have an effect on our children as well as ourselves.

The Arts

We now come to the part that the arts need to play in the Mormon home. To begin with, we need to recognize that a child is far more likely to appreciate good art if he is familiar, from infancy onwards, with good objects of the type I have been discussing. The infant may and should also experience the arts themselves: visual art may reach the eye, and music and the spoken word, the ear of the youngest child. Children are affected from the beginning by what they see and hear within the walls of their home. Their environment creates their taste.

We must not think when we are bringing up our children that their education can wait. It cannot. That doesn't mean that we should get our children to try to experience things that are beyond their age (although most children are more mature than most parents realize), but what it does mean is that we need to try and give the best to our children from the beginning. It seems to me that the age of eight for baptism and confirmation is well chosen. Children may become cynical and disinclined to accept things after the age of eight. Sin sets in very soon. So it is wrong to wait, just as it is wrong to bring up children ignorant of the Church and what they should do. There are modern parents who believe that they should leave all that kind of thing alone until their children are able to choose for themselves, but this is wrong.

My parents didn't always teach me in the right way, but somehow they managed. I was brought up during the First World War in a very small country cottage with about a hundred books in it. I read most of those hundred books from the ages of seven to nine. They were nearly all of them good ones. I had nothing else to read. There was no public library there, no newspapers. I never saw a comic. The outside world could not come in upon me in that little cottage in Essex; it wasn't there. I was in an artificial situation of restriction. I had to read those books or be bored. And so I learned to read them and enjoy them, and that was the basis of my education, the most important part of it. How valuable it is to be circumscribed—how valuable it is not to have too much choice! By the time I was ten and in London, I had had it firmly inculcated into me that only vulgar children read the then-equivalent of comics; I am sure I was a little snob. And, of course, a great many children are or can be snobs. But don't think that snobbery is necessarily a bad thing. If it enables one to dress better, to think better, to read better, there is something in it. What is wrong with it is the feeling that we are better than somebody else because we do better in a particular thing or things. We are never better than somebody else because we do this or that. We are only better in ourselves. The point is this: when I was young, it never occurred to me to read anything vulgar because by the time I was ten my basic taste had been formed.

Another example: my father and mother were both trained singers, and they sang good things—they sang their children to sleep with them. My mother's contralto arias from "The Messiah" are among the fundamental things that have remained with me throughout my life; I had them played at her funeral. I was put to the piano at the age of three, and I learned to read music before I could read a book. And I remember that after I had learned to read, I used to sneak a book on to the piano, play the music, and be reading the book at the same time—it was my way of getting through my practice. But when my father died and my mother had to find some means of earning extra money, she took to singing things which, perhaps, she would have preferred not to sing: such vulgarities as "The Bells of St. Mary's" or "Come to the Fair." At twelve or thirteen, I used to go and accompany her on the piano; I used to have to play those things. And at that age I already loathed them. I did not have to be told that they were vulgar; I could hear that they were.

For better or worse, the essential education is done in the family. Teachers hardly count; fathers and mothers do. Parents cannot and should not try to hand over to teachers the education of their children. So organize your family life, those of you who have families (and those of you who don't, plan to organize it, because being Mormon, most of you will have it, for better or worse)—organize your family life so that your children will grow up appreciating the best art there is. I ask you from the bottom of my heart, from the beginning, to interest your children in this art, whether it be visual art or music or literature. Put good things to look at about the house. Let your children listen to good music. Read good books to them. All this will help them become better people because good art of all kinds has a good effect on conduct: it cultivates our open-mindedness toward and charity for others; it leaves us ready for the new experience rather than the mere repetition of the old; it helps to keep us alive. It may be you are too late to start as thoroughly with yourselves as you would have wished to do, but you are not too late for your children and grandchildren.

I want now to discuss briefly three categories of art—visual art, music, and literature—in terms of their place in our homes.

Visual Art

The first point I want to make about visual art is that there is a difference between an original work of art and copies or pastiche of it, and it would be better to have on our wall an original painting by an unknown artist than several prints of world masterpieces. One problem with prints is that they are usually smaller than the originals. They may be two-thirds the size or half the size or even less than that, and size is important. Then, too, paintings are not two-dimensional, but three, and although the third dimension of depth is quantitatively slight, it is qualitatively of the greatest importance. Brush strokes are the same sort of thing as words in books. True, there are prints that endeavor to reproduce this third dimension and give us some sense of brushwork, but they cannot reproduce the quality of the originals.

Prints may be thought of as notes and reminders; a great deal may be learned from them about a work of art (and even reproductions of the best pictures are better than nothing), but they cannot give us the central fact of the experience. They will always be a little like the plastic toy or the molded glass. So just as we need to have a few practical objects of good quality in our houses, we also need to have at least one good original picture and/or sculpture. To know and feel the difference between an original and a print is an important step in artistic education.

Let me also say something here about the difference between nudity in a great work of art and pornography. To tell the difference, we need always to ask ourselves whether a picture enables us worshipfully to enjoy the wonder of creation or simply arouses lust. A completely unclothed figure may produce a feeling of reverence, while a partly clothed figure in a glossy magazine may be provocative or inane. Much painting of the nude must be rejected because, although it may be technically competent, it treats woman as a possession (e.g., Rubens and Renoir). In these matters, we need also to ask ourselves what it is we really do feel, which may be different from what the picture can enable us to feel. Because of the awe surrounding them, it is difficult to think of anyone's reacting with any sense of lust to the figures of Adam and Eve in Michelangelo's *Creation of Adam*. But it may take education to learn to appreciate Botticelli's *Primavera* as a tribute to the freshness of spring without improper lustful feeling. We cannot move faster than our educational level permits.

Music Radio and television, records and tapes—these allow us to bring music into our homes on an unprecedented scale. Unfortunately, there has been over the last few centuries an inverse relationship between technical expertise in producing, recording, and broadcasting music and the quality of the music being produced. Jazz and rock have now become a predominant moral problem for the whole of Western civilization. I find it difficult to see anything in most of the variants of jazz (ending at the moment with rock) except sex and violence alternating with self-pity. This music exploits musical rhythms in a deliberately excitatory way, and the original purpose of that exploitation was to excite to violence and/or sex. The fact that we suppress our inclinations in those directions doesn't mean that the music isn't doing that to us. Jazz rhythms are emphatic, but they are also disturbing and destructive. The spirit of this music is, as a whole, orgiastic, and its mere loudness is one of the ways in which sensitivity is lost (and, indeed, in which actual physical damage is done to the hearing). Jazz and rock produce violent sensations that lead to a desire for still greater violence, still greater volume. This music is demonic.

There is also something profoundly wrong with the incidental music of low quality that the radio and the TV frequently provide us with. Music that is intended to lull us, to soothe us, to put us to sleep, to make us forget what we ought to remember, is not the truth. It is the enemy of the truth. It is a drug. The object of art is to make us more awake, more vigilant, to make us notice more things, not to recline us on a kind of miserable, half-warm porridge of daily existence.

I do not say that classical music is the only good music, nor even that all classical music is good. There is strength in folk music, and there has to be strength from the folk in art in order that there may be really superior culture. Shakespeare did not despise the popular and the folk; he used it and made something superior of it. So I am not talking like a highbrow. The folk song is a fundamental experience of love and death, but it needs to be counterbalanced by the hymn that celebrates love and life.

As for classical music, let me begin by saying that there has crept into the classical music of the nineteenth and twentieth centuries an erotic and self-indulgent tinge that also affects some so-called religious music. Take Wagner: there is a sickly sexuality in *Tristan und Isolde;* there is a sickly religiosity in *Parsifal.* And can one say that the feelings evoked by *Parsifal* are any different from those evoked by *Tristan,* although the former is supposed to be centered on the sufferings of our Lord and the latter is a story of romantic infidelity? Erotic feeling shades readily into other self-indulgent feelings including, particularly, self-pity. Indeed, in *Parsifal* and *Tristan,* it is difficult to distinguish between the eroticism and the self-pity; they are blended. There is, in fact, very little music since the beginning of the nineteenth century which is not vitiated by what vitiates the whole of our society: self-pity, self-regard, self-esteem.

Tchaikovsky is another example. I know that he is a remarkably competent composer, but his most important music is a miserable expression of self-pity, and it does not have an enlightening, edifying, or upbuilding effect on anybody. Some of you may have read about his wretched life, and some of you may have even seen a more wretched film about it. The point is it is in company with his music: the sobbing of a deserted soul.

There is another set of emotions and attitudes that perturbs in some classical music: that of self-assertion, defiance, the dramatic gesture, the heroic. Self-assertion is liable to erupt into even the very best of Beethoven, right to the very end. It is there even in the last works, the last sonatas or quartets. They are wonderfully meditative, and then, suddenly, this kind of "I, Beethoven, am still here" is obtruded upon one. The self-assertion can be felt most keenly when Beethoven's last works are contrasted with the religious works of Bach, which are absorbed completely into worship. Since adulthood, I have never felt certain about anything in Beethoven—not quite certain. There is that streak of defiance. It is not despair; it is very often triumph. But even then there is a kind of grimness in it, a kind of determined self-assertion. It is, indeed, what most people probably like Beethoven for; but the heroism and defiance are hardly reconcilable with the spirit of obedience to the gospel.

As a reaction against the heroic and the self-indulgent, we often have in modern music a dry intellectuality, a negation, almost a cynicism. These are qualities in Stravinsky; they are qualities of so-called intellectual jazz.

From obsession with the erotic, the sentimental, the self-pitying, the self-assertive, the arid, and the violent, it is refreshing to return to the religious music of the seventeenth and eighteenth centuries, and particularly that of Bach and Mozart. These two in their musical practice exemplify the unity we find in the gospel of obedience and the following of a strict form with a sense of freedom and joy overflowing from the form. It is difficult to imagine better examples of this combination of discipline and freedom in a sense of liberated joy. These composers are capable of all the moods and passions but always in the same framework of faith. Theirs is not the triumph of self-assertion, but of worship. There is a passage in Herman Hesse's *Das Glasperlenspiel* (which has been translated into English under the title of *Magister Ludi*) about Bach's *heiterkeit.* I cannot translate this word exactly into English, but it is close to *serenity,* though not quite so "superior." Bach's extensive musical production and his twenty children of two marriages point to the kind of strength that lies behind his music: it flows on, develops, evolves, combines, spreads, goes up and down at the same time, but always comes back again as he dances his worship before our Father. There is no individual self-assertion there at all. And no choir sings these two composers better than our own Tabernacle Choir with its faith in the gospel; I wish it always sang such music.

Literature

Why do so few children in America today find it easy and enjoyable to read? It is because books are not an essential part of the sitting-room. It is because their parents do not read. It is because their parents do not even engage them in serious conversation, for learning to read cannot be separated from learning to speak. It is for a great many different reasons of that kind. But it all goes back to the family.

What did educated upper-middle-class people—and they *were* educated in the nineteenth and early twentieth centuries—what did they have? What were the major linguistic characteristics of their family life? The educated governess and the disquisitory meal table. Father and mother and children sat around the table, and discussion might begin on all manner of topics. Parents did not come down to the level of the children sitting around the table. The children were going to have to live up to a standard, and by degrees they did live up to that standard. They began to talk in a mature and educated way at a quite early age. This still happens in some families in upper-middle-class Britain. One still meets boys and girls of ten or twelve who speak with complete adequacy and fluency because they have been brought up in that kind of atmosphere; their parents have paid attention to their speech, and the children have been part of family conversation. This is not a matter of just one hour—and I understand that it is very often reduced to one hour—of family home evening. This is something which requires the presence of the head of the household at a fair number of meals throughout the week (and why not breakfast as well as dinner?) in order that the use of English in the household may be adequately maintained. Boys and girls from these more leisured upper-middle-class households of Britain, and of other European countries, came to the university adequate in speech, reading, and writing. We can see from the kind of letters written in the nineteenth century that people were adequate in this way. Quite ordinary people wrote good letters that were correctly punctuated and spelled and that were sensitive and discriminative in expression.

Now, about reading, it is all very well to read silently to yourself, but the right thing to do with anything worthwhile is to read it aloud to yourself or, even better, to others. Parents who are in the habit of reading to one another and to their children will find that their children respect reading and want to read. Children can even learn to read by being in an atmosphere in which there is reading, in which it is done with them there. They gradually come to follow on the page, and before you know it, they are reading. Children can do that by the time they are three-and-a-half, and they should. Other benefits aside, they would be much less of a nuisance if they could read by the age of three-and-a-half. They would have another means of amusing themselves. I think that the earlier a child learns to read, the better. There may be some children who wouldn't wish to read, but normally children up to a certain age are eager to read.

The most important thing we can read to our children is the scriptures. The scriptures can be a complete education, as has been shown by those in the past who truly educated themselves from the scriptures when they had no other education—people like John Bunyan, George Fox, and Joseph Smith, who is the greatest example. Joseph Smith was, of course, a great genius, otherwise he could not have got out of the scriptures the education that he did. But all of us can get something if we will but read the scriptures. And, indeed, by reading the scriptures thoroughly, we can get a better education than we can in any other way. Self-educated people who have read the scriptures are better educated than someone who has been through BYU or Harvard or Berkeley or wherever because the self-educated have been reading the word of the Lord and concentrating on it.

But, alas, the scriptures no longer occupy the place in our lives that they did with our forebears. We no longer read the scriptures aloud to one another daily in the family, as we should do, year after year, decade after decade, until they have sunk in and become part and parcel of ourselves. They are no longer a stable part of public education, as they were in Britain when I was a child: in my school, we had two scriptural lessons per week and a Bible reading in school assembly every single morning. Even in the Church we often prefer to read about the scriptures rather than to read the scriptures themselves. The result of this is that we do not readily appreciate the scriptures or get out of them all that there is to be got. Fewer and fewer people today are able to *feel* the scriptures; they haven't been brought up to do it. They don't know what is going on there.

The voices we hear as little children remain with us, so parents must read the scriptures to their children as early as possible. The child who hears the scriptures in the loved voices of his father and mother will come, through that love, to understand the scriptures and appreciate them in the best way. I heard the scriptures daily in my childhood: my father read us a section of the Bible before breakfast every morning. And I can still hear my father's voice in my ear. I think perhaps the first thing I can remember is the calling of Samuel: that is a passage greatly to impress a quite small child, although a small child may not yet fully understand any more than Samuel what it was all about. I can still hear my father reading me the account of the voyages and shipwreck of Paul, reading me the parable of the prodigal son. You must know that the emotion I feel about that parable is far greater because my father (who was killed when I was nine years old) read that to me from time to time, and it is with me for eternity, so I shall be able to thank him for it when I get to the other side. Before he died, I had heard my father read the scriptures for three or four years—I had understood them for those three or four years—and those passages are still in my mind.

Through the voice of their parents, children can hear and become familiar with the voice of the Lord. A stranger's voice on a tape will not do. Neither will the caricatured voice we hear from simplified scriptures do. I believe in giving the children the milk and meat of the scriptures and not other people's adaptations. There are things in the scriptures that can appeal to children from the age of four years onwards: e.g., the boyhood of Samuel, the story of David and Goliath, Luke's account of Christmas, the voyage of Paul to Rome. Those are good and very different examples.

Some may think that the language of the scriptures is too difficult for children, but the language of the scriptures can be built into children's lives if it is part of their daily existence. A family that reads the scriptures together regularly from the time when the oldest child is still an infant in arms will be helping the children, as they grow, to learn the language of the scriptures at the same time as they absorb the language of their home and environment. We need to remember that the Lord has given children faculties for learning language even greater than those of adults. I will not say that as a child I understood the scriptures immediately, but I absorbed the language of the scriptures and gradually came to understand it in the same way that I came to understand other parts of my own language. That was the most important part of my education, and indeed there is no reason why it shouldn't also be for Mormon children.

It is good for children to hear their favorite passages of scripture, and their other favorite stories, too, over and over. Repetition is important. Those children who want us to repeat the same story again and again each night are normal and healthy. As soon as they want a new story every night, something has gone wrong. We should not bring up our children to respond to the exciting, the thrilling. Americans don't get told this, but the thrilling and the exciting are bad. The thrilling and the exciting are a titillation of the nerves. To be moved is one thing; to be excited or titillated, a very different thing. If we bring up our children always to be wanting something new, then before we know it they will be hooked on drugs or racing cars or something like that because they will have to have a stronger stimulus each time until they finally bust. But if we inure our children to stability, to repetition, to normal life, if we get them interested in sameness and in the variety that can be found in sameness and exclude the exciting and thrilling, then they will live decent lives. But if they want always to have a thrill and titillation, their sex will go that way, their aesthetics will go that way, even their religious experience.

Let me now say something about children's literature. Fortunately, we have more good writing for children and more good illustrations for children's books now than ever before in history. So if we are good parents, we at least have the opportunity of giving our children better things than in the past have been available. It is my conviction, in fact, that in this age of bad art, terrible art, violence, sexual perversions, and all the other things that fill the mass media, the best literature that is being produced—you might even say the only really good positive literature that is being produced—is children's literature. I find myself, as I grow older, reading more and more children's literature because the rest is almost unbearable unless I confine myself to that written before 1800. The same can be said of the music, for that matter.

One of my colleagues on campus says that the only contemporary literature in the West that is any good at all is children's literature because it still preserves some vestige of proper moral standards. And I think that that goes very near to being the truth. I know that there are some screwy children's books, and they've been shown up in the press, but most books for children are based on sound Christian morality. That is one of the surprising things still about most children's books. It is astonishing that Christianity is not yet dead in a culture that has turned its back on it.

When I need comfort, at the more superficial level perhaps, I may take up a children's book. (When I need comfort at a deeper level, I take up the scriptures.) I may go back to a book that I read when I was a child, a book like Kenneth Grahame's *The Wind in the Willows* or A. A. Milne's *The House at Pooh Corner*, books that most of you know. Not long ago in Britain, I listened with my sister to a reading of the "The House at Pooh Corner" on television. It was a great experience after decades and decades to sit there and listen again to that story, its sound humor, its straightforwardness, its moral soundness.

If I were to rate a few of the better known English children's authors on a scale of one to ten, I would give Kenneth Grahame a six, A. A. Milne a seven, Lewis Carroll an eight, and Arthur Ransome a ten. I can't say very much about American authors because I am not as familiar with them. However, I do like Louisa May Alcott very much. She is the first American author I ever read (I read her at the age of seven or eight), and I shall go on happily reading her until I die, I hope. I am also glad to have discovered Sendak. He has an uncanny ability to illustrate nightmare. And in his pictures, he constantly uses images of terrible things together with images of the mother so that the mother overcomes the terrible.

We need to acquaint children with folktales, which are the classics of their own tradition. And we need to recognize that there is a great difference between a folktale and a fairy tale. A fairy tale is a make-over of a folktale. A fairy tale tries to make the world more pleasant than the folktale represents it, pleasanter than it really is, under the impression that the world will be bad enough for children when they come to it. The fairy tale represents life as something restricted and magically protected. The fairy tale does not help children at all.

If you turn to the original Grimm's folktales, you will find that the folk have profoundly understood over thousands of years that children must face up to nightmares and horror and cruelty. And since children have to face up to those things, the best place for them to do so for the first time is on a parent's lap, where they have a sense of security. If children are not "terrified" on their parents' laps, they will be terrified in their dreams when their parents aren't there. We know enough about children from a very early age to know that they have their nightmares and their horrors and their darknesses. If we don't give them those kinds of experiences, they still have them.

By becoming acquainted with folk literature, children may be educated. By that means, they may grow up facing reality. And if they grow up facing reality, there will be no crisis of confidence between them and society. Like people of earlier ages, they won't be taken in. The people in Shakespeare's time weren't taken in. They were politically sophisticated and realistic. They always knew the next day what had gone on at the palace, and it was what had really gone on, too.

My grandfather and grandmother certainly had the folklore of the past in a way that my mother and father did not because my grandfather and grandmother were not "educated," whereas my father and mother were half educated, which is the worst kind of thing to be. Either be completely uneducated or be educated. To be half educated and not recognize it is to be in the perilous state of mind that makes the *Reader's Digest* sell thirty million copies around the world. If you learn the folk tradition, you won't want to read the *Reader's Digest* because you won't want things predigested for you. You won't want to be bottle fed. Though the food has to be predigested for babies, it won't for you. "When I became a man, I put away childish things," Paul wrote (1 Cor. 13:11). Well, childish things are prevalent in my culture and in your culture. They are not so prevalent in German and Scandinavian cultures. Unfortunately, the Germans and the Scandinavians who have come to this country have adopted Anglo-Saxon culture instead of keeping their own more realistic culture.

One of the greatest disadvantages of fairy tales is this: they give to children the assurance that there are magical powers by which they can do all sorts of things without making an effort. That is ultimately what magic is about—not having to make an effort. Good literature with Christian values teaches children that they must try, that they must make an effort. And this is one of the most important things for children to learn. That is why an author like Enid Blyton, for example, is not good for children. I don't suppose she is much read in this country, but she has been read by so many tens of millions. Enid Blyton gives children morality, it is true enough, but she also gives them a magical world in which they do not have to make an effort to succeed because magic is there to help them out. That is the wrong kind of book.

When our children are twelve or thirteen, they should be able to begin reading some of the classics and go on reading them all their lives. I say "some" because it is difficult in the teens to get the experience of many of the classics. There are things that are no use trying to read at that age. I read *Faust*, part two, when I was seventeen and got very little out of it. I got plenty out of *Faust*, part one. I reread *Faust*, part two, at the age of fifty-four: the whole thing lived for me, and I was astonished at it. Half of my life lay in between the two readings. But I read *Don Quixote* (in English) at the age of ten and was enthralled by it; I read Plato's *Republic* at the age of twelve, and I didn't want to stop for a meal—the book gave me a sense of power I had never before experienced, a new way of comprehension. I read all of Shaw and Conrad between fourteen and sixteen, all Hardy by eighteen, all Lawrence by twenty. But best of all was Jane Austen. In my experience, girls can appreciate Jane Austen from the age of twelve, boys from the age of fifteen. Kipling can be read throughout the teens. (*The Jungle Book*, of course, can be read much earlier, around the age of six.)

Television

I want now to say something about television. The Lord has not ever given humanity so valuable an educational means as television. It could be marvelous. Sometimes it is used well, but for the most part it is used in vain. Think of the football games, the spoken account of what is happening pouring from the mouth of a hysterical commentator—or a pseudohysterical commentator, which is maybe even worse. The thing to do is to *play* games, not stupefy yourself by hours of watching them. Think of the soap operas that people waste their time with when they could be listening to good music. When you consider what television could have been used for, educationally and spiritually, its misuse is one of the most distressing things of all history.

What is the worst thing on television nowadays—the lies it tells about patent medicines or the truth it tries to tell about the news? Now, it is true that a great many people aren't taken in by television advertisements. Even many children are not taken in; they can see, for example, how ridiculous breakfast cereal advertisements are if the foolishness is pointed out to them. But we mustn't think of these things as trifles; they are not trifles. The interest of advertisers in teenagers has been severely destructive of teenage life. This is one reason why the Church is losing adolescent members. (What underlies our loss is the Mormon adolescent's illusion that there is a better kind of life outside.)

It is surprising how comfortable most of us feel, forgetting that they are not fiction, with the horrors that are almost daily presented to us on the television screen. I remember one TV program: the commentator said that a news film company had handed over two-thirds of its library to UCLA for research use, and then he showed one or two excerpts. One of the excerpts was the burning of the Hindenburg airship at LaGuardia Airport—panic, screaming, agony, death. The TV man commented, "A good, dramatic sequence, even in black and white." And what does a photographer do on such an occasion? Is it the photographer's duty to continue to photograph? I don't know what I could do on such an occasion except fling myself to my knees and pray to God. What else can be done when you are faced with a situation like that and you are helpless? People were running about like ants. How helpless we can be in such a situation is a reminder of what Moses realized, "man is nothing" (Moses 1:10).

The same morning on the same program, there was a report on a group of children suffering from progeria who met in Los Angeles and were submitted to the vulgarity of Disneyland (after all, Khrushchev had been submitted to it). The comment on this episode was, "It makes a fine story, doesn't it?"

And let me remind you of the photographer who, some twenty years ago in the Congo, came across a group of soldiers who had forty prisoners and bribed the soldiers to shoot the prisoners in order that he might photograph the shooting.

Well, those three episodes put news reporting at its worst into focus. What did Lear say? "Is there any cause in nature that makes these hard hearts?" (*King Lear*, 3.6.77). Sisters Goneril and Regan, prominent mass-media reporters in this, our time, have ceased to be moved by anything. They just record.

A central problem is this (I have noticed it even more with children than with adults): we cease to make a distinction between the fictional events on the screen and the real events on the screen. We see violent death in fiction frequently. Then we accept violent death in reality without a murmur because we have assimilated the two. We watch real deaths on the screen, like the death of a boxer, and don't think anything of it. We protect ourselves from the horror of what the world is really like by equating it merely with fiction—which is also horrible—but we are all so used to it as fiction that we take it as amusement. Horror has always been one of the principal amusements of mankind.

People in modern society, as those in ancient societies, watch great shows in the hope that somebody will be killed or hurt. Then they will have a thrill. People go to car races, for example, in the hope that there will be a fiery car accident and they will have the thrill of seeing somebody burned to death in front of them. It is the same kind of thing that led mobs to the Roman Coliseum to see Christians killed by lions. It is what makes people want to go to public executions. There is public execution in some countries still—in Iran, for example. When I lived there, they used to hang criminals outside the principal bank at 7:00 A.M., and ten or twenty thousand people would go to watch.

Television could have been a valuable educational tool, but for the most part, we have taken it and exploited it. And the question is, Can we go the right way after having gone the wrong way? Although repentance by an individual is not too difficult, repentance by a culture is very difficult. And repentance by the mass media, which are under the thumb of the advertisers, seems almost impossible, unless the advertisers repent. Luckily, your maximum viewing still seems to be at the age of twelve. From the age of twelve onwards, teenagers seem to watch less and less.

Of course, television has made young people quicker in picking up visual clues. When my stepdaughter was young, we would go into these continuous film performances in England—people just go into the English cinema when they want and come out when they want, and the films seem made accordingly. She could pick the clues up in a moment or two and could tell me what was going on. She was familiar with the screen, and she knew how to interpret its phenomena. That is a good development. Television does increase alertness to some things, but it increases non-alertness to others.

The essential trouble with television is that it reels on—it is and then isn't there. The book is always there, and we can go back to it again and again, and we should go back to it again and again—that is what we should do with all good literature; literature that we don't want to go back to is not worth reading. But the image on the screen is there and gone. This is dangerous; the flow of this medium and the permissiveness of our society are probably linked. Standards are things that stand, that hold, that stay put. Most of our society nowadays doesn't stay put—it flows. It flows in front of our dreamy eyes and into the labyrinth of our ears. If we don't look out, it will have a bad effect on both, and especially on the eyes and ears of our children.

The new vogue for videos enables me to end on a positive note: videos give parents the chance to *choose* what comes into the home. And children like to see videos again and again. The video library can lead to the book library. Children like watching with parents: if the parents are interested in good appropriate videos, the children are more likely to be so. This is a fashion and a technical development for us to use to the full: the opportunity to put on the screen what we want to put there instead of what the advertiser wants put there.

Let me quote, in conclusion, from the scriptures where the Lord says, "If ye then, being evil, know how to give good gifts unto your children . . ." (Matt. 7:11). It is remarkable how many evil people have given good gifts to their children because they (the parents) are not evil to their children. Perhaps some love of one's children survives when everything else good is gone. Our culture will survive by what we do for our children. Let us educate them in the home.

Disciplines

THERE IS A big difference between education and training. We train to achieve certain specific ends; we educate in order to prepare people for life so that they may deal creatively with the unexpected as well as the expected, professionally and otherwise. Education is a broader and more fundamental preparation than training.

These days we think of our universities as being there to train people to become lawyers, to become businesspeople, etc., whereas the sole purpose of the university should be to educate people. I remember my grandfather, who was a good watchmaker but a poor man, saying to me, "Arthur, get all the education you can. But never get it for anything else than its own sake. Don't get it for what it will bring you. Don't get it in order to improve your position. Don't get it in order to prepare yourself for life in the professional way. Get education." I have borne that in mind all my life (although when I joined the Church, I realized that education must ultimately be for the Lord's sake, not its own). My grandfather was a very poor man, but he understood that education was different from training. The working class in Britain understood that in the nineteenth century. There was an organization called the Workers' Education Association, which helped workers learn about the history of their country, about its literature, and so on. They appreciated that because they valued education. Nowadays, workers want specialist courses developed by trade unions that teach them to qualify for more pay.

We acquire education by learning from educated people the various disciplines that have traditionally been found to produce such people. Unfortunately, in the modern world, we are abandoning many of those disciplines, and as a consequence, we are losing educational ground. The fundamental point is Chesterton's: "If you want to remove a fence, first of all find out why the fence was put there." Otherwise, you may have a mad bull at you. The fence was there, and it has gone, and there are mad bulls all over the world just now.

What are the disciplines we need in order to become educated? It seems to me that there are three fundamental disciplines or categories of disciplines: first, language; second, mathematics; third, the arts, including athletics (the Greeks would have called it dance). These disciplines are ways in which we can express ourselves to the universe and can interpret the universe to ourselves. They are all open ended. Otherwise, we could not act creatively with them. If there were no such disciplines, there would be no free agency and there would be no eternal progression.

Language is the discipline we use for symbolic communication with each other. We might have used mathematics or some artistic medium, but language was chosen. "In the beginning was the Word" (John 1:1). So it is language I want to deal with first and then the other disciplines in their turn.

Language

Discipline in language includes discipline in speaking, reading, and writing. And I find at BYU, as I have found at universities in other countries, including Britain, that the problem of students' not being able to speak, read, or write properly is a tremendous one. Students' English is inadequate even at the graduate level because neither the earlier school education of graduate students nor their education in their families has brought them to the required level. To aggravate the problem further, even many faculty members do not know how to lecture or read or write. (The inability to lecture, incidentally, may be more common in Britain than here. Here there is greater social poise and greater social confidence than in Britain.) What ought to be done about this situation?

In the first place, the English department on any campus ought primarily to be concerned with the use of English on the campus, not with the study of English literature in the department. This means that English should not just be something gone through at the beginning and then dropped. It is something that must be pursued unremittingly, *pari passu* with the student's main studies, whatever the major subject, until the writing, speaking, and reading of each student are adequate. Secondly, all faculty members must collaborate in insisting on good reading and writing. All teachers on campus have to recognize that they have to be teachers of English as well as their own subjects. Indeed, the teaching of English cannot be divorced from the teaching of reasoning, the teaching of persuasion, the teaching of self-expression in all forms.

I consider my job on BYU campus, as I have considered my job on other campuses in the past, to be the job of teaching people to read and helping myself to learn to read better in the process. Learning to read is a lifetime process, and it increasingly has enemies. Its principal enemies at the moment are the mass media and that dreadful thing that our modern life has forced upon us, the need to read quickly. Our major task is not to learn to read quickly, but to learn to read slowly—slowly enough to have some understanding of what we are reading. The more quickly we read, the fewer our thoughts will be, but the more slowly we read, the more our thoughts will come thronging in. It is not the speed at which we read that counts, but the speed at which thoughts come.

The reading of books has to be firmly defended nowadays. A few years ago, I went to what was then called the Church College of Hawaii and talked to some of the people there about the trouble they were having teaching English. They told me they were trying to reduce the amount of reading in classes as much as possible. In biology class, for example, teachers thought that visual material was enough. Their object was to get the students through their examinations by using visual material. Teachers said, "Students don't have to read books. They can't read books anyway." That is cynicism or despair. That has nothing to do with the gospel. In the educational institutions of the Church, nothing but the best is due to the students.

Nowadays, many classes at the university level, if not most of them, have as their primary object the conveying of information that can and should be gotten from books. As I see it, if classes are used just to pass on information, they are replacing something else that ought to do that: the library. The more classes a university runs, the fewer books its students read, partly because they haven't so much time, but partly because they go to classes to get in predigested form the stuff that they should be getting for themselves directly from books, and not only textbooks, but monographs.

This applies, in my view, even at the undergraduate stage. Surely what needs to be done is to encourage and train students to read so that they can acquire information for themselves by reading. Someone once said to me, "We can't have a course in this subject because we haven't yet got a textbook." That seemed to me an extraordinary remark. Surely if there is a textbook, there is less need for a course; and if there is no textbook or no good one, that is just where a course is needed. Generally, courses and faculty/student interface are needed for the development of skills, the inculcation of method, the application of principle, the acquiring of attitude—to show how learning is organized, how it can stimulate and lead to discussion—not for information that students should be getting by reading.

There is a higher illiteracy as well as a higher education, and that higher illiteracy is becoming characteristic of modern European and American civilization. We read more and more and understand less and less, partly because we read too quickly, but also partly because during the years of our schooling we have not been submitted to any unremitting disciplinary training in the use of language. And I do not see how even so low as at the grade school level we can divorce true education from a certain amount of grind and insistence on detail and accuracy. Unless students get that kind of training, they will never learn to speak, read, or write properly.

Another point I want to make about language is this: it is unlikely that we shall be fully educated in our own language if we don't know another language. The major reason for learning a second language is not that it will enable us to talk to the people in a foreign country or to read their literature or to understand their culture; it is more basic than that. It is that we don't know our own language until we know at least one other. Knowing another language helps us to know from the outside what our own language is like. In the English public schools in the days of compulsory Latin and Greek, Latin verse writing and Latin and Greek translation from and into English gave a few thousand people in the United Kingdom in the nineteenth century some real knowledge of writing and literature. It may have been a grind, and it may have been that perhaps two-thirds of them did not like it, but the other third formed that great cultured British upper-middle class that produced so much good writing on all subjects.

This type of education, with its results, was also to be found in the nineteenth century in other European countries and also to some extent in the United States.

One of the most fundamental intellectual discoveries ever is that there are many different ways of saying things, and we can't know how many different ways until we get into a foreign language, especially some language like Chinese or Navajo that is very different from English. I remember my assistant, Cynthia Hallen, who served a mission in Bolivia, saying that she began to understand the gospel far more profoundly when she heard, read, and taught it, not in Spanish, but in Aymara, which is the principal Indian language in the part of Bolivia where she worked. Some of you may also know something of Indian and Eskimo languages. Those languages were first properly studied in the United States back in the 1920s by a man named Sapir, who wrote perhaps the most important book on language that we have. He was an anthropologist, and what anthropologists have to say about language is often more valuable than what philologists or linguists have to say about it. It is an accessible book, not too difficult to understand, but people don't read it much nowadays.

The experience of another language interacting with one's own can be very profound. I find myself at times thinking or talking in Swedish, French, or German, and I have discovered that there are various moods that are linked with those times. I don't need to go into biographical detail, but I am a slightly different person in each of those languages, and yet all of those persons are together in one person.

Mathematics

Numeracy is hardly less important than literacy. Numeracy means having the ability to calculate, which is essential to functioning in society, and also having some familiarity with the computer, which is also important nowadays. (I am convinced that humanists should all be taking courses in the use of the computer; if humanists let only the technologists and the scientists handle the computer, then the computer will not become as subtle, as interesting, and as valuable a tool as it should become.) But numeracy should not be the end of our mathematical knowledge. In mathematics, it seems to me, we do well to go as far as we can. We do well to get into calculus because as soon as we conquer that field we have approached the world of an alternate symbolic system to language. We do well to continue until we come to see mathematics as an art, as a game, as ultimately a form of spiritual exercise.

Mathematics may be seen as a sublanguage of ordinary language. A mathematician might express any important thing in ordinary language, but it would take much language to do it. Mathematics is shorthand for language. Mathematics enables us to manipulate symbols in a way that we shouldn't have otherwise thought. And once we have done it, we can then describe the results in ordinary language. But we couldn't have gotten there without the mathematics.

Mathematics is a fundamental way of dealing with the universe. It enables us to understand how the universe works in certain ways—not in all ways, but in certain ways. Not only that, but it is a way of controlling and operating the universe, a way of prophesying. This extraordinary power of mathematics is why mathematics has pulled the natural sciences with it, pulled the biological sciences with it, and pulled even the humanities with it.

Mathematics is necessary in order to make sense of recent natural science, which is very different from what science was, up until the beginning of the twentieth century. And it is not merely relativity we need to understand, but also indeterminism. Modern physics requires particles to be in two places at once. But how can anything be in two places at once? We are baffled. Physics has brought us to a point at which we are up against the veil. We are now producing paradoxical statements about the universe that are almost impossible to understand—such things as a positive universe going one way and a negative universe going the other way and the two interchanging in some sort of way as they go along. Statements such as these make mathematical sense, but they don't make common sense.

A lack of proficiency in mathematics, more so perhaps than a lack of proficiency in reading, is seen as a significant cultural and, therefore, social and political lack in this country. At the same time, even less is done about mathematics than reading. There is a deep-rooted prejudice against mathematics here in this country, as there is in Britain; I do not observe the same prejudice in Scandinavia and Germany. This may be because education in Scandinavia and

Germany is more oligarchic than it is in Britain or the United States. I would observe that it was traditional in the nineteenth century, when British education was oligarchic, for a talented person to read both classics and mathematics at a university.

I remember when I began studying math that I hated it, but the further I got into it, the more interested I became. I think I hated it to start with because in that day children were taught it in a routine way. Some children are taught it better now. I remember Zacharias, whom I once met at Oxford at a curriculum conference, saying that quite young children can learn the most fundamental mathematical concepts provided they are taught with three-dimensional shapes. A lot of investigation into the intellectual capabilities of young children is now being carried on. And there is no doubt about it that when children are three, four, five, or six they can learn a great deal. Sometimes it seems to me that our faculties before we are six years old are fantastically greater than what they are later. We ought to make more use of them. In the light of what Zacharias, Bruner, and others are saying about teaching mathematics and also physics to young children, and in the light of experiments in the Soviet Union, there is a great deal to be said for giving children the maximum intellectual stimulation they are capable of handling at any given age, and at any given age, they may be capable of handling more than we think. A great deal of time is wasted between the ages of three and six.

Arts

I want finally to say something about artistic disciplines. And let me first be clear what I mean by artistic disciplines. I mean, first of all, ability in the fine arts. Music, particularly, is very important, and I think everyone ought to learn to read music. A great many people can, but not enough. But I also mean, and Plato mentions this in *The Republic*, the dance. Under the dance, he included athletics and physical games of all kinds, as well as ballet and other forms of what we call dance. All these involve the kinesthetic expression of ourselves to the universe and the kinesthetic interpretation of the universe through ourselves to others and to ourselves.

The pattern is the fundamentally important thing. We may be rowing in a boat, moving on a football field, or playing tennis—however we are moving, we are fulfilling a pattern. The need to fulfill patterns is something so basic that we share it with the animals. Think of the ritualistic behavior of animals—the complex mating habits of birds, for example. Many of these behavior patterns have no apparent practical purpose. Apes take pleasure in running around in a figure eight. It is native behavior. It is a way of being that is in the blood. Kinesthetic expression may communicate in a more total way than other forms of expression. When we watch ballet dancers expand and contract as they perform, for example, our total self responds to that; our muscles and our minds together respond. At its highest level, ritualistic behavior may be a form of religious worship.

Participation in dance and athletics is a means of enhancing personal grace. Basketball players on the court move with ballet-like assurance. They leap around like young gods and goddesses. They really do. They are magnificent. Even in football, there are these superb examples of both individual and team plays. The unfortunate thing is that when the players come off the court, when they come off the field after the game is over, they slouch around like gorillas. That seems to be part of our culture. The poise that Asian and African men and women traditionally achieve in walking and moving is part of true education. If we were living in Nigeria or India or Southeast Asia, we should not sit as we do. We should sit formally, and that formality would be so ingrained in us that we should not slouch as we naturally do. In a good society, people walk about and sit as if they belong on this planet. In my country and in your country, we seem to care very little about this. But why should not we westerners show that we are children of God by walking and moving godlike? If the traditional Asian can do it, so can we. People have a right to demand some dignity both of themselves and of others. Dignity in dress is one aspect of this. But the telling point is the posture beneath the clothes rather than the clothes themselves.

I think Puritanism did away with grace by hatred of the body. That hatred is manifest when people hate to train the body, to use the body together with the mind, not realizing that the two are one. And we are told in the Doctrine and Covenants that they are one, that the spirit is a finer form of matter (see D&C 131:7–8). No other church would agree with us on that fundamental point.

Games and athletics should be for everybody. When they are professionalized and undertaken by a few, they don't necessarily have a good influence on the performance of all because the finer the teams and the better they play, the more likely everybody else is to feel that they could never measure up, and so why should they try. The reason why my country is not "good" at most internationally popular games, even though it developed most of them, is because it has gone on playing them in the old way—that is to say, as things for everybody to do and not to take too seriously.

We best begin as children to learn artistic disciplines. I was put to the piano at the age of three, and I learned to read music before I could read a book. I remember that after I had learned to read, I used to sneak a book on to the piano, play the music, and be reading the book at the same time—it was my way of getting through my practice. But I can never be sufficiently grateful to my father and mother for making me do that at that age because I can still read music at sight. I can no longer make my fingers follow it fast enough, but I can still read it.

The learning of any kind of artistic discipline requires a great deal of routine work. If you are learning to be a ballet dancer, for example, you have to concentrate for years on that bar. If you are learning to play the piano, you have to work on it for hours a day. Then, when you have worked and got control, the thing enters into you, and you are able to perform spontaneously.

In my widowerhood, when I lived with my sister's family, one of my comforts was to listen to my nephew at the piano. He would play and record a passage, listen to it, play and record it again, listen to it again; he might spend three or four hours playing and listening to just one passage literally hundreds of times. Then he would put several passages together to make a larger passage and play, record, and listen to that. He would, in this way, gradually build up to playing the whole piece. And after all that, he was ready when it came time to play that piece in public to do whatever it might occur to him to do, ready for the inspiration that would enable him to make a unique event of playing that piece. He had by the development of his technique brought himself to the point at which he could be spontaneous.

Raphael was once asked by the Pope for an example of his art, so he took his brush and made a perfect circle, just like that. The Pope was rather fed up, but it was a brilliant exposition of what Raphael could do. He didn't have to take his compass and work it out bit by bit. He just did it because he had done it hundreds, thousands of times before.

Complete spontaneity is the ability to respond to anything that the moment offers. That moment may be on the concert platform, on the field, on the stage. Complete spontaneity comes only from the most complete practice. It is dependent on discipline and hard work. It is not untutored and unprepared. Any artist knows that.

Conclusion

The most important subjects in any university are language and mathematics, and if students run away from those subjects, they cannot be educated; it is not possible to be educated without them—they are fundamental. When I first came to BYU and was an associate director of the Honors Program, I suggested that Honors students ought to have another language than English and they ought to have calculus. Students should also learn creative expression, including kinesthetic expression, in one or more of the arts. With these disciplines, students may leave the university with balanced and developed minds. Such disciplines can give a sense of wholeness to students' studies while they are at the university and, after they leave, a means to pursue those studies to the end of their lives.

Disciplines are acquired by long and hard work and best acquired when there is enthusiasm behind the work. And remember that that word "enthusiasm" originally meant a state of being seized by God. Where there is enthusiasm, and that is just another name for the passionate love of a subject, the effort can be untiring: the patience to achieve is part of the passion to achieve. The reward of acquiring disciplines is great. They open up life to spontaneity and grace. They may be means of worship.

Mechanization

We in the Church are often caught between the devil and the deep blue sea. The devil's side is the world trying to come in at the gates. The "deep blue sea" is the world washing in at the back door. I am more interested in the deep blue sea because it is more insidious and because it threatens the Church more than anything in Ohio, Missouri, or Illinois ever did. The deep blue sea consists of those who believe in the world and believe the world is reconcilable with the gospel and consequently advocate phenomena in the culture that are against the gospel. This deep blue sea may drown us, and the most awful thing about this kind of being drowned is that we may not know that it is happening. The cultural phenomenon I am here concerned with is mechanization, and I want to make some observations on its inroads into education and, in places, from education into the Church.

I was once surprised to discover that William Blake had a copy of Bacon's "Advancement of Learning," but I was not surprised when I later learned that Blake scrawled across the front page of it, "Welcome news to Satan." He might have written the same message across Descartes's "Treatise on Method." And what he said about Bacon's work and what he might have said about Descartes's was certainly what he thought about Newton's.

Scientists, however, are usually the most sober and probably the most intelligent people swimming in the deep blue sea. Scientists are usually modest about their propositions. They are well aware that our observations are observations that we make. Our eyes do not see the universe "as it is." They re-create the universe for us. It is the same thing with our ears, it is the same thing with all our senses. They do not reflect the outer world; they re-create the outer world. When we introduce ourselves into experiments, we make a difference—just as when an inspector of schools comes into a class, the class behaves quite differently from the way it does when the inspector of schools is not there. That is, I think, a good analogy to what happens in observation, in science of all kinds. We are not observing the universe anonymously.

Scientists are also aware of the difference between a hypothesis and a fact or a set of facts. Hypotheses are not true. And those scientists who have hypotheses that are so useful that they think of them as true are further from the truth than those who were superstitious before the rise of scientific thinking. A good scientist will always agree that science does not promulgate immutable laws but presents temporary or hypothetical explanations. The immutable laws remain those revealed for governing conduct, not the transient explanations of physical fact.

Physicists today, after two centuries of mechanical thinking, have had to face up to a nonmechanical universe that puzzles them intensely and puzzles all of us even more than it does them. Physicists have invented metaphors in order to try and convey their observations. But the difficulty is that what they are observing, for example, could be talked about as a wave and could be talked about as a particle and then perhaps talked about as an "undicle," but I don't know whether they are getting any closer to a model of the phenomenon by using the metaphors. The model eludes them, and so they find themselves having to rely more and more on mathematics. I am glad that mathematics is ultimately an art; on that I depend for the health of the universe.

Now I am perfectly well aware that mathematics has an uncanny facility for describing some of the things that the Creator does. It is perfectly obvious that some form of abstract thinking can operate on and affect the universe—can do something with it. When it is a question of the natural sciences, there seems to be no doubt about the effectiveness of this kind of thinking. But when we move across to the life sciences, the process has very different results because we are then dealing with life, with the organic. And yet the effort is to try to mechanize, even though our whole feeling about the origin of life, for example, is very different from our feeling about distances between planets and the origin of the universe and so on. I remember a film series on TV called "Life on Earth." Every single picture of life's beauty showed the inadequacy of the narrator's own theorizing about what he was showing. The whole process is much more complex than the mechanistic views of Darwin. And then the effort comes along to mechanize the social sciences. All this is the result of Isaac Newton's living before Darwin. Think to yourself what might have happened if Darwin had lived at the end of the seventeenth century and Newton had lived in the middle of the nineteenth. There would have been the most extraordinary differences. As it was, physics became the model for biology, and the two of them in their turn have influenced the so-called social sciences, which have taken up metaphors and jargon from the natural sciences. The social sciences are in their turn influencing theory and criticism in the humanities and the arts. But once we leave the college of physical sciences and move over to the life sciences and then to the social sciences and education and humanities and the arts, the cloud of glory that we trail behind us becomes cinders and ash.

In the social sciences, the problem is that there are so many variables that social scientists can almost never take them all into account, so they end up with simplistic theories. There are so many causes and so many effects that they have to make a selection, and in making that selection they may be going astray because they may be ignoring things that turn out to be much more important than they thought. In the moral sphere, this thought is very well exemplified in a couple of lines from T. S. Eliot's poem "Gerontion," "Unnatural vices are fathered by our heroism, / And virtues are fostered by our impudent crimes." That is a seriously grim thing to think about.

Psychology, sociology, and economics are fundamentally statistical. They deal with cases, not people. But cases are not people, and if theorists reduce people to cases, they lose the people. My old friend, the philosopher Hans Larsson, who died many years ago—he was born over 120 years ago—said, in 1894, under the shadow of Herbert Spencer, that if social scientists wanted to study the best models of humanity, they should go to the arts because the poet can give in careful, distinct nuance what the theorist cannot give in formulas.

The application of scientific mechanisms to the social sciences is also a denial of individual responsibility and individual choice.

What the laws of economics, sociology, and psychology mean is that people cannot individually decide what they want to do. What those laws mean is that there are certain ways in which people behave, whether or not they are converted. The concept of economic man, for example, is a deterministic construct. And I remember very well a lecture by John Covey, fourteen years ago now, in which he explained how wrong the concept of economic man is from the point of view of the gospel. And we should not in our church accept the concept of economic man because it is dead against the gospel. A Christian nation would not have people dying of hunger.

Behaviorism is a deterministic psychological theory that leaves out the essential responsibility of people for their own choices. It fails as a theory to explain higher forms of human behavior. We in Europe thought that you in America had got rid of Watson, only to learn that you had turned to worship the egregious Skinner instead. If you want to know in detail why I say egregious, read Noam Chomsky's scathing seventy-page review of Skinner's *Verbal Behavior*, which review appeared in the journal *Language* in 1959 and fully documents and demonstrates Skinner's linguistic naiveté. Behaviorism has infiltrated Church instructional material and may have a damaging effect. Behavioral objectives, for example, may ignore the state of one's mind and heart, and that is pharisaism. Such objectives may be suitable in the learning of certain tasks, but the trouble is, the more important a thing is, the more difficult it is to write a behavioral objective for it. I haven't the least idea what behavioral objectives I could possibly write for my Shakespeare classes. I hope those classes will have their effect in terms of what my students do for the whole of their lives. I believe that the principal weapon of the devil in education is mechanization. When the pupil's response ceases to be spontaneous and becomes drilled and mechanical, then the devil has taken over.

Some psychologists today are prepared to believe that homosexuals may be physiologically and genetically conditioned that way. They don't take into account the fact that the mind can profoundly influence the body, that the mind can change the body. Modern physiologists and modern psychologists are realizing that more and more. And above all, medical practitioners are realizing it more and more: the mind can change the body. We have to hang on to freedom of choice as a fundamental principle of Mormon doctrine. Mechanical explanations of human conduct are wrong because they rule out individual initiative.

In 1928, at the age of eighteen, when I first read Freud, I saw that the consequences of Freud are simple: either we are responsible for nothing we do and think, or we are responsible for everything. A person who is to become a God has to be responsible for everything—casual remarks and gestures, "random" activities, dreams. From this point of view, nothing human is accidental. Of course, if we took total responsibility for everything we did, we couldn't stand it; therefore, there has to be an atonement and a redemption.

The world today has tried to decide that we are responsible for nothing we do—in other words, that sin doesn't exist. (However, there is some indication that in some places, some people regret the absence of the word and think it ought to be brought back in again somehow; others take the view that sin is what other people do.) But sin is fundamental to our progress: it is, oddly enough, the way forward. Sin is the means by which we learn what not to do in order to learn what to do, and until we know about it, we know nothing—we are innocent. I don't mean that we must practice it; I mean that we must know about it. We should be realists. We shouldn't be such foolish optimists as to think that all of us are not sinners or such pessimists as to think we are all beyond salvation.

What is the status of psychological counseling in the Church? It is something that the Church has bothered itself about a great deal. What is fundamental is that there is an ecclesiastical authority in charge of each of us who has the right to inspiration about us. And the fact remains that that responsibility is ecclesiastical. Why is it ecclesiastical? Because what is fundamentally wrong with human society and human beings is not psychological, it is not economic, it is not political, it is not anthropological, it is not cultural. It is more fundamental than that. It is sin.

What lies at the heart of the Church's problem with the behavioral sciences, I believe, is this: the behavioral sciences deal with human beings by introducing a jargon that is incompatible with the scriptures, and the scriptures must be the basis of our dealings with human beings. One of my concerns in the Church at the present time, for example, is the word "goal." Now, I don't have any objection to the something hidden behind the word, but I don't like its psychological background and the mechanistic implication that our lives are to be directed by what we think up and fix in our heads. If setting goals does nothing else, it will tend to occlude the Holy Ghost. If we hold on to one goal in our life—to act righteously at every moment—then all the other goals will fall in place. But if we set up for ourselves tactical goals, they may very well get in the way of our strategic goal. The great goal is so difficult that every other goal should submit to it. Every time we make a decision to do something, it should be made in the light of eternity, not in the light of tomorrow or the next day. All decisions are in the light of eternity because all decisions take us one way or another. If we act righteously at one moment, the next moment will be right, but if we don't act righteously, the next moment will be wrong, and so it will go on, and we shall involve ourselves in sin. Whatever the world may say, time and again we have to come back to this: if we are good human beings, if we try to do the right thing, if we love the Lord, we shall do our work properly, we shall have the right relationships with our children, with our wives and husbands, with everybody. And we shall have all the problems of life, like death and absence and disease and things of that kind. But the fact remains that the gospel is the only way in which life can be rightly lived.

"Self-esteem" is another dubious notion that has come from a mechanistic psychological background. The idea is that when we act with confidence, it is because inside us is an "esteemed self." But the self is not the kind of thing we can get hold of to esteem. And if we try to esteem it, the self we are esteeming is not the self we are. And, indeed, I am extremely dubious about the self we are. I used to have a disagreement with my stepdaughter on this subject. She said, "We have to be what we are." And I said, "No, we cannot be what 'we are'; it is impossible. What we can do is become what we may." We are ourselves all the time, of course; we are ourselves in action at any moment. Nevertheless, we each have a central quality that can be damaged or enhanced by what we do. As the great founder of my former sect said, "There is that of Christ in every man." And that of Christ is obviously our fundamental self, the self we discover ourselves to have been, wanted ourselves to be, the self we need to find. And such finding is something that requires self-forgetfulness. Self-forgetfulness seems to me to be prime, not self-esteem as so many people think. Forget yourself, and you may become yourself. But if you are thinking about yourself, you have not forgotten yourself, and can, therefore, never be yourself, let alone ever become yourself. The fundamental mistake of the devil was to try to be himself. What lay behind his sin of pride was trying to be himself by being different from the Father, when his job was not to try to be himself, but to become himself by obedience to the Father.

The more one develops as a person, the more one wishes to be like the Father, as the Son wished to be like the Father. And the Son said, "He that hath seen me hath seen the Father" (John 14:9). We become ourselves through willing, joyful obedience. The gospel has no more use for self-esteem than it has for self-pity or self-regard. It is the devil in the guise of an angel of light: it is the opposite of self-forgetfulness. One of the mistakes we make over and over again in life is to go directly for the things we think are important. But if we aim at self-fulfillment, we shall never be fulfilled. If we aim at education, we shall never become educated. If we aim at salvation, we shall never be saved. These things are indirect, supreme results of doing something else, and the something else is service, it is righteousness, it is trying to do the right thing, the thing that needs to be done at each moment. G. K. Chesterton once wrote a famous poem about how to get somewhere. The final line of that poem is, "The night we went to paradise by way of Kensal Green." Kensal Green is a place in London where there is a cemetery. The principle applies everywhere.

I come now to linguistics and the humanities. Modern linguistics has fallen into the same errors as the social sciences. In the nineteenth century, people thought we could have a scientific study of language rather like the study of the universe. Mathematics was regarded as a kind of norm. Linguists were, of course, mistaken. Yet it still goes on. But it is a mistake because language is a human thing and cannot be tilted in that way any more than psychology, sociology, or economics can. These disciplines cannot be scientific.

Philologists, in particular, got an illusion—an illusion that Blake foresaw—that the proceedings of the humanities could imitate those of the natural sciences and produce something valid. Some of the more eager philologists wanted to prove theories instead of concentrate on details. It was discovered that the history of sounds seemed reducible to something like natural law. And so philologists became fascinated by the history of sound development: they thought that sound development might be a model for the way in which the rest of language developed. But though the linguists took the same thing up, there was a gap between the organization of sounds and lexis and syntax. The things are not parallel in the way that, according to this kind of natural-scientific approach, they ought to be. It doesn't work.

This is a problem of the kind of analysis. The linguists impose their own grids, their own generalities. They are anxious to prove theories. The virtue of good philologists is that they are never anxious to prove a theory. Chomsky is a case in point. Chomsky is really a mathematical logician; he is not a philologist. He is not a lover of language. He is a self-asserter in language rules that work because he selects the examples for which they are to work. Many linguists do that. But if there is something quite fundamental about philologists, it is this: they know that they must never make up their examples. They must always take examples from where they are; examples come from a matrix, and, indeed, they lose life as a result of being taken out of that matrix.

Nineteenth-century philologists were particularly taken with evolutionary theory. But evolution doesn't mean very much when you think of Homer, who in a sense is the original European writer and one of the very greatest from the beginning. We smile with contempt at the efforts of the French critics of the late nineteenth and early twentieth centuries who introduced Darwinian concepts in the development of literary forms as if they were biological forms—people like Brunetière, who tried to write the history of genre as if it were a branch of evolutionary theory. And it is incredible that a Frenchman could have been so naive, particularly since Darwin was not French. But we ourselves are making similar mistakes because time and again literary criticism generalizes from science, and not even contemporary science but the science of a generation or two back. Take the notion of archetypes. Archetypes go back via Jung and Freud to anthropological ideas held in the 1890s and early 1900s and exemplified in Fraser's *Golden Bough.* In the 1890s and early 1900s, there were two forms of anthropological generalizations. One said that human beings were spontaneously similar everywhere and, therefore, we find similar phenomena everywhere. The other said it all began in Egypt and went everywhere else. We have a reason in our church to look rather more favorably at the second of those; but whichever it was, Gilbert Murray and his successors took old-fashioned anthropology and applied it to literature. Fraser's *Golden Bough* is a collection of details, and we are then expected to look cross-culturally at the similarity of the details. But our modern anthropologists reject that, saying, "In each culture, the details have meaning in terms of that particular culture, not of their similarity across cultures." Yet these cross-cultural archetypes, for which Jung is mainly responsible nowadays, linger on in literary criticism. I lived many years in Sweden, where scholars are intensive students of folklore but look down their noses at Jung. Folklore is down to earth; archetypes are like Mohammed's coffin. When we introduce schemata, when we introduce generalizations and abstractions, when we introduce hierarchies, archetypes, and so on, we are replacing what we are studying with something else. Or even worse, we are conveying to students something other than is there.

It seems to me that to try to reduce something to order, even though it is human order, is not a wrong process, provided that we recognize that what we are doing is playing games. And I suggest to you that outside the gospel, human endeavor does consist in playing games of that kind. We should reduce things to law if we can (and the expression "reduce to law" is significant: we don't raise or edify things into law, we reduce them to law) but remember that the cases in which we can do so are limited. We should order what we can, but we should not presume to order something we cannot by making it analogous to what we can. We should not be so foolish as to say that because pigeons or rats behave in a certain way, human beings will behave in a similar way or that depriving young chimpanzees of their mothers is like depriving human children of their mothers. There is a naive entailment that draws people to become unscientific. It doesn't affect physicists much. It affects social scientists more and to some extent those in the humanities.

There is a deep wish to simplify, and that deep wish to simplify manifests itself as a deep wish to reduce to law. There seems to be a pleasure in precision, a pleasure in reducing to law, which is extensive among natural scientists and usually creeps most effectively into those pseudosciences that are trying to follow the path of the natural sciences. But to endeavor to reduce the universe to human law while failing to recognize that we are just dealing with observations is a process of great arrogance. The tendency to generalize is, ultimately, an assertion of the personality of the generalizer and may be accompanied by some form of sadomasochism. Granted that a touch of sadism is very good for the surgeon and for the dentist, possibly even for the schoolmaster, what is ignored when this takes place is some profound effect on the total individual and on each individual's emotions and way of feeling about things. We need to remember that there is always something that we have not caught in our rational explanations that the gospel has, and that the Lord has, and that the example of the Lord has, so that we are able to live with one another in that total way. We don't live with one another ultimately by reason. We live ultimately by faith. Reason is the servant of faith and not the master. If you turn that around, you become a rather simplistic-minded person. Alas, there are a great many simplistic-minded people in the world who think they are terribly sophisticated.

We know in our church (because we have been so taught) that law operates at different levels, including levels that we as yet have no apprehension of, though we may yet have. But we are going nowhere by saying law is ultimate because law has to be of the person, the person thinking, the person experiencing. The possibility of bringing together biology and sociology or physiology and psychology exists, but in a very limited way. What is fundamental is that however far we go, the gap between "natural law" and human life will never be closed; it will always be there. It is the gap which implies eternal progression.

We are always more than we can categorize ourselves as being. However much we may interpret ourselves, there is always something else beyond, just as however much we may interpret God, we have not comprehended him. Art is the example of beyondness to us in the sense that however much we may interpret it, there is always something else beyond that. We look at a picture throughout our lives, we listen to a piece of music throughout our lives, we read a book time and again throughout our lives, as we should do—especially the scriptures—and it is different each time. Something else comes in. We see something else there that we never saw before because we are a different person each time we experience a work of art. Even if we listen a number of times, for example, to a record of Toscanini conducting the Seventh Symphony of Beethoven, we have not got something that is the same every time we listen to it because we are different every time we listen to that record. Listening to a record, of course, is not quite the same as being in a concert hall where we have something that is totally new and totally different on both sides.

Musical ability is, strangely enough, something that frequently goes together with ability in mathematics and ability to play chess. Those three are, all of them, rational in principle, but we never, as human beings, know enough for them to be rational to us. Therefore, there is always a beyond. There is always something else in music other than what we have understood, and it goes on all our lives, and this applies to any form of the arts that has the infinite built into it. The infinite is there in mathematics in another kind of way—modern mathematics has developed to the point that we now know there are always more mathematical truths than any mathematical system can contain—and the infinite is there in modern physics. It is there in chess. The ability to play chess, after all, depends not merely on the faculty to see ahead in detail a certain number of moves, but on intuition—a sense of the grouping on the board, the distribution of power, and a sense of what happens in certain types of groupings.

A sense of the infinite—in God and in human beings—is most completely there in true religious experience, though, unfortunately, not in all religions. Religious movements like Calvinism and Jansenism in the Roman Catholic Church may be linked, via determinism, to the industrial and scientific revolutions. Pascal is an example of one in whom religious and scientific determinism met. He was a very good thinker, a very good writer, but desperate because he was entailed in law. And the fact that he was a mathematician made it more difficult for him. But the true gospel rescues us from this predestinatory mechanical world, and every effort in society to bring it back in order to quash our individuality or to dampen our enthusiasm is to be condemned.

We have a choice between the devil's world and the gospel world. The devil's world is a mechanical one. The devil's world is a predeterminate world. The devil's world is the world lived on the lowest possible level of law. The gospel vision is of a better world. The gospel wants something else, something more difficult to do and yet more simple to understand, and that is to live its life, the life of love. And then everything is right, and it doesn't matter what happens to us.

The Idea of a Mormon University

THE WORD *UNIVERSITAS* originally meant a guild, a community. One may expect of a guild or a community that its members are bound to one another with bonds of love or charity. (I don't think, incidentally, that the right translation of *caritas* is love. Love ended up a debased word after all the idolization of adultery in European nineteenth-century art. The Latin word *caritas* cannot be translated by "charity" either. It can be translated by the word "caring.") But there is another sense of *universitas:* universe—the whole cosmos. Let us keep in mind these two senses—love and totality. I shall refer to them again at the end.

The modern university goes back to the Athenian Academy. "Academy" was the name of the garden where Plato taught; it was a *hortus conclusus*, a place shut off from the rest of the world, where one might delight in leisured study and in discussion with other people. The Muslims took over the tradition of learning from the Greeks and developed institutions like the western university in Spain, in the Middle East, and in the Indian subcontinent. The first European universities developed in part because of the Arabian impulse. So Brigham Young University goes back to Plato's garden and the Muslim oases of learning.

The universities in Europe rose (though somewhat rebelliously) under the tutelage of the Roman Catholic Church. They were characterized by the heresy of celibacy. Celibacy was the norm for college faculty members in the Middle Ages. It was, of course, pseudocelibacy; it did not connote purity. One of the colleges at Cambridge used to be a nest of homosexuality. I once saw the then dean of that college order out of the chapel a young woman who was pushing a baby in a carriage—perambulators were forbidden in the grounds. That night he threw himself (or was thrown) off the roof of the chapel. The college now has female students and married couples who are fellows. But the celibate rule was not abolished at Oxford and Cambridge until the eighties of the last century, a hundred years ago.

The tradition of the celibate, of the monk, still influences the academic atmosphere, certainly in Europe, even in America. The academic as a celibate is uncreative—he may even choose academic life because he is uncreative. His prime traditional sin is *accidia*, that good old Latin term which means "sloth." In the traditional sense, "sloth" doesn't exactly mean lying in bed; it means not having the spirit to do what you ought to do, feeling listless and useless. And this is not merely a physical state, but a mental state, a state of the heart and mind. From the celibate academic tradition comes the related *odium academicum*—the celibate's sadomasochism, his taste for what he finds distasteful—and the *invidia academica*, the scholarly hatred of one's fellow scholars (exemplified by A. E. Housman).

From the celibate academic tradition comes the inbreeding of the modern university, the conceit and egocentricity of university faculty throughout the world, to which the relatives of university professors can testify. It is the tradition of the academic that they should be self-regarders, self-lovers, exhibitionists, narcissists, those who posture and clown for educational purposes. Their teaching is self-posturing before their students; their mannerisms develop into caricature until they turn into cackling, self-regarding old people. Not all teachers are like that, but I am afraid all too many are. And one of the reasons students don't learn as well as they would like is that they don't like the academic personalities of their teachers.

I have been a member of several universities, and I have visited some two hundred. And I can assure you that the outstanding feature of the faculty of universities is an extraordinary immaturity that springs from self-regard, the praise given by others, arrogance, the belief in one's own powers—any of these things will bring it about. It is more difficult to grow up when one is clever. The clever teacher is all important. He or she may have a spouse and children, but they have to give place to academic pursuits. Faculty get away from their families into research or conviviality. They are still in the root of their souls celibates.

Abraham Flexner's seminal book, *Universities British, American, and German*, published in 1930, analyzes the heretical idea of the university at its best. What lies at the bottom of Flexner's book is not what he saw in British and American universities, but what he saw in German universities. (Of course, German universities have had a considerable influence on American universities.) From the German university has come the idea of the supremacy of the professor and of research. It was the institution of a leisured, bourgeois society that was devoted to learning for its own sake and that made an idol of the study—the study, the isolation, the relief in sitting by yourself in a comfortable chair at a large desk, or the relief in involving yourself with experimental apparatus.

The university as ideally conceived in the nineteenth century and as still conceived, in part, in Britain, is a place where there is freedom from the community, where one may contract out of the community at large a place that is best represented by the ivory tower, the *hortus conclusus*, the garden. And notice that I say freedom *from* the community, not freedom *in* the community, not freedom to serve the community.

On the other hand, there is the Mormon tradition. For us, all learning is for God's sake, not for its own sake. As soon as we speak of learning for its own sake, we set up learning as an idol independent of God. The Mormon tradition is supremely one of work, work for the Lord and others—service. Work is the second great virtue. Caring or love is the first, and work should spring from caring. The object of a Mormon university must be to build the kingdom of God, to serve the Church in the full sense of what that implies. Because we believe in the Church, because we believe it to be the most important organization on this earth, because we believe it to be the instrument of God's will, because we believe that Christ is its head, we must therefore believe that any organization that the Church sets up must finally and ultimately serve the Church. We are servants in that full sense of the word as it is used in the New Testament. In the sense of ministers, of *doloi*, we are the servants of the Church.

The Academic and the Ecclesiastical

It is astonishing to a convert coming from outside this country to see how separate the ecclesiastical and the academic worlds on BYU campus are. In consequence of this separation, neither the academic nor the ecclesiastical side is as effective as it could be. One of the effects of the separation is to allow mediocre students or faculty members to use the academic side as an excuse for not doing what they should be doing on the church side and/or the church side as an excuse for not doing what they should be doing on the academic side. In some cases, students and faculty members may be victims of this conflict; in others, they may be hypocritical manipulators of the conflict for their own apparent advantage. One of the major mistakes that many of us make (and it may be that we make it on purpose, as many of our mistakes are made) is to argue that we have to do so many things. But we don't have to do them all at once. Nobody is requiring us to pay attention during the whole of our lives to all of the things we are supposed to be doing. We have our free agency to choose, and we should choose much more fundamentally and radically than we usually do.

The dichotomy between the ecclesiastical and the academic also leaves room for the interpolation of a third world that is not dominated by either the ecclesiastical or the academic world (and such a world has no right on campus): the social world is the third world into which the student escapes from both church and academic duties. Too many students, not being converted, find refuge in a kind of neutral social activity. The student comes to campus with ideas of how much time should be devoted to social activity—ideas derived not so much from the Church as from high school (or perhaps from the wards, too, because they may reflect the mentality of the high school). Indeed, the university itself also encourages the social aspect of a student's life; the university seems to expect the student to waste a good deal of time.

There is elitism on campus: athletic, social (clubs), and political (BYUSA officers and their staff). True, BYUSA officers do not have as much power as comparable officers at other universities, but in that very absence of power, they have exemplified empty elitism. They need to be made honest by being chosen, as Church officers are. Ours is not a democratic church. Why this imitation of apostate universities, an imitation of the world not necessitated by being in the world? Cannot the Lord's university be spared the unspeakable vulgarity of childishly run elections on which most sensible students turn their backs?

If this is the Lord's university, what room is there on campus for anything except our study and our work for the Church? What room is there for any other kind of "club"? There is too much pointless and random social activity, too much forgathering for purposeless and unworthy chat, too much lassitude and sloth. Dating is often a part of this rather than being a proper religious preoccupation. Much dating is pursued, not for serious reasons, but for erotic proximity, frivolous amusement, or prestige. Dating may also be pursued mechanically or with a conscious purpose to "marry," in the abstract as it were, or to manipulate oneself into marriage. There are too many wrong pressures on young women to marry, and these pressures come particularly from other young women on campus. This is degrading to the position of women. Coming into this kind of atmosphere may be a considerable letdown to many returned missionaries. Some find themselves unable to continue pursuing serious high purposes, and though as a body they raise the level of seriousness among students at BYU, they do find themselves making compromises that lower their spiritual level. Some may even become sources of cynicism and bad examples of dress and social life.

If the academic would regard itself as the servant of the ecclesiastical, then surely gospel culture would flourish at BYU more than it does. So much of what we have at BYU—from caps and gowns to the cougar—is inspired, not by the gospel, but by the surrounding culture. BYU is not the place for imitation of and subservience to the "culture" around us. We should give students an example of gospel culture, not world culture. Students come to BYU uneducated and uncultured. They are, of course, not uncultured in the more general anthropological sense: they come thoroughly processed in terms of dating habits, political thinking, and rock music. These they have absorbed from the culture around them partly because the Church members they have known and, above all, their own parents, have not understood the difference between the Latter-day Saint view of the world and the view of the world expressed in the culture in which they find themselves. But their experiences at BYU should not further confuse them.

If the proper relationship between the academic and the ecclesiastical were established, one result would be the upgrading of Church activities. It does not seem to me that Church activities on campus are superior to those in the rest of the Church; yet they surely could be culturally and educationally superior, and this surely would have some effect on their spiritual value. Family home evenings at BYU could be used for serious discussion of a type that both improves spiritual life and feeds into general education. Ward dramatic activity on campus could and should reflect a combination of spiritual and artistic values instead of reflecting the same low cultural standard of the members of the Church all over the world. When I first came to BYU and saw a certain amount of ward dramatic activity here, I said to myself, "In this large university there is a great opportunity to show the rest of the Church what drama can be like." And what is it like? Low-grade entertainment undertaken by exhibitionistic amateurs. Were the College of Fine Arts to serve the Church in all its activities as it sometimes does in music, then there might be some advance from road shows to something more like James Faulconer's *Akedah.* The academic could help the ecclesiastical on campus to be less *facile.*

There are many other obvious ways in which BYU could serve the Church: there is the preparation of missionaries, and this includes preparation before they even know where they are going; there is the teaching of English to speakers of other languages (English being the main administrative language of the Church and the language of most of its teaching), which President Kimball specifically urged on the occasion of the university's centennial; there is the analysis of exotic languages that the Church needs and that the linguistics department is not large enough fully to provide; there is the solving of translation problems (they will never all be solved, but progress can be made); there is the handling of cultural interrelations on a larger scale; and above all there is the need and the unexampled opportunity of keeping returned missionaries attached (as they often profess themselves attached) for the rest of their lives to the countries in which they have served. These are examples from the areas I know best. There are undoubtedly other examples in other areas.

The question that BYU administrators must ask themselves is, "To what extent should so-called pure research (which from our point of view in the Church is morally impure) be pursued on this campus?" All faculty members in conscience must ask themselves not only, "What am I to research?" but also, "What am I to research in light of the fact that I am a Mormon with such and such qualifications at this time in this institution?" "What is the gospel significance of what I am doing?" is what all of us have to ask ourselves.

Does what we teach at BYU contribute to the perfection of the whole Saint? There is confusion between worldly and Church values in the classroom, and this leads to sending out students into the world to compromise with the world as journalists, as lawyers, as businesspeople, as "televisionists," as teachers. Students who leave the university seldom realize that they are compromising because the only standard they have known at BYU is *already* a compromised one. Let me remind you of a sentiment of Brigham Young's with which you are all familiar: we must teach everything with testimony. Subjects at a university may support testimony, widen testimony, give evidence of testimony; they may be taught as testimony—testimony comes into them all. Testimony, therefore, is not to be shrouded in particular departments on the campus; it goes everywhere and permeates everything. Some of you may have read that apparently frivolous, but deeply serious, book called *The Double Helix*. It is about a young American at Cambridge who discovered something that turned out to have a deep significance for genetics—the form of a genetic molecule. He tells what happened during the days when he progressed towards that discovery. The book helps one to realize that great discoveries in science, like great artistic creations, come ultimately from—call it what you like—intuition or inspiration. Can anything worthwhile happen on any university campus without the Holy Ghost?

The Church has the task of teaching religious values without the support of the surrounding culture that other churches once had. If we were to teach more religious literature at BYU as part of general education, we should be helping the Church in this important task. But the English department at BYU teaches courses very similar to those taught in English departments in other American universities. And in most other English departments, not only in the United States, but throughout the world, the agnostic—not to say atheistic—trend has been more marked than in other departments; these departments habitually avoid a religious perspective in designing their curriculum and slight religious literature in their courses. Why should we be teaching what they teach, in either classical or modern literature, when their values are wrong? If their values are wrong, their selection will be wrong. Our task is not to accept agnostic literature. Our task is to say, "These are our principles; they are Christian principles. And in the light of these Christian principles, this is the kind of literature we should be teaching."

There is much great religious literature in the American and the British traditions, and it should have more place in the curriculum of the English department because some of it is very great literature. The Church's attitude to the apostate churches as a whole is clearly one of condemnation, and rightly so, especially from the point of view of their administration and their lack of authority. However, through the ages there have been good people who have been members of these churches who have made pious and highly valuable contributions in the arts. They were seriously concerned, and you learn by the time you get to my age that when people are concerned with serious matters, even if they occasionally bring the wrong doctrines in, they write better. At BYU, the great amount of this high-quality religious literature should be given space. We should be studying the many good sermons from the medieval period to the eighteenth century. We should be studying the English of the King James Bible in order to read it better. We should be studying the prose of Lancelot Andrewes, Bishop of Winchester and chairman of the Bible Translation Committee, who, according to Eliot, was the greatest prose writer in English. There is also religious literature in other languages. Who reads Bossuet's sermons when learning French? Yet those sermons are among the best things ever written. I think that departments in the College of Humanities ought to introduce things like religious poetry, sermons, theological treatises.

The religion department at BYU should help the Church bring members to the scriptures and keep them with the scriptures, teach them to read the scriptures for themselves and even to enjoy the scriptures (which most members for the most part do not do). The effective education of Latter-day Saints in the past was centered around the scriptures. Our current educational level would have been better if this had continued. There is no reason why it should not be resumed. It could lead to a great educational advance in the most important subject on campus—reading. Religious instruction in scripture reading is the key to the whole of general education at BYU. If students learn to read scripture properly, they will be prepared to read anything else. And yet, as far as

I know, there have been few, if no efforts, even to evaluate how well our students are really learning to read scripture.

The Lord's University

At present BYU is the Lord's university in principle and in part, in a glass darkly (see 1 Cor. 13:12). It has to become the Lord's university in the light. And yet many faculty members and some members of the administration seem to act on the assumption that (even if they do not know it), for the sake of public relations and the reputation of the Church, what this university has to become is a good *American* university. (Not that I think it should become a good *European* university. Emerson rightly castigated Harvard for imitating its European forebears and not thinking creatively on its own.) At the same time, they want this university to become better than other American universities. But in order to be "better," in the usual sense, than other universities, BYU would have to be comparable with them. Some people at BYU have no doubt tried to make it comparable with other universities and may have had thoughts of aspiring to the top ten and ultimately "best" of all. But this is thinking that is not simply in the world, but of the world. No: BYU has to be better than other universities by not being like them. Imitating other universities will lead us down with the Gadarene swine.

There is severe and dangerous moral decay in American universities and other universities of the western world. It is being followed fast by intellectual decay. And if we believe the gospel, we know that intellectual decay must follow moral decay. I have noticed in British universities that as the faculty members become less religious, more cynical, more agnostic, more atheistic, so they also become more interested in money than in their students. The more they earn, the more they seem to want to earn. (And that is true of nearly any member of society not under real gospel influence—few of us honestly dislike money, and yet it is a very good thing to be brought up to dislike.) They complain that they are not well enough paid and therefore have to earn money outside. I have seen acquaintances of mine get the TV bug, which means that instead of paying more attention to their students, they were off to London to participate in TV programs for which they got handsomely paid. And what happens is that where the faculty is cynical and self-centered, the students rapidly become cynical and self-centered, too, and the idea of the university of love, the idea of the bond between teacher and taught, disappears.

We in the Church know what is wrong with education today at all levels. Most people outside the Church don't know. But we know that education must be based on, trained in, grown from, and watered by religion. Education only has significance insofar as it is built upon the rock of a true and living religion. Spiritual development does not go hand in hand with intellectual development. The spiritual life must lead the intellectual life, and the intellectual life has to be a worthy partner to the spiritual life. It is within our own university that we have to look for the highest possible standards, and these, of course, are total standards. They are standards of spiritual and intellectual life together.

But we are so much like other universities, and we are striving so much to be like other universities, that if we are not careful we may share in the moral decline. That decline is discernible at BYU in the unwillingness of students to follow dress standards, directly against their word and promise, and in the reasons they give for not following them. It is discernible on the occasions when students cheat and in the reasons they give for cheating. (I understand some of them have had the effrontery to give reasons for cheating.) It is there in the obscene (and obscenely advertised) rock concerts, some given under the auspices of BYUSA. It is there, most pervasively of all, in the obsession with grades and the superficial success that they represent, in the triviality and inane conformity of so many who chase straight A's and frequently obtain them—the ones who get the scholarships and strive to retain them (at what expense, poor people?), the ones who get the good jobs and strain by compromising with the world to keep them (what shall it profit a man?), the ones who spend their intelligence and ingenuity during the years of their "education" on finding the easiest way through and spend the rest of their lives (poor souls—poor souls indeed) in the same boring, debilitating, and ultimately desperate way.

Our first step toward being the Lord's university on earth, our second, our third, and so on, are steps *away* from the habits and customs of apostate universities. We do not need to catch up with the world, the flesh, and the devil. If we are the Lord's, we are not of this world. If we fulfill prophecy, it will not be by imitating other universities but by taking note of what they do and, in the light or darkness of that, working out our own path. That path should ultimately be traced for us by inspiration and revelation, but it will not be traced for us at all unless we use ourselves to the maximum in the magnificent possibilities that are given us here. We are obligated, each of us, to make the best of ourselves in order that we may do the best for Christ, and that is as true of our intellectual work as of all other kinds of work we have to do.

It is useless to try to improve an institution irrespective of its people. An institution, however well planned, cannot be bad or good; it is the people in it who are bad or good. The Lord's university becomes better by having better people in it: students, faculty, and staff. Better people means converted people. The more converted people there are here, the more the Lord's university will become itself. How many people at BYU are now converted? Can we judge? Hardly, for conversion and testimony do not necessarily manifest themselves to the world. Certainly, valiance may be evidence of conversion, and those who are not converted are not truly valiant. But to human eyes, valiance can be simulated. Only the Lord knows the difference. If most of us were converted, there are things we should do here on campus—they would inevitably come out of the daily process.

Some of us sometimes have the temptation not to do the better that is in us because we are diligent at doing the not-so-good. It is a good excuse. I remember the Cornish poet Ronald Bottrall once saying to me (he was my chief then in Sweden), "The trouble with you, Arthur, is that you are the most lazy man I have ever met." And I looked at him in astonishment. "Yes," he said, "you are so keen to do everything that you don't stop to sort out the more important things you could be doing." I took that to heart. I have tried to think of that ever since.

Let me now come back to the idea of a Mormon university: *Universitas*—the guild, with its bond of love; *Universitas*—the whole, the totality, the teaching from testimony so that what we teach is a whole and springs from the whole mind. I would suggest that this university is the only university in the world that may become *Universitas Dei*, the University of God, and if I might give you a slogan for it, it would be "For God and our neighbor." I should like to think that this is the university of caring. I have just been rereading *Brand* (Ibsen's play—and Ibsen is the greatest of all modern authors), and the last line of this play is this: *Han aer Deus Caritatis*. This utterance comes out of the avalanche that is to overwhelm Brand. It means, "He is the God of Caring."

EFFECTIVE JOURNAL WRITING

State Street, monument
(with no redeeming feature)
to greedy ignorance.
Forgive the builders; but Christ
must atone for the buildings.

AHK
October 1980

Joseph Smith as a Writer

Joseph Smith was born and bred in difficult and limited circumstances among people who made the best of their circumstances—as so many thousands and tens of thousands of Americans at that time did under the influence of the religious force that impelled them. To give you some better idea of those circumstances, I want to refer to two books I have recently been rereading: *American Notes* and *Martin Chuzzlewit*, both by Charles Dickens. *American Notes* is an account of Dickens's visit to the United States in 1842; it was also published in 1842. *Martin Chuzzlewit* is a novel with an American setting that was published shortly after *American Notes.* Both *American Notes* and *Martin Chuzzlewit* give a drastic account of the America of those days; both contain vigorous and satirical criticism of the American society of the forties, the society that was persecuting the Church to the extreme. It is now over one hundred forty years since these books were published, and they are still worth our attention because they were written by perhaps the greatest reporter who ever lived (Dickens did years of reporting for newspapers and for Parliament) and because they provide us with an unexpected view of what America looked like to a European in the early 1840s.

Dickens came to America prepared to be impressed by its democratic institutions because America was far more democratic than Britain at the time. And he did actually find himself impressed by many American institutions—for example, by the New England factories, which were run in an admirable way, and by the hospitals and prisons, which he visited assiduously. He was impressed by the government in Washington. But there were other things that are startling to read and that were startling to me when I first read them as a boy of nine—for example, the universal habit of spitting in public, the mostly unpaved streets in the great American cities, and the thousands of pigs roaming all over the cities and living out of the garbage. The frontier was evident very soon after one left the seaboard cities; people were living and pioneering in very rigorous, very severe and difficult and poverty-stricken surroundings. It was a very hard life, indeed. You owe your prosperity now to the hard way in which those people worked under conditions of disease and poverty.

What we can get more from *Martin Chuzzlewit* than from *American Notes* is an account of what life was like in the Mississippi Basin. There was the same poverty as there was elsewhere on the frontier. Malaria was prevalent, and its impact on Church members in the Mississippi Basin must have been considerable. We find reference to the types who were tarring and feathering Joseph Smith further up the river or killing at Haun's Mill. Barbarisms, like those committed by some of the Indians, were perpetrated by American citizens on other American citizens. The sense of lawlessness is brought home by what Dickens as an outside observer had to say about conditions in the Mississippi Basin at this time. We tend not to realize the grim circumstances in which the Church grew up. The stories of persecution, the stories of torturing and deaths, are not exaggerated. This church was born in blood and baptized in blood; indeed, it is from the blood of the martyrs that the success of the Church has sprung. Life then was so different from what it is now that I wonder if we can feel sufficiently grateful about the difference or, indeed, if we should feel grateful about the difference when we see testimony flourishing in adverse circumstances rather than in prosperous ones.

Let me turn now to Joseph Smith himself. Joseph Smith had practically no formal schooling, just a few weeks. The outstanding thing about him is what he did with what he got: he translated the Book of Mormon, wrote the Doctrine and Covenants under inspiration, and accomplished other tasks that show the extent of his genius. The fact that he was inspired by the Lord does not diminish his achievements, just as the fact that Paul and Peter were inspired does not diminish their achievements. We owe our thanks to the Lord in everything; nevertheless, there are supreme geniuses among human beings. Some souls are far more equal than others.

We can see the contrast between Joseph Smith's limited education and the inspiration of his translation if we look at the 1830 facsimile edition of the Book of Mormon. It brings Joseph Smith home to us in a very different way from the verse-divided, modern-punctuated, spelling-corrected edition. Something comes out of that 1830 edition that affects us more than the post-1924 editions because we have from it the sense of the tremendous genius of Joseph Smith.

We must remember that those who founded our church were not greatly different from those early Christians in the meridian of time. They were plain, "uneducated" people. I think it is probable that Paul spelled correctly, but I doubt if Peter did. Nevertheless, Peter, like Joseph Smith, was a highly intelligent man. We have to remember that in those days the intelligent people of the lower classes remained at the social and economic level to which they were born; they were not promoted up through society as they are today. (I should say, "the *so-called* intelligent people." Intelligence tests reflect what society thinks, not what God thinks, and certainly not any kind of objective reality.)

Because Joseph Smith was a genius, he didn't need much formal instruction, any more than Shakespeare did. He absorbed knowledge about language and so was a fit tool through which the Lord revealed modern scripture with all the rhetorical richness of ancient scripture. Where did Joseph Smith absorb knowledge of language from? He had two major resources: one was the scriptures—and his principal education was from the scriptures—and the other was all the sermons he attended. We have no evidence of how much Joseph Smith read the scriptures in his youth, but he must have read a good deal because he must somewhere have gained the thorough knowledge of scripture which he demonstrated when he was in his twenties. We can see from his writing that the scriptures were a part of him as they were a part of many of his contemporaries, including his contemporaries in the Church. We know, of course, from his account, that he did go frequently to churches. And when he went around to those churches, he certainly did not hear men who spoke stumblingly. Their sermons would have been apostate sermons, that is true, but those were men who had had rhetorical training, who had been taught how to build a sermon and how to use the various rhetorical devices, men who were in touch with the rhetorical tradition of the scriptures. That is the tradition in which Joseph Smith grew up.

Joseph Smith was brought up in a rhetorical situation that has ceased to exist. He spoke and he wrote as people had always written and spoken from the beginning until the tradition began to be upset in the seventeenth century. From the point of view of language, Joseph Smith is closer in sympathy, nearer in mentality and education, to Moses and Isaiah than we are to him. The great divide has come since, not before.

When I read the history of Joseph Smith (his own account in the Pearl of Great Price), the person I immediately think of is the poet and critic Coleridge, who was writing in England a little earlier. Joseph Smith's language reminds me very much of the language that Coleridge often used at his best in the *Biographia Literaria*. That is not saying a little. Coleridge was perhaps the best English prose writer of that time. So if we take Joseph Smith's story irrespective of the message that it contains, if we just look at the writing, we conclude that this is a highly educated man. The reason Joseph Smith sounds like Coleridge, of course, is because Coleridge and the pastors and masters of New England read the same philosophical and theological authors. Coleridge was older than Joseph Smith, but, allowing for delay across the Atlantic (in those days information flowed from Europe to the United States), they were writing under the influence of the same authors.

When I was first brought to read Joseph Smith's story, I was deeply impressed. I wasn't inclined to be impressed. As a stylistician, I have spent my life being disinclined to be impressed. So when I read his story, I thought to myself, this is an extraordinary thing. This is an astonishingly matter-of-fact and cool account. This man is not trying to persuade me of anything. He doesn't feel the need to. He is stating what happened to him, and he is stating it, not enthusiastically, but in quite a matter-of-fact way. He is not trying to make me cry or feel ecstatic. That struck me, and that began to build my testimony, for I could see that this man was telling the truth.

Joseph Smith begins his story in his matter-of-fact way, setting out carefully the reason that he is writing this history and the facts about his birth and family. Then he moves from the matter-of-fact to the ironical, even the satirical, as he describes the state of religion at the time—the behavior of the New England clergy in trying to draw people into their congregations. He tells about reading the Epistle of James. He doesn't try to express his feelings. He gives a description of his feelings instead, which is a very different thing. Look at verse 12:

> Never did any passage of scripture come with more power to the heart of man than this did at this time to mine. It seemed to enter with great force into every feeling of my heart. I reflected on it again and again, knowing that if any person needed wisdom from God, I did; for how to act I did not know, and unless I could get more wisdom than I then had, I would never know; for the teachers of religion of the different sects understood the same passages of scripture so differently as to destroy all confidence in settling the question by an appeal to the Bible. (JS–H 1:12)

I am not good enough to write a passage as good as that. That is beautiful, well-balanced prose. And it isn't the prose of someone who is trying to work it out and make it nice. It is the prose of someone who is trying to tell it like it is, who is bending all his faculties to expressing the truth and not thinking about anything else—and above all, though writing about Joseph Smith, not thinking about Joseph Smith, not thinking about the effect he is going to have on others, not posturing, not posing, but just being himself. The passage continues as follows:

> At length I came to the conclusion that I must either remain in darkness and confusion, or else I must do as James directs, that is, ask of God. (JS–H 1:13)

Notice the coolness: "At length I came to the conclusion."

> I at length came to the determination to "ask of God," concluding that if he gave wisdom to them that lacked wisdom, and would give liberally, and not upbraid, I might venture. (JS–H 1:13)

Notice the rationality of it, the humility of it, the perfectly good manners of it.

> So, in accordance with this, my determination to ask of God, I retired to the woods to make the attempt. (JS–H 1:14)

Just imagine what a TV commentator would make of this sort of thing.

> It was on the morning of a beautiful, clear day, early in the spring of eighteen hundred and twenty. It was the first time in my life that I had made such an attempt, for amidst all my anxieties I had never as yet made the attempt to pray vocally. (JS–H 1:14)

Do you see how the tone is kept down, how matter-of-fact it is? Notice the effect of a phrase like "to pray vocally."

> After I had retired to the place where I had previously designed to go, having looked around me, and finding myself alone, I kneeled down and began to offer up the desires of my heart to God. (JS–H 1:15)

Plain, matter-of-fact, truthful, simple statements in well-mannered prose. This is no posture. We are not thinking of Joseph Smith; we are just waiting, waiting, waiting to hear. Do you see how beautifully this is built up, how the tension is built up by his being so modest, so well mannered?

> I had scarcely done so, when immediately I was seized upon by some power which entirely overcame me, and had such an astonishing influence over me as to bind my tongue so that I could not speak. (JS–H 1:15)

He is telling us about something terrible. But he is not trying to make us feel HOW TERRIBLE THIS IS. He is telling us that it happened.

> Thick darkness gathered around me, and it seemed to me for a time as if I were doomed to sudden destruction. (JS–H 1:15)

He felt he was going to be killed. But there is no excitement, no hysteria about this. He just tells us. Notice in particular the coolness of the phrase "for a time."

> But, exerting all my powers to call upon God to deliver me out of the power of this enemy which had seized upon me, and at the very moment when I was ready to sink into despair and abandon myself to destruction—not to any imaginary ruin, but to the power of some actual being from the unseen world, who had such marvelous power as I had never before felt in any being—just at this moment of great alarm . . . (JS–H 1:16)

Notice the expression "of great alarm." What would a posing sensationalist do with that? What kind of explosion would he devise, I wonder?

> . . . I saw a pillar of light exactly over my head, above the brightness of the sun, which descended gradually until it fell upon me. (JS–H 1:16)

"A pillar of light *exactly* over my head," "*above the brightness* of the sun," "descended *gradually*"—note the modifiers, the exactness. What he is trying to do is tell us what happened. He goes on in the same tone. He doesn't get ecstatic. He doesn't run over. He just goes on telling us just what happened in this astonishingly cool, and at the same time reverential, way. This is a visit of God the Father and God the Son to a boy of fourteen. But he is not in undue awe. He doesn't stare. He is not frightened. He was perhaps terrorized by what happened before, but he is not frightened of this. He doesn't lose his self-confidence, and at the same time, he is modest.

And then the humor: he returns home, leans up against the fireplace, and his mother asks him what is wrong. He answers, "I have learned for myself that Presbyterianism is not true" (JS–H 1:20). We have to remember that his mother had joined the Presbyterian Church shortly before this. How do you assess that as a conversation between a fourteen-year-old and his mother? All mothers know that sort of thing really happens to them with their teenagers.

The whole man is involved in this account, but the whole man isn't posturing and appealing to you to believe it. He is merely stating it, stating it with the whole of himself. The conviction is behind it. The emotion is there in perfect control. It is in the rhythm, the superb rhythm of that piece, and we won't get that unless we read it aloud. There is an extraordinary alternation of short and long sentences. Some of the sentences are long indeed—magnificent sentences—periods much better than Samuel Johnson could write. So there is this combination of a firm, convinced rhythm and a matter-of-fact statement drawing on all the resources of early nineteenth-century prose to produce a piece of prose better than anything Coleridge ever wrote.

Now there is no passage in mystical literature or in any other kind of literature concerned with visions that I know of which is like this, and therefore I am not prepared to give credence to other "mystical" passages outside the scriptures—I know the difference. I am thinking about St. Bridget, who lived in Sweden in the fourteenth century, and whose life I have studied in some detail; she had her ecstatic visions. I am thinking about St. Teresa, that great Spanish saint who wasn't quite sure whether Christ was her Lord or her husband. They don't compare with Joseph Smith. They attitudinize; they get into postures, contortions of mind, in expressing themselves. Not so Joseph Smith.

Now if you want to see Joseph Smith's temperament in contrast to another totally different temperament, compare the account given by Joseph Smith of John the Baptist conferring the Aaronic Priesthood on him and Oliver Cowdery (JS—H 1:66–73) with the piece of flowery journalese that Oliver Cowdery produced, which is in the footnote on the same page, right at the end of the Joseph Smith story. Oliver Cowdery produced a fireworks display. His is rhetoric in the false sense. He endeavors to persuade us and himself of feelings that he did not have. Joseph Smith simply describes the feelings he did have. Oliver Cowdery was capable of writing cheap journalese, but Joseph Smith wrote as a philosopher and rhetorician capable of comparison with the highest. He was a prepared vessel, prepared by the Lord, who knew Joseph Smith's capacity and helped him make the utmost of it. I think it is significant that Oliver Cowdery's account is in a footnote. It is of supreme importance to realize (one must know enough about language to realize it) that there is nothing vulgar in the scriptures anywhere. That is part of the evidence that the scriptures are the word of God.

I am asked sometimes, "Why don't we have any great literature now?" And we don't, you know; we may kid ourselves or other people may try to kid us that we do, but we don't. There were Homer, Virgil, Dante, Shakespeare, and Goethe; and there it seems to have stopped. There seems to have been no supreme figure since then. But I tell you there was one: Joseph Smith.

I only wish that I could know more about that fourteen-year-old boy. We do know a certain amount about him. But what would it have been like to have met him—to have discovered the reserved, reflective person that he was, yet with an enormous reservoir of power, with so much sense of humor, with such pleasure in physical contact with his fellow human beings. And who cares that he was a person with faults? There are plenty of odd things carried down by the purest stream that ever flowed. The faults are there and the condemnations are there—they are there in the Doctrine and Covenants. The Lord speaks to him and condemns him and Joseph Smith writes it all down for us. He doesn't pretend.

Think of Joseph Smith as a man who speaks to our time from eternity.

Journal Writing and Personal Histories

THE IMPORTANT THING to remember when writing a personal history or keeping a journal is that our descendants will be interested in the kinds of things that most interest us in the personal histories or journals of others. What kinds of things are these? First of all, the details of everyday life—details like our kitchen procedures and the way we treat our young children—because these things change so very much over the years. We are writing for posterity, and that posterity may extend for hundreds of years, and we can be sure that in one or two hundred years' time those details will be very different indeed. Our descendants will also be interested in the fundamental things—the truly fundamental things—birth, death, and marriage. So we also need to leave them true accounts of the most important things that happen to us.

Our descendants will want to know what seems old and ridiculous to us, what seems new and interesting, what surprises us, what distresses us, what bores us, but above all, what interests us. They will want to know about our reactions to events, people, situations. For example, they will probably look with some surprise at the women's movement of our time and be interested in what we really thought of it. They will wonder, "Why did these women have these problems? What were the frustrations in their lives which caused them? Why weren't they happy?" They will notice that women were more influential in the Church in the nineteenth century than in the latter part of the twentieth century, and they will be interested to know why. They will note the greater economic responsibility of women in the latter part of the nineteenth century than in the latter part of the twentieth and will want to know why there, too. We may not be able to tell them why, but we can give them the information from which they will be able to work out their own reasons why.

Just as we today can understand a former age much better than it could understand itself, so in the same way our descendants will understand our own lives better than we can, but only if we leave them the material by which they can do this. Let me tell you an incident from the life of one of my late cousins, which, from a historical perspective, I could understand better than he. This cousin lived in Tewkesbury and made gloves for George III and his family. One day at Weymouth, as my cousin was on his way to an early bath, he saw the king up the street. He felt the informality of the situation, which did not match the proper formality for an approach to royalty, so he turned a corner. My cousin said, "Soon after breakfast the king's secretary . . . came to my lodgings and smiling said, 'You need not hide yourself, the king . . . saw you turn such a corner this morning.' He then appointed 12 o'clock by the king's direction for me to have an interview with him." My ancestral cousin was self-conscious and created a situation that the king kindly and properly rectified. Though he didn't know it, he was caught between two patterns of Quaker behavior. A hundred years before, he would have walked up to the king, and, with his hat still on, stood before him and wished him a good morning. A hundred years later, he would have approached the king and behaved as deferentially as anyone else.

Our descendants will be interested in our genuine reactions, opinions, and feelings, not our conventional ones. I think, from this point of view, about the descriptions of deathbeds that my wife and I have in our family records from the eighteenth century, when it was a custom of the Quaker sect to describe in some detail the feelings of those who were dying. One very soon learns to distinguish the individual expressions from the clichés repeated from deathbed to deathbed. I am more interested in people who were not altogether content on their deathbeds and why they were not, than in those who expressed complete contentment, unless that contentment was expressed in an unusual language of simplicity and humility.

The older the personal histories and journals we read are, the less likely they are to be self-conscious, self-consciousness being a large-scale illness of the nineteenth century onward. When I look at the records of my own family members from the seventeenth and eighteenth centuries, I am impressed by the general lack of self-consciousness. They were absorbed into the group to which they belonged, the Quaker sect. They used the jargon of that sect just as we use the jargon of our church, but not self-consciously, and therefore it does not create a bad effect.

When we write, we need to be ourselves. We should not be misled by any teaching or cultural message we have received about being artificially cheerful or artificially anything. And we should not dismiss unpleasant matters from our minds. They must be faced, and our own responsibility for them must be assessed. Our responsibility is to tell the truth. We may need to reflect on how to put it down, but we should never reflect on how it will strike others, including our descendants. It is not for us to judge what we think will be good for them to read and what we think will not be good for them to read. The ways of salvation are not the ways of persuasion, but the ways of conviction. If we try to be truthful (and this is one of the few things we should try to be), then we are likely to convince. If we try to convince, we are less likely to be truthful. It is for us to set down the truth as we know it and think it, and it is for our descendants, not for us, to judge. Humility and honesty are two names for the same thing in writing. Try, therefore, humbly and honestly to assess your experience. Don't try and make your experiences into more or less than they were, and above all, don't think of your audience and try to appeal to it. All these are meretricious tricks.

In writing, we need to keep in mind the style in which Joseph Smith presented his own experiences. His manner is matter-of-fact and cool. He doesn't try to persuade us or work up our feelings. He may make us feel as a result of what he tells us, but he doesn't make an *effort* to make us feel. He does not attempt to do other than describe what happened, including how he felt. There is an important difference between expressing one's feelings and describing one's feelings. When we attempt to express our feelings, we nearly always find ourselves, instead, expressing the feelings we ought to have had or should like to have had or exaggerating the feelings that we really did have. The attempt is enough to cancel out our chance of success. But if we try simply to describe our feelings, we don't fall into these errors.

Abstract statements about our feelings are boring and don't really communicate. But a plain account may communicate a great deal. If we write down faithfully what happens to us, our feelings will come through and they will be felt indirectly and therefore truly. So rather than say how we felt on our marriage day, we should try to describe what happened to us on that marriage day. Our feelings will come through much better than if we just say how we felt. We are more likely to be able to convey to our descendants something of what we really were if we try to set down the truth about what happens to us, and the more concrete and more detailed it is the better, and the less abstract it is the better. It is a mark of genius to single out the little details that make everything come alive, and very often that happens, not because one seeks to do it, but because one is in the right frame of mind and has taken one's experience in the right way. Notice in the Joseph Smith story details like his leaning up against the mantelpiece when he gets home and the humorous remark he makes to his mother on that occasion.

In Joseph Smith, we have a man who is impetuous, generous-minded, sensitive, and tender. At the same time, the level of honesty he manages to reach in his story is an example to all of us, both men and women, of how sensitivity and honesty can come together. Another model for us is that most limpid and pure journal, John Woolman's journal. Another, to come nearer home, is Wilford Woodruff's journal. There are also the letters of Lucy Hutchinson, a truly great and humble woman who lived in the seventeenth century, and the Paston letters from the late fifteenth century—Agnes and Margaret Paston are particularly interesting people. There are the novels of Samuel Richardson, especially *Clarissa Harlowe* (written in letter style), and those of Jane Austen, of which the most impressive is the last, *Persuasion.* The letters of Queen Victoria can very profitably be perused. Above all, there are the letters of Madame de Sévigné. These letters of a great French lady to her daughter are, perhaps, the purest documents from a woman's hands that we have. They have been translated. However, they can only give their true atmosphere in the French. Look, too, at the correspondence of American women at the end of the eighteenth century before the affectations of the nineteenth century broke in.

A personal history always needs to be revised because what we think is most important in our lives changes as our lives go on. Certain experiences become less important as we grow older, and others become more important, more profound. Were we here simply to have certain experiences, life would soon be over for us. But we are here to live so that those experiences—for example, the experience of eternal marriage—may broaden and deepen and become richer as we grow older. Though we may think we understand the significance of eternal marriage at the time we are married, we may understand it much more deeply later. In fact, we may spend a lifetime realizing or beginning to realize what the real significance of an eternal marriage is. So just as we should go back constantly to the scriptures and to other great books, we should go back to the most important experiences of our lives.

The poet Wordsworth took some thirteen years to assess the significance of his first crossing of the Alps on foot. His first description of that experience, written in 1792 in his *Descriptive Sketches*, is a perfunctory, conventional description of no significance. His second description, written in 1805, is a very different one. He had got the real experience at last. He didn't know what it was until then. It took him all those years. Joseph Smith took eight years to get his account of the First Vision right. Certainly, the boy of fourteen had no full appreciation of that experience, but the young man ten years later was beginning to have a full appreciation of it, and ten years later than that his appreciation was at the full. Joseph brooded for years over those experiences and visions that he had in his teens. Inspiration may strike in a flash, but inspiration may not be fully felt or understood for many years. Inspiration may also go on over a number of years, as it did, for example, when Joseph Smith was working on the Inspired Version of the Bible. (Anyone who wants to know more about that can look at Brother Robert J. Matthews's excellent work.)

The greatest experiences of our lives need to be remembered and cultivated and thought of day after day. We don't want to tuck them underground. They are there for us to keep, treasure, observe, know, and live with. One of the greatest experiences of life is death, and that comes at the end, so we may well be appreciating that experience in the eternities and understanding more and more about it. I look forward to it. The most important experiences of our lives shape our lives—they are our lives.

Wholeness

Spared dissolution,
His body rose whole, but with
five wounds, by which, from
earth, ooze, ash, even air, we
all, however dead, shall rise.

AHK
January/February 1981

"As the Days of a Tree Are the Days of My People"

I DON'T EXPECT to be moved by introductions, but I have been moved by today's. Perhaps I can recover by saying about that finely rendered "Liebestod," which we have just heard, that I had to struggle for five years, from the age of thirteen to the age of eighteen, to rid Wagner from my soul. I literally trembled from head to foot when, sitting in the Westminster Congregational Chapel with my grandfather among 4,000 others, I heard on the organ for the first time the prelude to *Parsifal* (a "religious" opera). When I later heard *Tristan und Isolde*, I was surprised to find that the music was the same kind—in both works, erotic.

So, I would ask you today to pass from that fine rendering of unholy love to what President Holland mentioned from Alma: the song of redeeming love. And what I want to talk about today is learning the music of the song of redeeming love, for learning that music is the most fundamental part of our education. I know I have asked you to ask yourself questions, but I am not such a fool as to answer them. I leave you to answer your own questions, which have become yours through reading mine. That's how education works. But what I am going to try to do today is to say some things from which you can draw your own conclusions about your own education now and forever, because education is forever.

So I ask you to come with me now and leave this world that chews the cud of terrorism in its mass media, to leave a world that indeed exists in history and in scriptural history from the beginning,

Given as the commencement address at Brigham Young University, following a performance of the "Liebestod" in *Tristan und Isolde*, April 18, 1986.

from Cain onward: I would remind you in Isaiah of Rabshakeh before the walls of Jerusalem, cursing and despising the Jews; I would remind you in the Book of Mormon of the Gadianton robbers; I would remind you of the jailers whom Joseph Smith rebuked. All this hatred and violence is part of history, but only a minor part. Even the nightmare from which Stephen Daedalus says he is trying to awake is only a minor part.

The nightmare from which Daedalus was trying to awake, the nightmare from which thousands of millions of people in the world at the moment are trying to awake, is indeed the nightmare of history as the natural man sees it. But it is not natural for us to be natural; rather, it is natural for us to be supernatural. That is why the natural man is an enemy to God. But God has entered history for us, and God guides history; and that guidance, too, is what I am to talk to you about today. The song of redeeming love is the seed of history. And history is something that God, through his intentions and purposes, is always bringing to an unending close.

Love begins in the family. There are so many kinds of love for us: parental love, spousal love, filial love, the love of brothers and sisters, love between friends, love of animals; and the love of God's entire creation. Yet none of these loves is itself or can be itself unless it contains that element of the love of God, which is essential to all true love.

Love begins, then, in the family. And may I point out how much better love begins in a family that spreads its arms? I had the good luck at the age of nine, when my father died, to have my grandparents move in, together with a maiden aunt, and we formed a multigenerational family. That was my salvation in many ways: my grandfather stood in for my father. But for those who are happier in having fathers, remember this, too: how can a father show his son how a son should behave to a father unless the father behaves to his own father, that son's grandfather, how a son should be? Children love to meet their cousins. They feel their cousins are special to them. And I do hope that in a world that travels so much, and in a world in which people are a little casual about splitting their families and going to the ends of the earth, that we can remember that the multigenerational family has been the rule through the ages. Grandparents have lived on the family farm, for example, serving as the keepers and educators of the children while the mother and father did the work of dairying or doing outside chores. The multigenerational family is psychologically, economically, and theologically the right unit on this earth, the unit in which our love can learn to spread. And in that multigenerational family we can move back by studying its genealogy.

Those of you who now are leaving us should ask yourselves, "How much better am I now provided to study my genealogy than I was when I entered?" You had the opportunity here; did you take it? My wife and I have been strengthened in our faith and testimonies by the genealogy we have done. We have learned what happens when the hearts of the fathers turn to the children and the hearts of the children to the fathers. If that turning does not occur, a curse will befall humanity; we can see the beginnings of the workings of that curse more strongly than ever all over the world. I remember when, along with my wife, I first read an extract from a letter of a mutual fourth great-grandmother, Susanna Martin, daughter of a miller called Garton, who under the abominable Charles the Second spent twenty years in prison for his faith. Susanna Martin and her family were Quakers; she was a missionary. A mother of many children, she had afterwards gone up and down in England and Scotland and Ireland. She was overtaken by illness, and in 1735 she wrote her last letter. In that letter, she says she "had wrote this down" for the benefit of those that might come after her, when she was in the dust, so that they might know how good it is to serve the Lord and how sweet she had found his service. Every time I think of those words, tears of joy come into my eyes.

When in your genealogical researches you come across something like Susanna Martin's words, you will feel, as my wife and I felt, a great surge of gratitude to the Lord for allowing us to make that discovery and for the effect on our own souls. This gratitude comes from knowing that over the generations our forebears have struggled towards the light, and have now found it (their work has been done).

Thus we can extend our family back in time, and as we extend our family back in time, we can feel more and more love for that family. My grandfather was born in 1850; I remember him very well: he died at eighty-four when I was twenty-eight. There are undergraduates here today whom I have taught who will be in their early eighties in 2050. I have love for all those whom I teach, and a special love for some of them. Well, here we have an example of a love from my grandfather to me and from me to the youngest students among you, a love that stretches from 1850 to 2050—two hundred years. Now you will understand perhaps why I have called this talk "As the Days of a Tree Are the Days of My People." Isaiah uses that language to describe the Millennium (Isa. 65:22). But one of the major things I want to say today is that we can prepare for the Millennium in our hearts and in our society now: we are asked to do so before it comes. We can have some sense of the Millennium; we can sense some "bright shoots of everlastingness" before we reach it.

To prepare ourselves for the Millennium, we need to be able to think back and to imagine forward at the same time. The great French writer Charles Maurras said that when you come to an election you should not think of your immediate needs. Rather, he said, you should think of what your fathers wanted for this nation and of what your children and your grandchildren and your great-grandchildren will need, and then vote. But how many people do this? How many people, indeed, vote at all?

At this point, I want to mention the thing in family life that enables family love to grow most: the care and love and reading of the scriptures. That was the education Joseph Smith had, and that is why he was better educated than most of us in this hall, including myself; Joseph Smith was soaked in the scriptures. I was lucky that my father read us the scriptures daily before breakfast; I was lucky that I went into a school system in Britain that made religion and Bible reading compulsory so that we had two scriptural lessons per week and a portion of the Bible read to us in school assembly every single morning. This familiarity with the scriptures will die unless we keep it alive. Our most important immediate task is to make sure that familiarity with the scriptures remains alive in the family, for the family is where children gain the most essential education. The way in which families hand over their children's education to the school system nowadays goes directly against religious principles. The fundamentals of education are to be taught in the home, not in the school. So, even if you haven't yourselves yet read the scriptures thoroughly, remember what the Lord said, "If ye then, being evil, know how to give good gifts unto your children . . ."

(Matt. 7:11). Remember those words, and see to it—for some of you have children already, and most of you will have them—that you read the scriptures aloud in your family with the children there, even when they are young, even when they are months old, a year or two old. If you do so, your children will be under the influence of a scriptural atmosphere. Even now your children are learning their own language. Let them learn the language of the scriptures as part of learning their language, because childhood is the time when the Lord has provided language-learning faculties far better than we adults have. I am not speaking theoretically; it happened to me that way. When you have absorbed the scriptures, and only then, can you teach them with certainty to your children; and in your teaching, you should remember that "the scriptures" means the ancient scriptures, the modern scriptures, and what the prophets tell us now—all these things that confirm one another.

When you have the scriptures in your heart and your mind and your soul, then you have a means of measuring all things; you have a means for judging everything else. Above all, you have a means of judging words, both written and spoken. My grandmother left school at the age of twelve to become a kitchen maid; because she was neat and cleanly in her habits, she was promoted to parlor maid. She waited at table, and that is where, as a guest, my grandfather saw her and said to himself, "I'm going to marry that woman." My grandmother knew the scriptures. (She was a Peculiar Baptist with a capital "P." That is a very special thing: it means that you are absolutely sure that 999,999 people out of every million are damned. She managed to keep cheerful.) My grandmother wrote a good letter. She didn't make the same kind of spelling and punctuation mistakes that perhaps most of us in this hall do. Not only that, she had taste, and so had my grandfather, who was also a Peculiar Baptist; he was apprenticed as a watchmaker at the age of fourteen and was also soaked in the scriptures. He and she had taste in literature. Their taste was not what was taught them in school, but what they had got because they had the scriptures as their standard.

My grandparents did not read trashy stuff, and they did not like their children to read trashy stuff. I am afraid both my father and my mother read trashy novels—I saw some on the shelves; I even read them. And even at that young age, I disliked them intensely: I saw that those novels were trying to get hold of my feelings and work on them, and that is not what good art does. Good art does not manipulate. Anyway, I am afraid that my father and mother's marriage was not so satisfactory as it should have been, and one of the contributory causes was that, as young people, they got wrong ideas by reading the trashy novels of writers like Marie Corelli and Hall Caine. That terrible old poet W. B. Yeats said (call it to mind and let it remain in your hearts you yet unmarried), "Maybe the bride-bed brings despair, / For each an imagined image brings / And finds a real image there." Our marriages cannot be satisfactory unless we read and look at and listen to the kinds of things that will enable us to have a stable and sensitive marriage instead of opening up to the modern artistic and popular abominations that put ourselves in the center. What marriage can be successful in which our spouse is not more important than ourselves? Selfishness and marriage don't go together, nor can selfishness be unlearned very readily in marriage unless the process has already been started in the bosom of the family. We need to have learned to be unselfish *before* we get married.

Well now, let me extend from this need for reading the scriptures to what the reading of the scriptures enables us to do in other literature. My grandmother used to read to me. What did she read to me when I was seven or eight? Goldsmith—"The Vicar of Wakefield," "The Traveler," "The Deserted Village"—and Cowper. She liked these things. She was born in 1856, but her mind lived in the eighteenth century, and she found, quite rightly, most of the stuff written after 1780 pretty trashy.

You can judge what you ought to read of other literature by what the scriptures show you because the scriptures (I give you my testimony of this as a stylistician) are the best works ever written or spoken. Remember that. You can judge everything by the scriptures. You can judge a life of Abraham Lincoln by the inspired account of David given in First and Second Samuel and the first two chapters of First Kings. We know far more, and far more deeply, about David than we do about Abraham Lincoln. And always remember, when you go to even the greatest of other literature—to Homer, Virgil, Dante, Shakespeare, and Goethe—that only the scriptures are supreme. These great writers tell us much truth, but only the scriptures tell us the whole truth.

What goes for literature, the power to see what is good in literature because you are soaked in the scriptures, goes for the other arts as well. You will not want to look at bad things on your walls or listen to bad music (which most of you do) if you are soaked in the scriptures because such things don't fit. But you will love *The Messiah* (I mean the oratorio) because it springs out of the scriptures. My mother was a singer, and her contralto arias from *The Messiah* are among the fundamental things that have remained with me throughout my life. I had them played at her funeral.

We can, then, judge music and all the fine arts, once we have in our minds that firm and sound sense of what is good taste. I use the unsatisfactory word "taste," but a better word is difficult to find because "taste" expresses choice, and choice is the important thing. The ability to choose between good and evil exists in every choice we make: what we eat, what we look at, what we wear, what we read, and above all nowadays, what we watch on the tube.

Once we have the scriptures in our lives, we have world history from beginning to end. And that, too, is a means of putting history in order for us. The scriptures provide the way to approach the history of the past. We need to do so because, to go back to Isaiah's tree image, the tree is not simply the roots as the past and the trunk as the present and the branches as the future. Rather, the tree is the totality: the roots are still alive; the trunk is alive; the branches are alive; the roots are seeking the tree's sustenance; and the leaves are seeking the tree's sustenance—everything happens together. We may bear this tree image in mind together with other images of eternity like the ring, the eternal moment and the unending line. We must remember, however, the total tree, from the roots to branches—the tree of life, the tree of knowledge of good and evil, the tree of Jesse, the tree of the condescension of God. In our church, we believe that the spirits of the dead are not gone, that they have not vanished. They may indeed, as Brigham Young suggested, be here around us. But however the case may be, our church considers the past as part of our present in a way that no other church does. We do so because that is the relationship the Christian religion demands: the copresence of the past in the present to make the future possible. That future is a future of salvation, for the Lord has entered history and continually guides it.

To fully comprehend the relationship among past, present, and future, we must educate ourselves through good literature, good music, and good art. In particular, we must not neglect such education due to our preoccupation with practical things or inferior amusements. Being educated and having a moderate income is better than being boorish and having millions. My grandfather understood this fact. He—and I come back to him at the end of what I have to say—said to me once when I was about fourteen, "Git your education, boy, git your education; git all you can, but do it for its own sake." I have tried to live by that counsel; I lived by it until I joined the Church. Through the gospel, I learned that education was for its own sake in only one sense: the Lord's sake. I needed to learn for the Lord.

And so I come to the end of this address by asking you to ask yourselves the following questions, "Did I enter to learn? Did I enter to learn to love and love to learn?" You should have done; you could have done; you may have done; yet if you have not, you are not too late—it is never too late to learn. Having entered this university to learn, you now go forth to serve, but you go forth to serve with love. You go forth to love and serve. And the good love you bear contains both your love of God and the love God has for you, which is the essential part of your love for all those you love. Without that essential part, of course, our love is not the right love. All of us really know the right love. And I say these things in the name of Jesus Christ, amen.

Dreams

WE SEEM TO be agreed that what happens to us when we are awake is real and what happens to us when we dream is not. But that is a very stupid thing to think. Dreams are a part of our total mind and experience, and, more than we do, we need to ignore the difference between waking and sleeping, a difference that is a convention and only a convention. It is all going on underneath all the time, or on top, as the case may be. Remember what Tweedledee said to Alice when they found the Red King asleep under a tree. Tweedledee said, "Why, you're only a sort of thing in his dream!" And Tweedledum added, "If that there King was to wake . . . you'd go out—bang!—just like a candle!" The pen of a mathematician presents a profound philosophical problem in a story for children to hear. I read that myself when I was eight. It hit me hard, and I have never entirely recovered from it.

We find as we grow older that we wander from "dream" to "reality" and back again. And those of us who think ourselves sensible while awake will often find ourselves absurd when asleep. With me, it happens the other way around. I feel absurd when I am awake, so I am sensible when I am asleep. It is an alternative way of life. Sometimes my dreams are so vivid that I catch myself when I have woken up in the morning, at breakfast, thinking of something that hasn't "happened" at all: it happened in a dream.

As old age approaches death, the distinction between "dream" and "reality" becomes even less clear and less relevant. All sorts of unexpected things happen to people, and we need to know that so we can be prepared for similar experiences in our own lives. Death for most is not at all like it was for my uncle who simply said, "I'm going to die," and did, just like that, on the spot. All sorts of things happen, and they all have personal relevance. My father-in-law died at the age of 86. Shortly before he died, he was in the hospital with pneumonia. My wife went to visit him and found him outside his room, sitting in the corridor, looking out of the window. Well, she talked to him a bit, and she got him back into bed. And then, to her astonishment and even fright, he said to her, "Who was that woman with graying hair who was talking to me outside just now?" That was an important experience for them both. I spent part of the next day with him, trying to help him identify what had happened to him that day that he had "dreamt" and what had happened to him that he had "actually experienced." But, "really," the difference is pretty "immaterial." As I was saying to my wife, "Why do you bother about that?" We spend our lives in that kind of situation, of so-called mistaken identity. Our sense of certainty is a convention: we assume that certainty lies in sense-experience, whereas certainty lies only in the gospel.

My dreams are important and mean as much to me as my waking life. The two just run into one another as I write my verse. Let me tell you about one dream that I made into verse: I was walking along a road in a town at sunset. It was obviously summer and late in the evening, and some of the sun was coming straight down the road. And there was something on the pavement. It looked like one of these big yellow and black butterflies that fly about Provo in the summertime. I picked it up, and it wasn't anything of the kind—it was a bat. And not thinking about hydrophobia, I put the bat, if you please, into a great pink ear carved in a stone block that was on the side of a building. Well, there I left the butterfly, which turned out to be a bat, and walked on down the street. When I woke up, I made a verse about the dream because it was worth making into a verse. It was something that had happened to me. Most of the things that happen to me when I am awake are not worth writing about.

In 1964, I was in Ottawa at the Parliament House attending a conference, and there were a lot of people concerned because of a bat in the curtains in the corridor. And they called the janitor. The janitor wanted to kill the bat. I said, "You won't." I stopped him, and I took it outside and put it in the ivy. That is the only other occasion on which I had much to do with bats, except when I spent three weeks in Makerere, which is the university just outside Kampala, the capital of Uganda. And oh, the enormous fruit bats! There were tens of thousands of them. They looked like a lot of dead leaves on the trees, and imagine the trees waking up and finding bats instead of leaves on them every morning. Those are two experiences with bats, but I can't associate them in any way with my dream. However, I did have another dream once in which I was walking down the street of stone that was in the first dream. And it was in a west England town. It was the same time of evening. And I went down into a cellar, and there was Lazarus coming up out of the tomb. And I helped him up the steps into the sunlight, and he fainted. I dreamt that dream in 1951, a long time ago. And when I dreamed the dream about the bat, I linked it up with the dream about Lazarus because the landscape was the same. The Lazarus dream was another dream I made into a poem:

Dream as the Days Draw In

A corner of Cotswold stone
with a rusty bar sticking out.
I walk round the corner alone:
no-one about.
The sun glares on the bare street
hot, not bright.
What am I due to meet
at the coming of night?
What I shall meet is within,
but it will appear:
Lazarus white to the chin
with a dark stare,
and, trees with eyes in the gloom,
behind him all my dead.
In silence, in dread,
with that shadowy row
at first cock-crow
I too shall glide to my tomb.
And Lazarus, left for the light,
will he be I?
Can he inherit my sight,
let alone my history?
When he turns back my way,
can it again be day?

Dreams are the stuff of literature—we are all poets in our sleep. Dreams do what all poets and mythmakers do: bring together the unexpected and make new wholes. Freud was a poet, a mythmaker. We may feel uncomfortable about his theories until we realize that that is what he was. He played with images, handled characters, made myths into consistent wholes. Freud had a way of saying things that still need to be said. Most of them, incidentally, are comic, and one of the sad things about Freud was that he didn't feel comic enough, although he once said that a good cigar is sometimes a smoke—a cigar is not always something else. Freud's work stimulates people to think and is very useful that way. The Roman Catholic Church has found it useful. Freud's work points to facts, although it doesn't interpret those facts correctly—Freud was not a prophet, even though he was a poet. Myth is there, even in the natural sciences. The science of yesterday (Newton) is the myth of today. The science of today (Einstein, et. al.) is the myth of tomorrow. The science of tomorrow is the myth of today. It was Eddington who pointed out that the use of scientific terms like "atom," "electron," and "proton" is like the use of terms in "Jabberwocky." The more powerfully imagined the totalities that are thrown over experiences—the more dreamlike those totalities are—the richer the material we have to work with.

In 1913–14, the poet Yeats wrote a volume called *Responsibilities*. And this is the motto of the book: "In dreams begins responsibility." Well, Freud's *Interpretation of Dreams* was written in 1904. It wasn't translated into English until 1914. But Yeats was the sort of person who might have known about the book—he was in sufficient contact with intellectuals around Europe in one way or another. But "In dreams begins responsibility" is a profound saying, one that I have never forgotten. And it is not something that the scriptures deny, but something that the scriptures endorse. There are dreams and visions in the scriptures. After all, the ancient scriptures were written at a time when dreams were taken seriously. And I see no reason why they should be taken any differently now. Dreams may be the way that the spirit speaks to us. Dreams may present experience in a way that shows us where we are going and either endorse it or condemn it. Dreams, if we read them correctly, may prompt our moral responsibility, just as literature, in the same way, may also do. The responsibilities I shirk during the day, the month, the year, come back to me in dreams and bother me until I do something about them. My imperfect relations with others are warningly accentuated. A dream may refuse to let me get to a place where I want to go because to go there would be running away from where I am, which is where I ought to be. My dreams don't fulfill my wishes: they constantly stop me from fulfilling them. My dreams thwart me because I need to be thwarted. My dreams represent my whole mind, which may reprimand a refractory part. My dreams are a moral tutor. Not very often, when I do the right thing, they bring back someone I love from the dead—the sense of liberation and joy is greater than anything in my "waking" life.

My dreams are a reminder of what I could have been and what I still could be if I could in my waking life trust my whole self instead of niggling around with a part, for my dreams come from my whole self. They remind me that my whole self is still there, still whole. I don't say I am I, but my dreams tell me I am. Increasingly, my dreams travel through space and time, enabling me to see life as a whole. And how often have I gone to sleep while thinking of a problem and awakened to find it solved. Unfortunately, we often try to reason out a problem instead of sleeping on it.

Dreams should be a part of our waking lives. When we rise in the morning and prepare to pray, we should first try to remember the dreams of the night. If we don't remember them as soon as we wake, they are not likely to be there to remember.

How do you interpret a dream? How do you interpret a work of art? You proceed in the same kind of way. You don't approach a dream with a set of preconceived theories. You allow it to speak to you in the sense that you are speaking to yourself. It is above all the emotive ground tone of a dream that counts. A dream differs from a work of art in one important sense: it is itself the response to itself—the work is the response; we are the dream. But it is not just another experience: it is a creative experience, a whole experience. Dreams help to make us whole.

Atonement: The Only Wholeness

Article of Faith 3: We believe that through the Atonement of Christ, all mankind may be saved, by obedience to the laws and ordinances of the Gospel.

We Are Not At One

THE WORLD IS sick and most of us are sick—perhaps all of us are sick in some way or another. We need to be healed, to be made whole.

We are sick because we are not whole—we feel separated, we feel incomplete. To us who believe, the Lord is the healer, the one who makes us whole. Why, then, do we not feel whole? Why do we not feel at one?

In the first weeks of life, we still respond to our mother's heartbeat because it is the one that we know; then we lose our remembrance of that. We lose still further when we are weaned because we are separated still further. We separate ourselves further yet by learning to crawl, to walk, and so it goes on. Do we ever naturally feel whole again after birth? And does our mother? Does she not long to go on being one with her child?

Husband and wife yearn to be one with each other always and in all ways. Do we ever completely succeed?

Does the family feel at one? Is it not always struggling, even in its goodness, with the trammels of its badness?

Are we at one with our brethren? We have been told, "If ye are not one, ye are not mine" (D&C 38:27). What about the barriers of environment, race, creed, education, fortune? Can we be at one in a society that is not at one? How can we be at one with ourselves when we are aware all the time of the imperfections of society and our unfulfilled duty to help remove those imperfections?

Are we at one inside ourselves? Most of us feel more than one aspect of separation from others: the sense of inferiority, jealousy, fear, guilt, evil, suffering, death—all of them symptoms of separation. We have a sense of limitation and wonder whether it is our mind or our body or both that limit us. We feel pulled in several directions at once; we feel the need of having to choose the lesser of two evils. We are sick in body and mind—we have so much illness because we are not at one with ourselves. The number of illnesses regarded by the experts as having to do with attitude of mind—the psychosomatic illnesses—increases steadily.

And are we at one with God? How can we be at one with him unless we are at one with our family, with society, and with ourselves? And how can we be at one with ourselves, and with father, mother, brother, sister, husband, or wife, if we are not at one with God? If we were at one with God, should we not feel at one with all humanity?

But as Christians we know that the Lord is the healer, the one who makes us whole.

The Word *Atonement*

"We pray you in Christes stede that ye be atone with God" (2 Cor. 5:20, Tyndale's Version; the Authorized Version says "reconciled"). "To be atone" means to be reconciled. Romans 5:11 reads, "We also joy in God through our Lord Jesus Christ, by whom we have now received the atonement." In the Revised Version, the New English Bible, and the Jerusalem Bible, "atonement" reads "reconciliation." The German Bible's word is *Versoehnung*, whose usual translation is "reconciliation." The Basic English Bible says "at peace."

To be reconciled (2 Cor. 5:18, "God, who hath reconciled us to himself by Jesus Christ") we need a *mediator*. Christ is that mediator ("one mediator between God and men, the man Christ Jesus," 1 Tim. 2:5).

But Romans 5:11 is the only place where "atonement" is used in the sense of "reconciliation." Other scriptural references, particularly in the Old Testament, have a sense that is more familiar to us. The verb "to atone for" can mean "to be penitent, to pay for." We find, for example, in Leviticus 1:4 the sense "expiation" (appeasement by sacrifice); in Romans 3:24, "redemption" (which means "buying back"); and in 1 John 2:2, the word "propitiation" (meaning "making gracious"). On the day of atonement, the Jewish national sins were heaped on the scapegoat and he was driven out, "And the goat shall bear upon him all their iniquities unto a land not inhabited" (Lev. 16:22). The literal sense of "not inhabited" is—and this is significant to us here—"a land of separation."

Of all these senses, the one most familiar to us is that of "redemption." But it is the one in which we have lost the original sense of "buying back." It may be that in dealing with these things of the spirit we should not push the metaphor too hard. The sense "redemption" is not, after all, so very different from that of "reconciliation"; see, for example, "I know that my redeemer liveth" (Job 19:25), where the word *goel*, translated as "redeemer," could equally well be rendered by "vindicator" (New English Bible) or "mediator." In fact, if we think of and feel the word "atonement" with the right degree of imprecision or generality, we can reconcile the senses: we need to be made whole; we cannot be made whole without being reconciled to God; we are reconciled to God by the sacrifice of Jesus Christ.

Putting the senses together in this way, we are led to the meaning in which we understand the plan of salvation. Christ offered himself to make up for the transgression of Adam, the consequence of which was death. Christ sets all the posterity of Adam free from death (general salvation). "When Adam fell, the change came upon all other living things and even the earth itself became mortal, and all things including the earth were redeemed from death through the atonement of Jesus Christ" (Joseph Fielding Smith, *Answers to Gospel Questions*, 3:100–101; see also 2 Ne. 2:22). The animals and the elements, too, suffered death for Adam's transgression. But Christ also shed his blood (1 Pet. 1:19) for every person individually, and that is one reason why his Atonement must be infinite (2 Ne. 9:7). This salvation is for everyone who will repent, obey the ordinances of the gospel, and do good works (individual salvation); if a soul refuses salvation, such refusal means banishment from God's presence; if that soul commits the ultimate refusal, the second death is the ultimate punishment.

Members of the Church are familiar with these doctrines; they have been summarized above as a reminder. But what do these doctrines really mean? That because Christ rose, we also can rise? That Christ came to earth to show us the example of his infinite love and thereby conquer us by kindling our love (Abelard)? That

Christ showed us the example of what a perfect soul can be and that we can follow that example? That God became man so that men and women could attain deity (Irenaeus)? That Christ exerts on us the moral influence of his suffering? When we read such explanations, we are in part satisfied, but we are not satisfied altogether: such explanations do not account for the Atonement. They are merely rationalizations that we more or less understand. These helpful explanations and many other silly and heretical ones have concerned the apostate church throughout the ages. I have simply made a selection of some explanations that our church would accept.

But we should accept these explanations only with provisos. Can we rise merely because Christ rose? Can we imitate Christ simply because Christ has given the example? If God became man, can the human become God by human effort? What influence has the suffering of Christ so long ago on a world now so used to suffering *en masse*?

It would seem that our rational explanations can aim no higher than the level of the law of Moses. And "the law of Moses availeth nothing except it were through the atonement of his blood" (Mosiah 3:15).

And why the blood? To many modern persons, reference to Christ's blood is vulgar. But are they being realistic enough and robust enough in taking such a view? Archbishop Soederblom of Sweden once said that it took a barbarous thing like the Crucifixion to have any effect on barbarians like us.

That would seem to be true, but it, too, is not the whole truth. The Atonement is (for us as we now are) seen "through a glass, darkly" (1 Cor. 13:12). But it is a satisfying darkness, an eternally flowing well from which we can gain greater and greater meaning for ourselves and still find it inexhaustible. For is it not infinite?

Let us meditate together in our limitations on some of the things about the Atonement that we at least feel, and "know in part" (1 Cor. 13:12).

Separation

"For it must needs be, that there is an opposition in all things. . . . Wherefore, if it should be one body it must needs remain as dead, having no life neither death, nor corruption nor incorruption, happiness nor misery, neither sense nor insensibility" (2 Ne. 2:11). For this reason, Adam and Eve developed, after the Fall, the power to discriminate. For without opposition there is no choice. "Wherefore, the Lord God gave unto man that he should act for himself. Wherefore, man could not act for himself save it should be that he was enticed by the one or the other" (2 Ne. 2:16).

Hence the choice of Christ's plan of salvation, leaving us our agency. We are separated from God in order that we may *voluntarily* return to him.

But we are not whole as long as we are separated from him, though in this life repentance and good works may give us some sense of that wholeness, some premonition. And if we do not voluntarily return to him, we shall be involuntarily separated from him forever.

The more the separation or the opportunity of mortal probation, then, the more the opportunity for abundant life and also for sin.

Opposition is a fact of the universe, a fact by which the universe is, by which it defines itself, and by which it develops. But there is clearly a wrong opposition as well as a right one. The opposition of day and night is morally indifferent; the opposition of good and evil is not. Does not the sense of sin, of wrong opposition, cause the greatest separateness, the greatest distance from God?

We find this distance first in family quarrels, the struggle for power between spouses, between parents and children; in the bad-tempered husband and the nagging wife; in the stern face of a father exercising hypocritical authority over his teenage son; in the chill of a mother who no longer remembers what she was like at her daughter's age.

Family quarrels may last through generations. But is there not an image of atonement in the family through genealogy? Cannot the hearts of the fathers and the children be brought together from their long separation in the restoration of the oneness of the family through the generations, a family atonement? The family tree, the tree of Jesse, the tree of life, and the tree of the cross are all symbols one of another and of the love of God.

With all its imperfections, the family unit is close to salvation. Husband, wife, parents, and children have the opportunity of working out unity in separation; but casual, extramarital relations cannot do this. Sexual relations temporarily entered into only increase the sense of separation, of loneliness, of selfishness. Only through the unity of the gospel of Jesus Christ can a sense of lasting wholeness be achieved.

And so, with the prevailing sexual sins of this generation, we come to the sickness of society. We are members one of another and our action in sin shows it as much as our action in virtue. But we are not willing to shoulder our social responsibilities. Robert Musil, in his novel *The Man without Qualities*, shows us the erring inhabitants of Vienna centering their interest on an imprisoned sex murderer awaiting death. The murderer, being a weaker vessel, a kind of safety valve or scapegoat, has acted out the wicked fantasies of the population. For the same reason, in Forster's *A Passage to India*, when the Englishman asks the Hindu professor his opinion about who committed the assault on the young woman in the cave, the Hindu answers, "You did, I did, we all did." Those of us who have helped to build up the evil pressures in society or who neglect to do our best to combat them are partly responsible for the crimes that result from those pressures.

In a psychology manual, I once saw pictures of hundreds of children from Oslo at the age of four and then pictures of the same children again at the age of nine. The four-year-olds were bright and forward-looking and eager, their life shining out of their faces. The nine-year-olds were already dull and apathetic.

Daily we see the face and swollen body of famine in the newspaper advertisement and daily we turn our eyes away from it.

Worse than the sins that we recognize to be sins are those we do not recognize to be sins in our false atonement with this world—with the world of fashion, with its stupidity about cosmetics and clothes; the world of politics, with its naive ideas about what can be done without the help of the Lord. Whatever our political complexion, we need to remember that no political party preaches the United Order as we in the Church have had it revealed to us. Neither capitalism nor communism is reconcilable with that order. It is a voluntary giving up of self and all that belongs to self, to be entered into with joy.

Satan's solution was uniformity. We see this most clearly in the plan for a communist society (though no state in this world is yet entirely communist), but we should also see it in the dangerous monotony of mass production, both in the boredom of the work itself and in the commonplace nature of the product.

Some reconcile themselves to this world in terms of what they think to be its highest culture. But most art, and most modern art in particular, is an illusion. Only the greatest art with a religious impulse can truly support the gospel. Michelangelo's *Creation of Adam* can do so, as can Bach's *The Saint Matthew Passion*. But even Beethoven's harmony is only temporary, and the self-assertion constantly breaks through. And the most considerable artist of our time, Picasso, descended into ironical impotence and despair.

Art reminds us of another aspect of separation and sin, another thing for which we need atonement: the ugliness of our environment and ourselves. What window does not look out on something ugly that citizens have made? What man can look with approval at himself as he shaves each morning? Or what woman as she does her hair? And we constantly mistake certain kinds of ugliness for beauty, especially in our judgment of the beauty of women. We should remember that the Lord himself had "no apparent beauty" ("O God, the Eternal Father," William W. Phelps, *Hymns*, no. 175, based on Isa. 53:2), and many of us are insensitive to the radiance of loving and faithful eyes in a so-called plain face. The beauty of holiness is not skin deep. There is so much vanity from which we need to purge ourselves if we are once again to become whole through the merit of the Lord Jesus Christ.

The separation from God by which we identify ourselves with the world is worse than our separation from the world because we should be in the world but not of the world. Being merely in the world has its griefs and its trials, however. There is unhappiness at not being one with society; that unhappiness can be purged only by our becoming missionaries to our fellows. That is what the Church gives us the opportunity to do.

We come next to the separation of individuals within themselves. I cannot help thinking of it as the separation of mind and body because our culture has so insisted on this dichotomy that it is almost impossible to get rid of it, although it is not in keeping with the teaching of the Church. That is how most of us feel the struggle, often simplifying it to the tempting of the mind by the body, although it is obvious that the mind always begins temptation and corrupts the body, not the other way around. But to think of temptation, for example, as a struggle between mind and body is to simplify the problem to the point at which it seems readily soluble—but falsely so. In not following the gospel, we fall into hopeless divisions of ourselves and run always into the same cul de sac. We criticize our thinking in the same language as that in which we think. We analyze the situation between the individual and society in more and more subtle ways, only to realize that people intuitively and instinctively do as one operation what is a hundred to a sociologist or a social psychologist. We struggle on the moral plane because we cannot really believe in evil or a devil, and we regard our problem as a skirmish with ourselves rather than a battle with an inveterate adversary. We may be so frightened at the way we struggle with ourselves that we mask the deeper struggle and therefore find it impossible to resolve the more superficial one. The depth of our self-deceit is only exceeded by the depth to which the Lord descended to save us.

In the long run, our greatest difficulty is to be humble enough to put ourselves in the position to be saved, a position that may mean losing the self-concern of the struggle within ourselves and looking outward to be concerned with others and their struggles. The Good Samaritan was not divided against himself. But the Levite was (Luke 10:32); he only increased his concern about himself by his action in passing by on the other side.

Fear is a great separator of selves and of self. To be courageous at one level may involve being afraid at another—this helps to explain the difference between physical and moral courage. Most fears in the end are fears of oneself and can be conquered by bringing in the Lord as an ally.

And that brings us to separation from God. "It is a fearful thing to fall into the hands of the living God" (Heb. 10:31), but it is a still more terrible thing to fall out of the hands of the living God. To realize that Jehovah and Christ are one is to realize that the books Luke and Jeremiah are both part of the gospel and that the books Judges and Acts are both part of the gospel. Whatever the world may say about Jehovah being a savage tribal god, the god of the Old Testament and the god of the New Testament are the same person. We have to look at the documents to see that, and then the sternness of Christ and the mildness of Jehovah will come home to us, as well as the sternness of Jehovah and the mildness of Christ. They are the same God. Many people feel that when he looks at them, they are at one with his eyes of concern, but when he gazes at horizons, they do not like to feel that his eyes are as those of eagles. But what if people cannot see his eyes at all?

Yet with all the irritation at best and torment at worst of being divided against oneself, we need to remember that the prayer "suffer us not to be separated" (T. S. Eliot, *Ash Wednesday*) is a prayer against the destruction of our individuality, which is the most important of all things to us. The fear need not and should not be for the struggles we may have that come from the "opposition in all things" (2 Ne. 2:11)—we must admit these struggles into ourselves in order to be able to grow. However, that opposition is at its healthiest when we are not divided against ourselves, but we may find ourselves in opposition to someone else and discover the need to modify ourselves accordingly. It is better to conquer oneself in terms of reconciliation with someone else.

The words of the poet Yeats apply here:

> For nothing can be sole or whole
> That has not been rent.

The Incarnation

Christ is the only begotten of the Father in the flesh, and he *is* begotten of the Father in the flesh, and his spirit is united with his body in the same way as ours is—not added as a kind of loose inhabitant, but in union with the flesh.

By taking on a body of flesh, the Lord, like us, takes a step toward perfection. In so doing, like us, he extends his powers of sensation and perception. The only difference is that the greatest spirit has entered flesh begotten of the Father, and consequently his range is immensely wider than ours—his range for joy and grief, for good or for evil. With one side of himself the Lord experienced temptation more strongly than we can, and with another side of himself he was better able to resist it than we can. He was capable of experiencing more pain (as in Gethsemane) and more joy (as in his resurrection) than we are. He felt more profoundly and thought more deeply. Every answer to a trapping question is a turning of the trap on his adversary. Every action is appropriate to the situation and yet remains eternally true.

We can perhaps better understand incarnation (which we, too, have undergone) by the way in which, in our innocent state, we respond to the world around us and to the world of art. Every created thing is a symbol of its creator because it is the creator's handiwork. Everything that we ourselves make has something of ourselves in it. The realization of a thought or a state of mind in a work of art can give us some shadowy idea of what incarnation is. If incarnation makes the struggle harder, it also makes the creative achievement richer and more abundant, more palpable and concrete, more *there*.

Christ in his incarnation as man shows the possibilities of the human.

But Christ in his incarnation does not actualize those possibilities for human beings. Only with his sacrifice does he do that, and it is done only then on the assumption of our highest effort to help ourselves: the grace of God is given to those who work their utmost for the end which that grace enables humans to reach.

Gethsemane, the Crucifixion, and the Resurrection

What Winston Churchill offered the British people as their way to preservation, the Lord himself gave all peoples and every person to show them the way to salvation: blood, sweat, and tears. Christ's agony in Gethsemane takes over where his teaching may end, but his love continues. When his suffering caused him to "tremble because of pain, and to bleed at every pore" (D&C 19:18), it was not because of apprehension at his own death and suffering, but because he was taking upon himself the burden of all the sins of humanity from all times. In his trial and scourging and crucifixion he was to suffer still further for the gap between his teaching and the way people were treating him, but that was just a prolonging of the climax of suffering in Gethsemane when he accepted the cup with all its implications—implications that go far beyond not merely our thinking, but also our imagination. This in some way enables him to pay for our sins, to expiate them, to reconcile us with the Father, and to redeem us.

What, then, of the terrible panorama of history? Is it perhaps possible that the infinite Atonement of Christ paid, in part, for the suffering borne by those tortured throughout the ages: the individual murders from Cain onward; the mass killings by tyrants of so-called civilizations from the dawn of history to Hitler; the battles and massacres with carnage of millions and tens of millions; the blood of martyrs in Rome and in Carthage; the scarlet running out on the highways, in the mines, on the factory floor, in the field, and on the mountain; the blood of illness—the unexpected hemorrhages and the slow draining through the years; the blood of the innocent and the blood of the guilty; the blood of God's creatures slaughtered not for food but for amusement; the blood for which the lynch mob screams; and the blood shed by the painstaking surgeon? Could it not be that all that vast panorama of death down through ages past and through those to come was in the soul of Christ as he prayed in Gethsemane, and that it was for this suffering, too, that he shed blood through every pore in remission of our other terrible sins?

And the tortures he underwent: the physical torture of the crown of thorns, the sting of the scourging, the carrying of the cross; of the nails through the wrists and the palms of the hands and through the delicate bones of the feet; of the heaving of his chest and shoulders in the effort to breathe as he hung. Was this not the expiation for the agonies that humanity has savagely and pleasurably inflicted on itself: torture in the interest of the extracted confession; torture in the execution of so-called justice; torture in army huts; torture in prisons and private houses; torture by the secular arm with the consent, approval, and support of the apostate church? Death by fire, by heavy weights, by flaying piecemeal, by beatings, by piercings, by molten metal, and by other unspeakable ways? The witting and unwitting torture caused to animals (the burning alive of a captured cat at Halloween, the fish flapping in the bottom of the boat, the look in the eyes of a dying deer) and to men and women (the slaves in the labor camps of the East; the bedlams, the geriatric wards, and the battered babies of the West)? And the mental tortures: the deliberate mutual torture of countless marriages, the twisting of the knife in the wound of gossip, the murder of reputation and the suppression of opportunity by slander, the dragging down of leaders by rumor, and the deliberate frightening of the sensitive child? Were all these brought together in the mental agony of Gethsemane—the agony of comprising all these sins and sufferings? And the mental agony of the crucifixion—was it the agony of the knowledge that this is what we human beings could do to each other?

And the pain from disease and sickness, from cancer but also from arthritis, from toothache but also from meningitis—were all these pains and all this torture brought together to be suffered by one man, the Son of God, in the Garden of Gethsemane, and by a god, the Son of Man, on the cross?

Christ had to descend beneath and comprise anything that man could suffer, everything that man could do or inflict in the way of suffering, in order that he might understand the suffering we have borne and thereby be able to help us.

> And he shall go forth, suffering pains and afflictions and temptations of every kind; and this that the word might be fulfilled which saith he will take upon him the pains and the sicknesses of his people.
>
> And he will take upon him death, that he may loose the bands of death which bind his people; and he will take upon him their infirmities, that his bowels may be filled with mercy, according to the flesh, that he may know according to the flesh how to succor his people according to their infirmities. (Alma 7:11–12)

And then to suffer a greater separation than any separation ever suffered—the moment at about the ninth hour when he cried from the cross, "Eli, Eli, lama sabachthani? that is to say, My God, my God, why hast thou forsaken me?" (Matt. 27:46). Was it necessary that he also should suffer that last of separations, the separation of a Divine Father from a Divine Son in order to understand and stand for all those who, like William Cowper, had felt forsaken by the Father because of false doctrine or because they had themselves forsaken the Father? Christ had not forsaken the Father, but he had to have the experience of being forsaken. Such a moment is beyond our power to comprehend or imagine.

And then the Resurrection—the resurrection of the body to life everlasting—a resurrection from the greatest of agonies to the greatest of joys, the conquest of death for all and the conquest of sin for all those that will repent and seek eternal life by the grace of God.

The price: to suffer more agony than anyone; the achievement: eternal life for all those that can and will accept Christ; the motivation: love—the medium, the air, and the life of wholeness, of being at one.

Wholeness

The parts are not to be joined or sewn or glued together. There are no more edges and there is no more friction. Each part contains the whole and yet the whole is more than any part. Each part is fused and interfused with the whole, but the whole is more than the sum of the parts.

But what of the need for opposition in all things, and what of eternal progression? In this earthly life we may feel wholeness and oneness, this atonement—feel it fleetingly before the color of the experience changes and the harmony is gone, to come again and then to go again.

"For we know in part, and we prophesy in part. But when that which is perfect is come, then that which is in part shall be done away" (1 Cor. 13:9–10).

If we accept and live the gospel, we shall be made whole, we shall be glorified, we shall have traveled that much further on the pilgrimage of our eternal progression. What oppositions we shall then meet, what conditions for creation we shall then obtain, what new wholes we may rise to has not been revealed to us, and if it were we should not understand. But for the time being, if we have not a full understanding of divine or human love, we can be given the experience of it. We may have the supreme experience of it in contemplating the Atonement and in trying to live to be worthy of the love that it shows to us. Praise be to the Father and the Son that they are at one and that we may be at one with them, "As thou, Father, art in me, and I in thee, that they also may be one in us" (John 17:21).

God's Healing Wholeness

THE WORDS *heal* and *whole* are etymologically akin. The sense of "wholeness" and the sense of "healing" are held together in the New Testament expression "the man was made whole" (John 5:9). These words go back to the same root in Indo-European, and in the Germanic languages, they are close. Furthermore, *heal* and *whole* developed apparently separate significances of "curing" and "uniting," but while we take them as separate, we realize ways that these senses are clearly linked.

One variant of the two is the word *Heiland* (Old English *Heliand*), the main German word for "Savior." It is the translation of *Savior*, yet *Heiland* also means "the Healer," so the Savior is a healer as well. In fact, saving is healing and healing is saving; the dictionary's definitions of *salve* and *salvation* illustrate this fact. Furthermore, *Heilig* and *holy* are from the same root, meaning "holy," "heal," or "whole." Consider also the greeting words *hail* (English), *heil* (German), and *hell* (Scandinavian); all of these greetings mean "may you be well and whole."

Together with this etymological family, let us consider the word *atone* and the phrase "again bite of inwit." In the Middle Ages, those who translated the Bible and other theological materials into English did so (as the Germans still do when translating into German) by translating the verbal components of a Greek or Latin

Given as an Honors lecture February 2, 1992, being Candlemas Day, or the Day of the Purification of the Virgin Mary, but to the current world, groundhog day. The subject was propounded by the students, who felt a dialogue was needed at that time on campus because of the disputes about violence against women and children, abortion, feminism, and academic freedom.

word into English elements. Wycliff, for example, uses "again bite of inwit," meaning "remorse of conscience." "Again bite" is remorse; *morse* is "biting." You bite back, and you bite again and again (same dog). So having remorse is "biting back at yourself," like a dog at a flea. And *inwit* is a wonderful word for "conscience" because *inwit* has the sense of the Latin prefix *con*, which is an intensifier; *con-science*—conscience—means intense knowledge. The intensity is even stronger with *inwit* because *con* merely means "together with," while *in* means "right inside." *Inwit*, therefore, places the conscience right in the middle of the soul.

A term people muddle themselves about, for they cannot believe its etymology, is *at-one-ment;* "to make one," however, is exactly what *atonement* means. *Ment*, a suffix from Latin, makes *atone* into a noun; that's all *ment* does. But *atone* begins, like *inwit*, with Wycliff; he had *one* as a verb: "to one," which is daring. It then became *at one* (an adjectival or adverbial form) but retained its character as a verb; from *at one* came the abstract noun *atonement*. In the sixteenth century, Tyndale, a Bible translator, made the word equal to the Latin *adunire*, which means "to unite" (*ad* is an intensifier here). This translation approach, like "again bite of inwit," mirrors the Germanic process of translating component parts.

Unless we learn Greek and Latin, or some of both, we have not the same feeling of depth and strength about our language as the Germans are able to have. Simple Germans can understand the German words. Simple English people can't understand the Greek and Latin. *Conscience* is a difficult word to us. Its modern pronunciation has taken it still further away from its sense. But *inwit*, for somebody in the fourteenth century, meant something definite because it was part of the Englishman's own simple language.

Encapsulating foreign language inside their native language is a difficulty peculiar to English speakers. Other Germanic speakers keep their languages more pure, while Romance speakers—whose languages go back to Latin—better understand the Latin elements in their own languages than we do in our own. And the Mediterranean countries inherit a higher level of culture than Northern or even Central European countries. We join a service in a French-speaking branch, for example, and we feel how educated they are compared with us! Listen to their vocabulary.

I cannot deal further here with this interesting subject, but I wanted to give you this background of being "material" in our religion; that is to say, by concretizing, by historicizing, by being aware that our religion's language is made up of images and that etymology reveals every word as an image, we can learn that every word contains something more than we habitually ascribe to it. (I wish that etymology was taught in junior and senior high school; students at that stage would get a better grasp of their language.) I want you to have these details of the concrete because, ultimately, when we talk about God's healing wholeness, the Atonement is there as the whole healing.

We frequently speak mysteriously about the Atonement. And we frequently feel we don't know what it is. We may be confused among three questions: what the Atonement is, why it is, and how it is. The howness and the whyness are difficult to express in today's brief time, but the whatness is not. It is not difficult, that is to say, to list the things that the Atonement means. That is the way to approach anything when you cannot, as mostly we cannot in these matters, make a connotative definition: make a denotative definition instead.

What I shall do is talk about God's healing wholeness as a matter of our own souls, of our families, of groups to which we belong. Those groups include local groups like wards, groups within BYU, and BYU itself, enlarging out to the state and the nation and so on. The theme goes right through.

We have in our own church the ability to understand the particular etymology of *atonement* better than any other branch of Christianity. That is because we believe in the soul as a central concept. And the soul is not, to us, an alternative word for spirit, as with so many people. The soul is, for us, the union of spirit and body in this world so that the spirit may become flesh (incarnate) in order to gain experience and go a great step forward in eternal progression. Entering the flesh is not a way down and away as with Eastern religions; rather, it is a way on, a way up, because it provides experiences of varying sensation in many directions.

The word *sensation* may, in its turn, be refined into *sensibility*, a word not readily understood because many people think it means "being sensible" in the sense of "common sensibility." *Sensibility*, however, is the culture of the soul; this meaning appears clearly in the French *sensibilité*. (This is a meaning of *sensibility* that is gradually growing in English. We might substitute for it *sensitiveness*, but *sensitiveness* has not the European connotation of *sensibility*.) Soul, then, is the union, the *fusion* of spirit (finer matter) with body (coarser matter). We are not to think of the spirit as living in the body like a squirrel in a cage. Once we understand this sense, we realize that celibacy is an abomination from the Levant, whose inhabitants became so tired of sexual excess that, like St. Augustine, they welcomed privation. The pendulum swung from sexual excess to fanatical tyranny over self and others, from hair shirts to Inquisition.

You can see for yourself that being made whole, in the soul's context, has immediate sense (sense-play intended); it has psychosomatic sense. I dislike the word *psychosomatic* because it makes the division that I don't want to make. But if we think of *psycho-* as one end of the scale of individual matter and *-somatic* as the other end (for *psychosomatic* literally means "spiritual-corporeal"), and, if we can retain the sense of the individual's indivisibility, then we can talk about healing in a psychosomatic sense. Furthermore, once we realize that healing has to do with spirit and body together as soul—healing is healing of the soul—we cannot separate the processes of being healed in the body and being healed in the spirit; they belong together. And that is one of the significances, perhaps the great significance, of the Lord's miracles. We understand the inseparability of these healing processes more intensely when we know how the Doctrine and Covenants speaks of "soul" and "matter."

I want now to use this view, but I have to jump to and fro. When we are dealing with something like this, we cannot deal in strict order and say, "First I will deal with the self, and then with friendship, and then with the family, and then with groups." We can't do that because the thing works two ways. For example, if we were talking in terms of social science, we would begin with the group and finish with the individual. But in the Church we begin with the individual and end with the group, for from the beginning there were individual intelligences. The essential thing about these intelligences was that they were individuals, indivisible wholes. From the beginning we were male and female wholes. That, again, is not something taught outside the Church. When we, in our church, are able to heal, it is a healing of soul as body and spirit together; that healing cannot take place unless there is something working that enables body and spirit to be taken as a whole.

Once we have clearly in mind the idea that we are souls and that "soul" means the whole of us from top to toe, we think very differently about many things. Above all, we think differently about sex. I'm not going to spend much space on that—it's difficult to write or utter the word nowadays because of the abominable contexts it's got into. So we bring in that word *gender*, a grammatical term, as euphemistic for *sex* because we can no longer talk about the thing in terms of sex; we have to talk about it in terms of gender. We steadily lose depth and importance, for there is a link between sex and sacredness. Sex ought to be holy. It is a quality of soul, not a quality of body that we struggle with or use, but a quality of soul. And I don't want to say any more about it because it has to be kept in its proper place, and it's rarely kept there. We should not talk about it if we can possibly avoid it because it is too holy to be generally talked about. And the more we talk about it, the more we debase it and debauch it and take it casually. Such casualness is dangerous because sex is a sacrament. Sex has to be prepared for by instruction in the proper place, the place where sex is relevant emotively and religiously (but not scientifically): the bosom of the family. Furthermore, our children's home instruction should not commence so late that it comes after smut from little friends. Above all, that instruction should not speak of "sex," but of love.

Eliot in "Ash Wednesday IV" mentions interpreting dreams upward or downward:

> Redeem
> The time. Redeem
> The unreal vision in the higher dream.
> Redeem the time, redeem the dream.

Since we believe in soul and since we believe that the fundamental and final task of the soul is to learn to love and to learn to love more widely, deeply, intensely, and highly, then the word *love* must cover the whole gamut. And there is ultimately—insofar as we represent in ourselves the love of God (and that's a good phrase because it can be both objective and subjective genitive: it can mean our love for him and his love for us)—there is ultimately a point at which all forms of right love are inseparable.

Love is, insofar as it is God's love, in all forms of love, so I don't like to separate them in the way that people do. It is true that there is spousal love, parental love, filial love, sibling love, the love of friends and animals, and so on. I think all of them are ultimately acts of the soul, not of the spirit. That means that if we feel chary of touching others, of embracing them, there is something wrong with us, which may be partly at least the fault of contemporary society.

In these days of public shock at sexual abuse in the family (such abuse has always existed), touching others becomes a dangerous subject. The fact remains, however, that the soul expresses itself materially—it is "all matter" (D&C 131:8). I would hesitate to think that gestures of love such as facial contact, hugging (if you like to use a casual word for it—I prefer *embracing*), and so on are wrong. If you like to place those terms with sexual connotations for human touch at the bottom of the scale, you are missing the significance of what I'm saying. Remember that the young child develops better if constantly handled—caressed—by its mother. Likewise, if a father wants his offspring to have something of the same ease towards him, he would do well to participate in those activities that require close physical contact (bathing, changing diapers, and so forth).

Since it is in the family that we learn to love, it is also in the family that we learn to hate (as Cain demonstrates). Let me add something that people find difficulty in understanding. We have the pairs *hot* and *cold* and *warm* and *cool.* In the same way, we have the pairs *love* and *hate* and *like* and *dislike.* We can love and hate the same person. One of the difficulties about married life—and all relationships—is that the swing-over is so easy from love to hate and hate to love; the swing-over is easy because love and hate operate at a similar depth, one being of the Devil and one being of God. We can make life easier for ourselves if we realize that it is possible to both love and dislike the same person, "I love her/him, but I don't like him/her." I've never been in a situation in which I liked somebody that I didn't love, but I have been in situations in which I loved somebody that I disliked. Can we like and dislike the same person? For me the terms exclude one another. But I have to leave you to sort that out from your own experience.

I used deliberately *hot* and *cold* and *warm* and *cool* as a couple of pairs with *love* and *hate* and *like* and *dislike* in order that you might feel temperature (to speak metaphorically) in this matter.

A family is a whole when the relationship of the spouses is such that it leaves the children fundamentally at ease and not intense. Without that, it is difficult for a family to operate as a whole. As infants, we don't reflect on these matters, but we do all sorts of things that would be regarded as sins if we were not exempt until the age of eight—that's why we are exempt, and not because we are angels from heaven. We are both angels and devils until we reach eight years old; once we reach that age, we must act as responsible individuals. Given, however, that the young child is both an angel and a roaring egoist, making absolute demands, we can see for ourselves that love has to begin one-way and then become two-way. Of course, one cannot predict how or if love will become two-way in particular individuals. It may become two-way quite soon; it may take years; it may never happen.

It is difficult to be loved and not to love back. If we don't love back when we are loved, there is something in the way. And the something in the way is something that—from the age of puberty onwards, anyway—we need to reflect upon from the point of view of getting rid of egocentricity. Specifically, I have to repeat here what I constantly have to repeat on campus and elsewhere: there's something deeply wrong with the concept of self-esteem. We are individuals, and we are individuals forever, but self-esteem is not the cure for our imperfections, our lack of wholeness, our worry, and our trouble; rather, we must deal with these matters by self-forgetfulness. Newborn children are roaring egoists, but we can experience self-forgetfulness with some strength when we first fall in love. Otherwise we simply have self-assertion. If only adolescents could live their teens self-forgetfully instead of self-assertively! It doesn't very often happen; it's a struggle. It happens far more readily when the family itself lives in an atmosphere of good, relaxed love, when the family lives at ease.

We all know that most families are imperfect, including our own. But I will tell you two extreme stories that may put the normal in perspective. The players must remain anonymous, but they are real. When I was in the Honors Program, an aide sent me a young woman of nineteen who, he said, was unhappy but just needed a little love. For the first eighteen months that I knew this young woman—her parents were divorced when she was thirteen years old, and she had not seen her father (an alcoholic also into drugs) for seven years—I found myself pressing her to go and see her father. Whatever she might think, I believed, her father needed her and she needed her father. At last she went. She found that he loved her and she loved him. She came back confident. Within a few months she was on a mission but retained the tie with her father. She came back from a deeply felt mission poised and mature. (After this man's mother, who looked after him, died, he found himself without support; he then discovered he could support himself, recovered, and was reconciled to his family before he died. The key to his change was the love between him and his daughter.)

In contrast to the young woman I have just described, consider this sketch of a student—a member of the same "school" generation—I knew at the same time. His mother had been divorced three times and had four husbands. He was the son of the first husband; that first husband was an alcoholic. This student virulently hated his father. I could not get him to forgive or go to see his father. I think this young man was possessed. When he came into the study, my dog's hackles rose along her back and she used to growl at him: he couldn't come into the room without her growling. Well, he developed a heretical outlook, had a following on campus for a time, went into plural marriage, and is now lost to the Church.

These examples of the forgiving young woman and the unforgiving young man illustrate the kinds of relationships we need in our homes. We must make sure that the relationships in our families—particularly the relationships of daughters with mothers and sons with fathers—are relationships of love; these relationships cannot be ones of competition, possessiveness, or of struggling for freedom or power. We must be forgiving and ready to be forgiven.

The word *forgive* is not Latinate; it is straight English we can understand: *forgive.* The way to wholeness is to forgive and to be forgiven. Blake slightly overstates it to give it humor as well as love, "I forgive you, you forgive me, And so throughout eternity." But Blake's verse reminds us that forgiveness is an ongoing process, like repentance. *Re*pentance has the same *re* as in *re*morse, you see. And forgive *gives* itself, as in something that has to be done again and again, just as remorse. You bite yourself again and again, and in repentance you turn 'round and go back to where you started—or to a certain point on the way—again and again, daily, perhaps even hourly.

The absolute prerequisite for us to be whole is to have an open and unconcerned (that's an odd word to use here, but I mean what I say—let there be no tension)—an open and unworried—relationship with our parents and siblings. Incidentally, let me say one word about sibling love that isn't always understood. Sibling love is a very particular kind of love because we share with our brother or sister the same *two* parents. In that sense, sibling love is obviously a closer relationship from the beginning than any other relationship because we have both parents in common: we share the whole potential of our heredity, the whole tradition of our ancestry, in common.

Having addressed the family, let me go on to the group. The peer group seems inevitable in American society and in other societies that imitate American ways and arts. I suppose the inevitability of peer groups in this country has something to do with the economic demi-independence of adolescents here. When I was a teenager, I had no means to express myself in undesirable directions because I didn't have the money to do it with. In my teens, I saved the money I needed to go to concerts and theaters in London by walking to and from school instead of taking the bus. We appreciate things if we do them that way. I never knew I was a teenager until I was long past my teenage years. *Teenager* is an American expression and was exported to other countries from here. The teenaged peer group has got out of hand in this country and is, I suppose, the main source of its violence, both as training (for it becomes training) and afterwards in adult practice; that violence may be open like the mobsters or concealed like the boxers, footballers, matadors, police officers, soldiers, hunters, and macho husbands and lovers.

Peer groups exist in so-called primitive tribes, but they exist under ritualistic control. Our society has lost ritualistic control over the growing boy and girl—lad, girl, young man, young woman. Our Church ritual is sufficient in the temple but insufficient outside. We need to be more ritualistic, for example, about progress in the priesthood and the processes that young women go through. I think the Church is trying to do more about this problem as time goes on because Church leaders recognize it. For a comparison, one need only look at primitive societies to see the importance they give to the adolescent entering into maturity; those societies provide tribal ceremonies so that the adolescent gains a sense of awe followed by adequacy. Through tribal rituals, the adolescent is subdued into a sense of oneness and also fully accepted into the group.

The sense of oneness and full acceptance into the group needs something fundamental to be done about it. Unfortunately, what we find in American society is that teenagers seek that kind of relationship in their peer groups. Peer groups in American society—and increasingly in European society and, alas, in Russian and Asian society too (gradually it's extending)—become a matter of finding oneness (atonement) of the devilish kind: American teenagers seek oneness in the wrong group, a group which separates itself because it does not feel at one with the previous generation. The sense of oneness, however, ought to belong to the tribe as a whole, as part and parcel of daily living. In primitive societies, where oneness is shared by the entire tribe, no difficulty exists between the peer group and the family group because both have their place. The rituals of these societies (which often know more than we do about how to handle social things) keep young people in contact with the previous generation. That contact is not of an oppositional but of a collaborative kind. Primitive societies provide a sense of collaboration for adolescents, and the peer group arises from no sense of opposition to the adult society to which it now belongs. For our own LDS society, the introduction of some Marine discipline into the Boy Scout program might be an advance. Fear and awe are needed to open depth. Such discipline could well produce maturer young missionaries.

This parenthesis was intended to bring us back to self-forgetfulness. I can express it this way: other people should treat us as individuals and care for us accordingly, and we should treat other people as individuals and care for them accordingly, and to us they are individuals, but we should forget our own individuality because it will look after itself. This is about the gaining and losing of the soul in the gospel. Self-forgetfulness, in my experience, does not cure but rather ameliorates things like grief and sin. We make our sins too important (by ironic arrogance). We have a guilty sense of the past; we hang on to remorse instead of going on to repentance and freedom to act. Again and again when we repine about the past, we should be asking ourselves, "What should I be doing now? I should not be doing this; I should be doing something positive, throwing myself into work for the Church or whatever else is good because *then* I shall be developing myself."

But we do not develop ourselves by consciously trying to develop ourselves; we develop ourselves by doing the things that the Lord wants us to do. Thus, for example, Elder Dallin Oaks used to tell students here that the important thing for them was to give the proper attention to their education. That will cease to be a priority later, except in the sense that the whole world becomes an education. But it's the students' job to get ahead and do as well as they can; they must do so not for themselves but for the society to which they belong and the Lord they are going to serve. It is proper to become a lawyer (though many people do not think so). But for whatever you do, you must have a sense of vocation, of being called. A sense of vocation is itself an expression of the self-forgetfulness of which I speak. I know a dentist near here who spends much of his money in going off to up-country Mexico and teaching his skill there for no monetary reward. Self-forgetfulness in our vocation means that we can be at one with it, and that's an important part of being at one with ourselves.

If we are doing a job we don't like, we can't become a whole. Either we must learn to like our job or we must get another job. Many people make a mistake about this because they are presented with many different possibilities. For example, what I'm teaching is the exact opposite of the doctrine of worldly success. The success of the soul has little to do with material success. How can it have? After all, rich people may be good, but it is difficult (I know from a relative of mine) to be rich without paying much attention to how things are going. This relative of mine, who lived to be ninety-four, used to read the *Financial Times* first thing every morning. Her *Financial Times* was her prayer to her maker. She was kind and good, but she could have been outstanding in social work. Only vocation can excuse lengthy time taken, because only vocation means that we can work as to God and for God. Only in that way can we feel at one with God in our work.

I have been happy in this respect myself because I never asked for a job; my job came to me. It came only three times: the first for twelve years, the second for twenty-eight, the last for (to date) twenty-one. The first was my apprenticeship, the second my journeymanship, and the last my mastership. Few of my colleagues were concerned about the future. We enjoyed being with one another and discussing with one another, and that was our main education—not from the faculty, but from our peers. That was a right kind of peer group. And we used to have much serious discussion. We went to concerts and theaters together, discussed new books together, passed them around to read. A generation later, as a widower, I sometimes went up to Nottingham, where my niece was doing music up at the University. I was shocked at the frivolity of the conversation because it didn't fit in with the kind of way we used to talk. Sometimes we drank too much, but we continued to talk seriously when we were drinking. We never talked about jobs.

I come now to the most important thing I have to say here. We are all members of this campus. The tides are running cross at BYU at the present time, more so than I've known, and I've been here twenty-one years now. We must remember what the Lord said, "If ye are not one (at one), ye are not mine" (D&C 38:27). And if we aren't at one in our institution, we can't be at one in ourselves either, because we are members one of another. I refuse to be controversial in this context, but we must make a special effort with those who have hardened their hearts, feel rage and frustration, and are determined to reform things within their own span of time. Condemn sin but love the sinner, and do not commit the modern mistake (sin) of substituting for *sin* the words *mistake*, *error*, *misjudgment*, *misconception*, or even the phrase "another point of view." In a good society, *sin* and *crime* are synonymous (pun intended), but no existing society exemplifies that. Nevertheless, we have to restore that equation as far as we can. The American Constitution was founded—and the U.S. government long ruled—on the assumption that it was to work in a Christian society. Immigrants may worship or not as they please. They may worship in Christian ways or non-Christian ways. But non-Christians have no right to challenge the fact that the United States is still a Christian country—that would undermine the country's culture and civilization. It would be the task of a traitor.

A similar approach is appropriate on our own campus. Members of other faiths (and atheism is paradoxically a faith) may become members of the University, but they have no right to challenge the doctrines of the LDS Church here. That would be bad manners on their part. On our own part it would be disobedience. Objectivity is unattainable, but honesty is possible and right.

Wholeness implies that we must grow to appreciate the wholeness in both human and nonhuman things. (I remember how relieved I was when Gestalt-psykologie was promulgated in the twenties and thirties—at last psychology was saying it's the totality that counts.) Wholeness concerns being at one within ourselves, being at one with our family, and being at one with God's world, including nonhuman things. Being at one with nonhuman things, however, is not necessarily easy. I have found it difficult to learn to love certain things. I was an anachrophobic—it took me thirty years to love spiders. I learned to love snakes when there was a snake farm outside Karachi, and I sometimes took British scientists out to see it. Those snakes were so badly treated by the men that looked after them that I pitied the snakes in their agonized fear; I've felt pity for snakes ever since. We have a duty to learn to love God's creation and to cease to kill animals for sport, in preparation for the time when "they shall not hurt nor destroy in all my holy mountain, saith the Lord" (Isa. 65:25).

Ratiocination can impede our appreciation of wholeness; much division comes from ratiocination, from thinking, from arguing. Logic is a system, a system that varies from generation to generation. For me, as for scholars in the Middle Ages, logic is a part of rhetoric, a way of persuading people; it's a powerful way of persuading. Perhaps it is too powerful a way of persuasion nowadays, for many regard it as the main way of persuading. Logic can be useful in getting things ordered, like having a more complex index at the end of a book. Because logic is a system, however, we must take care how we apply it to our lives.

If we apply a system to life, we find the system doesn't fit. Every day, experts in economics, political science, and history are interviewed on TV: they don't agree. If logic were all-powerful, they would be able to agree. But they're not arguing, after all, within logic; they are arguing from premises that are outside logic. That's the point. It's like saying that you can apply chess as a way of looking at the world, and to a certain extent it works. But it would be better to use something more important than chess or logic. The supreme example is the language of the scriptures. A good counterexample is music, for it's the least accessible in terms of language. We live in music in a different way because there is no language in music. To translate music into language is to lose the pattern, the shade of feeling, that's unique. And so I come back to this point of sensibility. Meditation on great music awakens the deepest creative mind.

I said earlier that emotions can be worked up; I spoke of anger and I will speak of hate. There is a university disease that must have begun in Cairo, then spread to Italy, and then gradually came north in Europe: *invidia academica.* Literally, the term means academic hate, scholarly hate. Those poor wretches in the early universities were all supposed to be celibate. And celibacy has a remarkable facility for increasing hate. When we are celibate, we are more liable to hate (I think Pope John was a rare person). That hate can be overcome, but it's difficult to overcome. Hate can be directed at this or that; the hate is in us and we have to find something to direct it at, and there may be no logical connection between what we direct it at and what it represents. Something as powerful as hate goes right down through the strata of the mind (if we take that metaphor) to rock bottom. Hate is the fundamental evil, as opposed to love. Invidia academica is perhaps the most virulent sort.

The best exponent of invidia academica was probably the Shropshire Lad, A. E. Housman. He wrote good lyrical verse in imitation, well conceived, of the Latin. He despatched scholars. The trouble was he was nearly always correct. He was correct in nailing them for making their mistakes, for he knew more than they because he loved his subject: he took refuge in his subject. We need to look in our lives for the things we are doing in lieu of the things we should be doing. We direct our attention to something because we have chosen to do so, but the something doesn't correspond to our problem. We fix on it, but it doesn't spring directly from our problem.

Individia academica has become a tradition in universities. It is often regarded, not with horror, but with amusement. It's one of the causes of the current university decline, for it gets so easily mixed up with promotion or lack of it, salary or lack of it—all those things. If we don't get paid enough, we may find ourselves disgruntled, and that disgruntlement may take itself out on our colleagues or our family. It's easier to hate when we don't have enough money; it's easier to express our hate if we have too much.

"If ye are not one, ye are not mine." Controversy can be a game, but it's a dangerous one. In a university, scholars are usually interested above all in their subjects. Most of the things that they do are connected with their subjects. Their hates, loves, dislikes, and so on are all linked up with their subjects. In *this* university, which is a moral university and a deliberately moral university as a religious university, the problem is not simply in relationships about subjects, but relationships about fundamental things. But if things are fundamental, they obviously ought to be agreed upon.

Consider for yourselves when controversy appears on campus nowadays. Ask yourselves what the necessity is, where it comes from, what are its causes. If it has genuine causes, can we get together to solve them? If it has not genuine causes, can the people who are suffering from the controversy be relieved from it? Between human beings who share their religion, a situation should not exist in which we cannot come to some agreement about something, about parts of something. In the Middle East at the moment, for example, Syria and Israel have been talking about water rights. They might even manage to make an agreement about water, although they can't make an agreement about anything else; such an agreement would at least be something. The effort has to be towards agreement.

It does not do for me, on this occasion, to be specific. But it is for me to say, remembering God's healing wholeness, that we badly need God's healing wholeness at this university at the present time and that we should search ourselves to find out whether we have anything to do with other controversies. We should also find out whether we have our views for some reason other than the reason we should have for having them. And we should also remember, ultimately, that the solution is not gained by logical argument, by winning or losing an argument. That is superficial. The solution is only gained by mutual love and respect. That is the only way to wholeness in the community in which we exist now.

There is one other thing that I wanted to mention. Milton begins *Paradise Lost* with the phrase "Of man's first disobedience."

When you come to think of it, the word covers the multitude of sins. The disobedience of Adam and Eve is symbolic of all sin, not just what they did in disobeying about a specific thing. We disobey, and it always involves either something that we should be doing but are not or something that we are doing but should not. And so all sins are included. All the Ten Commandments come under disobedience and obedience. The whole gospel can be seen in these terms: obedience or disobedience. We either believe in authority or we don't. We can't prevaricate with it. We cannot gain wholeness by prevaricating with the authority that we've agreed to accept. We have to have an attitude of wholeness to that authority. We in our church know that this is true; all of us really know it. And we in our church know that in the outside world it is not so at the level of state and nation.

How can we feel at one with our country? Should we feel at one with our country? Is it possible to do so nowadays? There are occasions when Americans have felt at one. You felt at one when the Japanese bombed Pearl Harbor. The cynic might say you were manipulated into being at one. But the fact was that you were capable of feeling at one, just as we felt at one in England over Dunkirk. It was typical of the English to feel at one over a defeat rather than a victory. But it's a healthy thing to feel about a defeat. Think of the oneness that we have when we are defeated as compared with the oneness we have when we are victorious. Think how soon the jubilation over your hundred-hour war disappeared. It was the same with our little Falkland war. It was adrenaline: it lasted a little, and then it vanished. It didn't produce a genuine wholeness. This is a problem that I have to leave with you, this problem of feeling at one with our country. How can we feel at one with our country? To me, the answer seems to be to work for our country in self-forgetfulness insofar as we can.

Self-forgetfulness is the key to wholeness, to becoming at one with God's world, and each individual must become whole. The individual is of supreme importance. The individual is from everlasting to everlasting. But the individual exists by virtue of *others'* individuality. And that is why I say that individuals develop as they forget themselves; they do not develop by asserting themselves or thinking of themselves. And that's the fundamental thing about this soul of ours: if we can be at peace with ourselves and be at peace within the group, we can be so most readily by remembering that, as members one of another, we gain by remembering others and forgetting ourselves. Fundamentally, such remembering and forgetting is what love is all about.

Appendix: Reading List for a Lifetime

PEOPLE OFTEN ASK me for a reading list, so I have made a two-page list, which I have entitled "Reading List for a Lifetime." In some cases, I have listed a particular translation; in other cases, I have left it blank because they are all equally bad or indifferent, as the case may be. There are very few good translations. The ones I have listed are not at all good, but they are specific, and explicitness is a step toward goodness.

This list was originally generated for a BYU Honors Program seminar, an intensive eight-week course in reading the great literature of Western civilization. Actually, one should have read everything on the list before coming to the university, but better late than never. Students in the seminar took only this one class and were expected to read about three hundred pages a day, thoroughly and thoughtfully. Although I wouldn't revise it now, I might just concentrate on the scriptures and the five greatest writers: Homer, Virgil, Dante, Shakespeare, and Goethe. They are the supreme writers. They reveal the whole of life. I recommend the following as a good, basic reading list:

The standard works

Homer, *The Iliad* (trans. Richmond A. Lattimore), *The Odyssey* (trans. Emile V. Rieu)

The Bhagavad-Gita (The Song of God) (trans. Christopher Isherwood)

Aeschylus, *Aeschylus I—Oresteia* (trans. Richmond A. Lattimore)

Sophocles, *The Oedipus Cycle* (trans. Dudley Fitts and Robert Fitzgerald)

Plato, *Phaedo*, *The Republic*
Euripides, *Euripides One* (trans. Richmond A. Lattimore)
Herodotus, *The Persian Wars* (trans. George Rawlinson)
Virgil, *The Aeneid* (trans. John Dryden or Robert Fitzgerald)
Livy, *The Early History of Rome*
Josephus, *The Jewish War*
Plutarch, *Lives of the Noble Greeks and Romans*, and *Lives of the Noble Romans* (ed. Edmund Fuller)
Eusebius, *The Essential Eusebius*
Augustine, *The City of God*
Bede, *The Ecclesiastical History of the English People*
Dante, *The Divine Comedy* (trans. John D. Sinclair or Dorothy L. Sayers)
Geoffrey Chaucer, *The Canterbury Tales* (trans. Nevill Coghill)
Niccolò Machiavelli, *The Prince*
William Shakespeare, *Hamlet*, *Othello*, *Measure for Measure*, *King Lear*, *Macbeth*, *Antony and Cleopatra*, *Coriolanus*, *The Winter's Tale*, *The Tempest*
Miguel de Cervantes, *Don Quixote* (trans. Walter Starkie)
René Descartes, *Discourse on Method* (trans. Wollaston)
John Milton, *Paradise Lost*, *Paradise Regained*, *Samson Agonistes*
George Fox, *Journal* (ed. Rufus M. Jones)
John Bunyan, *The Pilgrim's Progress*
Jean Baptiste Racine, *Athaliah*, *Phaedra*
Molière, *Tartuffe*, *The Would-Be Gentleman*, *The Precious Damsels*, *The Misanthrope* (trans. Morris Bishop or Kenneth Muir)
Jonathan Swift, *Gulliver's Travels*
Antoine Prévost, *Manon Lescaut*
Samuel Richardson, *Pamela* (Part I), *Clarissa*
Montesquieu, *The Spirit of the Laws* (trans. Thomas Nugent)
Voltaire, *Candide*
James Boswell, *Life of Samuel Johnson*
Jean-Jacques Rousseau, *Émile*
Adam Smith, *The Wealth of Nations*
Edward Gibbon, *The Decline and Fall of the Roman Empire*
John Woolman, *Journal*
Johann Wolfgang von Goethe, *Faust I, II* (trans. Walter Kaufmann or Charles E. Passage), *Wilhelm Meister*
William Wordsworth, *The Prelude* (Books I & II)

John Jay, Alexander Hamilton, and James Madison, *The Federalist Papers* (ed. A. Hacker)
John Keats, *Letters* (ed. Robert Gittings)
Jane Austen, *Persuasion*, *Emma*
Stendhal, *The Red and the Black*
Søren Kierkegaard, *Fear and Trembling*, *The Sickness unto Death* (trans. Walter Lowrie)
Honoré de Balzac, *Eugenie Grandet*
Karl Marx, *Early Writings*
Henry David Thoreau, *Walden*, *Civil Disobedience*
Parley P. Pratt, *Autobiography*
Charles Dickens, *Little Dorrit*, *Great Expectations*
George Eliot, *Middlemarch*, *Daniel Deronda*
Gustave Flaubert, *A Sentimental Education* (trans. Robert Baldick)
Fedor Mikhailovich Dostoevsky, *The Brothers Karamazov*
Leo Tolstoy, *War and Peace* (trans. Rosemary Edmonds), *Anna Karenina*
Sarah Orne Jewett, *Country of the Pointed Firs and Other Stories*
William James, *The Varieties of Religious Experience*
Friedrich Wilhelm Nietzsche, *Thus Spake Zarathustra* (trans. Walter Kaufmann)
Henrik Ibsen, *Peer Gynt* (trans. Michael Meyer), *Rosmersholm*, *Ghosts*, *Hedda Gabler*
Thomas Hardy, *The Mayor of Casterbridge*
Henry James, *The Ambassadors*, *What Maisie Knew*
Anton Chekhov, *The Cherry Orchard*, *The Seagull*, *Uncle Vanya*, *The Three Sisters* (trans. David Magarshack)
Joseph Conrad, *Nostromo*
James Joyce, *A Portrait of the Artist as a Young Man*
Sigmund Freud, *The Interpretation of Dreams* (trans. James Strachey)
Thomas Mann, *The Magic Mountain*, *Joseph and His Brothers*
Marcel Proust, *Swann's Way* (trans. C. K. Scott Moncrieff)
John Maynard Keynes, *The Economic Consequences of the Peace*
D. H. Lawrence, *Women in Love*
E. M. Forster, *A Passage to India*
Franz Kafka, *The Trial*
Hermann Hesse, *Steppenwolf*, *The Glass Bead Game* (chapter 7)
George Santayana, *The Last Puritan*
Montaigne, *Essays* (trans. John Florio)

Index

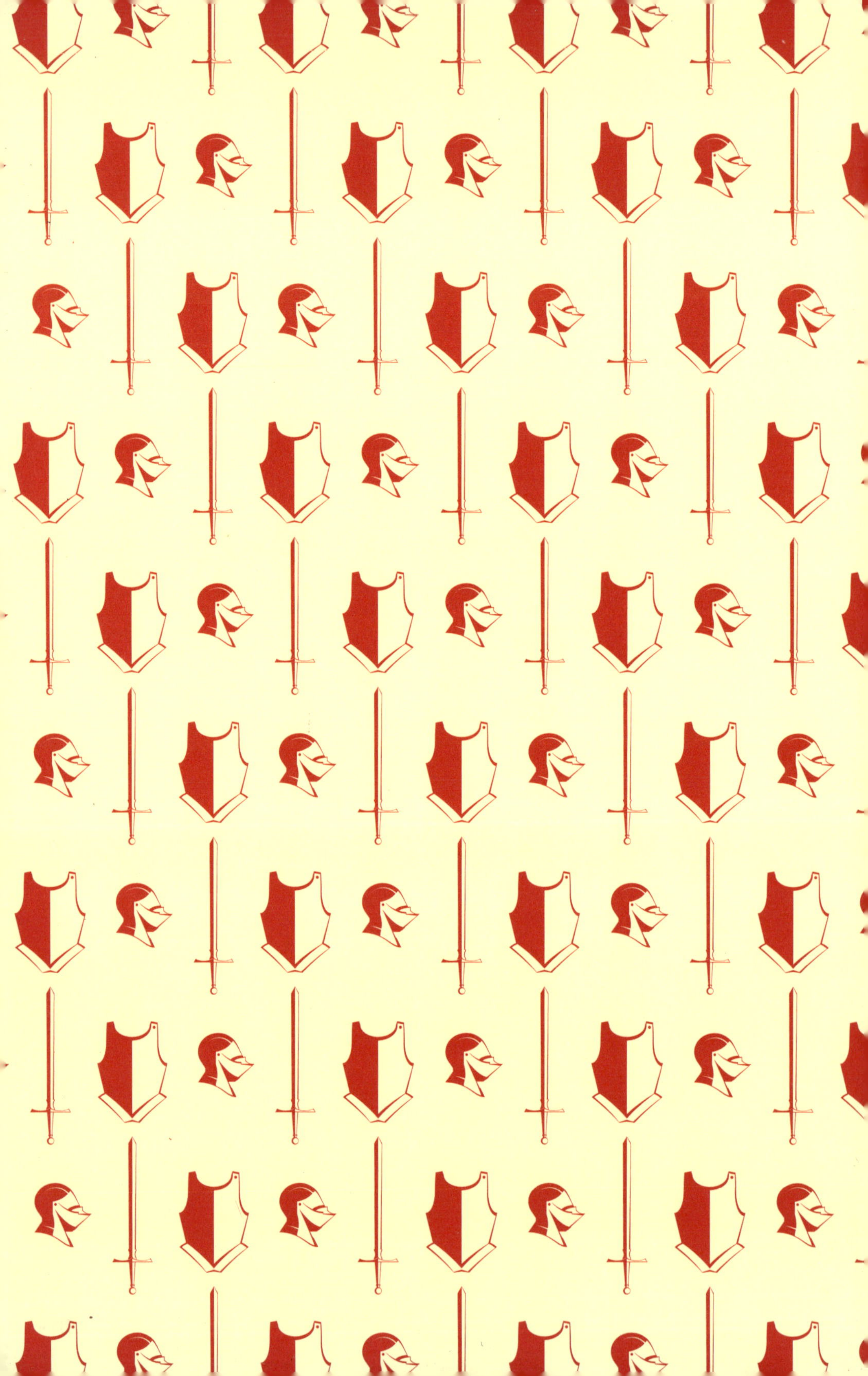